Caribbean Collections:
Recession Management Strategies
for Libraries

SALALM Secretariat
Memorial Library
University of Wisconsin–Madison

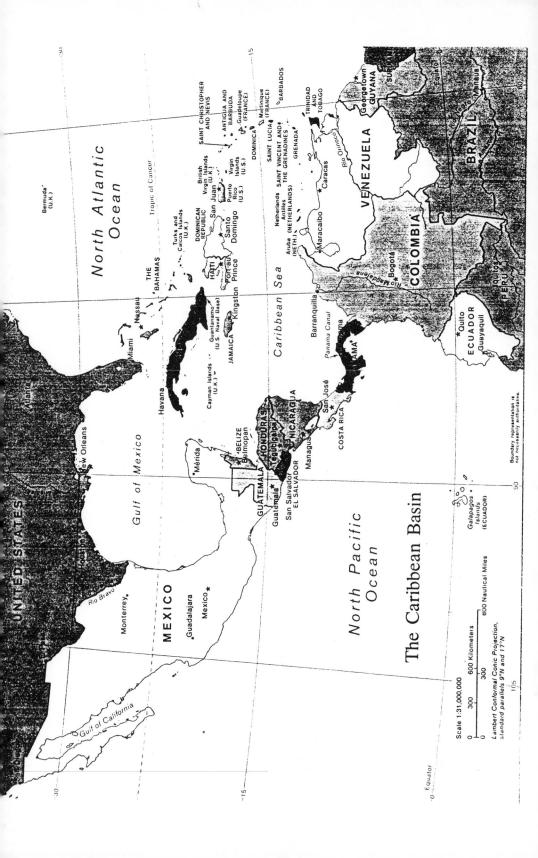

The Caribbean Basin

Scale 1:31,000,000

0 300 600 Kilometers
0 300 600 Nautical Miles

Lambert Conformal Conic Projection,
standard parallels 9°N and 17°N

Boundary representation is
not necessarily authoritative.

Caribbean Collections: Recession Management Strategies for Libraries

Papers of the Thirty-Second Annual Meeting of the
SEMINAR ON THE ACQUISITION OF
LATIN AMERICAN LIBRARY MATERIALS

held jointly with the

Eighteenth Conference of the
ASSOCIATION OF CARIBBEAN UNIVERSITY,
RESEARCH, AND INSTITUTIONAL LIBRARIES

James L. Knight International Conference Center
Miami, Florida
May 10-15, 1987

Mina Jane Grothey
Editor

SALALM SECRETARIAT
Memorial Library, University of Wisconsin–Madison

ISBN: 0-917-617-22-3

Dedication

These papers are dedicated to the members of SALALM and of ACURIL who, after many years, saw their dream of a conference of both groups together come true. They are dedicated particularly to Peter de la Garza, whose hard work—beginning with a feasibility study for the meeting and continuing through his service in Miami as Rapporteur General for ACURIL—made the stimulating experience of a joint conference possible.

Contents

Part Three. Grantsmanship

Part Four. Acquisition and Preservation

Part Five. Historiography and Bibliography

Part Six. Cuba

Preface

It is a great pleasure to present the papers delivered at the Joint Conference of the Seminar on the Acquisition of Latin American Library Materials (SALALM) and the Association of Caribbean University Research and Institutional Libraries (ACURIL) held in Miami, Florida, May 10-15, 1987. This joint conference marks a new stage in a long relationship between these two associations. The first meeting of ACURIL was held as an adjunct to the SALALM conference of 1969, and the founders of ACURIL based many aspects of their association on SALALM. Through the years, contact has been maintained by members of both associations. ACURIL is a regional library association serving the needs of the Caribbean in much the same way that the Association of College and Research Libraries (ACRL) serves the United States. It is a multilingual association with four official languages: Dutch, English, French, and Spanish. Its purpose is to facilitate development and use of all types of libraries, archives, and information services by assisting in the identification, collection, and preservation of materials. It supports a wide range of intellectual and educational endeavors in the Caribbean area. For ACURIL, the Caribbean has a broad definition, including not only the islands in the Caribbean Sea but also those countries bordering it.

In contrast with ACURIL, SALALM is a special library organization which began in 1956 as a seminar to discuss problems with the acquisition of library materials from Latin America. In 1968 it incorporated as a nonprofit organization. SALALM may be unique in that bookdealers are full active members in the organization. Over the years its focus on acquisitions has broadened to include the processing, preservation, and access to Latin American materials. The Caribbean has always been included in SALALM's definition of Latin America.

One SALALM meeting each decade has focused on the Caribbean. SALALM V in 1960, held at the New York Public Library, was the first. Alma Jordan, who served as the first ACURIL president in 1970, was president of SALALM in 1979, and that year chose

"Caribbean Studies and Libraries" [1] as her theme for SALALM XXIV. Eight years later, SALALM XXXII follows up on many of the topics discussed there.

Recession Management Strategies is the general theme of Part One.   Parts Two and Three examine Resource Sharing and Grantsmanship as strategies to help survive a recession.   The papers collected here offer no magic solutions to these problems.   If solutions had been recommended they would in all probability not fit all situations.   These papers do show a variety of methods for alleviation of problems.   Perhaps one of the most important outcomes was finding out that others, including parts of the United States, also suffer from the effects of poor economic times.   Useful ideas on cooperative efforts, the importance of creativity, and adaptability were discussed. Other catchwords were efficiency, innovation, dynamism, and inspiration.   It was emphasized to never lose sight of the main objective of service to the primary clientele.   The importance of detailed planning and setting priorities and the need to evaluate current practices with a potential for redefining activities are points that can be applied in any organization.

One area identified for special attention was staff and especially staff morale.   Human resources are sometimes an underrated and underutilized resource.   Another topic was technology: does it solve problems or create additional ones?   The possibilities for solutions can be found with libraries, within the environment of the parent institution, and between libraries on local, national, and even international levels.

Another question explored was what, if anything, can associations like SALALM and ACURIL do to help?   One role they play is to improve communications among their members and other interested parties through publications and especially through their meetings which provide a forum for discussions such as those in Miami.   The meetings allow people to make the contacts needed for workable cooperative efforts.   More than twenty-five countries and dependent territories were represented at the joint conference.   The chance to discuss problems face to face with others from the Caribbean, the United States, South America, and elsewhere was a wonderful opportunity.

---

1. Laurence Hallewell, ed., *Windward, Leeward, and Main: Caribbean Studies and Library Resources: Final Report and Working Papers of the Twenty-Fourth Seminar on the Acquisition of Latin American Library Materials* (Madison, WI: SALALM Secretariat, 1980).

During the meeting, exactly how valuable an opportunity this was became clearer as the isolation imposed by water became evident. Many of us in the western part of the United States bemoan the distances we need to travel between large cities with research libraries. For example, the University of New Mexico, a medium-sized research library, is the largest library in the state. It takes at least a day of travel to reach a larger resource collection. But the problems presented by land distances seem insignificant when compared with those over water. For Caribbean librarians who want to communicate and to cooperate with other institutions, the problem is often compounded by the need to work internationally. Associations like ACURIL and SALALM can help fight this sense of isolation.

The organizers of the meeting tried to serve the differing needs of the two sets of members. One goal was to present opportunities to learn from each other. Members from both associations were invited to participate at all levels of activity. Parts Four to Six reflect this variety in the papers presented. In Part Four, Acquisitions and Preservation are covered. The acquisition of government publications, which are often available only outside of regular trade channels, presents special difficulties. The two papers on this topic offer practical advice on acquiring these materials. Once an institution has acquired materials, it is presented with the problem of preserving them for future researchers. The preservation of materials is reaching crisis levels all over the world. But because of the poor condition of many Latin American materials at the time of publication, it is an even more pressing problem in these collections.

Scholarship on Caribbean history is of deep interest to the members of both organizations. Part Five, Historiography and Bibliography, is devoted to this area. Keeping up with the subject helps us to know if we are meeting the needs of our clients. It is especially helpful to hear from scholars from the Caribbean. The areas covered include Central America, the Francophone Caribbean, Puerto Rico, and Trinidad and Tobago. The most general paper in this section deals with women in the non-Hispanic Caribbean.

Within the Caribbean, the one country that probably provides the topic of most discussion is Cuba. Part Six brings together a look at research being done on Cuba in the nineteenth century with papers on Cubans in the United States. Three papers in this last category deal with activities at the University of Miami, one of the hosts of the joint conference.

These papers represent the formal presentations made at the panels and workshops. (At the end of this volume are listed the

substantive panels and workshops of the meeting.) The discussions
that took place after the presentation of the papers are not included
but can be found in the report published and distributed to the
members of SALALM.[2]   It is hoped that this joint conference
strengthened the bonds between the two associations and their
members.

                                                    Mina Jane Grothey

2. Charles S. Fineman, ed., "SALALM XXXII, May 10-15, 1987: Summary
Reports of the Sessions," *SALALM Newsletter* 15, supplement (September 1987).

Acknowledgments

These papers would not have been written but for the hard work of all the people involved in the planning for the Joint Conference of SALALM and ACURIL.

SALALM Executive Board for 1986/87

President: Mina Jane Grothey, University of New Mexico

Vice President/President Elect: Paula Covington, Vanderbilt University

Past President: Iliana Sonntag, San Diego State University

Executive Secretary: Suzanne Hodgman, University of Wisconsin-Madison

Treasurer: Jane Garner, University of Texas at Austin

Members at Large: David Block, Cornell University; Rafael Coutín, University of North Carolina; Russ Davidson, University of New Mexico; Marian Goslinga, Florida International University; Deborah Jakubs, Duke University; Sharon Moynahan, University of New Mexico

Rapporteur General: Charles S. Fineman, Northwestern University

ACURIL Executive Council for 1986/87

President: Alice van Romondt, Aruba National Library

Vice President/President Elect: Albertina Jefferson, University of the West Indies

Past President: Marie Françoise Bernabé, Bibliothèque Universitaire Antilles-Guyane

Executive Secretary: Oneida R. Ortiz, Biblioteca Regional del Caribe, Universidad de Puerto Rico, Río Piedras, Puerto Rico

Treasurer: Joan P. Hayes, Biblioteca Estación Experimental Agrícola RUM, Universidad de Puerto Rico, Río Piedras, Puerto Rico

Members: Vere Achong, Medical Library, General Hospital, Trinidad and Tobago; Jean Wilfrid Bertrand, Archives Nationale d'Haïti; Blanca Hodge, Philipsburg Jubilee Library, St. Maarten;

Venezuela; Neida Pagán, Instituto de Estudios del Caribe, Universidad de Puerto Rico, Río Piedras, Puerto Rico; Frank Rodgers, University of Miami

Rapporteur General: Peter de la Garza, Library of Congress

Local Organizing Committee

Chairman: Frank Rodgers, University of Miami

Co-Chairman: Laurence A. Miller, Florida International University

Editorial: Marian Goslinga, Florida International University

Exhibits: Ronald P. Naylor, University of Miami

Home Hospitality: Estrella Iglesias, Florida International University; Sara Sánchez, University of Miami

Public Relations: Paul Feehan, University of Miami

Registration: Tony Harvell, University of Miami

Secretariat: Carol F. Ahmad, University of Miami

Social Events: Antonie Baker Downs, Florida International University

Translation Service: Sherry Carrillo, Florida International University

Transportation: Jacqueline Zelman, Florida International University

Treasurer: Dale L. Barker, University of Miami

Part One

Recession Management Strategies

1. Recession Management Strategies

Antonito Gordiano Croes

I welcome this opportunity to address this distinguished group of Caribbean librarians and publishers during this joint conference. It is an honour to discuss the governmental authority's view on management in times of economic recession. I would like to see the librarian community focus its unique skills and resources on this very important task, since the future position of the Caribbean in this changing world depends in part on how well we can understand the nature of information management. Education is the vehicle through which this can best be accomplished, and I suggest that the librarians who recognize their responsibility towards domestic education would also recognize the advantages of exchanging information and experience with countries in our region.

The theme of this conference is well chosen. Exchange of information is the first step in international cooperation. As managers of information you are important, you are the ones who are the first in line to open avenues of cooperation. But this is not as easy task.

Apart from the constant rise and change in the public's demand for information and related services, government authorities and librarians are faced with two new problems: the constant change in the appearance of knowledge and information and the just pressure for still better terms of disseminating and sharing knowledge and information. The change in the appearance of knowledge and information is something we have heard a lot about, but we have seen so little of what is possible or what is still to come.

The traditional forms of acquiring knowledge will undergo great change, and definitely so with education. Newspapers, magazines, and books will probably get new functions which are not yet quite clear to us. Electronic mass media will grow in influence but change in scope to satisfy the ever-changing needs of people. These and other changes caused by the information technology and its revolutionary forms of generating and transmitting information, are intriguing. But they also pose serious problems for the independent and democratic development of especially small countries like Aruba. They surely form a problem or rather a challenge for our libraries.

The problem of sharing knowledge and information is as formidable as the need to acquire and use information and knowledge properly. If having knowledge means having power, then managing information means managing power, and that is what you as librarians do. Sharing information is the starting point of sharing power, which lies at the heart of democracy as it means the enabling of *all men* to manage their lives and their society in a rational and just way.

Thus the question is, how do we in the Caribbean, with our limited and sometimes shrinking resources in a seemingly everlasting economic recession, cope with the changes brought about by the information technology and at the same time assure a steady democratic development of our island countries? There are no tested strategies. Uniform approaches are unrealistic as they often neglect important characteristics of the different communities. The differences, for example, the homogeneity of the population, the literacy rate, and other relevant social and economic factors, exclude the use of uniform strategies. The common structural limitations and the often common goals of the Caribbean countries do argue, however, in favour of unified efforts to manage these new situations.

Aruba has limited natural resources and relies on imports for most of its requirements of food and consumer goods. It does have a well-developed infrastructure and a high standard of education. The attendance rates at the primary and secondary schools equal those in industrial countries. The attendance rates at institutions of higher education are constantly growing, but limited mainly by the small number of such institutions on the island itself.

Until recently, the economy of Aruba was supported largely by oil refining and tourism. In March 1985, the Exxon refinery closed its facilities owing mainly to the drop in oil prices and changes in the pattern of world oil trade. The closing of the oil refinery caused Aruba to suffer a severe loss of foreign exchange, public revenues, and jobs, which in turn put into jeopardy Aruba's long-term future. The island's gross domestic product is estimated to have dropped 17 percent between 1984 and 1986; foreign exchange earnings were cut in half; and government revenues plunged 40 percent.

At the same time Aruba attained a new political status. On January 1, 1986, Aruba became a separate entity within the Kingdom of the Netherlands. This new political status enables the government of Aruba to define and implement social, cultural, financial, economic, and monetary policies on its own. Before 1986, these matters were under the authority of the Netherlands Antillean Government. The impact of this new political status has been, on the one hand, the conspicuous stain caused to the already diminishing resources, and, on the other hand, the emergence of a complex decision-making process, which up until then was unknown in the Aruban bureaucracy. The country has encountered problems in the transition to this new situation, but it has managed rather well.

Aruba is a small country with a total population of about sixty thousand, 12 percent of whom are above the age of fifty-five and about 40 percent younger than twenty-five. It is a country with no university. All postsecondary education, except for the training of teachers for the kindergarten and primary education, takes place abroad. Information and training facilities for specialized professional groups are very limited.

The National Library is a government-funded and -managed institution. It functions as a department within the Ministry of Human Services. Although the day-to-day management of the library is in the hands of the director, the minister in charge is the one responsible for the general financial and personnel management and for the information-gathering and -disseminating policies and for enabling institutions like the National Library to carry them out. Changes in these policies are possible within the parameters set by the constitution and specific laws.

So there you have an open community going through its greatest economic crisis ever, with basic development needs growing and the usual organisations and institutions to satisfy these needs lacking. It is within this framework that one must see the position of the National Library in Aruba and its ability to cope with new demands and changes in terms of economic recession.

I am proud of the fact that at the beginning of 1986 our government adopted a general long-term development strategy based on the deepening and widening of our tourist industry and the diversification of the economy as a whole in those feasible areas. The Government of Aruba has been quite successful, thus far, in its policy, witness the increase in the number of hotel rooms, in the amount of carriers flying to Aruba, and in the number of tourists visiting Aruba. The figures are staggering. In sixteen months the amount of hotel rooms, either in construction or about to start, doubled from 2,000 to 4,000. The airline seats available almost doubled, and the number of tourists visiting Aruba is 25 percent higher than the previous year.

In less than eight months, 2,000 new jobs have been created, and the foreign exchange reserves skyrocketed to more than Af. 200 million, which is equivalent to six months of our import.

In order to strengthen this envisaged development, the Government of Aruba considered from the outset of its tenure that the competitive edge of Aruba in the international division of labour would be in its human resources. Therefore, it has been assumed that a sustained economic development would be viable only through a high quality of services and level of production. This, of course, implies an emphasis on the quality of education and of information services, such as those offered by the library, and a close relationship between the two. In addition, the strengthening of the education system and the disseminating of information and knowledge are assumed to be vital for a steady and real democratic government.

The Government strenuously has endeavoured to overcome the structural limitations and logistic constraints. One way has been to facilitate opportunities for prospective college students to continue their undergraduate programs abroad. A special fund has been created to promote the enrollment of students at overseas universities. Last year more than 200 students, equivalent to 2 percent of the total school population, were given the opportunity to study abroad.

Another way has been to strengthen the National Library.

The specific aims of the government for the library within this general strategy are to expand the scope and raise the quality of the services offered by the National Library, to bring the information and educational services of the National Library closer to actual and changing needs of the man in the street and the professionals, and to build an international information network in order to support the overall development strategy.

Again, there are a number of assumptions from which these specific aims come forth: To manage the impact of the new information technology in a critical way and to assure a good dissemination of all information available, a capable organisation was needed. The National Library turned out to be the best instrument to perform these tasks, because of its experience already accumulated, its internal facilities and organisation, and, not least, its international links. It was assumed that by expanding the scope and by raising the quality of the services of the National Library, a number of objectives would be achieved.

We would strengthen the image of the National Library as a multifunctional and professionally-managed organisation. This would in turn attract more and new users for its new types of information services. In our view, critical users of the information made available through the new services and information technology must be developed, for instance, in education, in case they are not already present. The expansion of the services of the National Library, and the enhancing of the quality of the services, meant more efficient use of the facilities and capabilities of the library. Most of all, the expansion of the services of the Library was a very efficient way of "filling the gaps" in the institutional, organisational, and logistic capacity of the community. By doing so the National Library achieved one of its main objectives.

Our policy was to emphasize and sustain the activities of the National Library in this respect and to eliminate whatever restrictions there were. The result thus far of this combined approach of the government and the National Library is that the National Library has evolved into a real cultural and information center, an open meeting place. In addition to the creation of this cultural and information rendez-vous, the National Library undertook specific efforts to reach out to the public at large. One of the means employed has been regular visits of the library buses to the several parishes in Aruba. The visits take place at strategic spots (e.g., schools and churches) and on scheduled dates. The efforts to strengthen the reading habits of especially the youth have been quite successful. The National Library in Aruba can best be characterized as an active and attractive center for a variety of activities. And this is mainly attributable to the creativity and the high morale of the director, her staff, and personnel. An example of the very important and successful activities of the library is its work with the very young. The various activities for children between three and twelve years of age have at least one objective and achievement in common, namely, to lower their fear of working with other children and grown-ups outside the home or the school and to develop an intellectual curiosity about the life around them. The educational value of these activities may be greater than is expected.

The strategy applied to the Aruba case, to manage the information and educational services of the library in a time of recession, was to capitalize on the existing strengths and creative manageable services required by the community within the existing facilities. In doing so we boosted the image of the library which in turn strengthened its capability even more. Internally the library also went through a process of adaptation to make the strategy work. There was a conscious re-definition of the aims and priorities of the library and a restructuring of the organisation. The latter resulted in an organisation in which at a certain moment each library worker has a personal responsibility in the decision-making process at some level. This involvement was essential in raising the morale of the people at the library.

The ability of the National Library to cope with the information needs of the community is one of the two main factors I consider essential in any strategy aimed at managing information in times of economic crisis. The other equally important factor is the regional and international cooperation in the gathering and dissemination of information. For the Caribbean countries, ACURIL is already performing a valuable function in that it links the member libraries. In doing so it addresses their limitations and complements their effectiveness. ACURIL is a very good example of cooperation toward reaching a common goal across national, political, historical, cultural, and linguistic barriers. Together with the International Federation of Library Associations, UNESCO, and the Caribbean Development and Cooperation Committee, ACURIL forms the structure of international and regional cooperation. In my opinion this form of cooperation is the most important instrument in managing the new information revolution. Without it the various countries in the region would each face insurmountable problems in dealing with the information revolution on their own.

To sum up, this is, in brief, how we handled the situation in Aruba: We have redefined the goals of the library in such a way as to respond more adequately to the real information needs in the community. We have given the library the space to pursue these goals in an active and creative way, involving all the personnel, thus boosting their morale. And we have strengthened international cooperation. The result has been the expansion of the services and activities of the library, which meant a change in its role in the community. The library has been converted into a cultural focal point. This new role is being supported by several private organisations.

Our situation is unique, as is so with each of your situations back home, and make the transfer of our experience to any other situation difficult. Nevertheless I hope that I have been able to inspire you also to look for solutions to problems within financial and organisational limitations. I am sure that we are not the only ones who have had success in doing so. The situation in some of your countries is at least as bad as ours, and I have heard that you have developed ways and means to survive which I consider admirable. I must say that you have done very well indeed. Remember—you are never given a dream without the power to make it come true.

2. Caribbean Collections

Yvonne V. Stephenson

The Information Society

It seems somewhat of a contradiction today, when mankind the world over has developed a scale of information needs unparalleled in history and information is said to be growing exponentially and publishing at an unprecedented level, that libraries and information and documentation units should be afflicted with a formidable combination of inflation, the falling value of currencies, foreign exchange crises, reduced grants, and severe budge cuts. The true significance of this dilemma confronting libraries in the Caribbean and elsewhere as we approach the twenty-first century should be viewed with deep concern.

We are in an age in which, politically and philosophically, education is considered a right of the individual, the same as any other human right. Along with this, there is the very strong rhetoric concerning the "right to read." The consequent spread of education has now had a significant impact on the Caribbean region in which many of our societies, once considered semiliterate or even primitive, have evolved with increased and sophisticated information needs. Noteworthy, too, is the introduction of technological innovations, which have stimulated a need for access to a range of information hitherto unknown. Politically, the demand for increased information is acute. Caribbean countries can hardly afford to go through a period of infancy in terms of the availability of information—like Topsy, they have to be "born big." Our young nations in the Caribbean must be at the bargaining table with the older and more developed nations, discussing and negotiating issues of common interest. There is perhaps no greater need for information than that of these countries which must be in possession of relevant information if the discussion at the bargaining table is to be a dialogue and not a monologue, or if there is to be equity arising from such meetings.

A very fundamental issue in the Caribbean is the need for information which must provide support for research and decision making which would benefit the economic, social, cultural, and scientific development of our societies. Libraries in the Region should be equipped to meet these needs. It is their Caribbean collections specifically which are under pressure in these circumstances. Inadequate finances—budget cuts, devalued currencies—have posed the severest threats to these libraries in honouring an accepted mandate—that is the collection of all works on the Caribbean produced within, or outside of the Region, with special responsibility for the comprehensive collection of works relating to the country in which the library is located.

How can libraries respond to this mandate?

Creativity

Robert Townsend, famed for his work *Up the Organisation* (London: Michael Joseph, 1970), stated:

> A tight budget brings out the best creative instincts in man. Give him unlimited funds and he won't come up with the best way to a result. Man is a complicated animal. He only simplifies under pressure. Put him under some financial pressure . . . then he'll come up with a plan which to his own private amazement, is not only less expensive, but also faster and better than his original proposal which you send back.

In considering Townsend's statement, one wonders whether in the context of our deliberations there might not be a challenge held out to us. The fact is that we live in times when much is expected of our services. We are expected to operate efficiently to meet the information needs of the organisations that we serve, along with those of the wider society, if we are not to be phased out of existence. This level of expectation can hardly be met effectively without reasonable provision of finances. Neither can it be met "cheaply." De Solle Price tells us in *Little Science, Big Science* (London University Press, 1963) that technical and scientific information is doubling its output every fifteen years. Hence the general dilemma referred to earlier—increased volume of publications and declining finances.

This is a real-life situation that must be confronted in a practical way if libraries and information services are to be effective. For this reason, my paper attempts a practical approach to the problem. There might be no absolute solutions, but it is hoped that ideas generated would stimulate the creativity and imagination alluded to by Robert Townsend.

Notwithstanding the fact that the focus of our attention is Caribbean collections, it must be recognised that we cannot divorce the problems of these collections from the general financial issues affecting their parent libraries. The operations of these collections must be recognised as an integral part of the Library's operations—problems of financing, space, technical expertise, staffing, which affect the general library also affect the specialised collections. It could be said, however, that in the long run, these problems, when applied specifically to Caribbean collections, could have a far more crippling effect than in the more general areas of operation.

The Challenge

The challenge confronting Caribbean collections is one not of survival but of growth and development: How do we develop in the face of the existing financial climate? How do we progress rationally and in a qualitative fashion? In different circumstances, one would solve a problem of collection development by following a purely logical procedure, identifying one solution—or perhaps a partial solution which librarians, very likely in consultation with a special committee or with key users—planners, decision makers, scholars, researchers—would design a strategy for action in which priorities are identified and "an essential core" of material established. On this basis one would operate a crisis budget aimed at securing the essentials identified. But this pattern of selectivity in the collection of Caribbean material on our history, culture, and indeed all areas of development must be considered as imperative in terms of collection development.

In our colleges and universities, studies and investigations into all aspects of the Caribbean are an inescapable fact. This is reflective of the times in which we live—when there is an urgency to understand ourselves and the problems of our societies. If we consider the general theory of human behaviour, we must be concerned with the evolving patterns in this area of our own societies. We must therefore have access to all pertinent information, if such a study is to be meaningful. How then could one decide what should not be acquired? The multidisciplinary approach to the coverage of Caribbean material requires a dynamic approach to collection development and one which is sensitive to the needs of our societies.

There should be no need for a justification of the comprehensiveness of our collection development policies. There should be considerable concern for the impediments which restrict such policies and consequently the development of these collections. We are faced with such problems as:

1. Publication Runs
    Comparatively smaller runs of Caribbean titles are produced, resulting in comparatively higher costs of these publications. This places considerable strain on already weakened budgets.

2. Accessibility of Publications
    The difficulties in the identification and acquisition of the range
    of material produced in the Region, already discussed in previous
    SALALM and ACURIL meetings, make financial planning
    difficult, more so in times of recession when adequate planning is
    a necessity.

3. High Cost of Material
    Reduced budgets, coupled with the lowering values of currencies
    and the high costs of publications, have led to considerable
    restrictions in purchasing.

4. Availability of Material
    The speed with which material becomes unavailable hampers
    collection development when funds are not readily available.

5. Finances
    Budget cuts and limited access to foreign exchange have generally
    restricted acquisition programmes.

Financing

Although there are ample reasons for concern about the finances
of libraries, our primary concern during this meeting is the development of our Caribbean collections in times of financial stringencies.
In examining this issue it is useful to review very briefly the financing
of such programmes in normal circumstances. Some questions to be
considered are as follows:

1. Do libraries have a special budgeting allocation for Caribbean
    collections?
2. If so, is this allocation a fixed percentage of the overall budget?
    How is the budget determined?
3. Is this material acquired with funds just skimmed from fixed
    allocations for other subject material?
4. Is Caribbean material acquired from a discretionary fund
    administered by the librarian?
5. Is Caribbean material accorded priority in the book budget?

The importance accorded Caribbean material should be reflected
in the way in which financial provision is made for the development of
these collections. The significance of such a provision is that it would
be the foundation on which adjustments could be made for the
financial management of these collections at all times and in all
circumstances. If, therefore, there is no recognisable budgetary pattern
within institutions, then there would be no ready basis on which plans

of any sort could be made. It is reasonable to assume that only when institutions, internally, accord some independent financial status to these collections, that logical financial planning or adjustments could be seriously addressed. The responsibility is ours to demonstrate by our financial planning, the importance we ourselves are prepared to attribute to these collections.

The bugbear of foreign currency which is gravely in pursuit of most of our libraries is perhaps the most formidable of financial issues to be confronted. It raises a number of complex issues which are almost beyond the control of most librarians. It is usually a national issue which envelops libraries and one which must be recognised as being the domain of economic planners. Nevertheless, this does not defy our ability to seek ways and means of acquiring at least some material.

Today nations are considering counter trade and barter. Can libraries benefit from these ideas? Notwithstanding the state of local publishing industries, the production of books at each national level could be considered in relation to their value for securing publications from outside of the Region. As long as such schemes are not considered to be in disharmony with national trade policies, they should be given serious consideration.

Librarians have already exploited Gifts and Exchanges programmes. I therefore do not deal with the subject, but merely persuade libraries to utilize such programmes to the fullest capacity.

Grants

For years grants have been a substantial source of revenue for libraries. Securing funds this way has now become a skill or a fine art which librarians must develop. Although such sources of funding have greatly expanded, the competitive nature of the game must not be underestimated.

Survival Strategies

Today in the Caribbean we are wearied by inflation, we are sceptical about the stability of our currencies for any fixed period of time. In the meanwhile, the growing scarcities of financial resources have weakened the foundations of the development of our library collections. Caught in this situation and confronted by spiralling costs and severe budget cuts, libraries are under pressure to attain their objectives. They must therefore be prepared to develop their defences and, in more positive terms, develop strategy which would be of practical value to them in seeking solutions to their mounting problems.

Susan Curzon identified eight strategies which libraries should develop if they are to confront the issue of recession or financial cuts. [1] I have modified them to the following in the light of some experiences in Guyana and in the wider Caribbean, and in relation to their adaptability to our situations:

1. Development of a Power Base
    Like all other organisations which must operate in a political sphere, libraries must seek to have a power base. What is suggested here is the establishment of useful contact with influential persons or with suitable pressure groups which are subtle and effective and which have a comprehension and an appreciation of the value of libraries. Libraries have an appeal for many serious groups because of our role and our involvement in education and in the social, economic, and cultural development of society. These support groups should establish the correct link for the governmental or political lobby. From practical experience, we are aware that in societies such as ours, this is an accepted way of getting action. Libraries must therefore explore this possibility.

2. Knowledge of Our Press
    In our society, the correct press coverage could stimulate the desired public opinion. One must, however, be realistic about the image one's library really has and the one it will project. We cannot convince the public that we are a crisis service like health or the police. It is for us to impress about our role in preserving a vital part of the nation's culture and its heritage; our mission in the organisation, in the dissemination of information, and in the encouragement of people to develop, to educate, and to realise themselves through knowledge of their present and their past. We can project the fact that this mission has worth and quality. The judicious use of the press can inform the public of the viability of Caribbean collections and services and of their fundamental role in shaping the quality of life and the development of the Caribbean peoples.

---

[1] Susan Curzon, "Survival Strategies for Library Managers," *Wilson Library Bulletin* 54 (December 1979), 224-229.

3. Public Relations Programmes
    Libraries have been far too modest and ultra-conservative about
    the valuable work they do. Take, for instance, the work done in
    supporting indigenous writings of our history, our culture, and so
    on, which are so dependent on the material assembled by our
    librarians; take the significant role we play, providing information
    which extends the work on the development of numerous strands
    in our society. As librarians, we speak to one another about our
    activities which are too often taken for granted. We need to be
    more visible and to promote the value of our service. Public
    relations should be a part of our library programmes. When the
    value of our libraries is accorded due recognition, budget cuts
    might be done more judiciously. At worst, when there are budget
    cuts, libraries should not suffer more than any other public
    service.

4. Alternative Strategies
    We need to be more prepared for budget cuts and should
    anticipate them in a practical way. One such possibility is the
    establishment of a small committee of the most creative persons
    to do an analysis of the operations of our Caribbean collections.
    Identify what must be sacrificed if the funds must be cut. There
    is a need to look at duplication or unnecessarily costly processes.
    The real key is to exercise creativity and to re-conceptualise the
    programme of our collection if possible. Too often we become
    very negative and depressed about cuts, and alternative strategies
    are never accorded the importance deserved.

Alternative Sources of Funding

Depending on the countries in which we live, our libraries are all
in various states of recession or depression, while the general
economies of most countries are battling with rampant inflation and
spiralling unemployment. In Jamaica, in 1970, the unemployment rate
was estimated to be 8.75 percent; in Trinidad 18.5 percent; in Barbados
7.35 percent; and in Guyana 12.2 percent. This gives some idea of the
state of our economies—a condition beyond our control. It is therefore
clear that libraries must take another look at all aspects of their
financial support and at the traditional sources of funding.

In recent times there has been much discussion among Caribbean
governments about the diversification of the economies of the Region.
Perhaps it is time that our libraries give some consideration to the
diversification of our sources of income. Funding for libraries has
always tended to be an estimated 80 percent from the central

government and 20 percent from the local government and other sources. But in real terms the monies allocated are infinitesimal in relation to the overall national budgets. The low level of support given to libraries presents a grim picture that cannot be improved with the state of the economy as it is today. Budget cuts and the declining value of currencies will only produce crises in our libraries.

Should libraries therefore consider the possibility of involvement in financial ventures? We have long accepted the fundamental creed of "the public library as the people's university," added to which we have developed a long tradition of our public library's being a service provided free of charge to the public. The concept of introducing a charge would immediately seem to negate this noble tradition and the fundamental creed of our public libraries. The debate on this issue is on, and there are groups of proponents and opponents of the idea of charges. I am of the view that most of us in the English-speaking Caribbean would not favour the introduction of charges in our public library service. But given the state of our economies, can we truly afford the services we would like to provide? Notwithstanding this, a review of certain elements of the service provided might stimulate an adjustment in our thinking.

It would seem reasonable that access to our institutions and to our book collections which are enjoyed by the entire community should always be a free service. One should therefore consider very seriously those services which are clearly tied to the personal or corporate research interest of our users. Could these be justifiably provided for a fee? This must be seriously considered because increasingly heavy demands are now being made on Caribbean collections for specialised information which is often required for the support of projects, some of which are funded. In these instances, many libraries undertake extensive searches and compile bibliographies and holdings lists. These services provided are specialised and are far in excess of what is provided to the average user. Why should these services be free? Why should not the library charge a fee for some of these ventures?

This growing use being made of our collections by persons involved in financial ventures must be given special consideration. It is clearly one area in which a fee could be justifiably considered. Other services such as photocopying could be operated to produce a surplus. Obtaining material from sources outside of one's country should be done on the same basis. This level of financial operation is one that libraries are unaccustomed to. But given the financial stringencies of the day, this should not be an unrealistic undertaking.

Whatever our position on this issue might be, some libraries in more opulent societies such as the United States and Canada are charging fees for a variety of services. A recent U.S. study has shown that over one in five libraries charge rental fees for some types of highly specialised publications; one in three for the loan of films; one in twenty-seven charge registration fees; one in sixty charge for admission to library-sponsored programmes. Many, of course, are charging for access to online database services. We in the Caribbean would do well to consider this development and its adaptability to our organisations.

This issue of supplemental funding is growing in popularity and is the subject of several articles. There has even been a call for research to identify and describe present and potential alternative funding options for publicly-supported library and information services in the United States.

Brooke Sheldon in her address to the 38th Annual Canadian Library Association Conference listed the following options open to all types of libraries for the supplementation of grants:

> Charge fees for the use of meeting rooms.
> Charge for space for exhibitions.
> Tap the private sector, foundations, and so on, for grants.
> Seek endowments.
> Institute needs assessments and other planning mechanisms to pin-point essential services.
> Streamline procedures.
> Engage in resource sharing and networking.

She culminated her address on this issue by reiterating the fact that we must not be deterred in our endeavours to convince governments of their responsibilities in maintaining a certain minimum level of fiscal support for our libraries. [2]

Policy Information

The prevailing economic circumstances must affect the fundamental policies which govern the character and the growth of Caribbean collections. The scope and quality of the services offered by these collections must be equally affected. There are also the major issues such as the policies which will determine the degree of

---

[2] Sheldon Brooks, "Constant Change: Libraries Respond to the Challenge," *Canadian Library Journal* 40 (October 1983), 303-307.

dependence or interdependence of the collections in our libraries on other libraries.

The fundamental policies referred to are those which will determine the financial management of our collections. Equally important, they will determine the quality of the service provided by these collections. In fact, they will determine not only the quality of these collections but also the general reputation of these collections and their parent libraries. Given the importance of these policies, it follows that their formulation should be given careful consideration.

To be specific: these policy issues—the options exercised in what is acquired and what is not, the decisions about the shape and character of these collections—are so vital that they should not be formulated in isolation but should include the views of the librarians concerned. Administrators and perhaps even the views of a few users might well be consulted on this all-important issue of policy formulation. Librarians concerned with Caribbean collections have a serious and inescapable obligation to state very clearly the facts that underlie each of the policy issues being considered. These issues should be stated clearly, unambiguously, and should be related to the more general framework of operation of its parent library.

There are no easy answers to the numerous questions which must be considered in the process of policy formulation in times of recession, but once questions are raised, responses should reflect the views of librarians, administrators, and users. This is no doubt a difficult process, but should nevertheless be pursued as the need for goodwill, understanding, and support is vital when a reduction in service, facilities, or structures is under consideration.

It is perhaps a common experience among libraries that key questions are not always raised with any conviction; and policy issues are often considered only in times of crisis. So often issues are raised at ineffective committees and at budget or estimates meetings which are only concerned with the restriction of financial expenditure. Ideally, these matters should be aired at the most important forum with parties most likely to be concerned or in some way affected by the developments. Purposeful exploration of the issues concerned, and decisions on key issues, would provide librarians with the measure of support required, and would be very useful in building an informed and supportive body of users, who could, in certain circumstances, constitute a pressure group at the wider national level, influencing financial administrators.

Ways and Means of Managing Libraries

Ways and means of managing in times of recession cannot be legislated. They have to be approached creatively. For this reason, my paper has been more concerned with the creation of relationships and an environment which would support creativity and expediency planning. I hold the view, however, that institutions which are run on the basis of standard management practices, utilising analytical techniques to improve their operations, are very likely in the best position to adopt even the most ad hoc of strategies for operating in times of financial crisis.

In the specific area of Caribbean resources, librarians must be much more conscious, and a great deal of emphasis should be placed on reliable data collection. There is a need to know very precisely the level of use of items in these collections over specific periods of time; there is a need to know the intrinsic value of individual items which are to be acquired with scarce resources.

If resource sharing is to be a strategy aimed at ensuring the availability of material, then careful planning, based on hard facts, and not just on arbitrary decisions, must underpin this plan. Recognising that resource sharing could be an area of potential conflict, careful negotiations must be worked out. Terms of such a programme would, in the case of a national plan, be dependent on local conditions, the number and type of libraries, and the extent of the financial issues. It is expected that in such arrangements factors taken into consideration would be the mission of each library involved—the infrastructure available in the co-operating libraries—in order to achieve a rational and logical sharing of responsibilities.

Most libraries should be able to establish very clearly the factors which would most heavily influence library expenditure on certain types of material, given budget limitations. This is vital if the concept of resource sharing is to be successful. The library's mission in relation to the acquisition of certain types of material must be very carefully formulated. The list of such considerations could be long and the answers of great importance.

Generally, the collection and the ultimate preservation of Caribbean material is an awesome responsibility. Libraries involved must be clear about their responsibility with respect to the national literature. They should also be clear about their responsibility, where applicable, for providing access to the more general publications of all types produced in the Region. If these responsibilities are to be met, then it is obvious that steps must be taken to ensure that notwithstanding the financial disabilities, libraries involved in resource sharing must be prepared—and able—to meet their commitment.

Recommendations

1. Have thought out clearly and in advance the priorities and essential functions of the Caribbean collections. Recognise that a traditional activity is not necessarily an essential activity. Flexibility and the willingness to accept innovations must be encouraged. With priorities established, goals and objectives should be set. A plan of action must be worked out, and there must be clear ideas about what should be cut when the need arises.

2. There must be good communication between library staff and administration in order to promote the library's views at several levels.

3. Good management information must be easily available. There must be the ability to back up advice or recommendations with facts and figures. Be prepared to demonstrate the impact of cuts in concrete terms.

4. Be prepared to maintain a certain level of service even at the cost of other things, for example, the provision of a single copy for reference as opposed to two additional copies for loan.

5. Strictest economy in operating costs must be observed.

6. It should be established whether library budgets are being reduced or literally being cannibalised to support other areas of the institutions.

7. In the case of research grants allocated to the university, a bid should be made to have a percentage allocated for library development; a formula should be worked out as an accepted policy.

8. Unlike decisions which must be made as to the proportionate distribution of a book budget, which at the very least would depend on the science/social sciences/humanities offering at a given university, the question of the acquisition of Caribbean material must be seen in a different light. The question of Caribbean material is one of needing everything, resulting in agonising decisions as to what can be excluded and the basis for such exclusions.

9. There must be a re-consideration of the introduction of fees for special services provided.

10. Carefully planned public relations programmes should be developed.

11. Libraries must be prepared to justify money invested in them.
12. The ability to tap funding agencies must be carefully cultivated.
13. Resource sharing must be more realistically pursued.

Conclusion

Our struggle to preserve the development of Caribbean collections is not just a struggle for a service or another cause. It is a struggle to preserve the core of our libraries. These collections answer our users' deepest need for culture, growth, and self-realization. For the librarians in the Region and the thousands of users who walk through our doors every day, we speak about a quality of life that says: "The preservation of the world of the mind is as crucial as the preservation of the body." We must employ every ability at our command to protect an institution of extraordinary value.

BIBLIOGRAPHY

Bassnett, Peter J. "Implications: Charges for Public Library Services." *Canadian Library Journal* 38 (April 1981), 57-63.

Curzon, Susan. "Survival Strategies for Library Managers." *Wilson Library Bulletin* 54 (December 1979), 224-229.

De Gerraro, Richard. "Escalating Journal Prices: Time to Fight Back." *American Libraries* 8 (February 1977), 69-74.

The Information Society: Issues and Answers. London and Phoenix, AZ: Oryx Press, 1978.

Library Advisory Council of England. "Libraries and Their Finance." *Journal of Librarianship* 8 (January 1976), 1-20.

Machlup, Fritz. *Information through the Printed Word: The Dissemination of Scholarly, Scientific, and Intellectual Knowledge.* Vol. 1, *Book Publishing.* New York, NY: Praeger, 1978.

Overton, C.D. "Value for Money in Government Library Information Services." *ASLIB Proceedings* 26 (June 1972), 325-336.

Peacock, P.G. "The Hidden Cost of Saving: The Effect of Cancelling Periodicals." *ASLIB Proceedings* 32 (April 1980), 167-169.

Sheldon, Brooke. "Constant Change: Libraries Respond to the Challenge." *Canadian Library Journal* 40 (October 1983), 303-307.

Smethurst, J.M. "Management, Research, and Academic Library Problems: A Way Forward." *Library Review* 31 (Winter 1982), 231-238.

3. In the Eye of the Hurricane: Libraries and Economic Recessions

Laura Gutiérrez-Witt

I was invited to comment today on economic recessions and their influence on library collections and services and what librarians can do to minimize their effects. Needless to say, it is not coincidental that I was asked to speak on this topic. Who has not heard of the much discussed and lamented slowdown of the Texas economy? Yes, it has been a shock to many people in Texas to learn that the gushers no longer flow green and gold!

Economic recessions are not new to Texas nor to any other state or nation, and their effect on libraries is well known and well documented. The library literature includes many accounts by library managers bemoaning low and ever-decreasing budgets, particularly since the 1970s. [1] No nation, no state, no institution, no library is immune to the vagaries of our global economy. Even the fabulously endowed Getty Museum and its Library have recently been cited as facing some uncertainty in funding and income owing to the Texaco-Pennzoil lawsuit.

Therefore, for University of Texas librarians the news in 1986 that funding was to be decreased rather than increased was not unexpected. Nor was the softening of the dollar abroad and the rise in foreign serial subscription prices completely unforeseen. The silver lining for Latin American acquisitions, of course, was that the dollar still bought quite a few books in Latin America. Nonetheless, a decrease of legislative funding for higher education in Texas still meant less money for every library, the Benson Collection included.

I do not intend to dwell on our experiences at Texas of the past two years since they follow the classic model of financial exigency and retrenchment that other libraries have undergone. Personnel hiring freezes, shortened hours, reduced acquisitions—thus far nothing too drastic, but over the long range these necessary measures will surely cause an erosion of collections, of services, of salaries, of staff morale. We face, then, a situation common to many if not all libraries at one time or another: how to minimize the effects of reduced funding, of slow or no growth, of diminished resources in general.

The obvious course of action is to adjust to a reduced standard of living and of spending over the long term. One writer has called that situation as one of existing in "genteel poverty." But does it really have to be so? Will a reduced budget necessarily mean a reduced role for the library? Faced with external political and economic factors such as less government revenues, inflation, the fall or devaluation of currencies, librarians certainly have cause to feel helpless and frustrated. In addition, library managers must also cope with price increases in published materials, with the rapid growth of information, and with increased demands for more materials and more services. Library buildings may need renovation, space for collections and for services may be in short supply, and the size of the library staff is probably insufficient to meet all needs. In actuality, the majority of these factors have been fairly constant for libraries during much of their history. One or another or several have plagued libraries continuously. But somehow it is difficult to accept a future of endless "genteel poverty," and we do not have to do so.

Despite the many factors beyond our control, librarians still do and can control how library resources and library budgets are used and conserved. Too often both resources and budgets are viewed as contingent on external forces. The availability of institutional funding may be a factor outside the library's purview, but librarians do control certain constant and very valuable resources: collections, buildings or space, equipment, and staff.

My participation on this panel, therefore, is personally timely. In the course of preparing these remarks, I reviewed the literature on library financial planning, and found, not surprisingly, that a corpus of materials has recently evolved covering the topic of this conference: recession strategies. The key concept common to much of this literature was planning. Planning in order to survive, live with, and even benefit from research, stagflation, retrenchment, austerity, or whatever term one chooses to describe the condition. Most of the writers, however, specifically stated that planning for austerity cannot take place without setting aside some traditional ideas of acquiring and providing information. Too often in the past, traditional modes of accomplishing goals have tended to limit library innovation.

Planning and innovation, therefore, are seen by the experts, that is, librarians who have experienced austerity and learned from it, as the two most important activities that must take place if libraries and their managers are to survive and benefit from budgetary decreases. If library managers can grasp some control of their future, uncertainty can be lessened and fulfillment of goals achieved.

Planning and the setting of realistic goals cannot take place in a vacuum. In order to plan for the future, it is necessary to review current goals, perhaps revise acquisition programs and services, certainly inventory resources. In short, data-gathering is the first important element in planning for austerity. This activity is not new to libraries; practically every library gathers statistics on circulation and reference, user visits through turnstile counts, original and edit cataloging, salaries, space availability, staff size and composition, and so forth. Budgetary documents also provide information of what and how financial resources are allocated. Annual reports recapitulate accomplishments of the past year and enunciate goals for the coming year. A recent Office of Management Studies report points out, however, that other data such as library staff/user ratios, acquisition dollars per FTE (full-time equivalent) student and per Ph.D. student, library expenditures per FTE student, technical services staff per volume processed, and public services staff relative to user statistics are rarely collected yet would be very useful to determine library support and the effect of a decrease of such support. [2]

Information about institutional programs is also essential for libraries confronting planned reductions. Often academic institutions have formulated plans for new programs without consulting the library, without regard for which resources are available, or what the cost of providing the research support for the new programs would be. A review of institutional programs and plans is imperative, therefore, in order to plan for a future of reduced funding for the library. One writer mentions trustee charters and bylaws, personnel manuals, policy and procedure handbooks, policy statements, minutes of administrative and academic councils, state or federal legislation, accreditation reviews, self-studies, and other similar documents as useful materials for identifying specific objectives of the library and determining priorities. [3]

In order to establish priorities for acquisitions and services, library resources need to be fully surveyed, and they are frequently more numerous than is apparent. Collections, buildings, equipment, and staff, each is valuable and represents a considerable investment for the institution. Maximizing the use of each is particularly essential during periods of financial difficulties.

The library collections exist to support research and teaching, but their use is dependent on many conditions. Are the materials cataloged and accessible? Are they in usable physical condition? Certainly, backlogged uncataloged materials are wasted resources. How can these materials be made available to the public even if full cataloging is not possible? And, lastly, are all the collections really useful to meet the needs of local clientele? Or are they outdated or simply no longer needed? Can some of these collections be traded or sold for needed materials? Some materials may be better used or needed elsewhere. A case in point was a collection of Bolivian materials that Northwestern University Library sold several years ago. The collection was not used locally because it was too esoteric. Its sale provided some ready cash and freed space and custodial staff.

When money is in short supply, collections do suffer. They simply do not grow if other sources of funding are not found. During the course of this conference, the matter of grants from external organizations or foundations will be considered. All too often the tendency is to neglect to look on campus for funds which might be diverted to acquisitions of library materials. Various programs on campus may have endowments that can be tapped temporarily. The support of faculty is particularly important in this search, since these individuals will know of research grant monies or other sources which might be available for the asking. During the University of Texas Centennial celebration which took place in 1983, a very large number of endowed professorships and chairs came into existence through the generosity of many donors. The Benson Collection is this year receiving some funding from accrued monies from one of these endowed chairs in U.S.-Mexico relations. Not enough to offset a 46 percent reduction in acquisitions funding, but every penny helps!

The other major resource that too many managers take for granted is the library staff. A library is nothing without these human resources, and during times of diminished funding and slower growth of collections, the staff becomes prime material to develop. Staff performance can suffer greatly when salaries fail to keep up with inflation. Nonetheless, it will be the staff who will determine that the quality, if not the quantity, of library services is maintained during periods of austerity. Staff training and job enrichment are means mentioned by writers to help maintain staff morale.[4] At Texas, a staff-sharing program whereby a staff member can volunteer to work in another department for a few hours each week has been in operation for the last several years, and currently it is proving to be an important means for staff members to learn new skills and to seek greater job satisfaction.

Another avenue in use at Texas is job enrichment and enlargement. Individual assignments and responsibilities are being expanded for a number of paraprofessional staff members. Individual supervisors are cautious about overburdening their employees, but most staff members are meeting the challenge of new duties exceptionally well.

At the same time, assignments are being reevaluated as are procedures and practices.

During periods of financial constraints, frequent and ample communication among library administrators, middle managers, and staff is particularly important in maintaining staff morale. Staff needs direct contact with directors as well as supervisors. Through library newsletters, staff meetings, social functions, group discussions, and so forth, directors and supervisors can relieve much doubt and uncertainty amongst the staff. Stronger links will be forged and greater loyalty will result if staff are kept informed of budget constraints and about initiatives designed to alleviate them. Staff also needs to be involved during all steps of the austerity planning process. One writer has pointed out that austerity conditions tend to lead to greater centralization in library functions owing to the search for economy, library directors often must take risky and seemingly arbitrary measures, and staff morale can suffer from the perhaps unfamiliar condition of reduced autonomy and increased accountability. Hence, communication is doubly important during this time. [5]

The other two types of resources, buildings and equipment, must also be surveyed objectively. Is space being used effectively in managing the book collection, in providing services to the public, in processing the materials? This is another area where staff from the Benson Collection and the other units of the General Libraries at Texas are working. Somewhere in University administrative files is a proposed plan for a storage facility that unfortunately is ranked very low on the list of University building priorities. It is incumbent on us therefore to conserve space as much as possible, to use every nook and cranny available!

The use of equipment should also be studied during times when replacements may not be readily available. What else does one do with an old typewriter except keep it serviced regularly? But when it is necessary to replace it, what then? Budgets rarely dry up completely. In acquiring replacements, equipment utilizing more sophisticated technology should be considered. So no one knows how to use it? What better way to enrich jobs!

Under the rubric of equipment comes that indispensable tool, the card catalog. At Texas the online catalog, named UTCat (what else?), is now the source for finding the most recently cataloged materials as well as most books and periodicals in all libraries on campus with only a few exceptions. Providentially, this system was operational by the time the second personnel freeze occurred in the spring of 1986 when practically the entire filing crew for the public catalog needed to be replaced and no funds were available for those replacements. Even though the full-feature online catalog is scheduled to be operational only by the end of 1987, the availability of an online catalog with minimal data—author, title, call number, location, and circulation status—meant that the public was still able to access most recently added titles rather than only those titles whose cards have been filed up to early 1986. Although some filing is continuing in some unit card catalogs, the Benson Collection included, filing has not been resumed for the main public catalog, thereby conserving funds and permitting the reassignment of staff to public services.

Similarly, in acquisitions of library materials, materials available in new formats that might save space and staff time should be given greater consideration. No one denies the space saved by conversion of newspaper files to microformat. Advances in information storage will probably make even microformats obsolete in the not-too-distant future; nonetheless, it behooves librarians to be informed of progress in this area. I am not convinced that the book will become obsolete, but much information presently preserved in printed format might last longer and be stored more efficiently in another form.

Lastly, I need to point out another possible means to alleviate the effects of economic decline which libraries are already using to provide information to their users, that of networking or resource sharing. The buzzword, cooperation, arises frequently in the literature. Few libraries can function in isolation. Most are members of bibliographic utilities, consortia, or associations whereby information and resources are shared. During times of financial difficulties, it is particularly important to turn to these contacts. Research materials no longer affordable for one institution might be available through interlibrary borrowing or some other means. The science libraries at Texas have been experimenting with a document delivery system that the University of Kentucky found to be a viable alternative to subscribing to seldom used highly specialized journals. This system is designed to provide articles from locally unavailable journals on demand at no cost to the patron: the articles are provided within 8-10 days by a vendor at a cost to the library of $8-$12 per article. Funds from the materials acquisition budget are being used for this project.

Planning for austerity may not always be possible before the fact. Certainly at Texas the suddenly diminished oil tax revenues seemed to come upon us before written plans could be compiled. The personnel freezes were imposed without much prior notice, and nothing could be done other than to reduce library hours as fewer staff were available to operate public service units. In terms of rising serial costs, all bibliographers looked closely at subscriptions and determined where the cuts would be made. Although not in written form, contingency plans did exist. More detailed plans are being made now to cope with the uncertainty of the coming several years. An article in the *New York Times* of April 15 stated that the Texas economy has probably bottomed out and that recovery will be gradual. [6] But meanwhile we wait for the governor and the legislature to agree on a budget for the state government, of which the University of Texas is a part, and pray (and lobby furiously) that friends of higher education will prevail. The library literature points out that austerity brings out the best and the worst in people and in organizations. But I prefer the words of a tough old Texan whom I heard speak last week, "Tough times don't last; tough people do!"

NOTES

1. John C. Heyeck, ed., *Managing under Austerity: A Conference for Privately Supported Academic Libraries, Summary Proceedings* (Stanford, CA: Stanford University, 1976).

2. John Vasi, *Budget Allocation Systems for Research Libraries* (Washington, DC: Office of Management Studies, Association of Research Libraries, 1983), p. 15.

3. Edward R. Johnson, "A Realistic Objectives Management Program." In *Austerity Management in Academic Libraries* (Metuchen, NJ: The Scarecrow Press, 1984), p. 163.

4. Joseph Z. Nitecki, "Creative Management in Austerity." In *Austerity Management in Academic Libraries*, p. 56.

5. Ibid, p. 51.

6. Peter Applebone, "Oil States Drawing Hope from Belief that the Worst Is Over," *The New York Times* (April 15, 1987), p. 7.

4. La gerencia de bibliotecas en tiempo de recesión

Virginia Betancourt Valverde

La crisis financiera del país, fundamentalmente producto de la carga del servicio de la deuda externa, que representa un 35% del presupuesto público, y de la drástica disminución de los precios del petróleo, de aproximadamente un 50% desde 1983, ha tenido serias repercusiones en el área de información. Sin embargo, cabe destacar que la existencia desde hace diez años, de un organismo normativo y coordinador del Sistema Nacional de Bibliotecas, que cuenta con el respaldo de una Ley y tiene el rango de Instituto Autónomo Biblioteca Nacional y de Servicios de Bibliotecas, ha permitido hacerle frente a esta crisis.

El Instituto Autónomo Biblioteca Nacional y de Servicios de Bibliotecas (IABNSB) como núcleo coordinador del Sistema Nacional de Bibliotecas ha definido una estrategia orientada al logro del reconocimiento colectivo de la importancia de la información para el desarrollo del país y, en consecuencia, de la necesidad de darle bases jurídicas al derecho a la información. Este objetivo general ha dado lugar a la aplicación de una estrategia de:

1. Propuestas al Ejecutivo de medidas para afrontar la crisis de índole jurídica, financiera y técnica.
2. Extensión al Sistema de Bibliotecas de la normalización de los procesos técnicos para mejorar la organización y el almacenamiento de la información y favorecer el uso intensivo y cooperativo de la infraestructura tecnológica disponible en el país.
3. Mayor coordinación con otros entes públicos a nivel nacional, regional y local.

Estos objetivos son:

I. Evaluar el nivel de desarrollo del Sistema Nacional de Información para lograr su adecuación a las nuevas necesidades del país y a la escacez de recursos financieros.

Este objetivo se ha cumplido progresivamente mediante las siguientes actividades:

1. Evaluación de los resultados de la Primera Década del Sistema Nacional de Información (1986-1987).
2. Proposición de un cuerpo de Políticas para el Sistema Nacional de Información (1987).
3. Discusión de los puntos 1 y 2 en el Seminario sobre Política Nacional de Información, realizado a fines del mes pasado, con la participación de organismos gubernamentales y académicos vinculados al área de información, el Congreso de la República y tres organismos internacionales.
4. Adopción por el Ejecutivo Nacional de las políticas propuestas en el Seminario y de nuevos mecanismos encaminados a fortalecer el Sistema Nacional de Información (1987).

II. Promover la producción y mejorar la distribución de materiales bibliográficos.

Para cumplimiento de este objetivo se han llevado a cabo las siguientes actividades:

1. Diagnóstico de la situación de la actividad editorial realizada por el Estado[1] y de los materiales divulgativos producidos por entes públicos.[2]
2. Promulgación del Decreto Presidencial N° 1528 sobre Políticas de Estímulo a la Industria Editorial (1987).
3. Creación de la Fundación Kuaimare para la distribución y venta del Libro Venezolano en una red de librerías de alcance nacional (1984).
4. Promulgación del Decreto Presidencial N° 1613 sobre distribución al Sistema Nacional de Bibliotecas del 20% de los ejemplares de cada título producido por los entes públicos (1983), mediante su entrega al Instituto Autónomo Biblioteca Nacional y de Servicios de Bibliotecas.
5. Política de adquisición preferencial de libros y revistas venezolanos para el Sistema Nacional de Bibliotecas Públicas (1985).

III. Mejorar el acceso a la información.

Este objetivo se cumple mediante las siguientes actividades:

1. Establecimiento del Control Bibliográfico Nacional desde la Biblioteca Nacional lo cual ha implicado:
   a. Adopción de normas angloamericanas por la Biblioteca Nacional, el Sistema Nacional de Bibliotecas Públicas y

las bibliotecas universitarias especializadas más importantes del país.

b. Producción, automatizada y regular, de la Bibliografía Venezolana por la Biblioteca Nacional, desde 1982 (7 volúmenes).

c. Producción y edición del catálogo colectivo de bibliotecas públicas (1986).

d. Producción y edición de las bibliografías retrospectivas de las 23 entidades federales del país.

e. Designación de la Biblioteca Nacional como Agencia del ISBN en Venezuela (1985).

2. Adopción, por la Biblioteca Nacional, de un Sistema Automatizado (utilizando los software NOTIS IV y Documaster) el cual, a partir de 1982, es compartido por el Congreso Nacional, la Corte Suprema de Justicia y la Universidad Central de Venezuela.

Desde 1985, se ha intensificado la participación de las Instituciones incorporadas al Sistema y de los ingresos al Banco de Datos Documental de Venezuela, el cual cuenta con 400.000 registros relativos a: Base de Datos Jurídico-Legal, Base de Datos Bibliográfica, Hemerográfica y Audiovisual, y Base de Datos de Autoridades.

3. Adquisición cooperativa, catálogo colectivo automatizado, registro de investigadores e investigaciones en curso en la Cuenca del Caribe (1985-1987).

4. Racionalización progresiva de la adquisición y circulación de publicaciones periódicas extranjeras especializadas en ciencia, tecnología, y humanidades mediante:

a. Elaboración en 1983 por la Biblioteca Nacional, de la primera lista automatizada de las publicaciones periódicas disponibles en 84 bibliotecas universitarias especializadas y en la propia Biblioteca Nacional del país. Se actualiza anualmente.

b. Asignación por el Ejecutivo de una cuota anual de 3 millones de dólares a cambio preferencial, a los cuales pueden acceder las bibliotecas especializadas y la Biblioteca Nacional.

c. Definición de criterios para la selección de colecciones de publicaciones periódicas en ciencias de la salud, con la participación conjunta de asesores científicos, autoridades universitarias y especialistas de la información.

d. Aumento del préstamo interbibliotecario.

5. Afianzamiento del Sistema Nacional de Bibliotecas Públicas integrado por 23 redes estatales con servicios que responden a políticas y normas comunes, mediante el énfasis en la calidad de los servicios y el congelamiento de la creación de nuevas unidades operativas y de las siguientes actividades:

   a. Incremento de un 25% del apoyo de los Concejos Municipales en la obtención de terreno, locales, dotación y en el mantenimiento de los servicios (de un 13% del total de los Concejos Municipales en 1983 al 52% en 1986).

   b. Obtención de 1.300.000 dólares a cambio preferencial para la adquisición directa de libros a editoriales de España, México, Colombia y Argentina, lo que significa una economía del 93%, respecto a los materiales adquiridos en plaza.

   c. Aumento del 204% de los títulos ingresados gratuitamente al Sistema Nacional de Bibliotecas por concepto de la ejecución del decreto 1613 relativo a la entrega del 20% de las publicaciones producidas por entes públicos (de 73.10 volúmenes en 1983 a 222.850 volúmenes en 1986).

   d. Campaña anual nacional de recaudación entre la ciudadanía de libros usados para bibliotecas públicas, desde 1986, bajo el tema "Si ya lo leístes pásalo."

6. Normalización de la identificación bibliográfica y de la organización de las Memorias de los Ministerios e Institutos Autónomos mediante la adopción en Consejo de Ministros del Manual correspondiente (1986).

IV. Promover el uso de la información.

Este objetivo se ha cumplido mediante las siguientes actividades:

1. Promulgación de la Resolución N° 335 de Ministerio de Educación sobre Política de Promoción de la Lectura (1985).

   a. Creación de la Comisión Nacional de la Lectura (1985).

   b. Reforma del Currículo de la Escuela Básica (1° a 9° grado) y del de profesionalización de los maestros a fin de asignarle una mayor jerarquía al proceso de aprendizaje de la lectura (1985-1987).

   c. Establecimiento en Bibliotecas Públicas, de Servicios de Apoyo al Docente en 12 de los 20 estados del país, con fondos provenientes de la Universidad Pedagógica Experimental Libertador.

    d.   Campaña televisivas de promoción de la lectura.

2. Exposiciones regulares de Fotografía Documental y del Cartel Venezolano en museos de la capital. Se editan catálogos en cada ocasión.

3. Producción de los siguientes boletines informativos especializados: *Bibliotecnia* (1984), *El Investigador Venezolano* (1984), *Red* (1986), *La Gaceta de Conservación* (1987), *Documentos para Conservación* (1987), y *Boletín ISBN* (1987).

4. Exposiciones permanentes de nuevas adquisiciones en la Biblioteca Nacional y todas las bibliotecas públicas del país.

V. Formar y perfeccionar los Recursos Humanos del Sistema Nacional de Información a nivel técnico y profesional.

1. Creación del Post-grado en Estudios de la Información en la Universidad Simón Bolívar (1986) con el apoyo del Programa de las Naciones Unidas para el Desarrollo (PNUD), de la Unesco y de la Biblioteca Nacional.

2. Formación continua de auxiliares y asistencia de bibliotecas para las 23 redes de Bibliotecas Públicas del país, capacitándose 510 funcionarios en el período 1983-1986, lo cual constituye el 50% del total.

3. Formación de 359 especialistas en salas infantiles (1983-1986).

4. Capacitación de 357 funcionarios en el área de información a la comunidad (1983-1986).

VI. Mejorar las condiciones ambientales, fortalecer los soportes y perfeccionar la manipulación de los materiales documentales, especialmente aquellos en los que se registra la memoria nacional.

1. Intensificación del asesoramiento permanente, desde el Centro Nacional de Conservación Documental, a Archivos, Museos y Bibliotecas sobre medidas de preservación (1981).

2. Designación de la Biblioteca Nacional como centro local de la IFLA en el área de conservación (1987) para América Latina y el Caribe.

3. Definición de lineamientos normativos para la construcción y ampliación de bibliotecas públicas (1983).

4. Mejoramiento sustantivo de la calidad del 77% de los locales que alojan las bibliotecas públicas del país y no fueran inicialmente construidas con ese fin.

Las estrategias, los objetivos y las actividades antes señalados demuestran la necesidad de enfrentar la crisis económica afianzando los vínculos de coordinación, normalización y armonización no sólo entre los diferentes componentes del Sistema de Bibliotecas sino con otros organismos afines que conforman, o deben conformar, al Sistema Nacional de Información.

Hemos combatido el aislamiento institucional, sectorial y nacional, y en consecuencia, hemos aunado voluntades para lograr:

Respuestas a necesidades, sentidas y no satisfechas por años, como las políticas de Estado de Promoción de la Lectura y del Estímulo a la Industria Editorial.

Maximización en el uso de un sistema automatizado cooperativo.

Participación de autores, investigadores y editores en gestiones de análisis y de la divulgación, por los medios de comunicación, de alternativas creativas para la solución de la crisis.

Desarrollo de proyectos demostrativos de coordinación institucional como el Fondo Cuenca del Caribe y la adquisición centralizada de compras a editoriales del exterior de materiales para todo el sistema de bibliotecas públicas.

Apoyo internacional a soluciones regionales tales como el Postgrado en Estudios de la Información y la asesoría a otros países de América Latina y el Caribe, en automatización, preservación y organización de servicios audiovisuales.

NOTAS

1. "Aproximación al estudio de la actividad editorial de la Administración Pública," 1979-1983.

2. "Evaluación de materiales divulgativos y para neolectores," Omar Belandria, noviembre 1986.

Part Two
Resource Sharing

5. There Is a Future for the Library

Dick Reumer

In the Netherlands, as elsewhere, library work has felt the adverse effects of the weak world economy. Authorities have made considerable budget cuts. The Netherlands used to have a library law aimed at boosting library development. Many hundreds of new branches were established, and tens of millions of books and thousands of librarians were added. There seemed to be no end to it. This heady period of prosperity fostered ambitious goals: the library had to have everything; it had to be in a position to supply anything to anybody at any time and any place. The profession became highly developed and specialized.

When the economic tide turned, however, this came to an end. The library law was repealed, and budgets were lowered considerably. Libraries entered into a period of panic, unrest, and uncertainty. But worse yet, a sense of defeatism and despondency hung in the air. Defeatism is more fatal than any economy measure. When at a crucial point, we should never throw in the towel, but instead develop a new élan through innovative policy-making, while preserving faith in individual capacity and in the specific social task of the library.

In the Netherlands, the enormous challenge of regaining that belief in individual capacity has been successfully met. The unique role of the library is once again recognized. While reductions of up to 50 percent have been made in, for instance, the socio-cultural budget, the national government has spared libraries from its budget axe and does not intend to cut it any further in the future. Of course, the government will still have to be asked to make the means available, and success will depend on political action.

Success can only be achieved by means of a combination of various tactics, including, for example:

Stringent protest against budget cuts.
A demonstration in the vein of the one causing 4,000 Dutch librarians to take to the streets some years ago.
Heightening public awareness through press, radio, television, and advertising.

Very direct, personal contact with those officials politically responsible, fostering a gradual development of views and ideas.

Approaching ministers on a respectful but even footing. Provoking political fights is useless and only serves to erect a wall against your requests. Political fights should be dealt with at election time.

Explaining what you want and why you want it very clearly, with an explicit selection of priorities.

Convincingly and enthusiastically drawing the attention of the government to the unique role of the library in today's society.

As a matter of fact, only five years ago many officials considered Dutch libraries with their troublesome and expensive facilities just another necessary evil. That image has changed. As our minister of culture explained recently, he has discovered from social, administrative, and political contacts just how strong library roots in society are. Libraries are sufficiently self-organized, being the most concrete and businesslike type of work within the nonprofit sector. To their further credit, libraries have adapted to changing circumstances through constant self-examination and flexible response to new developments. The results have been no new budget cuts, millions extra for innovation, and strong moral support.

Apart from government support, alternative sources of funding are now being tapped, such as:

1. Numerous grant facilities of a more general nature in the Netherlands and the European Community (project grants for the unemployed, promotion of expertise, training, energy saving, building, women's liberation, adult education.

2. Numerous private foundations that grant money for occasional projects, block grants for initial expenses or for investment.

3. Renting advertising space to firms, for instance, in display cases, on the sides of mobile library vans, reverse side of bookmarks, book bags.

4. Providing sponsorship opportunities, enabling the sponsor to polish up his own image while boosting the image of the library as well, by supporting membership campaigns, library promotion or financing of occasional activities such as an annual report or a special exhibition. (Of course, not every firm is considered for this kind of support.)

5. "Friends of the library" campaigns soliciting financial donations from private individuals or businesses.

6. Income from commercial activities, such as a library shop, commercial rental of recreation videos, book sales.

On this point I would like to advise libraries in developing countries to continue to appeal to international solidarity. Find out which countries provide your country with development aid. Try to obtain information from the various embassies involved. From there, establish contacts with library organizations in those countries to launch a joint effort to obtain development monies for library work. In my opinion you may also appeal for funds directly to some of the more wealthy national library organizations.

In this period of innovation new technological developments present a great challenge to the library. I am thinking first of all of the automation of the internal library organization, such as cataloguing, lending, and administration. Moreover, digital information has vastly improved the retrieval process, allowing for more effective and efficient use of information stored in databanks. These databanks require selection and wide accessibility. Most of the time they contain special information. Truly user-friendly databanks for the public at large are far too seldomly available. Here an enormous task is waiting for the public library, which, like no other institution, has the expertise at hand in collecting and retrieving information, and which, like no other institution, can guarantee multiformity and voluntary consultation—a unique starting-point for the future.

For this reason the NBLC, the Dutch Centre for Public Libraries and Literature, has set up its own databank of information for the general public in the Netherlands. Because this databank stores documents supplied by the NBLC to the libraries, such as periodical indexes, newspaper clippings, AVM information, and documentation kits, document delivery poses no problem. Simultaneously, a number of local projects have been launched to establish a province-wide network, shared by 100 libraries, and local databanks with information from local government and socio-cultural organizations, education, and industry. It is expected that these experiments will be greatly expanded in the future. The NBLC is also developing other databanks containing information such as public library policies, adult education and professional literature for libraries, and is furthermore consulting with third parties on setting up databanks on authorities, industry, tourism, consumers, food, social counsellors, and so on. In order to make it accessible in as user-friendly a way as possible, a so-called *chapeau* has been developed, which finds the right host and the right databank to answer the user's questions quickly and easily. Such innovations have, of course, totally revolutionized library work. Librarians are receiving additional schooling for this purpose through a special expertise programme.

Funding reductions increase the need for efficient management of the money available. I view the library as a business, which must take full regard of the costs of its services, and produce basic data on the production of, for example, bibliographical entries, loans processed per employee, effectiveness of the collection—in short, a cost-benefit analysis of the organization and its expenditures. For many years in the Netherlands the emphasis has been placed on offering a wide range of materials at a variety of levels and locations. That time seems to be definitely over. Choices have to be made, and priorities have to be set. No doubt, compromises will have to be made to what has always been considered the holy professional code. There will be a shift from autonomous local holdings to availability through a large network and from direct loans to referrals to information elsewhere.

Technological developments facilitate such a shift, but cooperation remains a must. Therefore, a psychological process of change will have to be initiated and a flexible attitude will be required from all employees, but training and education should also pay more attention to good business practices.

Consequently, the NBLC has made sound management a top priority in its expertise programmes. The shifts in tasks and functions entail the need for adequate coherent networks. In this connection central service is essential. Originally central service included local tasks that, for the sake of efficiency and quality, were usually carried out at a national level against cost price. In the Netherlands this structure results in savings of approximately $40,000,000. For example, the central service department annually supplies 13,000 Dutch book titles and bibliographical entries, 1,500 AVM titles and computer software, 10,000 record titles, 100 documentation kits, 3,000 newspaper clippings, and an index to periodical articles. The NBLC's own publishing department is a significant component not only for professional publications but also for gaps in the commercial supply, for instance, for minority groups and the mentally handicapped. Practically all libraries make use of this central service, even if it means that personal opinions and interpretations have to be set aside, and that participation in the universal document database system is necessary. In your countries central service could likewise provide solutions to many of your present problems.

Marketing principles will also play an increasing role in library policy-making. The library will have to become more customer-oriented, meaning that the users and their ages, sexes, professions, and social situations must be known. The NBLC has been regularly conducting national studies and has designed models, forms, and techniques for carrying out local research. Various practical improvements are resulting from these studies. Only through familiarity with the user and his desires and needs can priorities be set and priority groups be targeted. All of this information must be laid down in a policy plan, supported by figures framing the policy. Through better self-management the library can help to solve its own problems, thereby positively influencing the authorities to provide their indispensable cooperation.

When considering innovation policy, I am also thinking of promoting a higher profile of the library. Public opinion is of great importance to politicians and authorities. Show the library, show what the library has to offer. This can be done in various ways; let me mention but a few. We are frequently in the news on television and radio or in the papers. Moreover, forty times a year we have a commercial television spot during government broadcasting time. Another example, government information on all kinds of statutory regulations and grant programmes is disseminated through television spots and pamphlets. Since we now have these pamphlets in the libraries, the slogan "Get the brochure from the public library" is shown on television on two channels eight times every night. Furthermore, we are staging a national library day, for the fourth year in a row, with national and particularly local activities, such as parades, parties, performances, open houses, which will be adorned with nationally manufactured decorations, such as flags, banners, and stickers. We have a video promotion week. We organize children's book weeks and reading promotion programmes, in cooperation with a variety of institutions. To give an example, together with the educational broadcasting companies, we held a course on children's literature.

Each week we visit our Ministry and regularly attend parliament. We participate in national shows and exhibitions. More and more nonprofit institutions are distributing their publications or conducting their publishing activities through the NBLC and the public libraries. All of this involvement provides more publicity for the library, allowing it to project the image of an active and enthusiastic institution. Consequently, the popularity of the library has grown. Various studies have proved that the library's popularity is greater than that of sports, museums, socio-cultural work, and musical schools.

New techniques, better public relations, and more efficient management no doubt contribute to even better public service by the libraries. However, one is justified in asking whether we are always conscious of the fact that the user is our reason for being here. The glamour of public relations activities, the adventure of unlimited technological developments, and the seduction of a more businesslike approach can entice us into a sort of star-struck daze, infringing upon our commitment to the users. It is good to realize that these activities are no more than means, they are not ends in themselves. All of these efforts towards innovation will result in disappointment, in my opinion, if user-friendliness is not simultaneously emphasized in the library. Therefore, it is necessary to look at our housing, collection, arrangement, and retrieval system through the eyes of the user. It will then certainly become apparent that our professional standards are not in line with their wishes, meaning that we shall have to rethink all of our policies, if we wish to survive. At this moment in the Netherlands ten different experiments are being conducted examining such issues as the number of symbols on bookbacks, different subject headings, furniture adaptation, and the rearrangement of books according to interest or topicality. I do not wish to frighten you, but it may also prove interesting to learn more about the attainments of large department stores.

Finally, will the library itself survive? In my opinion it will, but with a totally different image. I am convinced that only such an innovated library can meet future challenges, handle new tasks, maintain its status, expand further, and present itself to the authorities as the indispensable institution that it is. In the Netherlands this new assignment has been accepted as a challenge. It is not going quietly, not without problems, not perfectly, and not always in total harmony. Yet the more the pieces of the puzzle are assembled, the more I become convinced that this innovative policy will mean an illustrious future for the library.

Thus, there is no time for defeatism; there is too much to be done.

6. Strategies for Resource Sharing

Daphne Douglas

Moving toward the end of the twentieth century, information handlers are finding that the circumstances of their environment have changed considerably. They no longer have the same resources, the same tools, the same infrastructures upon which systems and services were built at the turn of the century or even during the current century. Even the new developments of evidence after World War II have changed drastically in recent times and have presented states which demand complete rethinking and new approaches to the accessibility and provision of information. The theme of this conference is based on resource sharing and this session focuses upon strategies which are being employed or may be employed in order to promote this fully accepted activity in filling the needs of information users.

If I were to recite to you a listing of what is being done or planned in the English-speaking Caribbean, I would probably bore you to tears. For a description of systems, functional or planned, refer to the appendices of this paper.*

I present instead a few ideas in brief about this topic, ideas which may or may not be controversial and which might generate some discussion or argument.

Telecommunications

Resource sharing has to be based on communication and communication links. The common carriers and the value-added carriers have to be convinced that there is a market in the English-speaking Caribbean for their product. They also have to accept the fact that they have to cost data processing at a much lower rate than voice transmission. Again, they have to rework their existing channels to accommodate this newer form of use. It is said that much of the connections in the area were designed for voice and are really unsuitable for data transmission. This helps to hold prices at high rates.

---

*See also, Chapter 14, below: Maureen C. Newton, Grantsmanship: CARICOM's Programme of Activities.

Data transmission and interrogation of databases between computers is based on one of the following:

Standardization. Absolute matches or cloning between systems.

Compatibility. Ability to adjust differing components, such as by the use of switching systems.

Open systems interconnection. Linkages between totally differing systems.

In identifying strategies for interfacing equipment and software, it must be appreciated that the foregoing three stages are developmental in terms of cost. Anything other than standardization costs more money. Keep in mind that planning for standardization takes time to develop and implies compromise.

A possible strategy for more immediate implementation, while the slower process of building databases goes on, is the possibility of electronic mail systems, either by establishing local systems or by utilizing an existing one. It would seem that such links would facilitate resource sharing at all levels—systems could talk to each other, requests could be broadcast, multiple responses could be received if necessary, actual information could be transferred or even facsimiles transferred. The concept of gatekeeping on this basis could open up wide horizons, especially for the people of the Caribbean. Through an electronic interface, they could have in a shorter time, and probably with cost effectiveness, the best of all worlds.

Materials

Access to formally published materials outside the Caribbean can be had with comparative ease. What we lack is a clear understanding of the generation of information within the region and the media in which it is recorded. Where does it originate? In what format? What happens to it? Where is it located? How can it be retrieved? With the publishing industry in its unorganized state, no one is ever sure about the answers to all these questions. Government publishing lacks control and the non-conventional formats present problems. Until copyright and legal deposit laws are enacted and enforceable, a great deal of the resources that could be available for sharing are not available.

A conscious effort needs to be made at resource building. Resource sharing can be taken to the point where collections begin to shrink because the alternative has become the norm.

Tied to the above is the need for the coordination of collection development between the systems which are sharing resources. This rationalization may take the form of responsibility for certain categories of materials and also the passing of last or only copies to the authority named to specialize in the relevant subject.

The whole matter of what can be shared and what cannot needs to be delineated carefully. A happy circumstance is that the development of computer graphics and sound reproduction permits the transmission of images and audio-forms such as facsimiles and sound recordings. Thus single or precious copies can be made to feature in resource sharing. The alternatives to interlending original copies or copies in great demand need to be explored.

Retrieval Tools/Authority Files

Although it is not essential to maintain a database in order to support resource sharing, it has its usefulness. There has to be a measure of consensus in union cataloguing, though, and the development of authority files is a must. Standardization is of the utmost importance.

Referral Services

One of the alternatives to bibliographic databases is the use of referral services. It is necessary to know a great deal about the collections in the cooperating libraries as well as something about their collection development and loan policies.

Human Resources

Resource sharing has many facets, one of which is the human element which services it. Strategies should centre on the knowledge, skills, and attitudes the persons involved have acquired, because appropriate education, training, and experience are essential to the successful running of a service.

Research

Always in the forefront of strategies must be the methodology for continuous enquiry and assessment. Some items worthy of study and application are as follows:

Case studies or the study of suitable models of resource sharing.

The investigation of Open Systems Interconnection to facilitate interfacing of systems.

The evolving of switching systems to permit software compatibility.

The development of a means of evaluating services based on the identification of meaningful criteria for measurement.

Statistical collection and analysis pursued as an integral part of any cooperative system.

Overall, influencing the social, economic, and political climate in order to ensure acceptance and promotion of the activity is an important consideration. A great deal is being written about downloading from databases and trans-border data flow. The Caribbean countries have not enunciated any specific policies in this regard, and it is to be hoped that a liberal approach will be the norm at all times and in all cases. Promoting the case for learning from each other since the countries are similar in stages of development is a telling rationale.

I feel a kindred spirit with Lim Huck Tee when he spoke of bibliographic exchange at a similar conference recently. He opened his paper with these words: "The subject of this paper has a vagueness and imprecision about it that is both the bane of the paper writer and a source of delight, since any reasonable interpretation would be correct!" I close with the same thought. Maybe something has been of value, maybe not. What I hope that together we have done in this session is to stimulate the idea that resource sharing just does not happen; the infrastructures can be costly, and what we need is to give thought to how we are going to achieve the optimum conditions.

BIBLIOGRAPHY

Buchinski, Edwin, and David McCallum. "At the National Library: Network and Protocol Development." *Canadian Library Journal* 43:3 (June 1985), 131-134.

Dougherty, Richard M. "Research Libraries in an International Setting: Requirements for Expanded Resource Sharing." *College and Research Libraries* 46:5 (September 1985), 383-389.

Tee, Lim Huck. "Aspects of Asian Bibliography: 3. Bibliographic Interchange/Coordination in Southeast Asia." *International Cataloguing* 16:1 (January/March 1987), 4-6.

APPENDIX I

Extract from Background Paper Relating to the Development of an Information Policy for the Caribbean Area

Prepared by Fay Durrant

1. for submission to the Caribbean Community (CARICOM) and the Economic Commission for Latin-America and the Caribbean/ Caribbean Development and Cooperation Committee (ECLAS/CDCC).
2. as the basis for discussion during a consultation mission to the Caribbean funded by the International Development Research Centre (IDRC), January, 1987.
3. to serve as the framework for the formulation of a Regional Information Strategy.

General Objectives of Regional Systems

At the conceptual level and in the plan, the regional information systems have been assigned a major role in the transfer of information within the region. By the nature of the information which the systems manipulate, they can also be seen as having the potential for also playing a significant role in technology transfer.

The existing and proposed regional information systems have been briefly described below mainly in terms of their objectives, functions, and services.

The Caribbean Information System—Economic and Social Planning (CARISPLAN) 1979—

Objectives: The collection, processing and dissemination of information relevant to socio-economic planning in the region.

The Caribbean Documentation Centre of the United Nations Economic Commission for Latin America and the Caribbean (UNECLAC) was requested by the Member States of the CDCC, to establish an information network linking the libraries/documentation centres of their National Planning Agencies, and other organizations working in the area of socio-economic development.

Users: Policy-makers, planners, technical personnel, and researchers, of the Member States.

Services: Current awareness services, selective dissemination of information, abstracting and indexing services, reference services provided mainly from a database covering Caribbean and other relevant documents.

The Caribbean Information System for the Agricultural Sciences (CAGRIS) 1985—

Objectives: The collection, processing and dissemination of information relevant to agricultural development in the region.

The University of the West Indies, St. Augustine, Trinidad, was requested by the Caribbean Development and Cooperation Committee, to establish an information network linking the University of the West Indies Library (St. Augustine) to the libraries of the agricultural organizations of Member States.

Users: Policy-makers, planners, agriculturalists and researchers, farmers and other agricultural practitioners of Member States.

Services: Current Awareness Services, Selective Dissemination of Information, Abstracting and Indexing Services, and Reference Services from a database covering agricultural documents on and relevant to the Caribbean.

The Caribbean Information System—Patents (CARPIN) 1985—

Objectives: The collection, processing and dissemination of information relating to patents registered in the Member States.

The Caribbean Documentation Centre of the United Nations Economic Commission for Latin America and the Caribbean Economic was requested by the Caribbean Development and Cooperation Committee to establish an information service for the collection, processing and dissemination of information on patents registered in the region.

Users: Technologists and planners of industrial development.

Services: Reference services from a database covering patents registered in Member States.

The Caribbean Trade Information System (CARTIS) 1986—

Objectives: The establishment of a regional trade information network to support the development of intra- and extra-regional trade.

The Caribbean Community (CARICOM) Secretariat was requested by the CARICOM Council of Ministers to establish a regional trade information system initially linking the CARICOM Member States, and subsequently the other CDCC Member States.

Users: Exporters and exporting organizations, Trade promotion agencies, importers/exporters/investors, researchers, Ministries of trade/commerce.

Services: Dissemination of trade information from databases covering company profiles, market opportunities, suppliers' profiles, trade documents, trade statistics.

The Caribbean Energy Information System (currently in the planning stages)

Objectives: To implement one aspect of the Regional Energy Action Plan and to facilitate the sharing of information on new and renewable sources of energy in the Caribbean region.

Users: Policy-makers, planners, and technical personnel in the Member States.

Services: Dissemination of information relating to new and renewable sources of energy in the Caribbean region.

The Caribbean Network for Education and Innovation? (CARNEID) (currently in the planning stages)

Objectives: The development of an information network linking the educational institutions in the region—initially those of the English-speaking states.

The system will be established by UNESCO through its regional office in Barbados.

Users: Educational planners, policy-makers, researchers, and practitioners of the region.

The Health Information Network (currently in the planning stages)

Objectives: The collection, processing and dissemination of information on public health and medicine.

This network is expected to include statistical data, as well as bibliographical information services to the Member States.

Users: Medical and public health planners, researchers, and practitioners of the Member States.

The Association for Caribbean Transformation (ACT) 1982?—

Objectives: The collection, processing, analysis, and dissemination of statistical data on agricultural products and prices.

This network has been developed by the Association for Caribbean Transformation and initially links information units in Member States Trinidad, Antigua, Dominica.

Users: Farmers and other distributors of agricultural products.

The Disaster Preparedness Information Network 1982–

Objectives: The collection, processing and dissemination of information on long- and short-term methods of preparing for disasters. An important factor being dissemination through the most appropriate channels, and forms of language.

The regional Disaster Preparedness Office was requested by CARICOM Member States to establish an information network linking the regional office to the national Disaster Preparedness Offices.

Users: All levels of the populations of the region.

Services: Dissemination of all types of information to all areas of the population, using all available facilitating mechanisms.

The Caribbean Technology Consultancy Service (CTCS) 1984–95

Objectives: To provide an information service for the implementation of technologies in developmental activities in the region.

The Caribbean Development Bank was requested to establish the system providing services to users on request.

Users: Practitioners working in all areas where technologies are implemented.

The Caribbean Agricultural Development Institute Information Network (CARDI)

Objectives: The collection, processing, and dissemination of information in areas relevant to the cropping systems, and to the other research activities of the Institute.

The network links the national offices of CARDI which serve as points for dissemination of information.

Users: Farmers and other agriculturalists.

Services: Current Awareness and Selective Dissemination of information services from an institutional database, and through access to several external databases.

The Caribbean Basin Information Network (CBIN)

Objectives: The dissemination of information relevant to the Caribbean business community and to the trading partners in North America.

The network provides linkages between the Caribbean Chamber of Industry and Commerce, the national Chambers of Industry and Commerce, and the CBIN Centre in Washington, D.C.

Users: The Caribbean business community.

The Shipping Information System for the Caribbean (currently in the planning stages)

Objectives: The collection, processing, analysis and dissemination of statistical data relevant to the shipping activities of the region.

The CARICOM Secretariat has been requested to establish this system to provide shipping information services to Member States.

Users: Policy-makers, planners, and technical personnel of public and private agencies in the region.

International Referral System for Environment Information (includes Caribbean focal points)

Objectives: Providing access to sources of environmental information.

The system links the Caribbean national focal points for INFOTERRA with each other and with the global system.

Users: Policy-makers, planners, and technical personnel working in areas related to environment development.

Sub-regional Systems

The Organization of Eastern Caribbean States Information Network (OECS) (currently in the planning stages)

Objectives: To provide a facilitating mechanism for the flow of information between the Member States of the OECS, the OECS Secretariat, and with the other regional information systems. This system is expected to ensure that users have access to the documents held in the libraries, and documentation centres of this regional grouping.

The OECS Secretariat will be responsible for the establishment and maintenance of the system.

Users: Policy-makers, planners, and technical personnel of the OECS Member States.

APPENDIX II

Extract from the Working Document for the
Caribbean Network for the Exchange of Information and
Experience in Science and Technology (CARSTIN)
Consultation Meeting, Trinidad, December, 1984

I. Introduction

Three meetings requested UNESCO to carry out the preliminary
work leading to a major sub-regional project in science and technology
for development, including a component aimed at improving scientific
and technological information services. These three meetings were the
Second Meeting of Caribbean Ministers responsible for UNESCO
Affairs (St. Lucia, 19-20 July 1982), the First Meeting of Caribbean
Ministers responsible for Science and Technology (Jamaica, 5-7 April
1983), and the Second Meeting of the Science and Technology
Ministerial Sub-Committee (Antigua, 4 May 1984).

In considering the main deficiencies of the S & T information
sector in the Caribbean, [1] Ministers directed specific recommendations
to Caribbean States, among which were the following:

i)   development of effective system for providing direct access to
       information contained in external databases and for ensuring
       access to technological options;

ii)   establishment of mechanisms to ensure that information gathered
       is available to inform research and development activities;

iii)   development of the specialized human resources needed to man
       the technological information systems, consideration being given
       to flexible training mechanisms;

iv)   establishment of coherent mechanisms to ensure that all studies
       and reports stored in a central agency in a manner that allows
       easy retrieval, and ensuring that such documents are accessible to
       those persons and agencies who require them (with due regard to
       considerations of confidentiality);

---

[1] Among others, absence of an effective information system in the region, especially
a system for the gathering of information related to projects; need for documentation and
information centres to collate and disseminate information; absence of a mechanism to
identify information at the international level which had regional significance; need for
information systems to have a dynamic impact with all activities at the national level
(First Meeting of Ministers Responsible for Science and Technology, Final Report, p. 6).

v)   support for a network of technological institutions to share information and develop expertise.

Within this context, UNESCO, through its General Information Programme, has taken initial steps towards the establishment of a Caribbean Network for the Exchange of Information and Experience in Science and Technology (CARSTIN).

The immediate objectives of the project are to:

1.   build up national and regional S & T information infrastructure, by:
     -   strengthening bibliographic control of the country's own scientific and technological output and by establishing computerized bibliographic databases in S & T subject areas of interest to the Caribbean region;
     -   setting up a network of referral services with the creation and/or strengthening of referral nodes at the national level;
     -   stimulating and promoting the creation of non-bibliographic databases in science and technology of importance to development in the region;
     -   developing specialized S & T information services in high priority subject areas and strengthening the information compound of existing networks in the field of science and technology;
     -   introducing improved/new information services, in particular sub-regional selective dissemination of information services based on databases available in the region, access to databases outside the region and information support, including consolidated and repackaged information adapted to different user groups (development planners, decision-makers, government officials, research workers, technicians, etc.) concerned with S & T development;

2.   create a general framework for the exchange of S & T information and experience, by:
     -   developing and promoting the technical and organizational structures and capabilities for cross-border exchange of data, the sharing of processing facilities and the eventual interconnection of national S & T information services and networks to form the regional S & T information network;
     -   strengthening one selected institution or agency in each participating country to enable it to serve as the National Coordinating Unit for the Regional Network, and also strengthening institutions of sub-regional vocation to enable

them to become Centres for Regional S & T Information
Services;

- establishing or improving mechanisms for the exchange of
expertise and knowledge in specific subject fields of science
and technology;

3. enhance national and regional capacity for S & T information
handling and use, by:
    - training information specialists;
    - increasing the awareness and enhancing the capacity of
    potential users for their effective use of information and data
    through promotion of the use of existing systems and services,
    in particular those established by UN agencies, and sensitizing
    and orienting users in the use of these services.

APPENDIX III

Consultation Meeting on the Basic Principles and Action
Plan for a Regional Programme to Strengthen Co-operation among
National Information Networks and Systems for Development
in Latin America and the Caribbean (INFOLAC),
Santiago, Chile, December, 1986

Introduction

The meeting which was sponsored by the UNESCO/General
Information Programme and the ECLAC/Latin American Centre for
Economic and Social Documentation (CLADES) was held at ECLAC
headquarters in Santiago, Chile from 3 to 7 November 1986.
Representatives from the national institutions of the following
countries attended: Argentina, Bolivia, Brazil, Colombia, Costa Rica,
Chile, Ecuador, Guatemala, Honduras, Jamaica, Mexico, Nicaragua,
Paraguay, Peru, Uruguay and Venezuela. The regional and inter-
national organizations represented were: Latin American Association
of Development Financing Institutions (ALIDE), ECLAC, Educational
Development and Research Centre (CIDE), Inter-American Centre for
Research and Documentation on Vocational Training (CINTERFOR),
International Documentation Federation/Latin American Committee
(FID/CLA), Latin American Faculty of Social Sciences (FLACSO),
International Development Research Centre (IDRC), International
Federation of Library Associations and Institutions/Latin America and
the Caribbean (IFLA/LAC), Inter-American Institute for Co-operation
on Agriculture (IICA), Latin American Institute for Transnational
Studies (ILET), Organization of American States (OAF), UNESCO.

I. Objectives and Results of the Meeting

Objective 1: To organize a forum to exchange information on the
present situation and the outlook for interinstitutional projects and
co-operative activities in the field of information in the region.

Results:

1. The knowledge that the basic document prepared by UNES-
   CO/PGI ECLAC/CLADES has been well received in the region.
2. The opportunity to become familiar with interinstitutional projects
   actually being executed in the area of information in Latin
   America and the Caribbean.

- Experimental design of mechanisms to exchange information among databases structured with different formats (Instituto Brasilero de Informaçaõ Cientifica e Tecnologica (IBICT), Biblioteca Regional de Medicina (BIREME).
- Training for information users (University of the West Indies), National Library of Jamaica, Caribbean Community Secretariat).
- Workshop on the use of microcomputers and the Microisis programme in libraries (University of the West Indies, ECLAC/CDC.

3. Acquaintance with a successful case of international co-operation among "peers": the Joint Programme of Studies on International Relations in Latin America (RIAL).

4. Updated information on the policies of international co-operation agencies in the field of information: IDRC, OAS, UNESCO/PGI.

Objective 2: To examine the intercommunication and co-ordination mechanisms between national governmental and non-governmental institutions and regional and international organizations carrying out activities in the field of information.

Results:

1. The design of a number of flexible co-ordination mechanisms for INFOLAC (Co-ordinating Committee, Advisory Group, Technical Secretariat).

2. A consensus on the need for diversity and the gradual development of national INFOLAC liaison mechanisms.

3. The official constitution of a tripartite INFOLAC Technical Secretariat consisting of ECLAC/CLADES; OAS/DACT and UNESCO/PGI.

Objective 3: To draw up the action plan of the short and medium-term programme including proposals for interinstitutional projects to be executed at the international and regional levels.

Results:

1. Identification of schematic profiles of interinstitutional projects by subject areas of the programme (see the list in section III).

2. Short-term action plan
   - Organization of missions by consultants to define the project proposals, submit them to financing agencies on the basis of the schematic project profiles drawn up at the meeting.

- Organization of national meetings to promote and initiate action through INFOLAC.

II. Some Conclusions and Recommendations

It was concluded that:

1. The INFOLAC concept represents a new and appropriate work method for the national institutions and regional organizations in Latin America and the Caribbean concerned with information, whatever may be their legal nature, governmental, non-governmental or intergovernmental and whatever their development missions.

2. INFOLAC is a necessary instrument for promoting action in the field of information in Latin America and the Caribbean, because it is an open programme where any institution involved in information services in the region may participate.

3. INFOLAC emerges, at the end of the 1980s, as a viable initiative because the national institutions have matured and accepted a new style of institutional and co-operative action.

4. Whether INFOLAC will make an impact will depend on the level of commitment by the national institutions—with the collaboration of the regional agencies for co-ordinating information to initiation, growth and permanence in the region.

It was recommended:

1. That the national and regional institutions participating in INFOLAC should contribute to the formation of national groups of the Programme to ensure wide participation by institutions with different missions and legal nature.

2. That the governments of member countries should give INFOLAC steady and effective support.

3. That the member States should give their backing to the document on preparatory assistance presented to UNDP by UNESCO as the executing agency and ECLAC as the associated agency for the financing of the start-up of INFOLAC during the fourth programming cycle for regional projects.

III. List of Interinstitutional Project Titles

Area 1: Information Project Management

    1.1 Improvement of information projects and programmes management capabilities.

    1.2 Co-operative development of databases for administration of information projects and programmes management.

Area 2: Evaluation of Modern Information Handling Technologies

    2.1 Pilot project for linking data transmission networks among countries in the region.

    2.2 Evaluation of the impact of the new technologies on information services.

Area 3: Compatibility, Systematization and Interconnection of Non-numerical Databases

    3.1 Normalization of formats for exchanging machine-readable documentary information.

    3.2 Development of a union catalogue of periodicals published in Latin America and the Caribbean.

    3.3 Normalization of the terminology for the indexing and retrieval of documentary information in Latin America and the Caribbean.

    3.4 Development and exchange of software packages for the management of documentary information.

Area 4: Promotion of Information Services Utilization

    4.1 Information promotion and marketing.

Area 5: Training of Human Resources

    5.1 Comparative study of the activities to update and train human resources in information and documentation in Latin America and the Caribbean.

    5.2 Study of training programmes for high-level information and documentation specialists in Latin America and the Caribbean.

Area 6: Co-ordination and Promotion

    6.1 Pilot project on the start-up of an information system on information activities in Latin America and the Caribbean.

6.2 Development of a "Clearing House" for audiovisual, educational or promotional material in Latin America and the Caribbean.

6.3 Pilot project to experiment with the use of modern communication technologies for the monitoring and co-ordination of the INFOLAC programme.

IV. List of National Participating Institutions

Argentina: National Scientific and Technical Research Council (CONICET)

Bolivia: National Information System and Fund for Development (SYFNID)

Brazil: Brazilian Institute for Scientific and Technological Information (IBICT)

Colombia: Colombian Fund for Scientific Research (COLCIENCIAS)

Costa Rica: National Scientific and Technological Research Council (CONICIT)

Chile: National Scientific and Technological Research Commission (CONICYT)
Catholic University of Chile, Library System
University of Chile, Library System Co-ordination

Ecuador: National Council for Science and Technology (CONACYT)

Guatemala: Economic Planning Secretariat

Honduras: Senior Council for Economic Planning (CONSUPLANE)

Jamaica: National Council on Libraries, Archives and Documentation Services (NACOLADS)

Mexico: National Council for Science and Technology (CONACYT)

Nicaragua: Ministry for External Co-operation

Paraguay: Technical Planning Secretariat

Peru: National Co-ordination of Integrated Development Information Systems

Uruguay: University of the Republic, School of Library Science

Venezuela: National Library Autonomous Institute (IABN)

7. Building a Caribbean Bibliographic Database: A View from a Cataloguer's Desk

Nel Bretney

This paper documents some pointers that are considered pertinent to the topic, in the hope that the discussion which follows will amplify, redefine, and even refine the suggestions made. It is not meant to be a blueprint nor must it be construed that what is said is exclusive.

In my opinion a Caribbean bibliographic database is not a single entity but a composite or umbrella system embracing several databases or files. Cataloguing is considered in its broadest sense to include indexing. Looking at the topic within that framework, certain points must constantly be brought into focus: first, the multilingual nature of the area under review which comprises four official languages—English, French, Spanish, and Dutch; second, the disparity in library service and automation provision in the region; and third, the geographic separation of the territories involved.

State of the Art

The year 1979 saw the start of the Caribbean Information System with CARISPLAN based at ECLAC's Caribbean Documentation Centre in Trinidad. Focussing on development and planning, CARISPLAN relies heavily on input from members of the Caribbean Development and Cooperation Committee (CDCC). As a result Puerto Rico, Martinique, and Guadeloupe are excluded. Its publication, *CARISPLAN Abstracts*, is now available on line, but telecommunications charges may be a prohibiting factor. A subscription tape service may be warranted here. For subject retrieval the OECD Macrothesaurus is the authority, and time coverage is from 1970 onwards.

The agricultural component, CAGRIS, is the second network in the Caribbean Information System. Recently launched, with the University of the West Indies, St. Augustine Campus as a regional centre, it plans eventually to include all Caribbean countries. With AGROVOC as the thesaurus, CAGRINDEX will in future represent a regional input. Plans are already off the ground for CARSTIN, with emphasis on science and technology, and there is talk of a Caribbean education database.

Noteworthy also are *CARINDEX* and *CARICOM Bibliography*. The first, another cooperative effort, is an index to periodicals in the social sciences and humanities in the English-speaking area. *CARICOM Bibliography*, as it represents the national imprints of CARICOM member states, covers only the English-speaking territories. Their value in the Caribbean bibliographic database should not be underestimated, however, and some consideration should be given to providing abstracts in areas not covered by the Caribbean Information System.

Bibliographic Description

Underscoring this fragmentation of effort, if a Caribbean bibliographic database is to become a reality, is the need for exchange-ability of records. Some amplification is necessary here. In its *Reference Manual for Machine-readable Bibliographic Descriptions*, UNISIST stresses the paramountcy of an exchange format. Using as its guide *Documentation-Format for Bibliographic Information Interchange on Magnetic Tape* (ISO 2709), UNISIST states that its prime objective is

to serve as a standardized communication format for the exchange of machine-readable bibliographic information between bibliographic databases or any other type of bibliographic information services, including libraries. This objective implies provision for adequate description and identification of the bibliographic items referred to in the records exchanged, as a basis for adequate and efficient storage and retrieval of both the items and the related records. [1]

What UNISIST has done is to take the logical units or fields of a bibliographic record (analogous to "areas" in AACR2), expand them, and identify them separately by assigning tags, indicators, subfields, and field separators, all called 'content designators.' Next, documents were classified by type and, under each, mandatory and optional elements were designated. Form and choice of heading would be in accordance with AACR2.

Note that UNISIST's mandatory elements are not exclusive. There will doubtlessly be other data deemed necessary for retrieval purposes in a Caribbean bibliographic database, for example, location, availability.

Following is a summary of mandatory fields by document type:

Monographs (Single records): ISBN, author (personal or corporate), title, date, language, publisher, edition, collation, country of publication code.

Monographs (Multipart): ISBN, title, author (personal or corporate), date, language, publisher, edition, collation, country of publication code.

Monographs (Analytic): Title, author, host item, collation (analytic), language.

Serials (Analytic): Title, author, host item (title, volume, issue and date), collation (analytic), language of text.

Reports: Same as for monographs or serials with the addition of report number.

Theses/Dissertations: Same as for monographs with the addition of university or institution.

Patents: Same as monographs, with the addition of identification, person or corporate body responsible for their existence, and INID Codes (International agreed Numbers for Identification of Data).

Conferences: Can be treated either as serials or monographs as the publications warrant, with the addition of name, location, and date of meeting.

In 1982,[2] UNISIST adapted its manual to cater to two types of that required special treatment—research projects and research institutions.

Research Projects: Record control number, date of input of record, language of record, project title, official title, language of title, working language(s) of project, name of researcher, name of institution, address of institution, starting date of project, completion date of project, current status of project, and its code.

Research Institutions: Record control number, date of input of record, language of record, name of institution, address of institution.

With all document types, extensive optional elements have been added. Consensus on these would have to be agreed upon by participating members of a Caribbean bibliographic database.

Authority Files

It is essential that the maintenance of an authority file be carried out centrally, with members given responsibility for names emanating from their own countries. Some members may compile theirs manually; indeed, there is no alternative if the necessary computerized facilities are lacking, but it is recommended that authority files be automated to facilitate exchangeability and currency. Moreover, it is advisable that there be a linkage between the bibliographic database and the name authority by assigning a code to each name entry to act as a pointer to the relevant name in the authority file. The advantages here, as described by K. Klemperer,[3] are the saving of disk space since each name is entered in the authority file only once, the use of variant forms of name for retrieval, and the automatic selection of the authoritative form of name to appear in bibliographic records. Added to these are the ease with which corrections can be effected, since the change occurs only in the authority records, and the enhanced currency of the authority file since no new record can be added to the database without the corresponding name being established in the authority file. A. Di Lauro [4] lists additional benefits of linking name authority files to the bibliographic database. These are:

Verification and proofreading of text stored in the authority file need be done only once.

The creation of an inverted file becomes a possibility. Since each authority entry records the item numbers of their corresponding bibliographic records, easy access to these records is possible.

The agencies and branches of an institution can be searched online, once the relationships are incorporated in the institution's authority record.

In printed output products, the references to an institution listed in an authority file can be automatically generated.

In multilingual authority files, each user can select a corporate name in his own language and retrieve all relevant documents.

Series Authority (Including Journals)

Admittedly, a series authority is not as crucial as a personal or corporate name authority, but if a Caribbean bibliographic database purports to offer comprehensive access, some consideration must be given to the establishment of a series authority file.

Susan Matson defends the need to differentiate between a series and a serial in an authority file, for a collective title may be regarded either as one or the other with differing cataloguing treatment. She says:

A serial title is treated solely as a main entry within the bibliographic subsystem of a database. A series title, on the other hand, is included in the authority subsystem, which then directs its bibliographic handling not as a main entry but as an element of description and secondary access in bibliographic records that bear some other main entry. [5]

Other functions of a series authority could include:

The indication of changes in journal titles so as to provide the necessary references and linkages.

The listing of traced and untraced headings.

The indication of which series should be in a series field and which should be in a note.

The allocation of variant series headings that often occur in grey literature and the establishing of the accepted form.

The national bibliographic agency within each territory should assume responsibility for the maintenance of the series authority for material emanating within its borders. Computerization here is not urgent and can be earmarked as a long-term projection.

Subject Authority

By far the most important component in authority control is vocabulary control, since on it can depend the success of subject retrieval. Users' requests need to be translated into a language that has been previously devised to match the documents of information housed in a system of database.

There are three courses open to the producers of a Caribbean bibliographic database: the use of a natural language, thus avoiding controlled terminology, the construction of a thesaurus, and the use of thesauri already in print. The options are not mutually exclusive, but the least acceptable is the use of natural language alone as a basis of subject retrieval. Any standardization here is limited to what natural language itself imposes. Depending as it does on key words in context, synonyms and homonyms are not catered to and can lead to low recall and low precision for the user. Even with the use of word combinations and truncation, the possibility of limited retrieval still exists.

Thesaurus construction is the most laborious choice available. Using literary warrant [6] (word frequency or popularity in the literature) and/or user warrant (interrogation of the user to ascertain needs), this method is time consuming with or without computer assistance. After terms have been assembled, their hierarchical relationships have to be determined, including broader, narrower, and related terms. Finally, there is the alphabetical display. *Documentation: Guidelines for the Establishment and Development of Monolingual Thesauri* (ISO 2788) [7] is the standard to be followed and exemplifies the effort demanded, a task which is compounded in a multilingual thesaurus where conceptual equivalences have to be assigned as well.

The optimum solution, then, is the use of subject headings or descriptors already in existence. However, harmonization of imported thesauri with local exigencies and usage is a problem which will have to be confronted. Ongoing cooperation among participating members will be needed to decide on preferred terms and thus obviate the need for the user to go a step further in finding information; ensure maintenance and updatability (the dynamic nature of language and advances in knowledge make this a priority); and review earlier decisions in the light of current experience.

Whatever method of vocabulary control is adapted, focus should always be on the end user. For this reason, a Caribbean database, in order to enhance its retrieval capabilities, should permit some precision in information extraction. Cataloguing/indexing under major/minor subjects or primary/secondary terms reduces the incidence of noise and offers the user a choice between high precision and low recall or vice versa.

Printed vs. Machine-Readable Thesaurus

These terms "printed" and "machine-readable" are not mutually exclusive, of course, for a computerized thesaurus can generate a hard copy. On the one hand, the printed form has the advantage of making for wider distribution, particularly among institutions lacking the necessary hardware. Even in organizations where both are available, the portability of the printed form cannot be denied. Additionally, it is energy efficient, since no computing time is involved. On the other hand, the machine-readable thesaurus can be linked to the main bibliographic database (much of what was mentioned earlier about the linkage of the name authority applies here). It also makes for easy sorting and enhanced maintenance as additions, changes, and deletions are easily effected. It also has a quality control function as unrecognized terms can be readily identified and rejected. The number of postings per descriptor can be indicated up front, thus allowing the user to know in advance the productivity of a particular search. Equally important, it permits generic searches.

Abstracts

Although not regarded as mandatory, abstracts are beneficial adjuncts to bibliographic records. It is this task that differentiates the cataloguer from the indexer. The proliferation of the printed word makes it imperative for a researcher to sift through a vast amount of literature in the least possible time, and the abstract is a handy vehicle in this screening exercise. As pointed out in *Documentation: Abstracts for Publication and Documentation* (ISO 214),[8] abstracts also obviate the need to read the full text of peripheral documents.

The DEVSIS Study Team's Document[9] outlines two options in the writing of abstracts:

Descriptors embedded in abstracts. Here the descriptors are assigned and an indicative abstract written with the selected descriptors embedded in it.

Free text abstracts plus descriptors. Here the abstract is written independently (often by the authors of primary documents) with descriptors subsequently assigned.

ISO 214 lays down specific guidelines for the compiling of abstracts. Distinction is made between indicative and informative abstracts, with a stated preference for the latter. A combination of the two is sometimes warranted.

The level of detail demanded by an informative abstract often can be a bugbear to cataloguers who index over and above their normal duties. The problem can be aggravated if the subjects of the documents are unfamiliar. What would be preferable is DEVSIS's second option where authors of primary sources were urged to write their own abstracts, with indexers affixing the relevant descriptors. A self-instructional guide to abstracting could be prepared for distribution to authors to ensure conformance to international standards.

Centralized vs. Decentralized Cataloguing

In these days of cooperative networks, it is envisaged that there would be a devolution of responsibility in the work involved in a Caribbean bibliographic database. However, there are benefits to centralization which one should not overlook.

Centralized cataloguing is predicated on the assumption that the central coordinating agencies for the various databases would also act as depositories for material in their specialized fields. The advantages here are that cataloguing standards and quality control could be maintained; that document delivery would be enhanced, and that, since staff would be appointed full time to the task of updating the files, a faster throughput would be expected.

But looking at the situation as it exists in the region, decentralization has been given prominence. Each participating country has a focal point whose task it is to collect worksheets from local members to be forwarded to the central coordinating agency. Worksheets, however, are gradually being overtaken by disks. The benefit of this decentralization is that each member has a stake in the operation, and plays a part in its success. On the negative side is the varying levels of enthusiasm encountered among members which could affect output.

Looking into the near future as telecommunications charges, one hopes, are reduced in the region, the feasibility of allowing participating libraries to input directly in the database will have to be considered. No final decision should be taken without resolving the difficulties of quality control and duplicate entries.

Retrospective Bibliographic Control

What has been discussed so far relates only to current and future documentation. But a Caribbean database would be enhanced with access to retrospective material. The feasibility of such accessibility is demonstrated by the fact that some libraries have either computerized their cataloguing or are members of international bibliographic networks that offer magnetic tapes as one of their output products. The three campus libraries of the University of the West Indies fall into the last category. As members of OCLC and through the use of holding libraries' symbols, the U.W.I. will be able to identify and extract West Indian or Caribbean records when they undertake retrospective cataloguing. What's more, looking into the near future, OCLC will be redesigning its system [10] to offer additional features in its Cataloguing Subsystem. Subject headings and classification numbers will be available as new access points, and under new search qualifiers will be added country of publication, national library designators, government documents/nongovernment documents, publisher and place of publisher. This augurs well for a Caribbean bibliographic database.

But what of traditional subject authority tools like Library of Congress and Sears Subject Headings? It is essential that there be, wherever possible, uniformity of headings between current and retrospective sections of a Caribbean database. Tapping a network like OCLC that accommodates a variety of subject authorities will permit the use of traditional tools for the maintenance of card or online catalogues as well as local topical headings and index terms derived from controlled lists. The last two categories would appear only on the inputting library's archive tapes, part of which could be extracted to form part of a Caribbean database.

Putting it all together, a way must be found to include Martinique, Guadeloupe, and Puerto Rico. One can foresee a Caribbean bibliographic database which is totally online, but which offers print products. All participating members will have online access to current and retrospective files that make up the database. To become a reality, attention must be paid to exchangeability of records and compatibility of hardware and software. True, some cataloguing decisions will also have to be made, but the machinery (administrative if not in all cases technological) is already in place; for many of us, brought up in a manual tradition, are eager to grasp the new technology. Indeed, a Caribbean bibliographic database must not be regarded as a brickbat to be shunned but a bouquet to be accepted. Most cataloguers are ready for the receiving line.

NOTES

1. Harold Dierickx and Alan Hopkinson, *Reference Manual for Machine-Readable Bibliographic Descriptions*, 2d rev. ed. (Paris: UNISIST, UNESCO, 1981), p. 0.2.

2. Idem, *Reference Manual for Machine-Readable Bibliographic Descriptions of Research Projects and Institutions*, 2d rev. ed. (Paris: UNISIST, UNESCO, 1982).

3. Katherina Klemperer, "Designing a Database to Meet the Combined Bibliographic and Technical Requirements of a Large Public Online Library Catalog: Abstract," American Association for Information Science, *Proceedings of the 45th Annual Meeting* 19 (1982), 368.

4. Anne di Lauro and Maureen Sly, *Guidelines for the Building of Authority Files in Development Information Systems* (Ottawa: IDRC, 1985), p. 4.

5. Susan Matson, "Desiderata for a National Series Authority File," *Library Resources and Technical Services* 26 (October/December 1982), 332.

6. F. W. Lancaster, *Vocabulary Control for Information Retrieval* (Washington, DC: Information Resources Press, 1972).

7. International Organization for Standardization, Information Centre, *Information Transfer: Handbook on International Standards Governing Information Transfer, Texts of ISO Standards* (Geneva: ISO, 1977), pp. 397-409.

8. Ibid., p. 6.

9. DEVSIS Study Team, *DEVSIS, The Preliminary Design of an International Information System for the Development Sciences* (Ottawa: IDRC, 1976), p. 60.

10. *OCLC Newsletter* 161 (February 1986), 3.

8. Le partage des ressources: une première étape dans la Caraïbe francophone / Resource-Sharing: A First Step in the French-speaking Caribbean

Françoise Montbrun

Je n'ai pas voulu faire du communication sur ce sujet quit m'apparaissait plus approprié aux grandes bibliothèques. Or, a cette session il m'a semblé utile d'informer nos collègues de la Caraïbe de nos efforts, même s'ils renvoient pour caracteriser notre activité, a une image de pionnier, comme l'a justement souligné notre collègue de la République dominicaine. Parler de realisations de départ peut paraître hors de proportion avec la description de grands projets imposants que peuvent mener certaines bibliothèques, c'est cependant une occasion de souligner la différence des composantes de l'ACURIL. S'il me manque des éléments, je demanderai a mes collègues francophones présents dans la salle d'intervenir.

Nous representons des territoires petits et disperses. Nous avons peu de moyens et notre problème principal est celui du manque de ressources humaines qualifiées. Nous nous sommes donc donné pour objectif de réunir les partenaires professionnels et de mettre l'accent sur la formation.

Le contexte documentaire de la Caraïbe francophone s'organise comme suit:

Les Antilles et la Guyane françaises
1. A partir de pôle étude/recherche: la Bibliothèque de l'Université des Antilles et de la Guyane située sur les trois départements de Martinique, Guadeloupe et Guyane par ordre d'importance; des bibliothèques départementales, des archives départementales et des centres de documentation specialisés.
2. A partir du pôle lecture publique: Des bibliothèques municipales et des bibliothèques centrales de prêt desservant les campagnes par bibliobus.

Editor's Note: Translated from the original French by Charles S. Fineman, Northwestern University Library, Evanston, IL.

Haïti

1. Dans le domaine étude/recherche: la Bibliothèque Nationale, les Archives Nationales, la Bibliothèque de l'INAGHEI, la Bibliothèque de la Faculté de Médecine, la Bibliothèque de la Faculté d'Agronomie, la Bibliothèque des Frères de l'Instruction Chrétienne.
2. Dans le domaine de la lecture publique: un reseau de bibliothèque se met en place avec la Bibliothèque Nationale.

Les liens entre professionnels ont été crées par impulsion associative avec la création, en 1979, de l'Association des Archivistes Bibliothécaires Documentalistes Francophones de la Caraïbe (AABDFC) suivie de la création, en 1982, de l'Association des Documentalistes-Bibliothécaires de Centres de Documentation et d'Information des Etablissements Secondaires (ASSODOC). La Bibliothèque Universitaire a ensuite pris le relais institutionel en créant un Centre Régional de Formation Professionnelle avec le support de la Mission de Formation Continue de l'Université.

Qu'avons nous fait en matière de partage de ressources?

1. De la formation, grâce a une mise en commun des compétences.
2. Une publication: *Notes Bibliographiques Caraïbes* (imparfaite, mais seule existante).
3. Un catalogue collectif des périodiques antillais conservés aux Antilles et dont la partie concernant la Guadeloupe est publiée.
4. Un répertoire de chercheurs des Antilles et de la Guyane françaises (partie Guadeloupe terminée).
5. Le CCOH, Catalogue collectif des ouvrages haïtiens, sur fiches.
6. La mise en place d'un laboratoire de restauration et de microfilmage en Haïti.
7. Développé le prêt inter-bibliothèques.

Les réalisations actuelles prennent la forme suivante:

1. Formation continue, après la réflexion menée pour ACURIL XVII.
2. Journées de réflexion.
3. Répertoires.
4. Animations: manifestations autour du livre.
5. Une banque de données sur la documentation régionale. Ce projet est avancé en Martinique. Le premier recensement portera sur les fonds de la Bibliothèque Universitaire

auxquels se sont ajoutés ceux de Centre de Documentation du Centre de Recherches Caraïbes de l'Université de Montréal après le départ de cette dernière de la Martinique en decembre 1986.

Notre préoccupation doit maintenant se tourner vers une réflexion commune sur le développement des collections. Dans le contexte économique actuel, il est urgent pour nous d'établir une politique équilibrée d'acquisitions et d'intensifier les échanges. Ceci constitue déjà une seconde étape que nous ne pouvions franchir sans une mise en place de partenaires qualifiés et au cours de l'aquelle il nous faut tenir compte des facteurs suivants: les fonds existants, l'analyse des besoins, les moyens mise en oeuvre et les contraintes géographiques.

I had not intended to present a paper on the subject of resource-sharing because the topic seemed better suited to research libraries. At this session, therefore, I thought it might be useful to tell our Caribbean colleagues about our efforts, even if, in so doing, as our colleague from the Dominican Republic has so rightly said, they can best be characterized as pioneering efforts. Speaking about initial successes may be out of proportion, given the descriptions of large, major projects certain libraries may be able to carry out. It is, however, an opportunity to point out the differences among the members of ACURIL. If I lack specific information, I would ask those French-speaking colleagues who are in the auditorium to speak up.

We represent small and dispersed territories. We have few resources and our main problem is the lack of trained personnel. For this reason our objective is to bring together professional partners and to emphasize training.

In the French-speaking Caribbean, there are very few private libraries. The university/research and public libraries and archives are organized as follows.

Antilles and French Guyana
1. University/research: The Library of the University of the Antilles and Guyana, located in the three departments of Martinique, Guadeloupe, and Guyana (in descending order by size); libraries and archives of the departments and specialized documentation centers.
2. Public libraries: City libraries and central lending libraries serving the countryside with bookmobiles.

Haiti
1. University/research: The National Library, the National Archive, the INAGHEI Library, the Medical School library, the Agronomy School library, the library of the Brothers of Christian Instruction.
2. Public libraries: Under the guidance of the National Library, a public library system is being established.

Links among professionals were given a major boost in 1979, with the founding of the Association des Archivistes Bibliothécaires Documentalistes Francophones de la Caraïbe (AABDFC) (Association of French-speaking Caribbean Archivists, Librarians, and Documentalists), followed in 1982 by the founding of ASSODIC, the Association des Documentalistes-Bibliothécaires de Centres de Documentation et d'Information des Etablissements Secondaires (Association of Documentalist-Librarians of Documentation and Information Centers in Secondary Education). The University Library subsequently picked up the institutional reins by establishing the Centre Régional de Formation Professionnelle (Regional Center for Professional Training), with the support of the university's Mission de Formation Continue (Ongoing Training Mission).

What have we accomplished in the area of resource sharing?
1. Training, thanks to a pooling of talent.
2. Publication of *Notes Bibliographiques Caraïbes* (not the best, but the only tool of its kind).
3. Union catalogue of Antillean periodicals held in the Antilles; to date, the section on Guadeloupe has been published).
4. Directory of researchers in the French Antilles and Guyana; the section on Guadeloupe has been completed).
5. CCOH, *Catalogue collectif des ouvrages haïtiens* (Union Catalogue of Haitian Publications), on microfiche.
6. Establishment of a preservation and microfilming laboratory in Haiti.
7. Development of an interlibrary loan system.

Current projects include the following:
1. Continuing education, resulting from discussions at ACURIL XVII.
2. Discussion sessions.
3. Directories.
4. Book-related public events.

5. Data base on regional documentation. This project is under way in Martinique. The first census will cover collections held at the University Library and those of the Documentation Center of the Caribbean Research Center of the University of Montreal.

We should now begin to think together about the development of these collections. Given current economic conditions, we urgently need to create a balanced acquisitions policy and to increase exchanges. We cannot accomplish this second stage without trained partners. And during the course of our efforts, we must keep the following factors in mind: existing funds, a study of needs, utilization of resources, and geographical constraints.

9. Resource-Sharing Experiences in Puerto Rico and Possibilities for Expanding Resource Sharing in the Caribbean

Mariano A. Maura

Introduction

Library tasks should be summarized within the context of service. From this perspective resource sharing is simply an extension of service. Puerto Rican reality regarding interlibrary cooperation reflects the principle of service through a significant inventory of projects, even though some of them have yet to reach fruition.

Many factors should promote resource sharing among Puerto Rican libraries. For instance: a reduced geographical area, acceptable means of communication and transportation, increasing demand for library services, limited budgetary resources, and limitations in skilled personnel characterize the library environment in Puerto Rico. These limitations, added to other factors described below, induced the development of some early cooperative projects such as the union card catalog of the José M. Lázaro Memorial Library, an informal interlibrary loan program, and the union catalog of law libraries. These projects were later followed by the Puerto Rican Periodicals Indexing Project, the Puerto Rican Newspapers Indexing Project, and the Puerto Rico Newspaper Project.

Among the factors influencing resource sharing should be included the increasing number of new graduate programs during the last five years and the mushrooming of two-year colleges, which have stimulated graduate and undergraduate research. Development of online searching services has also influenced the degree of resource sharing among Puerto Rican libraries.

For the purpose of this paper, resource sharing encompasses three main resources: bibliographical, human, and, taken as one, equipment and materials. Chronological order is used to present several cooperative projects focusing on three basic issues: control of monographs, control of periodicals and newspaper, and effect of technology on resource sharing.

This paper is a summary of events that constitute, in my judgment, good examples of resource sharing in Puerto Rico. Certain technical factors hindering resource sharing are identified. Finally, the application of CD-ROM technology is considered as an alternative for coping with identified problems and for expanding resource sharing not only in Puerto Rico but also in the Caribbean.

Control of Monographs

In Puerto Rico, as elsewhere, interlibrary loans are the early evidence of cooperative efforts among libraries. Since the beginning of the 1950s a significant number of loans were carried out among the main academic libraries, despite a complete absence of tools facilitating interlibrary loan processes. However, in 1954 an evaluation report of the Middle States Association of Colleges and Secondary Schools included a recommendation for the development of a union catalog.

Unsuccessfully, the administration of the University of Puerto Rico (UPR) requested from the Legislative Assembly financial support for the implementation of the union catalog.

In 1959 Dr. José M. Lázaro, director of the UPR General Library at Río Piedras, met with the library directors of the UPR Mayagüez campus, Catholic University, and the Inter-American University. They reached some agreements concerning the organization, functioning, and maintenance of a union catalog which should represent the collections of all four institutions. The proposed union catalog was to facilitate the bibliographical control of both the collections and the interlibrary loans.

In the early 1960s, Josefina del Toro, director of the UPR General Library at Río Piedras, compiled instructions for developing standards to regulate the union catalog. Photocopy of the main entries of monographs was the mechanism used to create the union catalog. Over the years more collections were represented in the union catalog. At present, twenty-four academic institutions are integrated in this catalog, including 186,000 entries. Codes are assigned to each participant library so that location of entries is easily indicated.

In 1983 microfilming of the union catalog started at the José M. Lázaro Memorial Library, where it is located, but for some unknown reason the process was interrupted. At present, about 60,000 entries are still awaiting microfilming.

Another major attempt to produce a control of monographic collections by means of a union catalog started in 1976 under the initiative of Olga Alvarez, then librarian of the Puerto Rico Supreme Court. This union catalog includes the collections of three law school libraries (UPR at Río Piedras, Catholic University, and Inter-American University) and of other major legal collections.

Control of Periodicals and Newspapers

At least between the two major campus libraries of the UPR (Río Piedras and Mayagüez) the interlibrary loans program is a vigorous process reflecting an ever increasing number of transactions. Owing perhaps to the demands of graduate programs and the scarcity of resources, a significant number of interlibrary loan requests are for periodical articles. Therefore, more effective tools for bibliographical periodical control are needed especially regarding Latin American and Puerto Rican periodicals.

Some pertinent facts need to be taken into account when discussing periodicals in Puerto Rico. (1) Most Puerto Rican periodicals are not indexed by traditional indexes. (2) Resistance to reading English materials is a noticeable tendency among some portions of the population, especially undergraduates. (3) Acquisitions of periodicals represent a considerable portion of the library budget, which is hard to justify if usage is low. Within this framework the urgency for tools that can help is clearly understandable.

In 1976 a research conducted by Dolores Barreras found that several libraries were indexing the same periodicals, attributable in a sense, to the lack of communication among libraries. This was an even more dramatic finding, considering the economic crisis of that time. Showing awareness of that crisis, a group of librarians met and decided to coordinate an indexing project for Puerto Rican periodicals, the final product to be shared among the participants.

The Puerto Rican Periodicals Cooperative Indexing Project has the following objectives:

To provide access to the contents of Puerto Rican periodicals.

To standardize the process of periodical indexing, at least at the academic library level.

To avoid and reduce duplication in the indexing of Puerto Rican periodicals.

To develop a union list of Puerto Rican periodicals.

After two years of planning and organization, the Cooperative Indexing Project was initiated with great success. At present, nineteen institutions are participating, fifty periodical titles are currently indexed, each participant library has the responsibility for indexing specific titles, and 15,600 entries have been produced.

For many years the indexing of the newspaper *El Mundo* has been the major indexing project in Puerto Rico. This project is carried out by the Puerto Rican Collection of the UPR Library System, Río Piedras Campus, but for many reasons the project has been working behind time. Although the indexing of *El Mundo* is basically a bibliographical control tool, it is also profusely used by researchers and the library community. If published, its resource sharing potentiality should dramatically increase.

In 1983 a group of librarians from several UPR regional colleges decided to start a cooperative indexing project covering Puerto Rican newspapers. The following titles are currently indexed by the six participating libraries: *El Mundo, El Nuevo Día, El Reportero*, and *Claridad*. After a period of inactivity, new impetus has been imparted to the project, increasing the number of entries to a total of around 5,000.

A smaller but not less important indexing project has been developed by Professor Samuel Figueroa at the Puerto Rico Protestant Seminary Library. In almost one year the complete file of *Puerto Rico Evangélico*, considered the most important Puerto Rican Protestant periodical, has been indexed. The index, which covers from 1912 to 1973, and a thesaurus have been fed into a computer. After a special agreement, the Protestant Seminary will share this index with the UPR Library System at Río Piedras, receiving in exchange a microfilm copy of the *Puerto Rico Evangélico* file.

As a by-product of an in-house program installed in the José M. Lázaro Memorial Library, a list of serials that encompass all the titles in the UPR Library System at Río Piedras has been produced. Since 1984, the list, including holdings and locations, is shared with all the institutions who have requested it.

A plan, sponsored by the American University, is under consideration to develop a computerized union list of serials for all academic libraries in Puerto Rico. A computer printout of the list would be shared among libraries. Owing to the importance of this project strong support must be offered.

Perhaps the most ambitious project regarding bibliographic control of newspapers in Puerto Rico is the U.S. and Puerto Rican Newspaper Project which started in 1985. This project has been funded by the National Endowment for the Humanities and the UPR Library System at Río Piedras. It is based on a three-phase plan including: Phase I (Planning and survey); Phase II (Cataloging of resources and inputting data into OCLC-CONSER and other databases); and Phase III (Preservation of newspapers through microfilming). According to the

Performance Report No. 2 the Project "has as its ultimate goal to
create a Puerto Rican Newspaper Center. The Center has among its
various objectives the following: (1) to ensure bibliographic control;
(2) to facilitate preservation; (3) to promote sharing of resources in
order to provide the availability of and accessibility to all newspapers
on the island; and, therefore, (4) to satisfy the community's research
and information needs." [1]

Effects of Technology on Resource Sharing

Most of the technological applications in libraries involve a
significant level of resource sharing. Although an analysis of the
reasons behind that generalization is far beyond the limits of this
paper, a brief account of the use of technology in Puerto Rican
libraries emphasizes how resources are shared. One good example is
the development of online searching services. The experiences gathered
by the institutions that pioneered such service in Puerto Rico, namely
UPR Medical Sciences Library and the UPR General Library at
Mayagüez, have been shared with the rest of the library community by
helping others through the organization of new installations, by offering
demonstrations, and by training sessions.

Library automation projects represent important examples of
resource sharing. Here are a few.

UPR José M. Lázaro Memorial Library at Río Piedras

Since 1977 this library developed an in-house module system
starting with acquisitions, followed later by circulation and cataloging.
However, modules have never been fully integrated, which caused a lot
of problems. Perhaps this limitation blocked the possibilities of future
applications in other libraries, but even within this limitation the
system has been exposed to librarians from different institutions who
have learned, at least, what is not supposed to be done in a library
automation project.

UPR General Library at Mayagüez

In 1983 and 1984 a plan was developed for the integrated
automation of this library. After extensive considerations a Data
Research Associates (DRA) system called Atlas was selected. A partial
retrospective conversion is on the way. AMIGOS and OCLC services
are used for record conversion. A bibliographic database containing
70,000 records is almost ready, as well as the complete set of options
offered by Atlas.

The Central Administration Office of UPR is considering a plan for the automation of all their eleven campuses and regional college libraries. This project is part of a master plan which includes also four other components: student administration, personnel administration, office automation, and telecommunication network.

For the purpose of the library automation project a technical advisory committee was appointed. Six librarians from different campuses and regional colleges (including myself) and technical personnel from the Central Administration's Office of Information System are participating in this committee. At present, the Committee has finished a needs analysis which will be used as a basis for the request for proposal.

Ana G. Méndez Educational Foundation

Their library automation project started in 1983. Organization of the project was the responsibility of a committee integrated by deans of learning resources and directors of the libraries from the three affiliated institutions: Puerto Rico Junior College, Metropolitan University, and Turabo University. A project coordinator was included in this committee. After a year of analysis, where the needs and possibilities of the three institutions were considered, the DRA system was selected. They are using UTLAS for record conversion, and in the meantime Bibliofile is used for prospective cataloging and local conversion of records to MARC format, including original cataloging. They are planning to develop a public online catalog with bilingual subject-searching capabilities. A database with 37,000 bibliographic records is expected to be ready by late 1987. Software and database will be centralized at Metropolitan University, and the other two institutions will be connected to the central database by dedicated lines. Also, an Ethernet will be installed at Metropolitan University.

By the end of 1987 additional titles converted by UTLAS and new titles converted with Bibliofile will be integrated into the database. Then, public online catalog with a total of 80,000 records should be available.

In preparing the bilingual list of subject headings a special committee was created with catalogers from the three affiliated institutions. The whole project is an outstanding example of cooperative work.

Inter-American University

The library automation project was initiated in October 1986. After developing a need analysis and a request for proposal, Dobis-Leuven system was chosen. Retrospective conversion, done by UTLAS, is based on the collection of the Metropolitan Campus Library, the largest among the twelve libraries located in different campuses and colleges across the Island. When converted records are put into the database, 100,000 records including monographs, serials, and audio visual materials will be available to the rest of affiliated libraries which will use this database for retroconversion of their own collections. The system will be centralized. By the end of summer 1988 acquisition and circulation modules as well as a database with 400,000 records should be available.

Department of Public Instruction

A library automation project including fourteen school libraries has been under way since 1986. The participant libraries have been selected depending on the nature of their collections. Therefore, specialized school libraries are included in this project basically to share their strong subject-oriented collections (i.e., mathematics, science, social sciences).

Every library catalog is being photocopied. At the end, a union catalog of approximately 69,500 records will be gathered and ready to be converted into MARC format. The resulting database should be available to every participant library.

Different alternatives are under consideration to implement LIFENET (Library Involvement for Education Network), which is the name of this project. After a performance evaluation of LIFENET other specialized school libraries should be included.

LIFENET is only one of the components of a more sophisticated and comprehensive project called PRILINET which visualizes the development of a library network in Puerto Rico. The feasibility study for PRILINET, which includes different types of libraries, was conducted by King Research in 1984. Implementation of this project has been postponed owing to the lack of an appropriate infrastructure.

Over the years PRILINET has been considered a model of library network and resource sharing. Some problems pointed out by the King Research report have been solved, others have not. Based upon King Research's findings the major problems are the lack of bibliographic control and the need for exposing library holdings for people to be able to know about their collections. These two problems are still present, but now we have some advantages which were absent when King Research's report was written.

Consider the following factors:

Bibliographic control will improve as direct effect of the present library automation projects.

More records will have a compatible or standard format.

Records stored in mechanical databases are easier to copy and transfer to other media.

Data communication remains a difficult problem, as different system configurations might interfere with data exchange. Another negative factor is the still expensive cost of telecommunications.

To cope with the situation described, I would like to suggest CD-ROM technology as an alternative because of the following advantages:

Huge storage capacity.

Control over response time.

Relatively fast access time (less than one second).

Relatively inexpensive equipment (basically a 512 kilobyte micro-computer and a CD-ROM drive), hardware that can also be used for other needs.

Worldwide standards.

No deterioration from constant use.

A life expectancy in the order of 10 to 20 years.

Elimination of telecommunications costs.

Even when production cost of a CD-ROM is relatively high ($20,000 for each 100 megabytes of data), copies of the master disk cost $25 to $10 depending on quantity produced.

Implementation strategy should include the following steps:

Convert records from the shelf list to a machine-readable MARC tape.

Create authority control.

Merge tapes and authority control.

Press CD-ROM database master disk.

Select appropriate search software.

Following the structure established by PRILINET, a set of CD-ROM might be produced including union catalogs from a group of school, public, and academic libraries. Copies of the master disk might be shared among participant libraries.

A special service of interlibrary loans should be organized on the basis of phone request by using a password previously assigned to each participant library.

Because of the size of its participant collections and the availability of external funds, LIFENET should be used as a pilot project. If the evaluation of this project is positive, further arrangements should be made to extend the service. Other pilot projects might be developed in the Caribbean. Different experiences should be shared and compared in order to get a more standard medium of bibliographical data exchange.

Conclusions

Despite the evidence of resource sharing presented here, a lot more needs to be done in Puerto Rico.

More interinstitutional agreements are needed, as exemplified by the agreement between the UPR and the Ana G. Méndez Educational Foundation which includes a statement on library resource sharing.

Duplication and unnecessary expenditures caused by retrospective conversion projects would be reduced if the present isolated strategy is replaced by an enlarged cooperative program, perhaps based on CD-ROM applications.

CD-ROM technology should be considered as an alternative for sharing library resources.

Quoting Dr. Haydeé Muñoz-Solá, director of the UPR Library System at Río Piedras: "As one of our major problems is the lack of economic resources, Puerto Rican librarians as a professional group should be more aggressive in getting funds from private corporations. Also we have to make people aware of the importance of bibliographical control and we need to adopt a more dynamic leadership." [2]

We have seen our challenge. Let's face it.

NOTES

1. Luisa Vigo-Cepeda, *U.S. and Puerto Rican Newspaper Project; Phase I: Planning and Survey*, Performance Report No. 2 (Río Piedras, PR: University of Puerto Rico, Library System, 1986), p. 1.

2. Haydeé Muñoz-Solá, "Cooperación interbibliotecaria en Puerto Rico," Conferencia presentada ante la facultad bibliotecaria de la Universidad Católica, Ponce, PR (agosto 1985), 13.

10. Estrategias para intercambio de fuentes de información

Verónica Regus

El servicio de préstamo consiste en la entrega por parte de la biblioteca, de una publicación de su acervo, a una persona, institución u otra biblioteca para que en un tiempo determinado haga uso de ella con la obligación de devolverla cuando finalice el plazo convenido. Con este servicio ambas partes resultan beneficiadas.

A pesar de la larga historia que tienen las bibliotecas, los préstamos entre ellas son muy recientes. No es sino hasta 1971 cuando la American Library Association aprueba el primer código de préstamo entre bibliotecas, para que sirviera de guía a las bibliotecas de los Estados Unidos de Norteamérica.

En República Dominicana no existen hasta el momento antecedentes formales de organización de un servicio de préstamo interbibliotecario. Aunque se han hecho arreglos de cooperación conjunta entre bibliotecarios para intercambiar información y/o materiales bibliográficos.

En la búsqueda de precedente en nuestro país, encontramos que, del 12-13 de diciembre de 1955, en Ciudad Trujillo, hoy Santo Domingo, se celebró un Seminario Nacional sobre Préstamo Inter- bibliotecarios en República Dominicana. Se deduce pues, que en el país desde hace muchos años ha habido preocupación por organizar un servicio de esta naturaleza.

Debido a la crisis actual que enfrenta nuestro país en los diversos sectores de la sociedad, se impone la necesidad de que las bibliotecas y centros de documentación aceleren la utilización en forma coopera- tiva de sus colecciones, principalmente las publicaciones periódicas, que tienen un costo elevadísimo por la depreciación que está sufriendo la moneda nacional.

Tratando de buscar soluciones a estos problemas la Asociación de Bibliotecas Universitarias Dominicanas (ABUD), ha elaborado un proyecto para préstamos interbibliotecarios. En la primera parte el servicio será para las bibliotecas miembros, de ABUD, y en una segunda etapa se contempla que participen todas las bibliotecas y centros de documentación del país. Este proyecto ya elaborado podría servir de base para el futuro proyecto de préstamos internacionales.

Desde luego, no hay qué oponer el préstamo internacional al préstamo entre bibliotecas del mismo país. Indudablemente, el primero plantea algunos problemas que el segundo conoce poco o nada: duración de los plazos, reembolso de los gastos. Pero para aquéllos que admiten el principio del préstamo, el hecho de prestar fuera del país no es más difícil que limitar los envíos al territorio nacional. El país donde el préstamo interior funciona bien es así mismo el que mejor responde a las peticiones del extranjero. No se observará ningún progreso verdadero en el plano internacional mientras no se organicen mejor los préstamos en el interior de cada país.

Justificación del préstamo interbibliotecario

Es utópico pensar que una biblioteca pueda poseer la cantidad de materiales, que tan vertiginosamente se está produciendo en el mundo. De hecho, hace que el préstamo entre biblioteca sea tan indispensable como son los Canjes Internacionales. El préstamo es pues, el único medio gracias al cual los establecimientos pueden disponer temporal y rápidamente, de aquello que desean o pueden poseer con carácter definitivo.

No es una solución para todos los problemas que plantea el acceso a la documentación, sino una respuesta práctica a una necesidad de carácter limitado. El servicio de préstamo interbibliotecario deberá extenderse fuera de las fronteras del país cuando el material no exista en el mismo.

Problemas del préstamo

En realidad el préstamo se considera de un modo diferente según sea prestamista o prestatario. Una biblioteca rica en materiales bibliográficos, no debe menospreciar a otra menor, ya que en determinado momento ésta podrá tener materiales que aquélla no posee.

Para la biblioteca prestataria es evidente la carga que representa el préstamo, incluso cuando éste esté funcionando de manera óptima. En efecto, el envío de un material al exterior supone tres inconvenientes:

1. Se corre el riesgo de que la obra falte a los lectores del establecimiento a que pertenece.
2. El envío y la devolución del material son operaciones que exigen tiempo y personal calificado.
3. El préstamo al exterior deteriora los libros mucho más que la simple utilización en la sala de lectura.

No hay duda de que muchas veces se puede evitar el envío de volúmenes facilitando al solicitante una fotocopia de aquéllos que le interesa, sobre todo cuando se trata de artículos de revistas.

Uno de los aspectos que se deben dejar sentados en la reglamentación que rija este sistema, es la forma de pago por la cual el usuario costeará el servicio prestado.

Otro de los aspectos primordiales en la implementación del sistema, sería asesorar a los países que no tengan sus catálogos colectivos o bibliografías nacionales, a elaborar los mismos, ya que éstas son herramientas fundamentales para hacer frente a las diferentes peticiones que se produzcan.

Sugerencias para la implementación del sistema

Si queremos sacar las bases para el establecimiento del sistema de préstamo interbibliotecario, debemos, entonces, recurrir a aquellas instituciones que tienen largos años de experiencia en el área y que podrían aportar sugerencias y recomendaciones para su mejor funcionamiento.

Merece la pena mencionar el Midwest Inter-Library Center que fue creado en 1949. Más tarde el Centro prestaría cualquier obra de su fondo a cualquier biblioteca del país. Rápidamente el Centro se convirtió en el mayor y más completo de los Estados Unidos de Norteamérica. En virtud a la expansión que tuvo el Centro, modificó su política en 1961, abandonando toda restricción geográfica en la admisión de miembros y pocos años después cambió su nombre por The Center for Research Libraries, para así evitar la limitación regional.

Otra de gran importancia es la National Library of Medicine que posee el fondo más grande y más completo de la literatura médica de los Estados Unidos, y tal vez del mundo entero.

La Federación Internacional de Asociaciones de Bibliotecarios (FIAB), con su Comisión de Catálogos Colectivos y de Préstamos, esta función la ha venido desempeñando desde hace unos 50 años y tiene toda la intención de seguir expandiéndola.

Y por último no debemos olvidar que recientemente varias bibliotecas de carácter mundial han considerado un movimiento denominado DUP (Disponibilidad Universal de Publicaciones). Como su título sugiere, este movimiento tiene la esperanza de hacer de los préstamos interbibliotecarios un tema internacional con el propósito esencial de prestar, y coger prestado, materiales a nivel mundial. Dicho movimiento DUP está hoy en día alineando esfuerzo cooperativo entre bibliotecas de Gran Bretaña, Canadá, Estados Unidos, México y Sudamérica.

Si se lograse conseguir alguna consultoría de estos organismos, sería más fácil y rápido que este proyecto sea una realidad.

11. Resource Sharing in the Research Triangle: A Challenge Unmet

Deborah Jakubs

This decade marks the fiftieth year of cooperation among the research libraries within the Research Triangle, that is, the University of North Carolina at Chapel Hill, Duke University at Durham, and North Carolina State University at Raleigh. Our cooperative program for Hispanic materials dates back only to the very early 1940s. Rather than reiterate the history of the formal cooperation among our institutions, so well presented by William Ilgen of the University of North Carolina at SALALM's Chapel Hill meeting in 1984, I would 1 like to approach the theme of this panel from another direction. Although we work under what looks on paper like a clean division by country of materials in the social sciences and humanities published in Latin America, and our program is often praised as one of the first successful cooperative arrangements in the country, I contend that we have not yet lived up to the promise of cooperative collection development in the Research Triangle, despite significant efforts on the part of many librarians over the years. I would venture to say that this is a problem not only in North Carolina but also elsewhere. Why has cooperation not worked well? By addressing this question, I hope to point out the potential pitfalls of planning for resource sharing and to indicate issues to bear in mind when considering, as nearly all of us must these days, formal arrangements for building collections cooperatively.

First of all, resource sharing cannot work on the basis of general agreements. Careful planning, detailed assessment of collections and programs, realistic appraisal of potential for cooperation, in terms of both staff and money, and, perhaps most important, a mutual commitment to joint goals are required for any such arrangement to

Author's Note. I would like to acknowledge the special assistance of my counterpart at the University of North Carolina at Chapel Hill, William Ilgen, with whom I often discuss this subject, Pat Dominguez and Luke Swindler, also from UNC, who have shared their ideas from a paper they are writing on the topic of cooperation in the Research Triangle, and many others.

work.   Cooperative collecting policies must be specific, flexible documents, responding to subtle and not-so-subtle shifts in program emphasis. As such, they must be tended, evaluated, and rebalanced, all of which implies a significant commitment of time and close personal contact among bibliographers. Resource-sharing agreements do not work automatically; they must be carefully monitored and adjusted.

Ironically, it is easier to devise cooperative plans between institutions that are dissimilar in mission than between those that are similar.   It is, for example, clearer to identify Duke's collecting responsibilities vis-à-vis North Carolina State University, known for its strength in scientific and technical fields, than to elaborate our arrangement with UNC, very similar in mission and makeup.   Duke and UNC have faculty with very close interests. Our cooperative plan for Latin American acquisitions, which was initially devised in the 1940s based largely on research interests of the faculty on board at the time, ran into trouble, for example, when Duke lost and did not replace the Brazilianists who had been largely responsible for building up a splendid collection as well as the Andean specialist by the name of John Tate Lanning, a man who singlehandedly developed our collections on those countries. A generation or two of faculty have come and gone since then, and hirings have not taken into account the directions we have headed with our cooperative collection-building efforts. As a result, we have faculty at Duke who are interested in the countries "assigned to" UNC way back when our original plan was written up, some of whom are not interested in traveling the short distance of twelve miles to use the collections at our partner institution, and UNC finds itself in the same situation. Thus, we have built-in duplication of effort. Until we revise our cooperative scheme in light of the new programs and faculty interests, and find a way to encourage the universities, not just the libraries, to develop complementary teaching programs, we will not be living up to the promise of our history of cooperation or serving our institutions as well as we might. Some of the key factors are, however, at present out of the control of bibliographers.

One problem of cooperative arrangements is defining the range and type of materials involved. Do you cooperate from strength or marginality? Most often it has been the latter, since it has generally been agreed what the library must purchase in certain areas to support teaching and research. That leaves other, less critical areas to be split up among partners. In theory that may work well; it will not, however, save any money and may not build up unusually unique collections, since the areas of strength require significant funds, and collecting in those marginal areas falters, drops off, and revives depending on the budgetary situation. Today's marginal areas may be tomorrow's trends, however, so cooperative planning should be in the hands of bibliographers with a good perspective on the scholarship in a field and the ability to predict directions in that scholarship in the years to come.

Fluctuating funding from year to year at all three institutions has affected our ability to honor commitments made long ago. When a library is in budget trouble, often cooperative commitments are the first areas to be sacrificed. It is critical, therefore, that cooperative arrangements be made in the areas of each institution's greatest interest. Thus they will be protected for the future.

Resource sharing that works requires that attention to detail. It is important to define precisely—and this we have not yet done in the Research Triangle—what "responsibility" for collecting in a field means. For example, it is sensible for one institution to collect primary materials and large microform sets as well as census materials for the countries for which it is "responsible." In some cases it has worked out this way between Duke and UNC, but we are striving to be more specific in our documentation and in practice. This detail and the publicity that cooperative plans must receive among their clientele can improve the library's service as a whole by informing patrons of the strengths—and weaknesses—in the collections. Library users are happier when they know what to expect and where to find it.

The question of accessibility is of critical importance in the smooth functioning of cooperative plans. For example, Duke, UNC, and NCSU now share an online catalog that has made it possible to search the holdings of any of the three institutions from one place. This fact has made it imperative that we provide practical access to the materials at the neighboring institutions. Interlibrary loan is a possibility, but many patrons would like to be able to spend a day or part of one at one of the other institutions from time to time. What is keeping them from doing so? It is too difficult to find a parking place. So we have theoretical access but it is not real. A bus or van system such as that between Stanford and the University of California at Berkeley is one of our hopes for the future of resource sharing.

I could comment in much more detail on what makes cooperation work and on specific examples of our problems in the Research Triangle. In closing, however, I will say that cooperation to some degree between and among libraries is in everyone's interest; cooperative programs must be institutionally sanctioned and enforced, not just a preference of the libraries; and cooperation is a system. As such, it must be kept alive and dynamic for all parties concerned. Too many cooperative arrangements have become static, forgotten, taken for granted. It is time to re-examine resource sharing in the Research Triangle and to redesign, revitalize, and revive our program so it can be a true model for cooperative schemes everywhere.

Part Three
Grantsmanship

12. OAS Assistance in the Fields of Libraries, Archives, and Conservation in the English-speaking Caribbean

Susan Shattuck Benson

Introduction

The Organization of American States (OAS), headquartered in Washington, D.C., is the oldest international regional organization. It includes thirty-two member countries from the Western Hemisphere. It was formerly called the Pan American Union (PAU), which was created in 1889. It has political and technical functions. The political functions involve settling border disputes, monitoring human rights, and establishing international treaties. The technical branches of the OAS are concerned with problems basic to development in the fields of education, science, culture, economic, and social affairs. These include a wide range of projects concerned with libraries, archives, documentation centers, publishing, conservation, microfilming, and related advanced information technologies.

This report deals only with activities and projects carried out from 1985 through 1987. I present first a short overview of activities in the ACURIL member countries, and then describe in some detail two projects to give you an idea of how the system works.

General Overview of Assistance to ACURIL Member Countries

Learning resource centers are being developed as centers of learning for both school children and teachers. The model for these centers is described in a publication entitled *The Flexible Model for a National System of School Libraries*, which is published in English, Spanish, and Portuguese. Teachers are trained to use and operate libraries. Use of low-cost audiovisual equipment and furniture that can be built and maintained by a low-income community is emphasized. The methodology of the work was developed by librarians from several countries and in cooperation with the library school of the University of Costa Rica. After wide acceptance in the Spanish-speaking countries it is being adapted for use by the English-speaking ones.

The Center for Information for Industry (ICAITI) in Guatemala is sharing its experience and resources to assist all kinds of libraries in both the Spanish- and English-speaking countries to make use of microcomputers for technical processing and building of databases. A course was held there in 1986 on microcomputer use and another given in Trinidad and Tobago. Science documentation centers in all the countries are being strengthened or created and nationals taught to use microcomputers. The OAS's Inter-American Institute on Agriculture (IICA) located in Costa Rica created and maintains the AGRINTER database, which is part of the AGRIS global network. It provides all the Spanish-speaking countries with assistance in agricultural documentation.

In Central America the OAS is working with the countries to develop community libraries and cultural centers and helping improve the quality and quantity of materials for new readers by training people in government and social service groups in writing, design, and distribution of materials and in communication skills (7 courses between 1985 and 1986). The national libraries of Guatemala and Panama are being assisted to improve their public libraries and technical processing. Cultural surveys were completed in 1987 of Panama, Guatemala, and Honduras and a survey is underway of El Salvador to identify, among other things, the many different institutions that provide information services.

Through the Inter-American Project on Children's Literature (PILI) headquartered in Venezuela, assistance is being given to the Spanish-speaking countries in creation of documentation centers on children's literature. A thesaurus on children's literature has been developed that will be presented at a meeting in Venezuela in July 1987. Training in writing, illustration, and design of children's books is given. Through the Centro Universitario de Investigaciones Bibliotecológicas of the UNAM in Mexico, courses have been given to library school professors from throughout Latin America in research and evaluation techniques. With Radionederland the OAS is supporting a survey of the facilities in the English-speaking and Dutch-speaking countries to produce radio and television for children. At a meeting to be held in Barbados later in 1987 the results will be discussed to determine the kind of training and assistance the region will receive from 1988 onward.

DISC—Project to Develop Integrated Information Systems in the English-speaking Caribbean

This regional project is advised by librarians and/or archivists from the OAS English-speaking Caribbean member states who meet every two years to set the priorities for the following biennium. These meetings are also attended by other international and regional organizations, such as IDRC, UNESCO, CARICOM, Caribbean Development Bank, CERLAL, DLS/UWI. The first meeting was held in Jamaica in 1982 and the second in St. Lucia in 1984. The third and fourth planning meetings took place at ACURIL St. Croix and ACURIL Miami as a means to simultaneously support ACURIL and to give many Eastern Caribbean librarians a chance they would not otherwise have to participate in their professional association. The countries that participate in DISC include: Antigua and Barbuda, Bahamas, Barbados, Dominica, Grenada, Jamaica, St. Kitts and Nevis, Saint Lucia, Saint Vincent and the Grenadines, and Trinidad and Tobago.

In 1986-87 DISC's two priorities have been development of training modules for library assistants and training in archives and records management. The priorities requested for 1988-89 are in use of microcomputers for public libraries, creation of national databases and continued assistance to develop archives and records management.

DISC provides modest but ongoing assistance to the Department of Library Studies. For example, it has paid for staff research in the Caribbean, attachments for graduating students in libraries of the region, purchase of bibliographic materials, participation of faculty in international professional meetings. It provides one scholarship a year for an OECS student and sponsors national and regional courses taught by DLS staff. It also makes use of the faculty for technical assistance and coordination of some activities. For example, DLS is coordinating the development of a curriculum for self-teaching for library assistants which is being written by Caribbean librarians. The curriculum will be made up of a series of modules (a core of 10 with 2 electives). The purpose of the curriculum is to diminish the time librarians have to spend in training staff and to allow staff without going abroad to raise their technical level at a time, place, and pace convenient to the trainee.

Since the need for training is ongoing and ever-changing it was important to develop a mechanism for module development that would survive this particular project. Teamwork was deemed the approach that would come closest to accomplishing this. We hope the team has been developed through the five planning meetings held between 1948 and 1986. Staff of Caribbean institutions that have been concerned with library training such as those of Jamaica, Barbados, and Guyana have also been involved in the work.

In the field of archives-records management OAS is providing on-site training and advisory services at many different levels through a series of short missions which put primary responsibility for carrying out recommendations on national staff but provide reinforcement and further assistance. Each country presents a different situation and, although the methodology employed in each is similar, the content is individualized. It has found that taking one person from an institution to attend a regional course that covers a broad range of material in a short time is not cost-effective. The trainee frequently returns with new ideas to an institution that is not receptive to them and also without the technical manuals and support staff needed to advance. It is important that the policy-makers as well as the people who carry out the work understand their respective roles in implementing new procedures or techniques.   Thus, simultaneous, multilevel on-site training and assistance that embrace, for example, ministers, registrars, department directors, and clerical help have been adopted. Once work has been going on in several countries in this manner and common needs are identified, then regional courses are given in an appropriate context to carefully selected people. For example, UNESCO paid for participants in a regional course on records management at the DLS/UWI in March 1986 for which OAS provided the expert.

In the archives program we have begun with management of current records rather than historical and with legislation and laying out the plans for the national archives network. Once the archives are in place and the records management program underway we shall begin concentrating on management of historical records using Caribbean archivists as consultants. By then it is hoped that policy-makers will understand archives as important to economic development and government efficiency as well as to preservation of cultural heritage.

CENTROMIDCA—Inter-American Center for Restoration and Microfilming of Books, Documents, and Photographs

Through CENTROMIDCA, located in the Dominican Republic, technical manuals are being produced, advisory services given, and on-site training missions carried out that emphasize prevention of damage through proper storage and cleaning techniques. Countries are helped to set up restoration facilities and taught microfilming and basic repair of both paper and photographic materials. All of the English-speaking countries have been surveyed except Grenada, St. Kitts and Nevis, and the Bahamas who will be surveyed in 1988-89. A disaster preparedness course for the Eastern Caribbean countries was held in Saint Lucia in 1985 and given in Trinidad as a national course. Funds were given to the Caribbean Archives Association for a general course in conservation held in Barbados in 1986, which was supported by a variety of institutions. The eventual goal of this assistance is establishment in each country of cooperative facilities that can serve libraries, archives, and museums concerned with paper and photographic materials. A meeting will be held in September 1987 of conservators from Mexico, Venezuela, and Brazil in the Dominican Republic to form a consortium of institutions of excellence to assist the other countries and to create an inter-American association of paper conservators.

At the Seminar on Disaster Preparedness held in Saint Lucia the participants expressed need for a microfilm program. Based on their requests OAS is providing coordination and seed money to raise the funds necessary to carry out a large-scale project. The first planning meeting to this effect was held in May, 1987 with fifteen English-speaking Caribbean librarians and archivists and nine others from institutions interested in collaborating, such as the University of California, Berkeley, the Library of Congress, and the British Library. In 1988 we begin approaching foundations for the funds to begin the actual microfilming and simultaneous training of Caribbean microfilmers.

Technical Publications

With cooperation of a large number of librarians the translation into Spanish of the *Anglo-American Cataloging Rules II* were finally made available in 1985. (It may be purchased from the American Library Association for $30.) The *Lista de Encabezamientos de Materia para Bibliotecas* was produced through the Instituto Colombiano para el Fomento de la Educación Superior (ICFES) and made available in 1986. (It may be purchased from ICFES, attn. José Arias.) A variety of manuals on microcomputer use and database development were produced in both English and Spanish in 1985 and 1986 in cooperation with ICAITI (Guatemala) and are available from the Department of Scientific Affairs of the OAS. These include: *Acceso en Linea a Bases de Datos, Thesaurus Handling System, Sistema de Manejo de Tesauros, Organization and Operation of Technical Information Units, Organización y Operación de Unidades de Información, Operadores Booleanos en la Recuperación de Información, Comunicación de Datos, Boolean Operators for Information Retrieval* (self-instruction), *Data Communication for Information Units* (self-instruction), *Uso de Microcomputadoras en*

Servicios de Información. In process for 1987 are publications in English and Spanish on database design for self-instruction. The thrice yearly *Boletín de Micro-Informatica/Bulletin on Microinformatics* is being prepared in both English and Spanish and will be widely distributed beginning in June 1987. Manuals on microfilming and prevention of damage are in preparation and will appear in English and in Spanish by the end of 1987, as will a records management guide for the Eastern Caribbean countries. The *Flexible Model for a National System of School Libraries* is available in English, Spanish, and Portuguese. *Comunicación para Niños* was published through CIESPAL (Ecuador) in 1986. *Como Escribir para Neolectores* will be written by Daniel Prieto and made available by OAS Headquarters at the end of 1987. The two cultural surveys produced in 1986 were: *El Directorio Nacional de Panamá de Instituciones que Desarrollan y/o Difunden Acciones Culturales, Educativos y Sociales*, and *El Directorio Nacional de Guatemala de Instituciones que Desarrollan y/o Difunden Acciones Culturales, Educativos y Sociales.* The surveys of Honduras and El Salvador will be produced by the end of 1987.

For further information write to:

> On public and national libraries, and paper conservation in Spanish-speaking and English-speaking countries, and archives in the English-speaking countries:
> Susan Shattuck Benson
> Department of Cultural Affairs
>
> On science information and documentation:
> Oscar Harasic
> Department of Scientific Affairs
>
> On school libraries, learning resource centers, university libraries:
> Martha V. Tomé
> Department of Educational Affairs
>
> All are at:
> 1889 F Street N.W.
> Washington, DC 20006

13. Grantsmanship: CARICOM's Programme of Activities

Maureen C. Newton

Introduction

The term "grantsmanship" has been described as "the art of securing financial assistance given as by a foundation to an individual or institution for educational purposes."[1] The Caribbean Community Secretariat[2] does not fall into the Funding Agency category. Rather it can be perceived of in the role of an Executing Agency with the responsibility of mobilising on behalf of CARICOM Member States available financial and technical assistance at national, sub-regional, and regional levels[3] for the strengthening of existing national infrastructure. This paper highlights some of the more recent information projects and activities which are being developed by the Secretariat focussing particularly on developments during the past two years. It also shows how as Executing Agency the Secretariat has sought to mobilise resources for the benefit of Member States.

Historical Background

The involvement of the CARICOM Secretariat in the development of Information Systems and Services in the Region is derived from mandates given by the Conference of the Heads of Government of the Caribbean Community and the CARICOM Council of Ministers. Dating back to 1974, through initiatives by specific member governments and institutions, requests were made to the Secretariat for its involvement in:

1. A programme for the exchange of information on a regional basis.
2. The development of a programme for the promotion of regional library development and cooperation.
3. The establishment of a Regional Editorial Board to compile a Regional Bibliography of current imprints.

A second mandate arising out of the First Meeting of the Ministers Responsible for Information, held in 1981 requested inter alia the Secretariat to make proposals regarding policy guidelines and strategies for the development of an integrated Information/ Communication System for the guidance of Member States.

In all of the information activities embarked upon by the Secretariat in the execution of these mandates funds have been utilized both from the Secretariat's budget as well as from the resources made available through Funding Agencies. At a time when recession has impacted heavily on financial and human resources in all sectors including libraries and Information Units, causing constraints in the application of the new technologies in the provision of information services, the CARICOM Secretariat has been mindful of the developments taking place regionally and extraregionally and has tried to ensure that there is no duplication of effort in the implementation of its projects.

Assistance with the Development and Implementation of Plans

There have been instances where programmes of institutions overlap and would tend to cause duplication. Whenever this occurs, there should be consultation and joint action in order to achieve the same objective. Thus, when UNESCO's programme for assisting in the establishment of National Information Systems in the CARICOM States coincided with the Secretariat's activity in respect of the CARICOM LDCs, UNESCO was able to utilize the services of the Secretariat's Chief, Information and Documentation Section during 1981-82 to undertake a consultancy on behalf of Antigua and Barbuda, Dominica, Grenada, Montserrat and St. Vincent and the Grenadines.

The Secretariat followed up on that particular activity in 1983-84 by appointing a Regional Advisor in Information and Documentation who assisted in the implementation of the National Plans. Activities under this programme of implementation included:

The identification in consultation with the Permanent Secretaries and the Interim Co-ordinator of the National Information System, areas that were immediately implementable, as well as those that were crucial to the establishment of the information system.
The provision of assistance in setting up the Advisory Council.
Assistance in setting up the national agency or department responsible for the co-ordinated development of the system.
Conducting education and training programmes.

The organization of the Users of Information Workshops which were conducted in most of the CARICOM Member States was however done in collaboration with the Department of Library Studies, University of the West Indies, since that institution had already planned and had received funding for the development, testing, and evaluation of a user education package for planners within the Public Sector. This collaborative effort not only provided an opportunity for the sharing of expertise among information specialists but avoided costly duplication.

Regional Information Policy

With the large number of Information Systems being developed in the Region, for example, the Caribbean Information System for Social and Economic Planning (CARISPLAN), the Caribbean Trade Information System (CARTIS), the Caribbean Energy Information System (CEIS), the Caribbean Information System for Patents (CARPIN), the Caribbean Information System for the Agricultural Sciences (CAGRIS), the request for the Secretariat to make proposals regarding policy guidelines and strategies became a matter of urgency. In collaboration with the Economic Commission for Latin America and the Caribbean (ECLAC) which had also planned to develop an information policy for the Caribbean area, a joint CARICOM/ECLAC project sponsored by IDRC evolved.

This information policy seeks to provide a framework for the establishment of new systems; the necessary linkages between the information systems already in place; and a rationalization for the existing systems. The information policy will also address such areas as compatibility, overlapping, and standardization in the systems being developed. A draft information policy report has already been prepared and was discussed at a meeting which was convened in Port of Spain, Trinidad, May 27-29, 1987.

Sectoral Information Systems

In recognition of the need for information support in the execution of major sector programmes viz: trade, agriculture and shipping, the CARICOM Secretariat is currently involved in the development of three computerized information systems: the Caribbean Trade Information System (CARTIS), Agricultural Production and Marketing Information System (PROMIS) (name likely to be changed), and the Shipping and Trade Information System. These systems, which are all at various stages of development, are networking systems consisting of national nodes in each Member State with the Secretariat serving as the regional node.

A common methodology is currently being applied by the Secretariat in establishing these systems:

Visits to the Member countries to evaluate the existing situation in
terms of the identification of users and user information needs
and the evaluation of the existing infrastructure.

Convening workshops to consider mission reports and proposals for the
establishment of the system; computer systems designs and the
testing of the sample databases. This is followed by a process of
refining.

Finalising of project proposals and seeking of funds for the project.

While the proposed information systems are geared to provide
needed and timely information to particular target users, they are, in
effect, strengthening the existing National Systems. For example, under
the CARTIS project, not only will information services be provided for
institutions and individuals at the enterprise level (exporters, importers,
manufacturers, trade policy and promotion officials), but assistance will
also be given to the national nodes through the purchase of necessary
computer hardware and software; training for both users and staff in
the use of the software; consultancy services and the exchange of trade
information either by means of diskettes or online facilities both
regionally and extra-regionally.

The Agricultural Production and Marketing Information System
(PROMIS) is being funded by CIDA. The information provided under
the project will be primarily quantitative data dealing with products,
product availability, prices, and so forth. Like CARTIS, a training
component has been included in the project and will provide training
for both staff and end-users. A workshop to consider and refine the
project proposals was convened in Port of Spain, Trinidad, May 25-26,
1987.

The Shipping and Trade Information System is still in the
preliminary stages of development. This system will put in place
mechanisms for data collection, analysis, and dissemination of
import/export data at the enterprise level, taken from Customs warrants
and shipping data collected from ports.

With the coming on stream of these various computerized
Information Systems, the CARICOM Secretariat is seeking to improve
its own information services through an EEC-funded Information
Handling Computerisation project which will not only support the work
of the Secretariat but will also provide the base for the development
of end-user oriented sectoral information systems.

The Secretariat's current strategy for mobilising funds for the
establishment of regional systems which in turn will strengthen the
National Centres can be seen as the best possible approach to ensure

the uniform development of information systems in a region seeking to apply modern technology to the provision of its information services.

NOTES

1. *Random House Dictionary.* New York, NY: Ballantine Books, 1980.
2. Hereinafter referred to as the CARICOM Secretariat.
3. The terms "regional" and "sub-regional" used in this paper refer to the CARICOM Region and the CARICOM Subregion (OECS States) and does not include Latin America.

14. Project Formulation and Implementation: Outline of a "How to" Approach

Wilma Primus

In order to initiate funding for the development of a project, a project proposal must be formulated, taking into account, first of all, the policies or systems of values held by the parent organization. This avoids internal conflicts. In the case of projects to be implemented on a national or regional basis, where other institutions are expected to be involved, there should be a mandate or request authorizing the proposal and, where necessary, contractual agreements.

The Project Proposal

The project document should describe clearly and in specific terms the purposes, objectives, methodology to be pursued, and justification of the proposed budget.

Generally, the project document consists of the following sections:
Background
Objectives
Outputs—Activities—Inputs
Methodology
Budget and Notes on the Budget
Work Plan or Time Table

Background

The Background statement is a brief description of the institution, its legal status, by whom it is governed, and from where it derives its major income. The statement usually provides:

A brief account of existing facilities.

A statement of the institution's record of previous relevant project implementation and how the results were used.

The staff to undertake the project.

Why the project is necessary, what in general terms it hopes to achieve, and who and in what manner will receive the benefit. In other words, an outline of the mechanism for linking the project with the identified community.

Objectives

A project is not an end in itself but a means to a broader development objective. The project is expected to help in part to attain this objective through the achievement of its immediate objective. The immediate objective is what the project itself is expected to achieve. Although this appears very early in the document, it is often finalized after the proposal has been completed. These objectives must be sufficiently clear to be understood by all concerned with the project.

Outputs—Activities—Inputs

In order to achieve its immediate objective, a project has to produce certain outputs. These outputs can only be achieved by undertaking specific activities. Various inputs must be obtained to carry out the activities.

In order to derive resource inputs, time and cost, the work to be done and the expected work results must be broken down into levels and component parts during the planning process. Resource inputs are measured in terms of man-months or machine-hours, applying standard work efficiencies.

The resource planning for the project starts with:

A survey of the resources available within the organization or externally.

The degree of availability.

Price.

Work efficiency.

Methodology

The methods by which the objectives are to be reached should be described. What activities and work steps are performed, methods and techniques used to perform activities, interdependence of activities— whether they parallel, precede, or succeed. Sources should be stated; criteria for selection of personnel outlined. If consultants are to be used, their specific functions and methodology should be outlined. How the results will be evaluated. What are the criteria against which success or failure will be measured.

Budget

Separate budgets must be shown for each major institution involved. The Budget headings usually refer to Salaries, Travel, Training, Consultants, Publications, Capital Equipment, and overhead costs where necessary. The latter covers the cost of administration, rent and running costs of buildings, equipment and the like.

Notes on the Budget

Brief explanatory note to explain why each item is proposed and what its direct relevance is to the project.

Work Plan or Time Table

A management tool that serves to organize the implementation of a project on an efficient and coordinated basis and to review the papers and achievement of the project.

Negotiations for Funding

Before submitting the project proposal to the funding agency, it should be discussed, scrutinized and revised by the administration, especially in relation to institutional policies and resource commitments. Some funding agencies review the proposal with the recipient, indicating the areas that are feasible within a specific time frame and the components that they are prepared to fund. This exercise is based on experience and if done in the spirit of partnership can be highly beneficial to the recipient.

Finally a revised project document is agreed upon and appropriate contracts prepared and signed.

Implementation

Prerequisites for implementation should be identified in the project document and fulfilled prior to the start of the project.

The first steps should be:

1. Revise and secure agreement on the Work Plan and a framework for effective participation of staff from related institutions.
2. If indicated by the monitoring process, subsequently amend the Work Plan and Framework.

The Work Plan should provide a broad schedule of inputs, activities, and outputs for the entire duration of the project and a detailed schedule on a twelve-month basis. This should be extended and updated every six months on agreed periodic reviews.

The Plan should:

1. Indicate the scope and duration of each project activity.
2. Indicate the interrelationships between the different activities.
3. Describe the outputs of each activity or subactivity and the month or year to be produced.

4. Schedule the delivery of various inputs in relation to the different activities.
5. Schedule reviews for monitoring.
6. Schedule evaluation of the project.

Framework for Effective Participation of Staff in Other Institutions

A framework is necessary to ensure that the project, especially a national or regional project, is organized and implemented in a manner calculated to help achieve the broader goal of self-reliance.

It identifies and describes with respect to each project activity how the national and regional resources will be used to complement and reinforce each other, what will be the output of each activity, and in terms of institution building what knowledge and skills the national staff will possess at the completion of each activity.

The framework should be prepared in consultation with the institutions, taking into account skills at the beginning and at the end.

The framework is a means to provide effective participation at the national and regional level.

The Project Leader

The Project Leader is responsible for the entire project and must maintain the necessary personal contacts with the Administration, project staff, funding agency, and collaborating institutions.

The major responsibility of the project manager is to plan and control the execution of the project in such a way that the goals are achieved with minimum of resource consumption. This involves recognizing "danger signals" and potential future problems at an early stage so that preventive steps may be taken.

The major activities of the project leader are:

Add, change, delete activities in the Work Plan, thereby influencing work methods or technical solutions.

Substitute resource inputs.

Develop proposals for corrective steps.

Analyze causes.

Propose and select staff.

Order the execution of activities.

Make sure that resource inputs are in fact made.

Create and maintain a high degree of motivation.

Verify and authorize statements on resource consumption and on the contents and quality of outputs.

Collect and record project control information.

The person selected should have a knowledge and experience of the organization, the objectives and process of the project, the resource inputs, project management, and should preferably be recruited from within the organization.

15. The Mystique of Grantsmanship: Getting Started (in Post-Irangate America)

Ellen H. Brow

Now does not seem to be a particularly good time for fund raising or development activities in the United States. The NGL is at an all-time low. The NGL is, of course, the National Gullibility Level. This secret figure, calculated hourly by Ted Turner and only available to certain select insiders (actually, it is available online to anyone whose gullibility level falls in the 90 percent range), is probably not a very reliable measure of public support for libraries, librarians, or bibliographic master plans.

We live at a time when the extremes of obscene wealth and obscene poverty are so horrendous as to defy belief. As people in the middle, we need to:

1. Make sure our own strength and numbers increase rather than diminish.

2. Analyze the problems in such a way as to be able to convince the wealthy that it is in their interest to contribute to projects that enhance human growth by improving access to information.

There is an old folktale common to many cultures, that I know as Stone Soup. I'm sure you have heard it, so I just summarize it here:

> A weary traveler stops at the hut of an old woman and asks for food and a place to sleep. She agrees to let him sleep on the porch but denies having any food. He mentions that he knows how to make soup from a stone if she can supply a pot and water. As the water reaches the point of a low simmer, he mutters that it would be much better with a potato or a carrot, but since they don't have this, they will have to make do. And of course she finds a potato and a carrot.
>
> So, as he gently laments the lack of other foods, the old woman cautiously retrieves these ingredients from her cupboard until they have this wonderful tasty soup, made, of course, with a stone. She is amazed and delighted to have learned how to make soup from a stone; and the weary traveler can go to sleep with a reasonably full tummy.

His priority was to eat. Her intention initially was not to be ripped off; but then it was to learn how to make soup from a stone. As grant writers we need to make soup from a stone, to change the

109

priority of the funders, to make the funders want to learn how to make soup from a stone. As soup makers (or grant writers) we may be looking for salt, potatoes, the soup bone (money, encouragement, access to national priorities) and we may be doing this as individuals, as a formal professional group, as an informal professional group, or for our home institution, should we be fortunate enough to have one. We may seek funding from government, from foundations, or from individuals or families.

First: We need to know what we want to do and why we want to do it.
Second: We need to know who is giving away money and why.
Third: What are the procedures for asking?
Fourth: (This relates to the first.) What are our strengths? (What can we do with our stone?)
Fifth: (This is the stone soup part.) We need to convince, listen, change the proposal, test the viability of the project. This happens both at home and in the offices of the foundation.

Even though as librarians we disdain the political process most of the time, it is important to emphasize that fund raising, getting funded, is part of the political process, regardless of the source of the funds. Whether you are talking about hunting for money in the government sector, foundation, or private sector, you are talking about convincing others that what you want to do is important, that it will promote their own agenda, that you are competent and resourceful enough to accomplish what is proposed, and that the project will enhance the reputation of the funding agency. Especially for these reasons, it is important to make sure that there is a good match between the donor and the project, between the donor and your library, your university, your colleagues.

There are some irrational aspects to fund raising that are apparent if you are anything other than a full-time fund raiser or development officer. The greatest irony is that you probably have a problem because you are short of money, space, time, or staff, or all four. But preparing a grant proposal takes money, space, time, and staff (not to mention patience, timing, persuasiveness, diplomacy, even charisma, unlimited high-quality Xeroxes, a good word processor, a back-up typewriter, and, yes, even a good therapist). So, in order to get the money to solve your problems, you augment them by turning your attention to something else which may or may not pay off. It's not unlike spending your last dollar on a lottery ticket; but the odds of winning are probably better, and there are ways to improve your odds.

Come to think of it, lottery money comes with fewer strings attached, so you may prefer that option.

Let's suppose you know what needs to be done, you've figured out what it would cost, and you can spiel off the local, national, international, and stellar benefits that will accrue to almost everyone except your children, spouse, and coworkers who will only see you in rare moments of uncontrolled grumpiness, should you be so blessed as to be funded.

The next step is even more complicated than the first. Who is it that might be interested in funding what needs to be done? This stage has a lot in common with the Easter egg hunt. If you remember childhood, especially when you were the youngest in the hunt, others would find an egg or several eggs and you would run to that spot and you would never find anything. So, even though it sounds risky, it's important to find new sources, to look for support in different places, to try to learn to think like the Easter bunny--or for that matter, make friends with the Easter bunny and suggest some hiding places. In more concrete terms:

1. Explore the resources of the development or research support office on your campus and make friends with them. Take them to lunch, buy them flowers, name your firstborn male child after them. Read their materials, subscribe to their bulletin, listen, explain, fantasize, listen.

2. Read newspapers and all the stuff that lists new projects, foundations, and so on: *Humanities*, the *Federal Register*, the *Chronicle of Higher Education*, as well as general library literature. Keep a stack of this stuff in the bathroom.

3. Check out printed and database sources that index funding sources. This approach has serious limitations because the coding may be too precise and cause you to overlook a big general fund that would actually be easier to approach than the narrowly specific fund.

4. Write proposals early and ask grant makers to critique them. Send them summaries or general descriptions and ask them for their reactions. Sometimes if they are patient enough, or encouraging enough, they will reach a point of enthusiasm for the project that will enable them to defend it, or they will become advocates for the project in front of the board. Don't send proposals cold. Don't write them the night before the deadline.

5. Get your proposal critiqued by others at your institution and elsewhere so that there is enthusiasm and support for what you are trying to do at home. If you have dissenters who don't agree

with what you are doing, there may be a fatal flaw in your logic. Maybe outside money isn't needed—just some minor internal adjustment to bring about the results you are looking for. You can also discover some internal obstacles that would make the proposal impossible to carry out. It could conflict with university policy. You will follow up many false leads. It is important to be able to recognize a "real" impediment and one created by a "tired" bureaucrat who just can't cope with any more complexity in his or her life.

Once you have written the proposal with the help of a cast of thousands, you should request letters of support from relevant individuals who are in a position to benefit from the effort and in a position to evaluate the quality of the proposal.

After you've been turned down, be sure to ask for the criticisms of the readers or the board in order to learn from your mistakes. It may be that they just had too many good proposals. This is a good reason for looking for funds in new places. You can pretty well judge that if it is a source that has gotten its name in all these lists and directories, then it is a source that will be so inundated with requests as to be choking on the quantity.

Realize that the individuals who make the final decision change over time, so that what failed miserably with one group of people may work with others. Stay in touch with people you know who serve on boards or work for foundations. This improves your chances of knowing when their priorities correspond with yours. Imagine yourself in their shoes.

Even though you need to be flexible, you also need to make sure that your own priorities stay paramount. If you have to change the project too much in order to get the money, you are wasting your time and theirs.

Look for ways to accomplish big things with just a little bit of effort. Show that you are fully utilizing existing resources. Do as much as you can on your own without outside funding because it is much more efficient. There are fewer strings attached. You will have to resort to complexity, but aim for simplicity.

Reason, I believe, would say that we build on strength; but we also respond to national, regional, and local priorities. In all of this process there is the danger that we will be destroyed by the coupon syndrome. Those of you who have done time as housewives or homemakers will know what I'm talking about. Magazines and newspapers are full of coupons that will save us money on all sorts of products. We are flooded with articles in the homemaking literature about superhomemakers who have managed to pay for their BMW with the money they saved by conscientiously clipping and using absolutely every coupon that ever came within their reach. I bet there are some of you in this audience right now who have expired coupons in a drawer at home, and that you wake up at 3:00 a.m., sit bolt upright in bed, and say "My Pampers coupons expire at midnight on Friday!" The same thing has been done to us in this whole area of fund raising and grant writing. We read of super fund raisers who have raised literally millions, and we are intimidated by the June 1st deadlines, the dreadful critical problems that scream for solution. You need to remember that you, as one tired, sometimes depressed, individual, cannot possibly do it all at once; that if you want to do something too much, it will fail, or funders will distrust you, or you will be too inflexible. Stay humble and remember that your agenda may not work for others.

I would like to close by pointing out that there aren't enough grant-writing jokes. Maybe this could be remedied by someone writing proposal? For lack of anything better, I would like to paraphrase Groucho Marx and ask: "Who is buried in the grant's tomb?" The answer is: We aren't sure, but we think it is the principal investigator (PI), along with efficiency and probably sanity; but no one can remember who the PI was.

INSPIRATIONAL READING ABOUT FUNDING SOURCES

Bauer, David G. *The Complete Grants Sourcebook for Higher Education.* 2d ed. New York, NY: American Council on Education; Macmillan Publishing Co., 1985. 465 p.

Chronicle of Higher Education. Washington, DC: Chronicle, 1966–. Weekly.

Coleman, William Emmet. *Grants in the Humanities: A Scholar's Guide to Funding Sources.* 2d ed. New York, NY: Neal-Schuman, 1984. 175 p.

Consortium of Social Science Associations. *Guide to Federal Funding for Social Scientists.* New York, NY: Russell Sage Foundation, 1986.

Directory of Research Grants. Phoenix, AZ: Oryx Press, 1987.

Federal Register. Washington, DC: U.S. Office of the Federal Register, National Archives and Records Administration, 1935?–. Daily. (Available online: Mead Data Central, Westlaw, etc.)

The Foundation Center Source Book Profiles. New York, NY: Foundation Center, 1983–. Quarterly with annual cumulations.

Foundation Fundamentals: A Guide for Grantseekers. Patricia E. Read, ed. 3d ed. New York, NY: Foundation Center, 1986. 239 p.

Foundation Grants to Individuals. Loren Renz, ed. 5th ed. New York, NY: Foundation Center, 1986. 288 p.

Humanities. Washington, DC: National Endowment for the Humanities, 1980–.

International Communications Industries Association. *Foundations Grants Guide for Schools, Museums, Libraries: Grants with a Slice for Communications Technology Products*. Fairfax, VA: ICIA, 1984. 62 p. (3150 Spring St., Fairfax, VA 22031)

Margolin, Judith B. *The Individual's Guide to Grants*. New York, NY: Plenum Press, 1983.

Proposal Writer's Swipe File: 15 Winning Fundraising Proposals. Washington, DC: Taft Corporation, 1984.

16. Successful Proposal Writing, or, Living the Soft (Money) Life

Barbara G. Valk

In an era of ever-declining resources for area studies programs the ability to write successful grant proposals has become more important than ever. Given the intense competition for limited funds that exists today, it is virtually impossible for a proposal to succeed on its intrinsic merit alone; the project must also be carefully planned and meticulously presented. Although writing abilities and styles vary tremendously among individuals, there are some basic tenets of successful proposal preparation which, if followed, will vastly enhance the funding probability of any worthwhile project. The following remarks are based on eleven years of personal experience in funding my own salary—and that of my staff—on the "soft" money that I have obtained from grants and the profits earned from grant-funded publications.

Plan Ahead

The point that cannot be emphasized strongly enough is to plan ahead. It is absolutely imperative to plan the project to the smallest detail in terms of both concept and execution before attempting to obtain a major outside grant to support it. If the project is large, which is to say that it will cost more than $50,000 and/or require more that a year to complete, the structuring of a small pilot project is recommended to determine the extent of the work involved and to help overcome the unexpected obstacles that inevitably arise when new ideas are first put to practice. Start-up funds for pilot projects are relatively easy to obtain from on-campus sources, such as library staff development funds and departmental research grants, and the benefits to be derived from the exercise can be invaluable: having learned from one's initial successes and mistakes, it is possible to prepare a far more thorough, effective proposal than when operating on theory alone; moreover, presentation of the results of the pilot project will lend credence to the value and feasibility of the larger project for which major funds are requested.

Even relatively small projects should be allowed to gestate for six months to a year from conceptualization of the initial idea to submission of a proposal. During this time the Principal Investigator (P.I.) should concentrate on refining the original concept, planning all the details of its execution, and preparing a workable methodology.

Discussions with respected colleagues are also valuable at this stage of the process. Not only are such discussions likely to reveal new insights into the problem, but they also help the P.I. to articulate his or her own ideas more clearly. One should beware, however, of accepting all advice offered; proposals prepared by committee are seldom successful. Rather, it is best to discuss the project on a one-to-one basis and to accept only those ideas that seem to enhance the original overall plan. Keep in mind that the person who presents the proposal is the one who will be responsible for executing it.

Find the Right Funding Agency

There are relatively few funding agencies that regularly support bibliographic projects in the area of Latin American Studies. Of these, the largest is the National Endowment for the Humanities. [1] Through their Reference Materials Tools and Access Program NEH awards outright and matching grants of up to $100,000 or more for bibliographic and reference publications, catalogs, databases, microform projects, and other related efforts that make new sources of information accessible for advanced research in the humanities. The U.S. Office of Education Title IIC Program also awards very large grants, but they are available only to qualified research institutions for library-wide or interinstitutional bibliographic projects. [2] The Tinker Foundation supports research in Latin American Studies, but in recent years their focus has shifted away from bibliographic works. [3]

For other potential sources of support review carefully the national *Foundations Directory* [4] and, if available, the equivalent statewide directory of foundations. [5] These publications have subject indexes that help to identify which funding agencies support projects in specific areas of research.

Likely sources should be reviewed for funding priorities, the focus of grants awarded in recent years, and typical funding levels. Make a list of the most promising ones and obtain the name and telephone number of a program officer for each, if possible. Write or, preferably, telephone the program officers, giving them a brief, articulate description of the project. If the project does not fall within the current guidelines of their program, take the opportunity to ask if it may be appropriate for another of the agency's programs, or if the person may know of another agency that funds projects of the type proposed. If the project description is received positively, ask for a copy of the program's proposal guidelines and offer to prepare a brief, preliminary proposal for review.

Give Them What They Want to Hear

Read all proposal guidelines carefully and follow them precisely. Determine the agency's primary funding priorities and focus the proposal to address them as closely as possible. Organize the written proposal in sections that respond directly to specific questions presented in the guidelines, using as section headings wherever possible the words given in the guidelines. If a preliminary proposal is prepared it should be brief—no more than three to five pages—but it should be well written and should incorporate all of the basic elements that will be presented in the final proposal, including a budget. One never knows, particularly when dealing with a private foundation, whether the "preliminary" proposal may be accepted as final. This happened to me once: After acknowledging receipt of my "preliminary" proposal I heard nothing further from the program officer, nor did she respond to my letters. A year later I received a check in the mail for the full amount of the support I had requested.

Submission of a preliminary proposal should always be followed a few weeks later by a telephone call to the program officer, as many of them are willing to offer helpful advice for modifying the proposal to meet better acceptance by the agency. Needless to say, any advice given should be taken with the utmost seriousness and should be incorporated scrupulously into the final proposal, even if it entails altering some basic elements of the original plan. Program officers tend to be the best judges of what is both feasible and fundable.

Writing the Final Project Description

The final proposal is simply an expansion of the preliminary project description and budget. Again, the project description should be organized in a way that answers clearly and fully all of the questions set forth in the program guidelines. Each question should be addressed in a separate section, and each section heading should reflect the wording used in the guidelines. Be sure to explain in detail not only the significance of the project as it relates to the program's funding priorities and how it differs from any other work previously done on the subject but also how the work will be carried out, who will do it, the qualifications and responsibilities of each of the participants involved, a time frame for completing each stage of the project, how the results of the research will be disseminated, and why the requested funds are needed.

Many people find some of these sections more difficult to write than others. In such instances, ask a colleague who has been successful in proposal writing for assistance in preparing the difficult portions of the project description. In my experience people have always been very willing to help.

Some other important considerations to remember when preparing a project description follow.

Be thorough and articulate. Keep in mind always that only the author of the proposal understands exactly what the project is about and how the work will be carried out. To convey this understanding to others it is essential to explain every phase of the plan clearly and precisely in layman's terms. This is often hard to do, for the more one knows about something oneself, the stronger the tendency to assume that the reader will also know it, and hence, fail to explain it adequately. To combat this problem, ask someone from a completely different field to read the proposal and then to describe it to you in detail. Anything that is unclear to that person should be revised until it is completely comprehensible.

Be a salesman. Be sure that the reader is made fully aware of the importance of the project. There is always a section of the proposal designated specifically for project significance, and this must be prepared as carefully as the methodology. Begin by providing a brief historical background for the proposed work, place it in the context of current research and, most importantly, demonstrate how the project will advance scholarship in the area(s) of the agency's primary concerns. If a work is not considered of major, relevant importance it will not be funded, no matter how well it may be conceived and articulated. To reinforce the value of the project, sprinkle qualitative adjectives liberally throughout all portions of the narrative description.

Be redundant. Reviewers typically receive a number of proposals to evaluate in the midst of a busy schedule and therefore sometimes fail to read each one as carefully as they might. Thus, if an important point is presented only once, it may easily be missed. To avoid so potentially damaging an oversight, the repetitive techniques of in-depth advertising are highly recommended. Define the basic elements of the project in the first paragraph of the introduction, then briefly reiterate the same positive message—particularly with regard to project significance—from a different, appropriate perspective in each section of the proposal. If possible, include also a concise, well-written abstract. A harried reviewer may not read beyond that!

Budgets

Plan well ahead to determine realistically how much money will be required to carry the project through to completion in the time allotted, and do not underestimate costs. Keep in mind when preparing the budget such items as normal salary increases; inflation rates for travel and services; incidentals such as mailing charges, telephone calls, copying fees, and so forth; and necessary equipment purchases, such as computer software or a laser printer. Consult with the library's Budget Officer and/or a University Contracts and Grants Officer to decide how best to meet any necessary cost-sharing requirements and to determine University overhead charges, current employee benefit rates, and other indirect costs.

When this has been done, sprinkle throughout the direct cost line items a small "fudge factor" of up to 10 percent of the total project budget to allow for unforseen expenses such as higher-than-average salary increases or the chance that a sum will be awarded that is less than the amount requested. A project will never be granted more money than asked for, and the chances are great that actual project costs will exceed even the full amount sought, no matter how carefully the budget has been planned.

After a realistic overall budget has been prepared, determine the maximum and average funding levels of the agency to which the proposal will be sent, and review the guidelines carefully to identify the kinds of costs the program will and will not fund. Design the specific project budget to conform to these norms.

If an agency from which funds are being requested does not award grants large enough to cover all of the project's costs, consider applying to several sources for partial funding, or request small grants to be used as gifts for federal matching funds. Gift and Matching Grants are strongly encouraged by large agencies such as the NEH to help relieve the increasingly tight budgets allotted annually for outright awards.

Supporting Documentation

Computer guidelines. Some agencies, such as NEH, require a section in the proposal that describes any automated systems that will be used to prepare the project. The purpose is to ensure that the software and equipment selected are appropriate to the project's needs. The library's Systems Director or other knowledgeable person should be consulted to help draft this section, as an apparent lack of technical knowledge can defeat an otherwise excellent proposal.

Sample pages. Include a few, carefully prepared sample pages of any proposed publication, whether or not they are required. Sample pages will give the reviewer a clear idea of the end results of the research without requiring an extensive use of imagination. If the samples are attractive and well written, they can greatly enhance the project's narrative description.

Letters of support. Judiciously selected, well-written letters of support from well-known colleagues, project contributors, publishers, and/or relevant professional associations can add considerable credence to one's own often-repeated statements of a project's worth. It is wise to solicit more letters than will actually be used in the proposal and to include only those that speak best to different aspects of the research and/or represent a variety of prospective audiences.

Reviewers. Some agencies, such as NEH, require the P.I. to submit a list of people qualified to review the proposal. If presented this opportunity, use it wisely. Confer, if possible, with one or two close colleagues to obtain suggestions for appropriate names representing a broad spectrum of institutions and project-related specialties. Next, telephone each of the individuals, describe the project concisely, and ask if he or she would be willing to write a strong letter of support. Listen carefully to the response; if you sense any hesitation, do not include that person in the final list of reviewers no matter how "influential" the individual. Even one slightly negative review can place a proposal in jeopardy; if the negative comments proceed from one's own chosen reviewers the results will be instantly fatal.

Following Up

Try to discover when the proposal will be reviewed and the earliest possible opportunity for obtaining an indication of its success or failure. If no word has been received within about a week after that date, telephone the program officer to inquire about its status. If the project was funded, a great deal of suspense will be relieved. If it was not successful, it is often possible to find out why the proposal failed and to revise it accordingly for prompt submission to another agency.

When awarded a grant, use the money wisely. Spend as needed to accomplish the task, but beware of depleting the funds before the project is finished. Generally speaking, it is best to spend conservatively until a clear picture of the project's actual operating costs begins to emerge. Time is not generally a major factor; if the research takes longer to complete than originally proposed, most agencies will be willing to extend the length of the grant as long as reasonable progress is shown, but they will seldom award additional funds. Regularly submitted progress reports, required by many agencies, complete the follow-up process and help to consolidate good relations that can prove invaluable when submitting other proposals in the future.

In summary, this paper has attempted to dissipate the somewhat mystical aura that often surrounds the concept of proposal writing and to show that it is, in fact, simply a learned narrative technique that ascribes like any other to certain basic tenets. Once you have mastered them, you are on the way to living the "soft money" life.

NOTES

1. National Endowment for the Humanities, Division of Research Programs. Reference Materials Program: Tools and Access. Washington, DC 20506. Telephone (202) 786-0358.

2. Department of Education, Library Education Research and Resources Branch. Title IIC: Strengthening Library Resources. Washington, DC 20506. Telephone (202) 245-9530.

3. Tinker Foundation. 645 Madison Avenue, New York, NY 10022. Telephone (212) 421-6858.

4. *The Foundation Directory*, 10th ed. Loren Renz, ed. New York, NY: The Foundation Center, 1985.

5. In California, see Melinda Marble, *Guide to California Foundations*, 4th ed. San Francisco, CA: Northern California Grantmakers, 1981.

17. Fund-raising in Context: Some Broader Issues of External Support

Dan C. Hazen

Other papers have explicated the mechanisms of fund-raising, and offered practical advice on locating monied sources and preparing grant applications. I now explore a number of perhaps less tangible aspects of the process: the changing framework within which our appeals are shaped; appropriate bases from which we might seek outside funds; how to select activities appealing to external agencies. I do this first by touching on the general context of fund-raising in the contemporary United States, and then by surveying some yet-unresolved issues in grantsmanship.

Where Is the Money?

Several phenomena condition philanthropic and public funding in today's United States:

Various functions formerly assumed by the national or state governments have been reassigned (or relegated) to the private sector. Privatization has in most cases reflected ideological commitments to "limited" government and fiscal conservatism. In some instances, such as de-institutionalization of the mentally and physically handicapped, it has also responded to special-interest arguments for reform. The effect has been to increase substantially the range of needs that can only be met through outside funding.

Individuals whose basic needs are not being met—the sick, the homeless, the hungry—are increasing in numbers and visibility. Old and especially new epidemics—AIDS, Alzheimer's, and their like—are likewise increasingly obvious. As these highly visible areas of need become more prominent, philanthropy in support of research and education often takes a back seat.

Corporate, private, and governmental philanthropy are all unstable. Articles in the *Chronicle of Higher Education* and the *San Francisco Chronicle*, for instance, suggest a phase of private sector retrenchment. [1] Profit squeezes, corporate takeovers, changes in tax law, stock market swings—all are reflected in philanthropic activity. To cite a few concrete examples from the San Francisco Bay Area, corporate donations from Chevron slipped from $27 million in 1985 to an estimated $19.7 million for 1987. BankAmerica Corporation's donations have tumbled from $7.4 to an estimated $3.0 million over the same period. Expanded funding needs are not inevitably matched by growing philanthropic resources.

Educational, research, and public service institutions have all geared up to exploit organized philanthropy. Almost all universities now have development offices. Most have likewise formalized their fund-raising plans, priorities, and strategies. As always, individuals are free to pursue grants for their own projects. But wide-ranging (and generally expensive) efforts to meet the broader needs of institutions or of disciplines must normally conform to externally ordained priorities. Many universities assign their libraries a relatively low spot among their development priorities. Within libraries, and excepting the enduring librarian/donor fascination with rare books, fund-raising priorities more and more focus on automation, preservation, and space. These priorities only occasionally dovetail with those of Latin Americanists and Latin American Studies.

Grant-giving fashions change, sometimes rapidly. Twenty years ago, agencies like the Ford Foundation were pouring massive sums into area studies. Other targets are now in vogue. Moments of Latin Americanist opportunity, such as the upcoming Columbian quincentennial, will continue to arise—but these seem unlikely to transform the generally diminished stature of area studies funding.

Philanthropic protestations notwithstanding, monies tend to flow most liberally to rich, prominent, "elite" institutions. Some of the reasons are entirely defensible, others perhaps less so. To begin with, larger institutions have specified staffs to advise and assist throughout the fund-raising process. In most cases, they also control already substantial resources and expertise in the areas for which funding is sought—and it usually is cost effective to build on strength. Less clearcut factors include networks of personal contacts between foundation managers and the development office staff at prominent institutions, the geographic concentration of funding agencies in major metropolitan areas (which leads both to greater familiarity with neighboring institutions and reliance upon faculty and staff at those institutions as referees and for advice), and the reputation of major institutions as it may sway outside reviewers.

For all these reasons, area studies fund-raising is increasingly demanding and competitive. Defining a grant-based project is a major undertaking, and even the best effort may not meet with success. Both the direct and the indirect costs associated with the quest for external support should be borne in mind.

How, and When, Do We Get the Funds that Are Available?

The response to the first query—where is the money?—has been a litany of reasons for its short supply. This extremely tight funding panorama injects a problematic element into the whole enterprise: devising strong and convincing proposals must be a paramount concern. The organizational basis for our funding requests and the activities for which we seek support are equally crucial.

These interrelated considerations carry practical as well as theoretical implications. On the practical side, for instance, if major funding agencies are already "spoken for" within some institution, further fund-raising is simply impossible for a person whose base is limited to that institution. He or she must either substitute strictly personal appeals or work within a consortium. Some such consortia can already exist. The Latin American Microform Project has thus received about $250,000 from the National Endowment for the Humanities to preserve Latin American ministerial *memorias*. Consortia can also be ad hoc creations, generated around particular projects. The Associated Music Libraries Group was established by several North American music libraries in order to attract funds for retrospective conversion. (Since music libraries tend to house their own technical processing staff, they are able to initiate proposals covering library operations beyond the purview of most area bibliographers.)

Consortia can provide an attractive alternative to locally based fund-raising efforts. They will generally guarantee a wide impact. They also afford some promise of quality results insofar as they join the separate strengths of their members. They may minimize indirect grant costs, which at many institutions exceed 50 percent of direct project budgets. Conversely, however, creating a viable consortium can be time consuming and fraught with difficulties. Joint action demands a consensus among all participants, and the politicking requisite to such consensus can be daunting. The logistics alone of communication among various individuals and institutions can hinder progress. While the consortial approach can provide an effective vehicle for grant applications, it demands a great deal of time and energy.

The fund-raising issue, however, is not simply one of logistical possibilities—of juggling names and institutions and thereby creating new bases for entrepreneurial activity. Choices among fund-raising stratagems and tactics must be matched with the more elevated consideration of how projects can best serve the entire scholarly community. Here a few related issues come to the fore.

A successful fund-raising proposal may attract funds to a second-rate effort, and simultaneously preempt appeals for a more definitive project. For instance, an institution might receive preservation microfilming money to film its periodicals. Such institutions should attempt to complete their files by borrowing missing issues from other libraries—but they may not. In the latter case, the filmed sets will be incomplete. Fill-in filming, while feasible, is likely to be logistically difficult (particularly if master negative standards are maintained), and unattractive to funding agencies. The recipient institution will have received and spent grant monies, and preserved its holdings—but the project will not have accomplished all that it might. Should we be satisfied that something has been done, or should we be concerned over an incomplete endeavor?

Another way to approach this question is through reflection on an actual case. Appeals for outside monies often entail a process, at once political and conceptual, of reconciling the agendas of several actors. The library at Berkeley, for instance, has defined bibliographic automation—which encompasses retrospective conversion of its manual catalog records—as its highest priority. Nationally, the Association of Research Libraries has recognized the importance of bibliographic automation, and also of Latin American Studies, by naming Latin American materials as one of four pilot areas for retrospective conversion.[2] With SALALM, though, we have determined that the provision of timely and complete cataloging for current Latin American imprints, not retrospective conversion, is our highest priority for bibliographic access.

The Association of Research Libraries has requested SALALM to endorse its RECON proposal. We did so. We were also requested to act as an independent agent in seeking and administering RECON funds. We did not. From an ARL perspective, the second request was as logical as it was economical: ARL would be freed to pursue its own grants for other projects, while the beneficiaries of RECON would take on at least limited project responsibility. For SALALM, the ARL invitation seemed an attempt to preempt our organizational agenda—an agenda that, we feel, reflects the consensus of the discipline's scholars and librarians. (That SALALM does not have a more fully articulated plan for bibliographic control and for other needs with Latin American librarianship, of course, suggests a continuing weakness within our own ranks.)

Berkeley, finally, has eagerly embraced ARL's RECON plans, since participation will further the institution's automation goals. For a bibliographer at Berkeley, the crosscutting priorities of different institutions with which we are affiliated translate, most immediately, into a somewhat schizophrenic personal reaction. On a broader level, the Latin Americanist and RECON communities' rather disjointed response to this possibility may both compromise the immediate funding project and muddy the waters for future joint efforts. Finally, and in the absence of fuller and more timely Latin Americanist-RECON collaboration, the project as currently envisioned may well fall short of achieving all that any of us would wish. The project does not now include some major Latin American collections, and its proposed areas of RECON responsibility do not always reflect an ideal distribution of collection strengths.

This RECON example reveals a mosaic of crosscutting agendas and priorities. The process by which we might lead in establishing a Latin Americanist consensus agenda among organizations, or in achieving planning coherence, or even in adequately communicating our own intentions, remains incipient. In the meantime, our fund-raising efforts may falter for want of appropriate background and expertise, or properly placed enthusiasm, or correct time. Both local and national aspirations may thus remain unaddressed. As a first step, it appears essential that we better define and more assertively project our own agenda.

Proclaiming the need to consult with all the appropriate actors in our projects and proposals leads naturally to the question of Latin Americans' proper place in our activities. As Latin American librarians, we are inevitably dealing with the region's cultural patrimony. On one level, a mechanical expansion of procedures workable within North America may fail: polling Latin American repositories to complete serial sets for preservation microfilming, to follow the hypothetical example advanced above, would be prohibitively complex. In the near term, we might more fruitfully consider ways to share the results of our fund-raising successes with our Latin American colleagues. Might computer tapes of machine-readable bibliographic records be provided to the region's national libraries and perhaps to the Columbus Memorial Library as well? Should we provide duplicate sets of preservation microfilm? LAMP has pursued mutually beneficial filming projects with Brazil's National Library whereby equipment, supplies, and completed microfilm have been exchanged for access to and preservation of needed scholarly resources. The bases for these exchanges are different from those just suggested, but the process seems similar.

Specific arrangements to incorporate Latin Americans within our activities—particularly where these activities result in a product usable beyond a single institution—will vary between activities and countries. However, our concept of service to the profession and to the region might well become more generous. To begin with, we need consensus among ourselves. We must then convince both our supervisors and the funding agencies.

All the issues raised so far may deserve attention, but they also remain thoroughly subordinate within the fund-raising process. The more immediate imperatives of local mandates and of simple expediency instead predominate. As more and more line librarians find fund-raising within their job descriptions, pressures intensify to apply first and ponder later. Easy rationalizations can assuage our occasional pangs. One of the most notorious, and facile, stands consideration of excellence and consensus on its head by asserting that we are remiss in hesitating when we have a project ready to go. Texas may have stronger collections than Podunk—but if Texas hasn't gotten to its needs first, that's tough luck. If we don't press ahead, the work may not get done at all: half a loaf is better than none.

Such arguments are, of course, in large measure indictments of those hearing them. Why haven't "they"—why haven't we—organized to have our own priorities and possibilities more fully in hand? This would help ensure that needed projects engender "full-loaf" proposals. The qualitative weight of such broad, solid proposals will, in turn, naturally squeeze out deficient plans. The prerequisite is clear: our criticisms cannot be taken too much to heart if we simply accept the process through which we are bypassed in the formulation of other projects and proposals.

It may not be immediately possible to respond to all these reservations and complications. We may not be able to educate our administrators, or outside funding agencies, about the need of Latin Americanists for fully productive and defensible projects. Most funding agencies are expected to give money away in exercises defined more by a finite pool of applications than by the realm of ideal possibility. We are, in fact, both capable of and responsible for developing and pursuing our own agenda of projects and priorities—with or without outside funding. We are not simply at the mercy of the priorities and politics of other organizations.

Moving ahead to design projects and to seek funds—within SALALM, within LAMP, through new groupings and consortia—is thus both feasible and necessary. A planning exercise to define medium-term goals and priorities may be our first step. We should work to construct programs of regional, national, and international impact, programs that will provide lasting support for Latin American Studies. By transcending the single-institution context, this kind of activity will also help mitigate the elite-institution funding bias mentioned above.

The final difficulty, however, may again be local. Most of us are evaluated, paid, and promoted on the basis of our service to our institution. The very substantial time and energy required to prepare viable grant proposals that transcend the local framework—for projects that respond most directly to Latin Americanists rather than home institution agendas—may not produce professional payoffs. Many administrators and librarians, moreover, would argue that scholars benefit most as the specific needs of real users in particular institutions are addressed: Latin Americanist goals, inconsequence, should not be addressed by more than occasional forays beyond our campuses.

If, as I believe, a vision transcending our local institutions is not only useful but indispensable for Latin American Studies, some of these assumptions and assertions must be challenged. The Latin Americanist library and scholarly community may also need to consider alternate means of publicizing and rewarding extra- and pan-institutional endeavor. Our philanthropic and cooperative impulses may otherwise founder on the rocks of personal and professional survival.

NOTES

1. "Bay Area Charities Feel Pinch" and "Flow of Corporate Philanthropy Slows," *San Francisco Chronicle*, May 3, 1987, pp. D1-D2 (Business Section); "Health of Foundation Philanthropy Assessed in New Study of Giving by Rich Americans: It Seeks to Document Economic and Social Reasons for Slowdown in Birthrate of New Funds," *Chronicle of Higher Education*, May 6, 1987, pp. 33-34.

2. Apparently reacting to lukewarm foundation response to its RECON grant proposals, ARL has more recently downgraded its RECON program to a "clearinghouse" operation which does not enjoy direct staff support.

Part Four
Acquisition and Preservation

18. La adquisición de publicaciones oficiales procedentes de la región del Caribe en la República Federal de Alemania

Sabine Zehrer

En Alemania se entiende bajo "publicaciones oficiales" todas las publicaciones editadas por entidades oficiales o semioficiales de la República Federal de Alemania, de los Länder (estados federados) y de los municipios. Al examinar los índices de las bibliografías más importantes de este sector, se muestra que en los EE.UU. se suele utilizar la misma definición. [1] En estas bibliografías está indicado todo el material editado por cuerpos legislativos, la administración de justicia, la administración en general así como por academias y sociedades científicas.

En la República Federal de Alemania existen bibliotecas determinadas que se dedican a la adquisición de publicaciones oficiales alemanas. Ya que su distribución está sujeta a la ley, los editores de dichas publicaciones tienen que proporcionarlas a estas bibliotecas. De ese modo las dos Staatsbibliotheken (Bibliotecas Estatales) de Berlín y de Munich y la Deutsche Bibliothek (Biblioteca Alemana) de Francfort reciben todas las publicaciones oficiales de la República Federal de los Länder (estados federados). Las Landesbibliotheken (Bibliotecas de los Estados Federados) y algunas bibliotecas escogidas reciben todas las publicaciones editadas por los Länder (estados federados) y los municipios. [2]

Las publicaciones oficiales del Caribe en bibliotecas alemanas

Sin embargo, respecto a la adquisición de publicaciones oficiales del Caribe no hay ninguna organización tan sencilla como la anterior. Hasta 1984 la Staatsbibliothek (Biblioteca Estatal) de Berlín trató de adquirir las publicaciones oficiales editadas en todo el mundo. Ya cumplía esta misión antes de la Segunda Guerra Mundial bajo la denominación de Preußische Staatsbibliothek (Biblioteca Estatal Prusiana), continuando con esta tradición después de la guerra. Obligada por la Stiftungsgesetz (Ley de Fundación) promulgada el 25.7.1957, [3] le cupo completar sus fondos antiguos, completándolos con la adquisición de publicaciones de los respectivos ramos especiales. La producción mundial de publicaciones oficiales, sin embargo, siguió aumentando, razón por la cual en 1984 la Staatsbibliothek (Biblioteca Estatal) tuvo que darse cuenta de que, debido a razones organizadoras y a la falta de personal, ya no le era posible coleccionar todo este material por sí sola. Hasta entonces el programa de adquisición de publicaciones oficiales fue fomentado por la Deutsche Forschungs-gemeinschaft (Fundación Alemana para la Investigación Científica). Esta fundación dejó de financiar ahora dicho programa, declarando que la adquisición de publicaciones oficiales tendría que realizarse por una biblioteca que se dedicara a coleccionar todo el material de una región y por otras bibliotecas que coleccionaran todas las publicaciones de un ramo especial editadas a nivel mundial. [4] En virtud de esta exigencia hoy en día no hay solamente una biblioteca sino varias a las que ha sido confiada la adquisición de publicaciones oficiales del Caribe. El Instituto Ibero-Americano de Berlín es la biblioteca que se dedica a coleccionar las publicaciones de la región latinoamericana y, por consiguiente, también del Caribe. Fue fundado en el año de 1930 y tiene la misión de coleccionar toda la literatura interdisciplinaria de Latinoamérica, incluidas las publicaciones oficiales. Además del Instituto Ibero-Americano hay también otras bibliotecas que están encargadas de adquirir publicaciones oficiales del Caribe. Se trata de bibliotecas especializadas en diferentes campos de investigación como por ejemplo geografía, biología, arte, etc. Entre ellas figuran bibliotecas universitarias tan famosas como las de Göttingen, Tübingen, Heidelberg, etc. La mayor importancia entre estas bibliotecas especializadas la tienen las cuatro bibliotecas centrales: la de Kiel (economía mundial), la de Colonia (medicina), la de Bonn (agricultura) y la de Hannover (tecnología). Coleccionan todas las publicaciones oficiales relacionadas con su ramo especial. [5] A las bibliotecas de los Institutos Max Planck de Hamburgo, Heidelberg y Freiburg les corresponde coleccionar las publicaciones jurídicas, especializándose en derecho civil, derecho internacional y derecho penal. Además de coleccionar publicaciones jurídicas generales les incumbe también la adquisición de publicaciones oficiales editadas por el poder legislativo, el ejecutivo y el judicial.

Bibliografías

La bibliografía periódica más importante respecto a publicaciones del Caribe es la bibliografía de la Caribbean Community (CARICOM), la *CARICOM Bibliography*. Recopila periódicamente las publicaciones de los estados miembros de la CARICOM: Antigua y Barbuda, las

Bahamas, Barbados, Belize, Dominica, Granada, Guyana, Jamaica, Montserrat, St. Kitts/Nevis, Santa Lucía, San Vicente y las Granadinas, y Trinidad y Tobago. Además de esta bibliografía hay las bibliografías nacionales que se editan periódicamente: *National Bibliography of Barbados*, *Guyanese National Bibliography*, *Jamaican National Bibliography* y *Trinidad and Tobago National Bibliography*. Estas cuatro bibliografías no pueden considerarse como publicaciones suplementarias, ya que todos los datos publicados en ellas figuran también en la *CARICOM Bibliography*. Pero tienen la gran ventaja de ser publicadas con anterioridad, de modo que es posible encontrar los títulos de las publicaciones oficiales editadas por estos cuatro países más pronto que las de los demás países.

Todas las publicaciones antes mencionadas aparecen con una demora de uno a tres años. Se editan cada dos o tres meses en forma de acumulaciones anuales, siguiendo su clasificación las normas establecidas por la Dewey Decimal Classification. En ellas están catalogadas todas las publicaciones editadas en los respectivos países, con excepción de las publicaciones periódicas. Estas sólo quedan indicadas cuando se trata de su primera edición, o de la primera edición después de haberse cambiado el título o de informes anuales. Puede considerarse como desventaja que las bibliografías *CARICOM Bibliography*, *Guyanese National Bibliography*, y *Trinidad and Tobago National Bibliography* tampoco incluyan publicaciones oficiales como por ejemplo revistas, leyes y debates parlamentarios. Sólo la *Jamaican National Bibliography* cataloga este material, indicando en el prefacio de la acumulación anual una relación de las memorias presentadas a la Cámara de Representantes. Las publicaciones oficiales de Cuba figuran en la *Bibliografía cubana* editada por la Biblioteca José Martí cada dos meses. Esta bibliografía cataloga periódicamente el material cubano, registrando los libros por materia y las publicaciones periódicas por título.

No hay ningunas otras bibliografías periódicas de esta región, pero existen unas fuentes excelentes donde se pueden encontrar publicaciones gubernamentales más antiguas, como por ejemplo *A Guide to the Official Publications of the Other American Republics* que se publica por entregas. Presenta volúmenes de Cuba, de la República Dominicana y de Haití. Otro material cubano figura también en las dos obras de Carlos Trelles: la *Bibliografía del siglo XIX* y la *Bibliografía del siglo XX*. El material de Haití está compilado por Michel S. Laguerre en *The Complete Haitiana*. Otra bibliografía excelente es el libro de Lygia Maria F. Ballantyne, *Haitian Publications: An Acquisition Guide and Bibliography*, que incluye una relación de librerías y editoriales así

como una lista de editores oficiales junto con los títulos editados por
ellos. Para toda la región hay la bibliografía de Stojan Albert Bayitch,
*Latin America and the Caribbean: A Bibliographical Guide to Works in
English.* Además existen varios catálogos importantes de librerías:
*Catalogue of the West India Reference Library, Catalog of the Cuban and
Caribbean Library* y *Catalog of Government Publications in the Research
Libraries, the New York Public Library, Astor, Lenox and Tilden
Foundations.*

Cómo se pueden adquirir publicaciones oficiales

Conocer la importancia de adquirir publicaciones oficiales es una
cosa y verse confrontado con la realidad de comprarlas es otra. Aun
cuando sea posible encontrar un título con la ayuda de una de las
bibliografías antes mencionadas, es a veces muy difícil adquirirlo. Sólo
puedo describir como el Instituto Ibero-Americano de Berlín adquiere
las publicaciones oficiales.

No hay solamente una agencia en un determinado país, sino
existen varias agencias. Pues, en caso de que usted encuentre un
librero caribeño que venda publicaciones de esta región, es necesario
asediarle con ruegos para que se esfuerce en proporcionar también las
publicaciones oficiales. Las publicaciones oficiales de la región del
Caribe perteneciente al Commonwealth pueden comprarse a la librería
británica Blackwell, las de las Antillas Neerlandesas y las de Suriname
a la librería Martinus Nijhoff y las de Martinica y de Guadalupe como
departamentos de Francia a la editorial alemana Dokumente Verlag
que está especializada en editar publicaciones francesas. El Instituto
Ibero-Americano compra las publicaciones de Barbados a la librería
Alan Moss en St. Michael. En el caso de Cuba tratamos de recibir
monografías de Ediciones Cubanas, pero esto sólo funciona en el caso
de publicaciones periódicas. Las monografías las compramos a librerías
españolas: Fuentetajas Promociones y Puvill Libros S.A. Hemos
establecido, sin embargo, muchas relaciones de canje con instituciones
oficiales de Cuba: Casa de las Américas, Comité Estatal de Estadísticas,
Biblioteca Nacional José Martí, Ministerio de Salud Pública y
Universidad de la Habana. A través de la librería Editora Taller, C.
por A., con la que mantenemos un contrato de blanket order,
recibimos las publicaciones de la República Dominicana. Además
existen relaciones con las siguientes universidades que nos proporcionan parte del material deseado o sea en calidad de canje o en
calidad de donación: Universidad Central del Este, Universidad Católica
Madre y Maestra, Academia de Ciencias de la República Dominicana,
Universidad Nacional Pedro Henríquez Ureña, Universidad APEC y

Universidad Autónoma de Santo Domingo. Mantenemos relaciones de canje con el Caribbean Community Secretariat que nos envía material de Guyana. A través del Haitian Book Centre recibimos material de Haití y además existen relaciones de canje con la Bibliothèque Nationale d'Haïti y el Institut Haïtien de Statistique. En el caso de Jamaica compramos las publicaciones a la librería Bolívar Bookshop. Existen también relaciones de canje con la National Library of Jamaica, el Ministry of Agriculture, la Geological Society of Jamaica y la University of the West Indies. El material de Puerto Rico lo compramos a la Librería Hispanoamericana con la que mantenemos también un contrato de blanket order. Hemos establecido además relaciones de cambio con las siguientes instituciones: Commonwealth of Puerto Rico, Universidad Interamericana de Puerto Rico, Universidad de Puerto Rico e Instituto de Cultura Puertorriqueño. Las publicaciones de Trinidad las compramos a la librería J. C. Sealy, The Bookshop, y aparte de eso existen también relaciones con el Ministry of Agriculture, el Ministry of Energy and Natural Resources y la University of the West Indies.

Libreros, universidades, academias y las otras instituciones antes mencionadas que nos sirven de fuente para adquirir publicaciones oficiales no son colaboradores permanentes, ya que no envían el material regularmente. Siempre hay que tener en cuenta que se puede perder el contacto, siendo, pues, necesario buscar otras fuentes. Creo que es posible mejorar las condiciones para adquirir publicaciones oficiales de la región del Caribe.

NOTAS

1. Vladimir M. Palic, *Government Publications: A Guide to Bibliographic Tools, Incorporating Government Organization Manuals: A Bibliography* (London: Pergamon Press, 1977), and *A Guide to the Official Publications of the Other American Republics* (Washington, DC: Library of Congress, 1945-1948), nos. 1-19.

2. Ralph Lansky, "Die Pflichtexemplar–und Amtsdrucksachen berechtigten Bibliotheken in der Bundesrepublik Deutschland und in Berlin (West)," *Zeitschrift für Bibliothekswesen und Bibliographie* 22 (März-April 1975), 136-142.

3. "Gesetz zur Errichtung einer Stiftung 'Preußischer Kulturbesitz' und zur Übertragung von Vermögenswerten des ehemaligen Landes Preußen auf die Stiftung vom 25. Juli 1957," *Bundesgesetzblatt* I (1957), 841-843.

4. Anita Stauch, "Der Sammelschwerpunkt Amtsdruckschriften," *Zeitschrift für Bibliothekswesen und Bibliographie* 31 (1984), 466-467.

5. Giesela von Busse y Horst Ernestus, *Das Bibliothekswesen der Bundesrepublik Deutschland: Eine Einführung* (Wiesbaden: Otto Harrassowitz, 1968), p. 76.

APÉNDICE I

Bibliografías y catálogos de bibliotecas
para averiguar el título de publicaciones
oficiales del Caribe

Ballantyne, Lygia Maria F. C. *Haitian Publications: An Acquisition Guide and Bibliography*. SALALM Bibliography, no. 6. Madison, WI: Secretariat, SALALM, 1980.

Bayitch, Stojan Albert. *Latin America and the Caribbean: A Bibliographical Guide to Works in English*. Coral Gables, FL: University of Miami Press, 1967.

Bibliografía cubana. La Habana: Consejo Nacional de Cultura, 1917/20 (1970)—.

CARICOM Bibliography. Georgetown, Guyana: Caribbean Community Secretariat, 1977—.

Catalog of the Cuban and Caribbean Library, University of Miami, Coral Gables, Florida. 6 vols. Boston, MA: G. K. Hall, 1977.

Catalog of Government Publications in the Research Libraries, the New York Public Library, Astor, Lenox and Tilden Foundations. 40 vols. Boston, MA: G. K. Hall, 1972-1976.

Catalogue of the West India Reference Library. 6 vols. Millwood, NY: Kraus International Publications, 1980.

Guyanese National Bibliography. Georgetown, Guyana: National Library, 1973—.

Jamaican National Bibliography. Kingston, Jamaica: National Library of Jamaica, Institute of Jamaica, 1975—.

Laguerre, Michel S. *The Complete Haitiana: A Bibliographic Guide to the Scholarly Literature, 1900-1980*. 2 vols. Millwood, NY: Kraus International Publications, 1982.

National Bibliography of Barbados. Bridgetown, Barbados: Public Library, 1979—.

Trelles, Carlos Manuel. *Bibliografía cubana del siglo XIX*. 8 vols. Matanzas: Impr. de Quiros y Estrada, 1911-1915.

_____. *Bibliografía cubana del siglo XX*. 2 vols. Matanzas: Impr. de Quiros y Estrada, 1911-1915.

Trinidad and Tobago National Bibliography. Port of Spain, Trinidad: Central Library of Trinidad and Tobago, 1975—.

APÉNDICE II

Lista de direcciones de los libreros y de
las instituciones oficiales de la
región del Caribe (una selección)

Barbados

Alan Moss
4, Hopefield Close
Paradise Heights
St. Michael
Barbados

Cuba

Ediciones Cubanas
Roberto Díaz Cabrera
Dpto. Publicaciones Periódicas
Apartado 605
La Habana
Cuba

Fuentetaja Promociones
Desengaño 13
28004 Madrid
España

Puvill Libros S.A.
Boters 10 y Paja 29
08802 Barcelona
España

Biblioteca Nacional José Martí
Plaza de la Revolución
La Habana
Cuba

Casa de las Américas
3 RA. y G
El Vedado
La Habana
Cuba

Comité Estatal de Estadísticas
Centro de Información Científico-
Técnica
Gaveta Postal 6016
Ave. 3A No. 4411 Playa
La Habana
Cuba

Ministerio de Salud Pública
Centro Nacional de Información
de Ciencias Médicas
Dpto. Planificación de las Fuentes
de Información
La Habana
Cuba

Universidad de la Habana
Dirección de Información
Científica y Técnica
Dpto. de Selección y Adquisición,
Sección de Canje
La Habana
Cuba

Guyana

Caribbean Community Secretariat
Bank of Guyana Building
P.O. Box 10827
Georgetown
Guyana

Haití

Haitian Book Centre
Post Office Box 324
Flushing, New York 11369-0324
USA

Bibliothèque Nationale d'Haïti
193, rue du Centre
Port-au-Prince
Haïti

Institut Haïtien de Statistique
Port-au-Prince
Haïti

Jamaica

Bolívar Bookshop
1 Grove Place
P.O. Box 413
Kingston 10
Jamaica

The Geological Society of Jamaica
c/o The Department of Geology
University of the West Indies
Mona, Kingston 6
Jamaica

Ministry of Agriculture
Hope Gardens
Kingston y
Jamaica

National Library of Jamaica
Institute of Jamaica
12 East Street
P.O. Box 823
Kingston
Jamaica

University of the West Indies
Library
Mona, Kingston
Jamaica

Puerto Rico

Librería Hispanoamericana
Apartado 20.830
Avenida Ponce de León 1013
Río Piedras
Puerto Rico 00925

Instituto de Cultura Puertorriqueña
Biblioteca Central de Puerto Rico
Apdo. 4184
San Juan
Puerto Rico 00905

Commonwealth of Puerto Rico
Department of Labor and Human
  Resources
Bureau of Labor Statistics
414 Barbosa Avenue
Hato Rey
Puerto Rico 00917

Universidad de Puerto Rico
Biblioteca General José M. Lázaro
Recinto de Río Piedras
Río Piedras
Puerto Rico 00931

Universidad Interamericana de
Puerto Rico
Departamento de Ciencias
Sociales
Apdo. 1293
Hato Rey
Puerto Rico 00919

República Dominicana

Editora Taller, C. por A.
Isabel la Católica 309
Apartado de Correos 2190, Z-I
Santo Domingo
República Dominicana

Academia de Ciencias de la
República Dominicana
Apdo. 932
Santo Domingo
República Dominicana

Universidad APEC
Av. Máximo Gómez No. 72
Apartado Postal No. 59-2
Santo Domingo
República Dominicana

Universidad Autónoma de Santo
Domingo
Biblioteca
Santo Domingo
República Dominicana

Universidad Católica Madre
y Maestra
Biblioteca
Santiago de los Caballeros
República Dominicana

Universidad Central del Este
Circunvalación
San Pedro de Macorís
República Dominicana

Universidad Nacional Pedro
Henríquez Ureña
Biblioteca
c/o Sra. Carmen Iris Olivo
Apartado Aéreo 1423
Santo Domingo
República Dominicana

Trinidad

J. D. Sealy
The Bookshop
22 Queen's Park West
Port of Spain
Trinidad

Ministry of Agriculture
Lands and Food Production
Central Experimental Station
c/o Arima Post Office
Centeno
Trinidad

Ministry of Energy and Natural
Resources
The Permanent Secretary (Library)
Port of Spain
Trinidad and Tobago

University of the West Indies
St. Augustine
Trinidad, West Indies

West Indies

Blackwell's
B. H. Blackwell LTD
Broad Stret
Oxford, OX1 3BQ
England

Dokumente-Verlag Ruppert
  Schmidt
Postfach 1340
7600 Offenburg
BRD

Martinus Nijhoff
P.O. Box 269
2501 AX The Hague
The Netherlands

19. Acquisition of Government Publications on the Caribbean Area: References and Addresses

Alan Moss

References

CARICOM Bibliography. Georgetown, Guyana: Information and Documentation Section, Caribbean Community Secretariat. Biannual.

Catalogue DOM-TOM, 1987. Paris: Institut National de la Statistique et des Etudes Economiques.

Directory of Publishers, Printers and Book Sellers in the Caribbean Community. Georgetown, Guyana: Information and Documentation Section, Caribbean Community Secretariat, 1980.

Downey, J. A. "The Acquisition of Social Science Literature from the Anglophone Caribbean: A British Perspective." *Library Acquisitions, Practice and Theory* 9 (1985), 121-145.

Guyanese National Bibliography. Georgetown: Guyana National Library. Quarterly.

Henry, Maureen, comp. *Directory of Publishers, Printers and Booksellers in Trinidad and Tobago.* St. Augustine: The Library, University of the West Indies, 1986.

Jamaican National Bibliography. Kingston: National Library of Jamaica. Quarterly.

Moss, Alan. *Acquisitions Guide to Barbados.* St. Michael: Main Library, University of the West Indies, 1986.

National Bibliography of Barbados. St. Michael: National Library Service. Annual.

Trinidad and Tobago National Bibliography. Port of Spain: Central Library of Trinidad and Tobago. Quarterly.

Addresses

The Book Place
Cr. Beckwith and Bay Streets
St. Michael
Barbados

Caribbean Imprint Library
  Services
P.O. Box 350
West Falmouth, MA 02574
USA

Joe Chin Aleong
P.O. Box 128
San Fernando
Trinidad

Mrs. C. P. Frey
c/o Cedar Valley
St. Thomas Post Office
Jamaica

Government Printing Office
Bay Street
St. Michael
Barbados

Sales Section
Government Printery
110, Henry Street
Port of Spain
Trinidad

Institut Nacional de la Statistique
et des Etudes Economiques
(INSEE)

Division DOM-TOM
18, boulevard Adolphe Pinard
75675 Paris Cedex 14
France

Service Interrégionale Antiles
  Guyane (SIRAG)
B.P. 863
97175 Pointe-à-Pitre Cedex
Guadeloupe

Service Régionale de la
  Guadeloupe
97102 Basse-Terre Cedex
Guadeloupe

Service Régionale de la Guyane
81, rue Christophe Colomb
97306 Cayenne Cedex
Guyane

Service Régionale de la
  Martinique
B.P. 605
97261 Fort-de-France Cedex
Martinique

20. Book Preservation and Conservation in the Latin American Collection

Mary Noonan

Introduction

The topic of book preservation and conservation is becoming increasingly important as librarians attempt to maintain a healthy collection within set budgetary limitations. The longevity of books and the qualities of durability and permanency should be important considerations of acquisition.

Most of the current preservation and conservation activity in libraries is concerned with materials that already show significant signs of deterioration. Many of these materials are beyond help, and microforming is the only method of preservation. If proper planning occurs, however, the library should be able to anticipate potential problem areas and perform preventive maintenance. For example, if it is known that books from certain countries or publishers generally have weak bindings, the library can take precautionary measures, such as rebinding or storing books in a special area to extend their longevity.

This paper reports on a study that examined the paper quality and binding strength of a representative sample of recently published Latin American monographs. The purpose of the study was to determine the acidity level found in the paper and the binding quality of recently published Latin American publications. Knowing the physical condition of new books being received from Latin America, librarians could begin preventative measures to increase the longevity of the Latin American collections. [1]

This study was conducted on books received in a medium-sized research library in the United States (Brigham Young University) between September 1983 and August 1984. Owing to an administrative decision, most books received from Latin America during this time period were not cataloged but given an accession number and placed in a public holding area, arranged by acquisition date. Since most of the books from the Caribbean were not kept in this area they were not part of the study. The books in the study were generally selected for the library by blanket order agents. The book subjects were almost

143

entirely on Latin American topics from the humanities and the social sciences. Included were books from commercial, university, institute, and governmental presses. Excluded were popular fiction, juvenile books, textbooks, and items not written for the university-educated person. Also not included were esoteric materials such as pamphlets, broadsides, and periodicals. The books used in the study can be considered representative of monographs published in Latin America found in university libraries.

The population from which the random sample was obtained totaled 2,659 books. To achieve randomness, a systematic (kth items) sample was used with every eleventh book on the shelf being retrieved. A total of 472 monographs were collected for the sample. The proportions actually selected from each individual country were very close to the population proportions determined necessary from each country. The sample represented 18 percent of the population. Each book in the sample was then tested and analyzed for paper acidity and binding characteristics. (See table 1 for the total used from each country.)

Table 1. Population and Sample of Books Tested

Country	Number of books in population	Number of books in sample	Percentage of population
Argentina	566	102	18
Bolivia	32	6	19
Brazil	794	127	16
Central America	152	28	18
Chile	29	5	17
Colombia	143	24	17
Cuba	15	2	13
Ecuador	106	16	15
Mexico	334	63	19
Paraguay	20	6	30
Peru	127	20	16
Uruguay	181	37	20
Venezuela	160	36	23

Paper

When cellulose fibers are beaten in water, they develop a fuzzy surface that enables the fibers to stick together and form a sheet of paper when dried. By the time the fibers have been pulped, bleached, and sized, various chemicals will have been added, causing a variety of reactions with the hydrogen, oxygen, and carbon composition of cellulose. Some of these reactions contribute to the acidity level that inevitably results in the deterioration of paper when exposed to air, moisture, heat, or light.

Groundwood

Four different chemical tests were used to measure the level of acidity in the paper. The first test determined groundwood content. Groundwood is pulp produced in a paper manufacturing process where wood is mechanically "defibered" without chemically removing the impurities, one of which is lignin. Lignin residue results in weak paper that deteriorates quickly when exposed to light and air. Paper with groundwood content is generally used for newspapers and paperback books for which preservation beyond a short time period is not expected. Testing for groundwood involved placing a thin line of phloroglucinol with a glass rod into the gutter margin of a book's page. If groundwood was present, the line turned a deep purplish red. If not, it turned cream colored or remained unchanged. If this test proved positive, no other acidity tests were conducted since the presence of groundwood indicated the presence of high acidity in the paper and an average lifespan of about ten to twenty years. Table 2 and chart 1 indicate the findings of the study. [2]

Of the 472 books tested, 91 (19 percent) were found to have lignin in their paper. In looking at the cross tabulations of countries with groundwood, Venezuela had the highest percentage of ground-wood paper, since 21 of the 36 books tested (58.3 percent) contained lignin. Ecuador and Central America also showed high percentages of books with groundwood paper, 43.8 percent and 39.3 percent, respectively. (Owing to the limited number of books examined from Central America, they were combined in order to be statistically significant.)

Brazil had a very low percentage of groundwood, with only 1 book out of the 127 tested containing groundwood (.8 percent). Uruguay had the next lowest percentage with 1 of the 37 books (2.7 percent) tested possessing lignin. The low percentage from Mexico was a surprise since the literature suggested that they used a high percentage of newsprint in their books.

Table 2. Groundwood Content of Books Studied

Country	Number of books tested	Number of books with groundwood	Percentage
Argentina	102	25	24.5
Bolivia	6	1	16.7
Brazil	127	1	0.8
Central America	28	11	39.3
Chile	5	0	0.0
Colombia	24	8	33.3
Ecuador	16	7	43.8
Mexico	63	9	14.3
Paraguay	6	0	0.0
Peru	20	6	30.0
Uruguay	37	1	2.7
Venezuela	36	21	58.3

pH

Two further chemical tests were conducted to determine the levels and degrees of acidity in the remaining books. The chemical properties of paper are measured by determining the amount of pH (hydrogenium) in the paper. Paper has acidic, neutral, or alkaline characteristics. The measurements for pH range from 1 to 14—7 being neutral, 1 being very acid, and 14 being very alkaline. Paper with a pH of 7 lasts twenty times longer than paper with a pH of 4.8.[3]

The tests for acidity involved using two different types of chemicals. The first, bromcresol green, could only indicate a pH level of below 5.4. For those books above 5.4, a further test was made by using chlorophenol red. This test indicated three general levels of pH: (1) below 6.0 (still acidic), (2) between 6.0 and 6.7 (mildly acidic), and (3) above 6.7 (near neutral, or alkaline).

Table 3 and chart 2 indicate the results of the two acidity tests. Three hundred books (63.42 percent) were found to be in the below 5.4 category and thus printed on very acidic paper. A low 4.6 percent were found to be above the 6.7 category or printed on neutral or nonacid paper. Argentina was the only Latin American country with more paper above 5.4 than below—39 above and 38 below. Still, when further tests were taken, of Argentina's 39 books above 5.4, 25 were

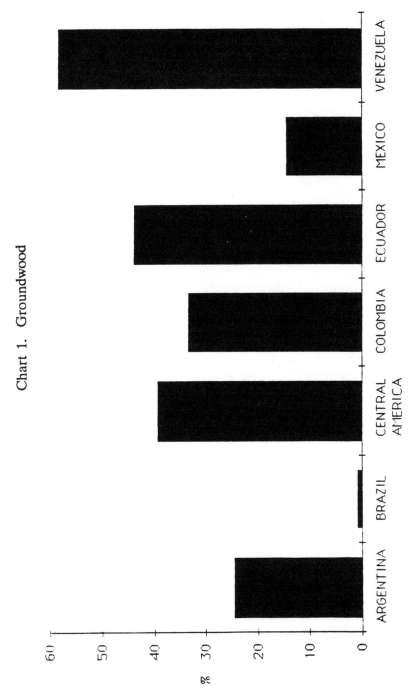

Chart 1. Groundwood

Table 3. pH Level of Books Studied

Country	Number of books tested	pH level <5.4	>5.4	<6.0	6.0-6.7	>6.7
Argentina	102	38	39	25	14	0
Bolivia	6	6	0	0	0	0
Brazil	127	112	5	5	1	2
Central America	28	17	0	0	0	0
Chile	5	4	1	1	0	0
Colombia	24	14	2	1	0	1
Ecuador	16	9	0	0	0	0
Mexico	63	43	12	7	3	2
Paraguay	6	6	0	0	0	0
Peru	20	12	2	1	1	0
Uruguay	37	28	8	4	2	2
Venezuela	36	11	3	1	2	0

still below the 6.0 mark which indicated acidic paper. The remaining 14 books fell in the mildly acidic category. Most of the countries showed a substantial amount of books with pH below 5.4 rather than above. Examples are Brazil with 112 of the 127 books falling below 5.4 (88.2 percent). One hundred percent of the books from Central America and Ecuador fell below 5.4. Twelve of Peru's 14 books, or 85.7 percent, were very acidic.

The high level of acidity found in paper used for Latin American books can be seen by combining the results of the groundwood examination with the pH test. As indicated in table 4 and chart 3, most books from Latin America are published on paper with high levels of acidity. Only Argentina with 62 percent has a low percentage, whereas all of the other countries were close to and above 80 percent. Books from Bolivia, Ecuador, Paraguay, and Central America have been printed on paper with a high acid content.

Alum

The final test of acidity was to determine the presence of alum in the paper. When wood is the principal ingredient in the paper, a chemical agent has to be added for sizing purposes. Sizing enables paper to resist water so that when it is printed or written upon with water inks, feathering will not occur. A popular sizing agent is alum.

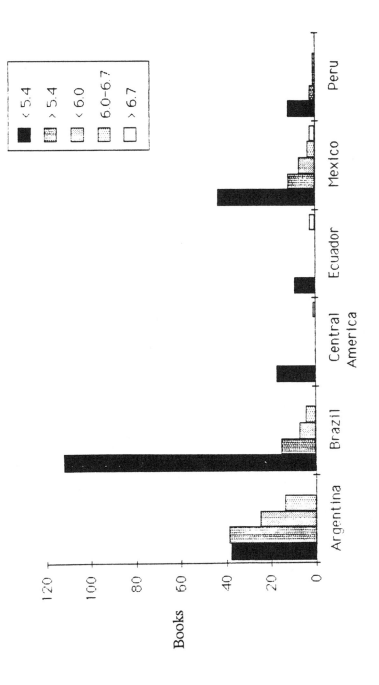

Chart 2. Acidity

Table 4. Total Acidity of Books Studied

Country	Groundwood content	pH < 5 content	Total	Percentage of acidity
Argentina	25	38	63	62
Bolivia	1	5	6	100
Brazil	1	112	113	89
Central America	11	17	28	100
Chile	0	4	4	80
Colombia	8	14	22	92
Ecuador	7	9	16	100
Mexico	9	43	52	83
Paraguay	0	6	6	100
Peru	6	12	18	90
Uruguay	1	28	29	78
Venezuela	21	11	32	89

Unfortunately, alum introduces acidity into the paper. Though there are now available alkaline sizing chemicals, many paper manufacturers continue to use alum in sizing.

The chemical aluminon was used to determine the presence of alum. Two hundred and six books, or 59.4 percent of the sample, showed signs of alum content.

Bookbinding

Guidelines for Quality Binding

Not only should a book have durable, acid-free paper, it needs a good outer covering to protect those pages as well. According to the Committee on Production Guidelines for Book Longevity, setting guidelines of assessing bindings is a difficult task because of the scarcity of research about binding longevity, the changes in binding methods, and the variety of binding materials available. The committee's recommendations target adult hardbound books. Their recommendations for evaluating bindings include leaving a 5/8-inch inside margin, that it be sewn through the fold leaf attachment, and that the cold emulsion polyvinyl acetate (PVA) or cold-plus-hot adhesive method be used rather than the hot-melt method. For the actual covering they suggest that strong acid-free endpapers be used, as well as an acid-free

Chart 3. Total Acidity

crash.   Cloth covers are preferred where the grade of cloth is appropriate for the size and weight of the book.   The grain of the cover material, boards, and endpapers should run parallel to the hinge to minimize warping. [4]

The binding quality of the books was examined to determine how well the books will stand up to use over time.   They were also examined to determine whether the items were physically constructed to allow for a second binding, if necessary.   The elements examined in this phase of the study were the following: (1) primary cover protection, (2) cover of the joint, (3) leaf attachment and glue condition, and (4) gutter margin.

Primary Cover Protection

Observing the types of primary protection can be useful in determining if rebinding will be necessary in the future.   Of the total sample, 455 books (96.2 percent) were protected by limp covers, leaving 15 books (3.2 percent) having rigid protection and 3 under "other." Although rigid bindings are the ideal, many limp bindings have a satisfactory life expectancy before rebinding would be necessary (table 5).

Table 5. Primary Protection of Books Studied

Country	Rigid binding	Limp binding
Argentina	1	101
Bolivia	0	6
Brazil	5	121
Central America	1	25
Chile	0	5
Colombia	1	23
Ecuador	2	14
Mexico	2	61
Paraguay	0	6
Peru	0	20
Uruguay	1	37
Venezuela	2	34

Cover of Joint

The joint of a book refers to the outer hinge. This is where stress is placed on the book from opening and closing. Therefore, the material that covers the joint is an important element to observe. Most joints of the books were protected by the same material as the covers. Three Uruguayan books had paper covers with stronger paper tape protecting the joints. All of the Latin American books, rigid or limp, were covered with paper. None of the books had leather protection.

Leaf Attachment and Glue Condition

A third area examined was that of the leaf attachment. The most preferred method of binding is to have the leaves sewn together through the fold, resulting in good openability of the book. It also allows for the book to be rebound without having to cut the paper. The second preferred method is that of an adhesive binding using a PVA cold emulsion. The PVA cold emulsion has proven to have longevity, but does take a long time to set. Consequently, book publishers often use adhesives that require a hot method of setting, that, though much faster in the production process, results in the glue becoming brittle and breaking within about ten years.

Two hundred and eight (44 percent) of the books in the total sample were attached by being sewn or stapled through the fold (i.e., sewn through the folds of the signatures), 214 (45.2 percent) had adhesive binding, and 38 (8 percent) of the books were stapled through the side. The sewn-through-the-fold method opens fairly easily and provides for easy rebinding. Brazil and Uruguay were the only countries with more books attached by the sewn-through-the-fold method than by adhesive. Brazil had 82 sewn-through-the-fold books, 43 adhesive, and none stapled. Uruguay had 19 sewn-through-the-fold, 4 adhesive, and 14 stapled. The three areas with very high percentages of adhesive books were Central America with 72 percent (18 of 25 books), Colombia with 79.2 percent (19 of 24 books), and Peru with 68.4 percent (13 of 19 books) (see table 6 and chart 4).

Unfortunately, a test does not exist that will determine adequately whether hot or cold processes were used in the binding of the books with adhesives. All of the books, however, were physically examined to determine immediate problems that existed in the binding. Of the 210 adhesive books, 68 (32.4 percent) displayed problems with glue cracking, leaves glued improperly, spines falling apart, and other binding difficulties that would require preservation assistance with limited use.

Table 6. Leaf Attachment of Books Studied

Country	1	2	3	4	5	6
Argentina	38	2	51	6	2	2
Bolivia	3	0	3	0	0	0
Brazil	82	2	43	0	0	0
Central America	3	0	18	4	2	1
Chile	4	0	0	1	0	0
Colombia	3	0	19	2	0	0
Ecuador	5	0	6	5	0	0
Mexico	29	0	33	1	0	0
Paraguay	4	0	0	2	0	0
Peru	5	0	13	1	1	0
Uruguay	19	0	4	14	0	1
Venezuela	12	0	23	1	0	0

1, sewn or stapled through the fold; 2, oversewn/cleatsewn; 3, adhesive; 4, stabbed; 5, unknown; 6, other.

Gutter Margin

The width of the gutter margin was measured to determine the percentage of books that could not be rebound in the regular method. Normally 1.3 cm (about 5/8 inches) is a good width. Books having gutter margin widths of 1.3 cm or above totaled 74.9 percent, with 25.1 percent falling below 1.3 cm. The gutter margin width is of special concern for books with adhesive binding because they generally require cutting off part of the gutter margin. Of the adhesive-bound books, 29.3 percent fell below the desired 1.3 cm category.

Summary

As a result of the study, the following conclusions were made:
1. The most serious preservation problem for recently published Latin American books found in the collections of university libraries is that of paper deterioration attributable to a high acidity content. This study shows that even though the Latin American publishing industry has undergone important changes in some areas during the past twenty years, one area not affected has been an improvement in the process of making paper. Consequently, without preventative measures, the majority of the recently published books in Latin America will not last

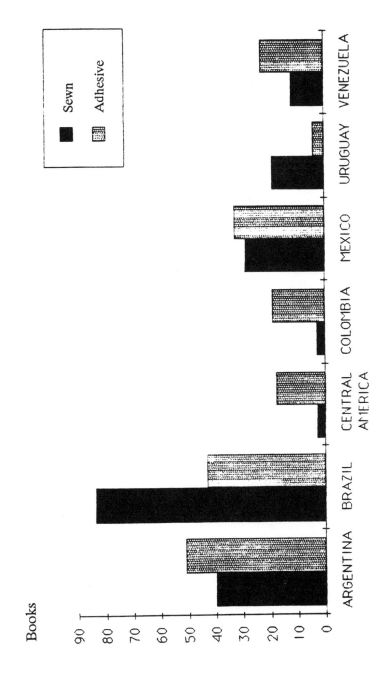

Chart 4. Leaf Attachment

beyond fifty years. Unfortunately, that is an indication of the lack of influence librarians have on the Latin American publishing industry.

2.   The problem of binding continues to be a concern, but not to the degree that it has been in the past. Binding quality has improved over the past few years and the maintenance of Latin American books has become easier. This study does point out that, as in the past, the responsibility for the final step in the completion of the publication process of Latin American books lies not with the publisher but with the individual. This final step that includes placing a rigid cover on the books has been traditionally left to be completed by the consumer and continues to be so. Although not appreciated by librarians, it tends to be an economically reasonable and effective practice for publishers and consumers alike in Latin America.

NOTES

1. For a study with similarities see Gay Walker, Jane Greenfield, John Fox, and Jeffrey S. Simonoff, "The Yale Survey: A Large-Scale Study of Book Deterioration in the Yale University Library," *College and Research Libraries* (March 1985).

2. Gerald W. Lundeen, "Preservation of Paper Based Materials: Present and Future Research and Developments in the Paper Industry," in *Conserving and Preserving Library Materials*, Kathryn Luther Henderson and William T. Henderson, eds. (Urbana-Champaign, IL: University of Illinois Graduate School of Library and Information Science, 1983), pp. 73-85, and Roy P. Whitney, "Chemistry of Paper," in *Paper—Art & Technology*, Paulett Long, ed. (San Francisco, CA: World Print Council, 1979), pp. 36-44.

3. Joseph J. Thomas, "Alkaline Printing Papers: Promise and Performance," *Library Quarterly* 40 (January 1970), 102-103, and Leonard Shatzkin, "Publishing on Permanent Papers," *Library Quarterly* 40 (January 1970), 121.

4. Council on Library Resources, Committee on Production Guidelines for Book Longevity, *Book Longevity: Reports of the Committee on Production Guidelines for Book Longevity* (Washington, DC: Council on Library Resources, 1982), pp. 16-17.

21. Preservation, Conservation, and Disaster Control in the Wellcome Institute for the History of Medicine

Robin Murray Price

The International and National Nexus

As flower children of the '60s and therefore, like me, obsessive readers of the *Whole Earth Catalog*, you will remember, I am sure, that "there is nothing so powerful as an idea that has reached its time." To say that of preservation and conservation is perhaps to trivialize that vigorous observation. But within the international and national context of preservation, it is the synchronicity that is important, not the sequentiality. International resolutions often have the appearance of initiating acts. Experience demonstrates that they are always subservient to action.

That observation will prevent us paying more attention than is due to the UNESCO/IFLA/ICA Conference in Veldhoven, Holland, in October 1985, which early proposed conservational selectivity rather than comprehensiveness (now a fashionable concept for many librarians; indeed a recourse of desperation as urgency increases), or to the IFLA/UNESCO meeting in Vienna of April 1986 which proposed the setting up of the IFLA Conservation Section and the Core Programme on Preservation and Conservation, and whose major contribution to the priority of conservation was the recognition of embrittlement—a problem of major importance in the United States where (it has been estimated) some 30 percent of stock is affected. Owing to shortage of funds and the familiar inertia of international institutions both the IFLA Conservation Section and the Core Programme have yet to be fully implemented. In the meantime there are informal links on conservation issues between Library of Congress, Research Libraries Group, Bibliothèque Nationale, and the British Library National Preservation Office and many other bodies. A pragmatist like myself would say that such links are far more important and effective. In a word, the international girders and cross-beams are in place: the building has yet to be walled and lived in.

As generality decreases, so particularity increases. The British Library, made aware of the problem, but slow to implement its solution, commissioned Dr. F. W. Ratcliffe, Cambridge University Librarian (of whose work I cannot speak too highly), through its Research and Development funds, to report nationally on the problem. His careful research appeared as the clear-sighted *Preservation Policies and Conservation in British Libraries* (London: British Library, 1984), which recommended the setting up of the National Preservation Office (NPO) within the British Library, a body whose Council he now chairs. The NPO claims to be no more, in the usual British tradition, than an advisory, liaison and co-ordinative body. It has, however, in its brief existence since 1984, defined its first objectives and largely fulfilled them. The NPO issues excellent information leaflets, has computerised lists of conservation suppliers, and has brought to the market (i) a cradle overhead photocopier to reduce damage to valuable codex material, (ii) an electroluminescent copier, invaluable for some applications, and (iii) an image digitiser which, though in the opinion of many still in the development stage, demonstrates much promise.

There is, not surprisingly, necessary cross membership between the National Preservation Advisory Council and the Library Association Subcommittee on Preservation and Conservation under the redoubtable chairmanship of Barry Bloomfield of the British Library. The Subcommittee, founded in 1982, regards its preliminary work in raising awareness in the profession, defining syllabuses for the implementation of teaching in library schools, assisting IFLA's care programme, and assisting the NPO, as largely done if not still in course of satisfactory action. It now aims to establish a National Register of Microforms, to identify priorities at the national level, and to assist in the development of programmes on national preservation and conservation. In this the enterprise of the academic libraries of Scotland in entering the Conspectus programme will certainly assist. There is of course much else which would take too much time to tell. Not least that the battle for acid-free paper for book production in the U.K. is being waged and won; and that the Standing Conference of National and University Libraries (SCONUL) has set up its own Advisory Committee to consider and report on this major problem within its area of interest.

The Wellcome Institute

The Wellcome Institute for the History of Medicine has been doing most of what follows for some time. Our preliminary disaster programme was for instance set up in 1979; and since 1965 we have been organically developing from the antique model of reparative bookbinding, through paper conservation, to a full team of three conservators headed by an experienced and dedicated conservator who keeps in close touch with developments and colleagues in his field. The conservation laboratory has become an integral part of our activity; so much so, and so much is it regarded as a major part of our continuity, that its work has been included in our recent exhibition in the Institute, *A Vision of History*, and will continue to be so included in future exhibitions on our resources.

We include far more than the Latin American interest which for the purposes of this Seminar I happen to represent. The Institute, privately financed, though recognised for teaching purposes by the University of London through University College, was set up through the practicality, genius, and vision of the American-born [Sir] Henry Wellcome [1853-1936]—the last of the great business moguls—whose Will provided for continuing bio-medical and clinical research and for an Institute for the history of medicine and allied topics. This extraordinary man, perceiving the unity of all studies, collected books, manuscripts, pictures and objects from all cultures at all times for the furtherance of the study of man and his healing. His Trustees, acting through the Institute and Library, have continued to collect and make available materials on these topics, and to acquire collections and whole libraries whenever possible. You will not be surprised to learn therefore that we now possess well over 400,000 printed monographs on this recondite theme from 1467 to 1987, as well as some 6,000 Western MSS, 11,000 Oriental MSS in some 43 languages (with a very large collection of Sanskrit materials), at least 100,000 iconographic items (prints, drawings, watercolours and oils), 100,000 autograph letters of physicians, surgeons and scientists, a rapidly growing Contemporary Medical Archive (since 1900), together with the comparatively few (but often exceedingly rare) items within the collection of Americana. Riches indeed, and presented in numerous forms, from palm-leaf to human skin, to animal bone and vellum and watercolour. You will understand that our Conservator did not reel with horror when casually asked the other day to conserve a unicorn's horn. All in a day's work.

Preservation

Administration—co-ordinative, and integrative, and imaginative—is vital. We regard its centre as naturally at the Deputy level: at the node, in brief, of policy and its implementation, of access to finance to carry out policy, and at the administrative interconnection of all stages in the library process from stacks to subject specialist, from Library

Director transversely to Administration, Building Engineers and
Security.

The ideal is prevention of chronic and acute damage.

Air-Conditioning

Whenever possible, temperature and humidity controls are
installed in our seven strong rooms; they are also installed in the more
confined reading areas. In certain closed reading areas forced filtered
ventilation is used, both for the sake of the materials as for the equally
perishable staff and readers. (Artificial means breed artificial disasters.
We have had a class demonstration of this when in our picture store
the thermostat ran out of control—over a weekend, of course—the
humidity system failed, and condensate resplendently flooded the floor.
Result: some damage to one picture; and another, on wooden panel,
by virtue of extreme dryness and heat, deflected by some four inches.
This is the reverse side of perfect conditions, which I quote for your
benefit.)

Fire

Books do burn, and exceedingly well. In our major strong room
we have installed a Halon system which is said to extinguish an
incipient fire automatically within seconds. In concentrations higher
than that necessary for extinction of fires it is highly toxic to the
nervous system. It is also expensive. But its speed, since we have as
yet no sprinklers, is vitally necessary.

Throughout the building there are gamma-ray (POC) detectors
which automatically set off building fire alarms, and which connect with
a computerised network for instant summons of personnel and with
identificatory signals both on a central building control panel and at
the immediate site. Time loss should therefore be negligible.

Manual extinguishers, more in number than officially required, are
placed at all strategic sites, clearly identified as to use and regularly
checked for efficiency. Staff are to be regularly instructed in their use.
Hoses, too, are available for instant use.

Water

If not *ab initio* by flood from roof, down-pipe or drain, water will
certainly find its way to the valuable library resource by way of the
insistent and searching hose of the fireman.

We do all we can to prevent both these contingencies: *First,* we
have built bund walls (engineers' jargon for waterproof partitions) in
our stacks to contain waterways so far as possible, as well as the

humidity apparatus (which requires water). These walls have saved us massive loss several times in times of rainstorms of unusual tropical violence. *Second,* other waterways, impossible so to contain, are doubly encased; and the moveable stacks have hoods over them and rubber seals at the sides to prevent as much ingress of water as possible. *Third,* we have installed the American system Liqui-Tect, to give instant alarm to the same computerised system. *Fourth,* not book is housed below 9 inches from the floor—a height which gives much volume clearance before acute damage is reached.

Light

Until very recently, light has been too little regarded. Stack lights are not left on past the moment of use. Showcases in library rooms are curtained unless being viewed. Levels in major exhibitions, which we now run some three times a year, are never above the recommended 50 lux in showcases, which are themselves mounted in a darkened and low spot-lit exhibition area.

Photocopying

Viewed as a curse, not a blessing for valuable materials, photocopying is not permitted for pre-1851 books. Thereafter, each application is looked at on its conservational and copyright merits. Readers are not encouraged to suppose that they have any right to lend a hand in the deterioration of books which belong also to future generations, nor to think that microfilming is not almost as deleterious. Microfilming therefore is not necessarily a valid alternative. We shall all have to return to memory, that excellent filter of the meritorious from the meretricious, and to cards and notes. Good for us and good for posterity.

Security

Like all the other danger points, security is under constant scrutiny. A video system watches all salient areas. Staff are aware of nefarious practices and watch for them. Identification procedures have been tightened up, and invigilation rotas are maintained for the rare materials reading area. Everything is locked that can be locked, and procedures are maintained for placing and recovery of keys at appropriate times. Consideration is being given to greater stringency, at present limited to some degree by the building's double rôle of public and office use. Book signal systems are being scrutinised, and electronic locks for limited hands-free access to certain areas will soon be installed. Coats and bags are not allowed in the Library. Other measures have long been in hand which it would be a breach of security to relate. Constant vigilance in both the administration and immediate practical sense is our watchword.

Good Housekeeping

Required are serial dusting and sweeping of the stacks, and dusting and dressing of books to the right in the reading areas. The whole place is kept as scrupulously clean and tidy as possible. Dust damages: it also encourages the proliferation of book pests. Its regular removal will ensure ideal conditions; and if an outside infestation occurs such vigilance will lead to its early recognition.

I pass therefore to the more immediate and practical.

Conservation

Inhouse

Formally, we rotate focus of one of the conservators' time on one department for approximately a year. Thus: a concentration of work is possible; a one-to-one relationship between conservator and librarian develops to the advantage of both; and work can be dovetailed so that when one department is ending its share in conservational time another is beginning. The system so far works well, and each functioning department has a year's share within rather less than every two years. Acid-free boxing is being carried out for some printed books, and, as space develops, for the western MSS collection. Only precious and rare materials are so treated. We show conservational films to staff and readers to remind everyone of our priorities. Indeed, I much recommend the British Library film, hireable, *Keeping your Words*, to your attention for this purpose. We are on the look-out for further such material. A film on disaster prevention, provision and planning would be invaluable: one is being planned by the British Library. Microfilming of stock has not been instituted on a conservational basis as yet; nor indeed have we yet entered the CD-ROM technology, though we keep it under survey. The latest information suggests that the disc has only a life of some ten years: conservationally it is therefore as yet a poor runner.

We consult with each other all the time: this is the cement which enables us to operate. The same cement could equally well appear under *Informal* conservation, which must include expectation of care. Among our unusually bibliophilic specialist staff there is scarcely a need to emphasise the value and fragility of the book and the ways in which it must not be used. Support staff are made aware of the same need. The conservator has been asked to give talks and advice within the library to both staff and readers whenever it is deemed necessary.

Among academic and other readers, owing to our increasing caution in photocopying, microfilming, to our insistence on environmental control, and to the shewing of the British Library National Preservation Office film, we continue to emphasise that the book is a precious, irreplaceable and frangible artefact.

Outhouse

We use commercial conservators, of proven skill and integrity, where the scale of the problem and the possibility of a semi-mass approach justifies it. Post-1850 publications and early United States imprints, for example (notorious for poor paper in the experimental period of American paper production and equally notorious for particularly acidic bindings), are first-class candidates for such semi-mass conservational means; as also runs of early periodicals. Modern periodicals are of course also sent outhouse, as also special volumes to special binders. In the future we are likely to send palm-leaf volumes and iconographic materials outhouse once training routines in our laboratories for the outhouse conservators have been completed. All this releases the few inhouse conservators to concentrate on the more specialist and demanding work on rare materials not allowed outside the building.

We keep a watching brief on mass-deacidification processes; a process which we are far more likely to hire than to purchase. We have to be among the first in the field in the U.K. to test such a system, since the need among nineteenth-century medical texts is particularly dire.

Disaster Control

Prevention

To the points I have already made, further duties are added.

A regular check that fire precautions are observed; that fire equipment is tested; and that it is adequate and appropriate to the area protected. Regular tests of POC detectors and their systems of alarm, and of Liqui-Tect detectors, are carried out.

A regular fire practice, using extinguishers, making clear to staff the indications for use of water, CO_2, and foam and powder extinguishers.

An occasional and unexpected fire drill during which the building is emptied of all staff and readers as rapidly as possible, and valuable items made secure in the limited time available.

A meeting on occasion onsite with the local fire station officers,
principally to point out major areas of concern, and to explain the
disastrous effects of unnecessary water.

A regular check to ensure that electric wiring is up to standard in
every part of the building.

A regular check on contractors' employees, including building, painting
and cleaning staff. These frequently pose a fire and security risk.

A regular check by building engineers that gutters, down-drains, and
main drains are clear. Any blocking will mean disaster. Roofs
and gutters must be checked frequently during building work:
builders' rubble left to choke drains is responsible for many a
crisis.

Provision

Provision means foresight of needs in the event of a disaster.
Among the essentials are the provision of:

An address list including telephone numbers of administrative,
conservational, specialist, engineering and security staff to be
called on instantly in an emergency. The list is regularly updated
on the word processor, and distributed to all staff as listed.

A checklist, continually updated, of the contents of all rooms, in
particular of the stack rooms containing irreplaceable materials.

Insurance of all valuable items; in our case, of the whole stock.

A regular check on disaster provision materials. Such materials,
subject to human attrition, are locked in a safe by accessible place,
and means of access provided for appropriate staff. The store
contains, *inter alia*, plastic freezer crates (stacking according to the
module of the freezer store for which provision has been made,
see below), freezer bags, kitchen towels, newsprint, blotting paper,
buckets with squeegee compartments, squeegee mops to fit them,
sponge squeegee mops, pusher-bladed brooms, torches (regularly
re-batteried), dustbin liner bags, dustbins, soft sponges, and hand-
held sprays.

A regular check that emergency equipment is available, including
electric pumps and at least one standby diesel pump; also
industrial blow-heaters and industrial fans. Building engineers
advise on and pursue these items for purchase or emergency hire.
Some of them are instantly hireable through standby arrangements.

Most importantly, external provision is made for *blast-freezing* against
the time of disaster. The Institute permanently hires space in a
freezer store in case of necessity. A small permanently hired area,
useful for a minor emergency, provides some priority for a larger

area if the need arises. We plan to order sufficient plastic stacking crates to provide for the full use of our hired space.

Equally importantly, provision is made for *vacuum-drying*. Few places carry this out. UKAEA (Harwell), well-practised in the remedial action for the Taylorian Institute flood of 1979, provides a back-up service for the Wellcome Institute. The facility is renewed annually on an updated estimated basis at the beginning of every year.

Staff are made aware that disaster provision exists, and that the obvious ways of dealing with material after fire or flood are not necessarily the best. Expert curatorial and conservational advice is to be sought before moving anything. Soaked film materials are, for example, best packed immediately in clean water and sent at once to a film laboratory for restoration. Soaked leaves of items on loaded paper are to be separated at once and interleaved with plain dry tissue or plain newsprint until air-dried.

Planning

We have set up a Disaster Action Group (DAG) composed of the Librarian, Deputy Librarian, Administrator, Conservator, Building Engineers, Estates Services (Security), Building Managers, Property Manager, and Staff Supervisor, to take direction of disaster prevention, provision and planning. Before planning is possible, prevention and provision routines, as indicated, have to be in place.

Many libraries will very properly want a highly structured plan appropriate to their highly structured situation. We believe, after careful discussion and having laid the groundwork of prevention and provision and continued expert consultation, that we are firmly placed to react sensitively and rapidly to the demands of an unexpected situation. It is better in our view to remain flexible than to box ourselves in with a plan which in the event may not answer our needs. We therefore follow the broad lines of the model disaster control plan in Appendix 1 of the admirably informative and practical *Planning Manual for Disaster Control in Scottish Libraries and Record Offices* by John McIntyre and Hazel Anderson (1985). Its disaster reaction flowchart outlines all possible events from notification of the emergency to final assessment of the measures, including restoration, to overcome it. It underlines the need to call in the Building Engineer and the DAG at the first stage of the disaster to assess and stabilise the situation, and to determine the likely requirements and support services. It foresees the need to call in the disaster team once that assessment is made, and to call upon the conservator and on the specialist curators whose areas are affected. Teams are then organised and informed how they should deal with the material involved, and the appropriate support services such as the blast-freezing and cold storage and transport services (already set up for such an emergency) informed. Emergency equipment is moved to the area, undamaged stock protected, and damaged stock sorted into separate categories for air-drying, freezing, and for immediate specialist processing. Each category, so far as possible, should be listed before processing. Air-dried material should in particular be dealt with promptly within 48 hours to avoid fungal growth. Coated paper must be interleaved at once, and the interleavings changed as often as possible until the book is absolutely dry. Sorting for restoration of all three categories follows, until damaged areas are themselves returned to full use.

The same model plan, which I recommend to your attention, usefully lists disaster equipment, emergency procedures, guidelines and procedures for salvage teams, and it emphasizes the need, if time allows, to make up damage lists to identify the contents of crates of damaged material. It has also designed a damage list which requires little modification.

In order to reserve library and conservational time and energy for their regular duties informal arrangements have been set up with a well-known and responsible firm of commercial bookbinders and conservators to ensure their instant support in case of an emergency; and we are investigating the possibility of similar arrangements with a firm of expert conservational salvagers to carry on with immediate matters of salvage under curatorial and inhouse conservational supervision.

Implicit in the whole disaster exercise is a close control of prevention, provision and planning, in particular of the procedures maintained for daily action in the early and urgent stages of a disaster. The Disaster Action Group is required to act across all administrative levels both to attract informed advice and to give clear directions as to the resolution of chronic and acute problems.

The practice of one library, aware of its national and international rôle in the preservation of its unique material for the future may provide some food for thought for your theory and practice. Since I am here to learn, I would be grateful to receive comments, to know of your experience, and to hear of any improvements we may make.

Part Five

Historiography and Bibliography

22. Recent Research in the History of Trinidad and Tobago: A Review of the Journal and Conference Literature, 1975-1985

Margaret D. Rouse-Jones

This paper examines the journal and conference literature on Trinidad and Tobago which appeared in the period between 1975 and 1985. It is useful to look at the work done during these years because the two major vehicles for publication of recent research in Caribbean history appeared continuously throughout this period. The *Journal of Caribbean History* which is the only journal specializing in publishing material in Caribbean history [1] has appeared uninterrupted since 1976. An Annual Conference of Caribbean Historians, another major forum for researchers, has been taking place since 1969. For the most part the papers of these conferences have not been formally published, although the Main Library of the St. Augustine Campus of the University of the West Indies has been systematically attempting to collect them. In a review of the historical writing for the period from 1940 to around 1970, Woodville Marshall has indicated that for the Commonwealth Caribbean as a whole the volume of writing has greatly increased in scope and has also revealed new perspectives. [2] This paper updates Marshall's review for Trinidad and Tobago in particular, focusing on the journal and conference literature.

The list of references at the end of this paper consists of eighty-one items on a variety of topics related to the history of Trinidad and Tobago. Numbers in square brackets throughout the text refer to the items in the list. Some of the items are interdisciplinary in nature but they have been included because the historian increasingly draws on the methodology of the other social scientists in analyzing his data. These

---

Author's Note: I would like to express my thanks to Dr. Bridget Brereton, Head of the History Department, University of the West Indies, St. Augustine, for useful discussions and for making available copies of papers and reprints. The staff in the West Indian Division, the Main Library, University of the West Indies, St. Augustine, have been very supportive and have assisted in locating items and checking references.

studies also contain information which is relevant for social history. For example, the items in the area of linguistics [43] [44] [77] [78] which examine the origins of names and the use and development of Creole language in Trinidad fall into this category. A general index to the subjects covered by all the items is given in Appendix 1.

It is evident that a wide variety of themes and subjects has been the focus of the research. In this paper the discussion focusses on a few of the topics: aspects of the pre-emancipation era; the post-emancipation period; immigration and the East Indians; education; women; biographies; Tobago. Generally the paper shows that "the area of historical knowledge [still] is constantly being enlarged," [3] with the impetus having been provided by available avenues for discussion and publication of research. In addition to the Annual Conference of Caribbean Historians, at least five other conferences have been held during the period. Work has also been published in a range of journals within and outside the region.

A glance at the authors will confirm Marshall's findings that a group of historians rather than a lone voice has been making a significant contribution to the task of historical reconstruction and reinterpretation. [4] Seven of the historians who have been writing on Trinidad and Tobago before 1975 have continued in the tradition. [5] It is interesting to note however that within the ten-year period some dozen or so other historians have been added to the pool of those researching and writing on the history of Trinidad and Tobago.

The Pre-Emancipation Era

The early settlement period of Trinidad's history is a period about which not much has been written hitherto. Arie Boomert's work [10] [11] during the past decade has brought to light much information on this period of the island's history. Using manuscript maps Boomert traces the history of the Arawaks during the sixteenth and early seventeenth centuries and throws light on their relationship with the Spanish. His archaeological research, in addition to un-earthing evidence of the fact that Trinidad is the oldest settled island of the West Indies, has also pointed to other archaeological sites known in Trinidad which still remain to be excavated in order to provide further evaluation of artifacts of its Amerindian past. His use of archae-ological data to elucidate historical fact demonstrates the possibilities and potential of the interdisciplinary approach.

Although slavery has been a popular subject for the historian within recent times, the institution in Trinidad has not been the focus of much attention by scholars. [6] Trinidad's experience of slavery was different from that of the other colonies. It became a slave society much later, the first sugar estate being established on the island in 1787. It was only after the British conquest of the island in 1797 that the slave population doubled. In 1813 a Register of slaves in Trinidad was created as a result of the concerns of the abolitionists in Parliament who felt that slaves were being smuggled into the colonies. The information relating to the slaves in this Register—their physical characteristics, place of residence, occupation, and so on—provides the basis of the source material for the articles on the physical stature of slaves in Trinidad by Gerald Friedman [27] and Barry Higman [33] [34]. Higman's work on height of different groups of slaves in Trinidad [34] reveals that those born in the New World as well as those originating from the Senegambia region of Africa were taller than other Africans. The tallest slaves were Creoles from the British Caribbean colonies which did not grow sugar. This led Higman to deduce that there was a correlation between the short stature of slaves and life style on sugar plantations.

Friedman's work [27] seemingly extends Higman's analysis by introducing other measures—work routine and material well being—and lends some support to Higman's conclusion that the Trinidad slaves were shorter due to overwork and malnourishment. However in summarising his explanations he states that "it is not yet possible to measure the separate effects of overwork, poor diet and disease on the stunting of Trinidad slaves' growth" and also that "there is little direct evaluation on what the Trinidad slaves were eating" so that the findings can only be taken as suggestions or conjecture although the relationship between diet, disease, overwork and the physical condition of the individual is well known.

Higman's study on the slave family patterns [33] also uses the 1813 Registration of slaves. He sets out to test the relationship between specific African origin and slave family structures in Trinidad in 1813. Although the data has its limitations Higman is able to draw several conclusions. The analysis shows that the majority of African-born slaves in a newly settled plantation society were isolated from any formal family system. Extensive intermarriage resulted in an almost immediate loss of cultural identity of distinct ethnic or tribal African groups. African families contrasted strongly with those of Creoles and a tendency to matrifocality was observed.

Although these studies shed light on very specialized aspects of the institution in Trinidad, research pointing to a more comprehensive study of slaves in the island still remains to be done.

The free coloureds in Trinidad, an important group in the society, have been the subject of research by Carl Campbell [21] [22] [23]. Under the terms of the famous Cedula of Population of 1783, a sizeable number of free coloureds, sufficient to constitute a separate group, came to the island. Campbell's article on the rise of the free coloured plantocracy in Trinidad 1783-1813 [23] shows that under Governor Chacon they had access to land. By the 1820's scores of them had inherited parcels of land given originally by the Spanish government to their white fathers or grandfathers. They also played an important role in establishing the pattern of subsistence throughout the island, being rural dwellers, unlike their counterparts in other territories. When Governor Woodford took over the governorship of the island in 1813 he wished "to establish a settled society, institutionally fixed, racially defined and graduated in terms of social ranks." His measures to define the population more sharply along racial lines operated strictly against the free coloureds whom he felt had been allowed to get out of control. The most serious proposal which he made to control them was in the area of land policy. He suggested the passage of a law which would restrict the amount of property which coloured children could inherit from white fathers. Nothing came of his suggestions, but he did effect two measures, one of which related to the registration of all land titles which seemed to have a direct effect on the free coloureds. Generally his efforts failed to reduce their socio-economic position, but they were aware that they were the target of prejudice from the governor himself.

In the third article Campbell [22] examines the part played by Francis de Ridder, a free coloured Roman Catholic Priest who was instrumental in championing the cause of the free coloureds by challenging the Roman Catholic Church which supported the institutionalization of prejudice against them.

One historian has noted that an examination of the free coloured group in any society is a measure of Frank Tannenbaum's well known thesis regarding the relationship between ease and frequency of manumission and the relative mildness of slavery. [7] In the case of Trinidad, the examination of the circumstances related to their presence in the island serves to highlight the peculiar nature of Trinidad's historical experience.

The Post-Emancipation Era

The Post-Emancipation period in Trinidad was of particular importance because of the island's historical experience. The fact that it had become a British colony only ten years before the Abolition of the slave trade and had been newly opened up for sugar meant that it always had a labour problem. [8] At the time of emancipation there was still a considerable amount of land still awaiting cultivation. Brian Blouet's article [7] examines the land policies adopted by planters and other colonial authorities with regard to the ex-slaves, whom they feared would set up small subsistence farms on the large tracts of unforested crown lands which were uncultivated, uninhabited and beyond the limits of effective administration. The planters therefore attempted to manipulate the laws so as to keep the labouring classes landless. This was with a view to keeping them dependent on the sugar plantations for a livelihood, thus ensuring their labour supply. It was subsequently discovered by a Committee of Enquiry into the quantity of land occupied by squatters that squatting had become prevalent. It was therefore decided to make small plots of crown land available cheaply. This scheme implemented under Lord Harris was intended to guide the expansion of the agricultural areas. However, the uncertain financial situation of the country at the time coupled with the absence of the basic administrative framework operated against the implementation of a complex land settlement programme.

Kusha Haraksingh [132], examining the labour situation on the plantation following emancipation, analyses it in the context of the annual rhythm of sugar cultivation and the unique situation in Trinidad. He shows that following Emancipation owners and managers of sugar plantations in Trinidad were engaged in a process of rationalisation which involved tailoring the labour force to the fluctuating seasonal demands of sugar production. Some freed men were induced to remain on estates in specialist occupations. Others were removed from the estates, but enough stayed in the vicinity of the plantations to provide a pool of labour which helped to maintain the level of production. While rationalisation was in train, the planters continued to insist that there was a shortage of labour and that the more the freed men earned, the less they worked. The complaints laid the ground for the replacement of a free labour force by labour not so free at low wage levels. Both these goals were to be fully achieved under the scheme of Indian indentureship which began in 1845.

Migration and the East Indian Experience

Migration which was the theme of one of the major conferences held during the period under review has been recognised as one of the major characteristics of West Indian society. [9] For Trinidad in particular it played an important role in the society from the end of the eighteenth century. However, it yet remains an area requiring comprehensive study: in particular intensive research is yet to be done on the migration of Europeans, Chinese and Syrian Lebanese. [10]

Over the last fifteen years the East Indian immigration to Trinidad and the implications of the experience has produced a series of articles. The research has been advanced by the organization of Conferences on East Indians in the Caribbean in 1975, 1979, and 1984. [11] It is not possible to summarize the research here, but particular aspects of the East Indian experience will emerge in the discussion on education and women.

Research done by Brinsley Samaroo [58] [59] and Angela Hamel-Smith [28] on education as it relates to East Indians has furthered our knowledge of education in the post-emancipation period. Their work also gives an insight into the factors affecting and the nature of the interaction between Indians and other groups in society. This was one area in which Marshall had indicated that information was lacking. [12]

Brinsley Samaroo's work [58] makes the point that although the ward schools had been originally set up in the 1850s for the purpose of bringing about the socialization of the East Indians into the value system of the predominant culture, this group, for several reasons, had not made any significant attempt to take advantage of these schools. Their reasons included fear of conversation, illiteracy in English, fear of derision by the rest of the school population. In addition to this the continued importation of East Indians into the colony was an important factor in maintaining cultural solidarity among the East Indians as a group and thus lessening their need for interaction with other racial elements in the society. This attitude on the part of the East Indians with regard to education caused the government and the planters to give tangible support to the work of the Canadian Missions which began in Trinidad in 1868. They saw the school as the major agency of conversion and employed various means to maintain the interest of the East Indians in schools. One of their methods was to establish in 1890 special Indian schools, the teachers of which were to know both Hindi and English. The syllabuses in these schools included considerable information from the religious experience of the missionaries in Canada, and the material proved to be more interesting than that which was offered in state schools. However, it was because of the vagueness and uncertainty regarding education in Trinidad and Tobago at the time that Canadian missionaries had a free hand. The influence of their efforts in education was discernible in their century—Presbyterian East Indians "were in the vanguard of the East Indian entry into the professions, business and politics" [58].

Hamel-Smith's paper [28] focuses on primary education and East Indian women in Trinidad. Following on from Samaroo's work, Hamel-Smith gives a more detailed insight into the education of a sub group within the East Indian community. She notes that the Canadian Mission schools constantly complained about the fact that East Indian parents were reluctant to send their daughters to school. This was as a result of their cultural system: a Moslem or Hindu girl was earmarked for early marriage and thus the academic subjects taught in formal education systems were considered to be of low priority. This view was reinforced by the belief on the part of the male that the female mind was incapable of learning non-domestic skills. The wives of the missionaries counteracted this problem by establishing residential schools for Indian girls where they were protected from early marriage and also trained to be "suitable wives and partners for young Presbyterian converts." Hamel-Smith reports that these schools were successful in their aims. Time eroded the cultural values which were hostile to the education of women, and by 1950 the attendance rates of East Indian females in primary schools was almost on a par with that of the men.

Carl Campbell's article [18] examines specifically the College Exhibition System in Trinidad and Tobago in the period 1872-1938 and in part extends the work on East Indians by Samaroo and Hamel-Smith discussed above. The College Exhibition System was considered to be one of the socially important education practices in Trinidad and Tobago and functioned as a vital instrument of upward social mobility. His analysis shows that many black and coloured children were able to elevate their social status through this means, but this applied to East Indians to a lesser extent. The pattern which Campbell's research revealed was that pupils of certain leading schools in Port-of-Spain won most exhibitions and very few if any East Indian children attended these schools. The system evolved in an era of competition in education, and it in turn had a great effect on maintaining the competitive nature of the education system in Trinidad and Tobago. College Exhibition winners who then became Island Scholarship winners demonstrated even more forcibly the potential of the education system as a lever of upward social mobility.

With regard to the question of the integration of the East Indian into the society, Samaroo, in another paper [59], examines the role of the Canadian Missions as an agent of integration in Trinidad. He makes the point that the missionaries' attitudes served to alienate the East Indians from the African community. By preserving the racial separation the missionaries reinforced the exclusiveness of the East

Indians and contributed to the separation which continues to have an effect on Trinidad and Tobago today.

Gerard Tikasingh's article [69] which focuses on another aspect of the East Indian experience looks at social change in the emerging East Indian community.   He shows that although the East Indians did attempt to maintain the continuity of the social organizations and institutions which they brought with them, their attempts to recreate a traditional Indian community within the parameters of the society's generally western orientation were not successful.   Certain key social institutions—the structure of caste, the traditional institutions of social control, Hindu religion, the family—underwent fundamental changes. The result was that the Indian community of Trinidad developed a social reorganization which was essentially different from that of traditional Indian society.

Women

It is particularly interesting to note that three of the writers have focussed on women. [13]   Rhoda Reddock's work [57] on Indian women and indentureship between 1845 and 1917 seeks to correct the strongly adhered to myths and untrue generalizations about the character of immigrant Indian women.   Reddock identifies two commonly held myths: that Indians unlike Africans migrated as families, and, as a result of this and others, the Indian family system could be maintained in its traditional fashion, and secondly that the Indian women who migrated did so under the power, authority and control of their male relatives and that they were of a docile and tractable character. Reddock's study clearly explodes these myths. The recruiters tended to prefer single men over family groups or individual women. She shows that the majority of Indian women who came to the Caribbean came as individual women and not as wives or daughters as has been commonly believed. Many were Brahmin widows who were subject to the stigma of impurity in India.   The other most popular type of female Indian immigrant consisted of women separated from their husbands for whom prostitution or destitution was the only remaining alternative in India. A smaller proportion of the women who came were already practising prostitutes or unmarried pregnant women seeking a new life. As Reddock argues, the motives which caused these women to emigrate were themselves a manifestation of their independent character and strength. Thus she explodes the commonly held image of the docile meek Indian woman arriving five steps behind her husband. The intentions of these women however did not coincide with those of the planters or the Indian man in the colonies, and as early as the recruitment stage attempts were made to control the situation. Like their African counterparts the women came as workers. In discussing education, Reddock's work also emphasizes the point made by Hamel-Smith regarding the influence of the Canadian Presbyterian' Indian education system over Indian women.

David Trotman's work [75] analyzes the pattern of crime and criminality among women in late nineteenth century Trinidad. He shows that the female population at this time was young, unmarried and predominantly Creole with a substantial rural component, these being non-Trinidadian immigrants from India and the other British West Indian territories. Where they had settled in the urban areas they were marginally employed. The statistics related to crime can only be understood against this background with its peculiar demographic, residential and occupational characteristics.

In considering the incidence of crime, residential factors did not seem to operate, in that both urban and rural women were vulnerable to three particular types of crime: assault, rape and wife-beating. Trotman's analysis however is fuller in details about East Indian women, and this may be a function of the fact that more detailed records were kept of their activities. Using prison records and newspaper reports Trotman shows that although some women were committed to prison in the nineteenth century, a greater number were brought before the courts and were probably fined rather than committed to imprisonment. As was the case in his examination of women as victims of crime, criminal activity among women reflected their socio-economic status. Women did participate in all types of illegal activities, but were more prone to gender-specific crimes such as prostitution, the crime about which Trotman gives considerable details. Working-class women were most frequently charged with indecent behavior, riotous and disorderly conduct and the use of obscene and profane language.

Biographies

Biography has been commonly regarded as a vehicle of history, and several studies have come out in the historical writings of Trinidad and Tobago in the last ten years. Mention has already been made of Carl Campbell's work—the free coloured Catholic Priest Francis de Ridder. [22]

Campbell has also written about Captain J. O. Cutteridge [18], who was director of education in Trinidad and Tobago for the period 1921-1942. This is a most valuable contribution to the scholarship in the area of education. Using a variety of newspapers and other sources he gives a detailed account of Cutteridge's career on the island. Although Cutteridge did bring about many improvements in the area of education, his textbooks which dominated the elementary curriculum for thirty years or so came in for criticism, a phenomenon which was previously unheard of.

Charles Warner acted as Solicitor General and Attorney General between 1832 and 1870, and his influence was greater than that of the real governor; he is also the subject of Campbell's research [17]. His official career was closely linked with the colonial government's handling of problems of the post-emancipation period.

Bridget Brereton throws light on Sir John Gorrie [15] and John Jacob Thomas [12]. Gorrie, a Chief Justice during the period 1885-1892 who left his mark on the countries where he served, as a political and social reformer who believed in equal justice for all regardless of their class or colour. He felt that the courts were the only means whereby the tendency of white capitalists to exploit labour could be checked. As Chief Justice he reformed judicial proceedings and took a prominent and conspicuous part in politics. Although he failed in his basic objective to make Trinidad and Tobago a more just society, he did open the Supreme Court to lower class suitors and reformed many procedural abuses. Brereton describes John Jacob Thomas [12] as an "unusual Trinidadian." He was a self-made, self-educated man, representative of the black and coloured middle class which was emerging in Trinidad in the years after Emancipation.

Kelvin Singh's work [64] on Adrian Cola Rienzi examines his contribution to the labour movement and the establishment of trade unions in Trinidad and Tobago. Earlier works have presented him as a middle class opportunist who exploited the labour movement and betrayed both Butler and the movement. Singh argues that these views are based on propaganda rather than fact. He shows that Rienzi's involvement in the labour movement had started as early as 1925 and that he founded the Trinidad Citizens League in 1935, of which Butler was a member. The latter subsequently founded his own party which was responsible for precipitating the 1937 disturbances. Singh argues that it was while Butler was in hiding that Rienzi took the initiative and played an important part in the establishment and legitimization of the trade unions, withdrawing from the labour movement only when he got caught in a web of rivalry with Butler and his party.

Another East Indian who was influential during the 1937 labour disturbances, Mitra Sinanan, is the subject of a biographical paper by Sahadeo Basdeo [3]. Basdeo shows that Sinanan played an important role in the development of political consciousness among East Indians.

As a law student in London he identified with the anti-colonial struggle. On his return to Trinidad as a barrister-at-law he worked closely with Adrian Cola Rienzi and became involved in local politics. Following the 1937 labour disturbances Sinanan defended Butler and won the case following an appeal. His efforts towards Afro-Indian solidarity had provided leadership to the East Indian community at a crucial moment in the country's history.

Finally, but by no means of least importance in the area of biography, are several studies on Dr. Eric Williams, late Prime Minister of Trinidad and Tobago. His death in 1981 precipitated a series of articles about the man who was also an important historian but who as head of state for twenty-five years played a prominent part in the recent history. In 1984 a conference was held on the contribution made by his classic work *Capitalism and Slavery* and several papers which were biographical in nature were presented. Using a variety of sources and approaches the several writers have attempted to arrive at an understanding of the character, personality and contribution of Williams. Colin Hope's article [35] briefly examines some of his major works. It draws heavily in part on Elsa Goveia's critiques of one of Williams' earlier works and concludes that Dr. Williams had serious ambiguities in his character which he was never able to resolve. Ian McDonald's memory and tribute [48], written on the night after Williams died, is a personal and somewhat emotional reminiscence of someone who regretted that he had never met the man but whom he feels that "history . . . will choose to stand in greater suns."

Ken Boodhoo's work [8] examines the economic ideas of Eric Williams as expressed in his works *Capitalism and Slavery* and *Massa Day Done*. He makes the point that Williams felt it was the task of the PNM "to right the injustices of the Massa" and the economic policies which were dominant in Trinidad since 1956 were mainly a reflection of Williams' thoughts and ideas. In another article, co-authored with Ivan Harnanan [9], Williams' contribution as a scholar is assessed and his position on the Federation, Caribbean Economic Community, the mainland Caribbean territories and Cuba is also examined. The writers conclude that Williams' vision of the region was unique—a vision which was based on his knowledge of history and on a desire to rehabilitate the dignity of the black man.

Richard Sheridan's [63] study of Eric Williams in part goes much deeper than writers discussed so far. Himself an economic historian, Sheridan examines the schools of historiography and the preparatory courses Williams took and the works he read which influenced him in his writing of *Capitalism and Slavery*. He argues very convincingly that in addition to the influence exerted on him by his reading of other scholars he brought to the study of imperial history motives and experiences that had been shaped by the reality of his Trinidad boyhood. Williams "wanted to condemn the educated class of Britain and the wider English-speaking world with the sins of omission of their forefathers and use this weapon to achieve racial, political and social justice."

Paul Sutton [67] focuses on the many-faceted aspect of Williams— economic historian, developmental economist, political 'theorist,' social critic and practical educator—and then assesses how all these aspects were combined in the concept of the nation of Trinidad and Tobago, the key to understanding Williams as a political man.

Howard Temperley's [68] article examines Williams' scholarship, with particular reference to his treatment of the abolitionists. According to Temperley, Williams pays tribute to them but at the same time he seeks to minimize their achievement.

Cuthbert Joseph, who was at one time a minister in his government [42], in assessing the contribution of Eric Williams to education, shows that Williams saw education as a fundamental economic, social and cultural right. His approach took into consideration not only the development of the individual as a free human being but also the economic, social, cultural, spiritual and psychological needs of the regional and the national community. His party manifesto declared that "to educate is to redeem," and under his administration the education system in the country was considerably expanded at the primary, secondary and tertiary levels.

These studies have been based on personal reminiscences, analyses of his writings and also on Williams' autobiography. However, as the passage of time puts distance between historians and Williams and his era and as more source material comes to light, further studies should come closer to separating the legend from the reality.

Tobago

On the subject of Tobago, it is true to say that the research has lagged behind that for Trinidad. This is apart from the fact that prior to 1889 the two islands were two separate entities. The work done by Keith Laurence [45] [47] and Bridget Brereton [14] are on very specialized topics.

Laurence's research on the 1801 Tobago slave conspiracy [45] brings to light the fact that none of the ringleaders of the conspiracy had any specific cause for complaint and their main aim was probably to escape from enslavement. One of the leaders did also indicate that one of the aims was the total annihilation of the white and coloured people by a regular and systematic attack. However Bryan Edwards' assertion that the leaders intended to turn against those Negroes who did not join in the revolt has not been substantiated. Laurence also suggests that the whites in December 1801 were preoccupied with the information that Tobago was likely to revert to French rule and this fact may have accounted both for reduced vigilance on the part of the whites and also an incitement to the slaves. A particularly interesting side is the comparison which Laurence puts forward between this conspiracy and a slave riot reported in Trinidad in December 1805. The aim of this conspiracy was to get rid of white and free coloured inhabitants.

Tobago is one of the islands which changed hands several times during the colonial period. Laurence's other piece on Tobago [47] examines the British decision to give the island back to France in 1982 only to recapture it the following year. He shows that this temporary take over was due to diplomatic blundering on the part of Britain's representatives in the face of French desire to maintain a great overseas empire.

Brereton's study on the "Belmanna riots" in post-Emancipation Tobago [14] places the riots in the context of protests which occurred in the Windward Islands at that time. Disputes over wages were a chief source of conflict between labour and management. Other grievances and oppressive conditions on the estates precipitated the act of protest by both immigrant and Creole labourers.

The foregoing review of the literature on specialized topics in the history of Trinidad and Tobago has shown that scholarship has advanced, knowledge has increased and myths have been explored. The breaking of new ground has also revealed avenues for further scholarship. Historians of the islands have generally been using a variety of sources and techniques of analysis. As new records become available and oral sources are identified and tapped, it is hoped that the gaps will be filled and new light will be shed on the grey areas.

Postscript

This postscript highlights some of the issues related to collection development and exploitation with particular reference to the type of literature under discussion. It also takes into consideration the theme of recession management strategies.

It is a well known fact that information about conferences can be elusive and the acquisition of conference papers can be a particularly difficult business for librarians [17] especially when the papers are not published formally. In the case of annual meetings which are held at the same time every year, for example the Conference of the Association of Caribbean Historians, it is more possible to acquire papers. Where the conference is irregular it is easy to miss information, and in instances where there is a special conference, for example the Conference on Migration and Culture Contact in the Caribbean or the Conference on Capitalism and Slavery in the British West Indies which was held in Bellagio in Italy, it is not inconceivable that librarians both within and outside the region may well have been unaware of the occurrence of the conference. The fact that no papers were published officially places the librarian in an even more difficult position with regard to acquiring copies of them. It is therefore very important to maintain good liaison with all faculty so that they are forthcoming with information about conferences with which they are involved and would play an active part in ensuring that copies of papers reach the library. Experience has shown that if the librarian has the information in time it is possible to get papers or photocopies. Once some time has passed papers are either not available or very costly. This situation also highlights the importance of cooperation between librarians in the region both with regard to information sharing and to acquisition of material.

With the limited avenues for publication for scholars in the region the librarian is also faced with the problem of 'scatter' of information in a range of journals. This study has shown that research on Trinidad and Tobago in the last ten years has been published in at least twenty different journals, more than half of which originate outside the Caribbean region. [18] This has implications both for acquisitions and bibliographic control. Libraries are constantly faced with the spiraling costs of serial subscriptions. In the case where the library does not take the journal it may be possible to request off-prints from authors. In cases where there is no access to computerised databases or proper indexing services which would bring to the user's attention the existence of the article, then other tools—accession lists, current awareness bulletins or in-house indexes—have to be created and/or used to meet the need. This also applies to conference papers. [19] The librarian should also be aware of the overlap between conference papers and journal literature: in some instances conference papers have subsequently been published in journals. [20] Researchers may also publish the same or a slightly modified version of a paper in two different places. [21]

These are some considerations which might be kept in view as we implement our recession management strategies for the development and exploitation of our Caribbean collections.

APPENDIX 1

Sources of Journal and Conference Literature Discussed

Journals

African Studies Review

American Journal of Physical Anthropology

The Americas

Boletin de Estudios LatinoAmericanos y del Caribe

British Journal of Sports History

Bulletin of Eastern Caribbean Affairs

Caribbean Quarterly

Caribbean Studies

English World-Wide

Ethnic and Racial Studies

The History Teachers Journal

Journal of Caribbean History

Journal of Caribbean Studies

Journal of Family History

Journal of Imperial and Commonwealth History

Military Affairs

Naturalist

Nieuwe West-Indische Gids

Social and Economic Studies

Social Science History

Conferences

Conference of Caribbean Historians. This conference organized by the Association of Caribbean Historians has been held annually since 1969 during the month of April at different venues throughout the region.

Conference on Capitalism and Slavery in the British West Indies: The Contribution of Eric Williams, held in Bellagio, Italy, May 21-25, 1984.

Conference on Migration and Culture Contact in the Caribbean, held at the University of the West Indies, Cave Hill, Barbados, April 4-7, 1984.

East Indians in the Caribbean: A Symposium on Contemporary Collection and Political Issues. Three meetings have been held so far at the St. Augustine Campus of the University of the West Indies: June 25-28, 1975; September; 16-23, 1970; August 28-September 5, 1984.

APPENDIX 2

Brief Guide to Topics Covered in List of References

American business interests,
76

American soldiers, 52, 53

Amerindians, 10, 11

Biographies, 3, 8, 9, 12, 15,
17, 19, 21, 22, 35, 42,
48, 49, 63, 64, 67, 68

Diplomatic relations,
Venezuela, 65

Sport and culture, 16

East Indians, 2, 3, 4, 24, 25,
26, 28, 30, 30A, 36, 37,
39, 46, 57, 61, 66, 69,
70

Education, 17, 18, 19, 20, 28,
42, 50, 59

Free coloureds, 21, 22, 23

Immigration, 46, 50, 51, 54,
55, 56, 57

Labour, 1, 2, 3, 4, 5, 30, 30A,
32, 38, 40, 60, 64

Law, 24, 36, 39

Linguistics, 43, 44, 77, 78

Peasants, 62

Pre-Emancipation society, 21,
22, 23, 50, 72

Post-Emancipation society, 7,
14, 30, 32, 73

Press, 13, 58A, 61, 70

Religion, 22, 25, 26, 37, 58,
59, 74

Slaves, 27, 33, 34

Sugar industry, 29, 31, 32

Syrian Lebanese, 51

Tobago, 14, 45, 47

Williams, Eric, 8, 9, 35, 42,
48, 63, 67, 68

Women, 20, 28, 57, 75

World War I, 58A

World War II, 52, 53

NOTES

1. For background information on this journal and a cumulative index of all material which it has published see Margaret D. Rouse-Jones and Annette Knight, "Cumulative Index, Volumes 1-19," *Journal of Caribbean History* 20:2 (1985-86), 192-216.

2. Woodville K. Marshall, "A Review of Historical Writing on the Commonwealth Caribbean since c. 1940," *Social and Economic Studies* 24 (1975), 271-307, esp. p. 271.

3. Ibid, p. 271.

4. Ibid, p. 273.

5. See, e.g, works listed by Bridget Brereton, Carl Campbell, Barry Higman, Howard Johnson, Keith Laurence, Marianne Ramesar, Brinsley Samaroo, Gerard Tikasingh. These historians all appear in Marshall's listing.

6. Marshall, "A Review of Historical Writing, p. 280.

7. Edward L. Cox, *Free Coloureds in the Slave Societies of St. Kitts and Grenada, 1763-1833* (Knoxville, TE: University of Tennessee Press, 1984), p. xi.

8. Bridget Brereton, *A History of Modern Trinidad, 1783-1962* (London: Heinemann, 1981), p. 77.

9. Marshall, "A Review of Historical Writing, p. 282.

10. Two reviews on migrant groups in the region as a whole already exist. See Marianne Ramesar, *Migrant Groups in the Caribbean: A Topical Essay and Introductory Review of the Literature* (St. Augustine: Institute of Social and Economic Research, University of the West Indies, 1978); and Alvin Thompson, "A Historiographical Review of the Literature on the Economic, Social and Cultural Aspects of Migration in the Commonwealth Caribbean, c1838-c1938," paper presented at the Annual Conference of Caribbean Historians, April 1984, p. 1.

11. See items 2, 3, 4, 24, 25, 26, 28, 30, 30A, 36, 37, 39, 46, 57, 66, 70.

12. Marshall, "A Review of Historical Writing, p. 284.

13. This is significant, too, because a programme in women's studies has now been introduced at the St. Augustine campus of the University of the West Indies.

14. Elsa Goveia, "New Shibboleths for Old." Review of Eric Williams, *British Historians and the West Indies* (Trinidad: P.N.M. Publishing, 1964), in *Caribbean Quarterly* 10:2 (June 1964), 48-54.

15. Brereton, *History of Modern Trinidad*, Preface, p. ix.

16. For an interesting discussion of the position of social history within the Caribbean see B. W. Higman, "Theory, Method and Technique in Caribbean Social History," *Journal of Caribbean History* 20:1 (1985-86), 1-29.

17. Workshop on Conference Literature in Science and Technology (1980: Albuquerque, New Mexico), *Conference Literature: Its Role in the Distribution of Information* (Marlton, NJ: Learned Information, 1981), p. 44. I am grateful to Lutishoor Salisbury, Librarian, Engineering and Physical Sciences Division, University of the West Indies, St. Augustine, for drawing this publication to my attention.

18. A list of journals and conferences is given in Appendix 1.

19. For a general discussion of the question of information retrieval in our particular context see Margaret D. Rouse-Jones, "Solving Reference Questions in the Caribbean: The University of the West Indies (Trinidad) Experience," *International Library Review* 18 (1986), 327-335.

20. See, e.g., items 2, 22, 30, 33, 38, 45, 64. See also Marshall, "A Review of Historical Writing, pp. 273, 288.

21. See, e.g, works by Annette Palmer, 52 and 53.

BIBLIOGRAPHY

Note: Three additional papers have been located since this paper was presented at the conference. They have been added at 30A, 56A, and 76A.

1   Basdeo, S. "Colonial Policy and Labour Organization in the British Caribbean, 1937-1939: An Issue in Political Sovereignty." *Boletín de Estudios Latino Americanos y del Caribe* 31 (1981), 119-129.

2   _____. "Indian Participation in Labour Politics in Trinidad, 1919-1939." Paper presented at "East Indians in the Caribbean: A Symposium on Contemporary Economic and Political Issues," St. Augustine, Trinidad, September 1979. Also published in *Journal of Indian History*, Diamond Jubilee volume (1982), 179-198.

3   _____. "Mitra Sinanan and Political Consciousness among Indians in Trinidad in the Thirties." Paper presented at the Third Conference on East Indians in the Caribbean, St. Augustine, Trinidad, August/September 1984.

4   _____. "The 1934 Indian Labour Disturbances in Trinidad: A Case Study in Colonial Labour Relations." Paper presented at "East Indians in the Caribbean: A Symposium on Contemporary Economic and Political Issues," St. Augustine, Trinidad, June 1975.

5   _____. "The Role of the British Labour Movement in the Development of Labour Organization in Trinidad, 1919-1929." Paper presented at the Eleventh Conference of Caribbean Historians, Curacao, April 1979.

6   _____. "The Role of the British Labour Movement in the Development of Labour Organization in Trinidad, 1929-1938." *Social and Economic Studies* 31:1 (1982), 40-73.

7   Blouet, Brian W. "Land Policies in Trinidad, 1838-50." *Journal of Caribbean History* 9 (May 1977), 43-59.

8   Boodhoo, Ken I. "Eric Williams: Economic Ideas and Policy." *Journal of Caribbean Studies* 3:1,2 (1982), 27-39.

9   Boodhoo, Ken I., and Ivan C. Harnanan. "The Caribbean Vision of Prime Minister, Dr. Eric Williams of Trinidad and Tobago." *Journal of Caribbean Studies* 5:1,2 (1985/86), 17-30.

10   Boomert, Arie. "The Arawak Indians of Trinidad and Coastal
      Guiana, ca 1500-1650." *Journal of Caribbean History* 19:2
      (November 1984), 123-188.

11   _____. "Our Amerindian Heritage." *Naturalist* 4:4 (1982),
      26-61.

12   Brereton, Bridget. "John Jacob Thomas: An Estimate." *Journal
      of Caribbean History* 9 (May 1977), 22-42.

13   _____. "The Liberal Press of Trinidad, 1869-1895." Paper
      presented at the Ninth Conference of Caribbean Historians,
      Cave Hill, Barbados, April 1977.

14   _____. "Post-Emancipation Protest in the Caribbean: The
      'Belmanna Riots' in Tobago, 1876." *Caribbean Quarterly*
      30:3/4 (1980), 110-123.

15   _____. "Sir John Gorrie: A Radical Chief Justice of Trinidad
      (1885-1892)." *Journal of Caribbean History* 13 (1980), 44-72.

16   Burton, Richard D. E. "Cricket, Carnival and Street Culture in
      the Caribbean." *British Journal of Sports History* 2:2 (1985),
      179-197.

17   Campbell, Carl C. "Charles Warner and the Development of
      Education Policy in Trinidad, 1838-70." *Journal of
      Caribbean History* 10 & 11 (1978), 54-81.

18   _____. "The College Exhibition in Trinidad and Tobago,
      1872-1938." *History Teachers' Journal* 2 (March 1983),
      43-52.

19   _____. "Education and Black Consciousness: The Amazing
      Captain J. O. Cutteridge in Trinidad and Tobago, 1921-42."
      Journal of Caribbean History 18 (1984), 35-66.

20   _____. "Good Wives and Mothers: A Preliminary Survey of
      Women and Education in Trinidad, 1834-1981." Paper
      presented at the Social History Workshop, Department of
      History, University of the West Indies, Mona, 1985.

21   _____. "Ralph Woodford and the Free Coloureds: The
      Transition from a Conquest Society to a Society of
      Settlement, Trinidad, 1813-1828." *Journal of Caribbean
      Studies* 2:2,3 (1981), 238-249.

22   _____. "The Rebel Priest: Francis De-Ridder and the Fight
      for Free Coloureds' Rights in Trinidad, 1825-1832." Paper
      presented at the Eleventh Conference of Caribbean
      Historians, Curacao, April 1979. Also published in *Journal
      of Caribbean History* 15 (1981), 20-40.

23   _____. "The Rise of a Free Coloured Plantocracy in Trinidad 1783-1813." *Boletín de Estudios Latino-Americanos y del Caribe* 29 (December 1980), 33-53.

24   Daly, Stephanie. "The Development of the Law Affecting East Indians in Trinidad and Tobago." Paper presented at the Third Conference on East Indians in the Caribbean, St. Augustine, Trinidad, August/September 1984.

25   Forbes, Richard Huntington. "Arya Samaj as Catalyst: The Impact of a Modern Hindu Reform Movement on the Indian Community of Trinidad between 1917 and 1939." Paper presented at "East Indians in the Caribbean: A Symposium on Contemporary Economic and Political Issues," St. Augustine, Trinidad, September, 1979.

26   _____. "Hindu Organizational Process in Acculturative Conditions: Significance of the Arya Samaj Experience in Trinidad." Paper presented at the Third Conference on East Indians in the Caribbean, St. Augustine, Trinidad, August/September 1984.

27   Friedman, Gerald C. "The Heights of Slaves in Trinidad." *Social Science History* 6:4 (Fall 1982), 482-515.

28   Hamel-Smith, Angela L. "Primary Education and East Indian Women in Trinidad, 1900-1956." Paper presented at the Third Conference on East Indians in the Caribbean, St. Augustine, Trinidad, August/September 1984.

29   Haraksingh, Kusha. "Cane Farming in Trinidad, 1919-1938: A Quantitative Exploration." Paper presented at the Ninth Conference of Caribbean Historians, Cave Hill, Barbados, April 1977.

30   _____. "Control and Resistance among Indian Workers: A Study of Labour on the Sugar Plantations of Trinidad, 1875-1917." Paper presented at "East Indians in the Caribbean: A Symposium on Contemporary Economic and Political Issues," St. Augustine, Trinidad, September, 1979. Also published in *Journal of Caribbean History* 14 (1981), 1-17.

30A   _____. "Estates, Labour and Population in Trinidad, 1870-1900." Paper presented at the Tenth Conference of Caribbean Historians, St. Thomas, U.S. Virgin Islands, 1978.

31 _____. "New Technology and Plantation Development in Trinidad, 1875-1980." Paper presented at the Twelfth Conference of Caribbean Historians, St. Augustine, Trinidad, March/April 1980.

32 _____. "Sugar Estates and Labour in Trinidad, 1838-1845." Paper presented at the Eleventh Conference of Caribbean Historians, Curacao, April 1979.

33 Higman, B. W. "African and Creole Slave Family Patterns in Trinidad." Paper presented at the Tenth Conference of Caribbean Historians, St. Thomas, U.S. Virgin Islands, 1978. Also published in *Journal of Family History* 3 (1978), 163-180.

34 _____. "Growth in Afro-Caribbean Slave Populations." *American Journal of Physical Anthropology* 50 (March 1979), 373-385.

35 Hope, Colin. "Dr. Eric Williams—His Work and Life: An Overview." *Bulletin of Eastern Caribbean Affairs* 7:3 (1981), 25-28.

36 Hosein, Fyard. "The Reception of Matrimonial Islamic Law in Trinidad and Tobago." Paper presented at the Third Conference on East Indians in the Caribbean, St. Augustine, Trinidad, August/September 1984.

37 Hydal, Maulana Mustapha Kemal. "The Religious Experience of the Indian in Trinidad: The Muslim Experience." Paper presented at the Third Conference on East Indians in the Caribbean, St. Augustine, Trinidad, August/September 1984.

38 Jacobs, W. Richard. "The Politics of Protest in Trinidad: The Strikes and Disturbances of 1937." St. Augustine, University of the West Indies, Department of Government, 1973. Revised version of a paper presented at the Fifth Conference of Caribbean Historians, April 3-13, 1973. Also published in *Caribbean Studies* 17:1,2 (1977), 5-54.

39 Jha, J. C. "The Background of the Legalisation of Non-Christian Marriages in Trinidad and Tobago." Paper presented at "East Indians in the Caribbean: A Symposium on Contemporary Economic and Political Issues," St. Augustine, Trinidad, September, 1979.

40   Johnson, Howard. "Oil Imperial Policy and the Trinidad Disturbances, 1937." *Journal of Imperial and Commonwealth History* 4:1 (1975), 29-54.

41   _____. "The Political Uses of Commissions of Enquiry (1): The Imperial Colonial West Indian Contest. The Foster and Moyne Commissions." *Social and Economic Studies* 27:3 (1976), 256-283.

42   Joseph, Cuthbert. "Eric Williams and Education in Trinidad and Tobago." *Journal of Caribbean Studies* 3:1,2 (1982), 41-47.

43   Laurence, K. M. "Continuity and Change in Trinidad Toponyms." *Nieuwe West-Indische Gids* 50 (1975), 123-142.

44   _____. "The Survival of the Spanish Languages in Trinidad." *Nieuwe West-Indische Gids* 54 (1980), 213-228.

45   Laurence, K. O. "The Tobago Slave Conspiracy of 1801." Paper presented at the Thirteenth Conference of Caribbean Historians, Guadeloupe, 1981. Also published in *Caribbean Quarterly* 28:3 (1982), 1-9.

46   _____. "Indians as Permanent Settlers in Trinidad before 1900." Paper presented at the Conference on Migration and Culture Contact in the Caribbean, University of the West Indies, Cave Hill, Barbados, April 1984.

47   _____. "The Restoration of Tobago to France in 1802." *Journal of Caribbean History* 16 (1982), 1-9.

48   McDonald, Ian. "Eric Williams: A Memory and a Tribute." *Journal of Caribbean Studies* 5:1,2 (Fall 1985/Spring 1986), 51-56.

49   Martin, Tony. "Marcus Garvey and Trinidad, 1912-1947." Paper presented at the Twelfth Conference of Caribbean Historians, St. Augustine, Trinidad, March/April 1980.

50   Newson, L. "Foreign Immigration in Spanish America: Trinidad Colonization Experiment." *Caribbean Studies* 19 (1979), 133-151.

51   Nicholls, David. "No Hawkers and Pedlars: Levantines in the Caribbean." *Ethnic and Racial Studies* 4:4 (October 1981), 415-431.

52   Palmer, Annette. "Black American Soldiers in Trinidad, 1942-44: Wartime Politics in a Colonial Society." *Journal of Imperial and Commonwealth History* 4:3 (1986), 203-218.

53   _____. "The Politics of Race and War: Black American
        Soldiers in the Caribbean Theater during the Second World
        War." *Military Affairs* 47:2 (1983), 59-62.

54   Ramesar, Marianne. "The Impact of the Indian Immigrants in
        Colonial Trinidad Society."   *Caribbean Quarterly* 22:1
        (March 1976), 3-18.

55   _____. "Patterns of Regional Settlement and Economic
        Activity by Immigrant Groups in Trinidad: 1851-1900."
        Social and Economic Studies 25:3 (1976), 187-215.

56   _____. "The Role of the British West Indian Immigrants in
        Trinidad, 1870-1921."   Paper presented at the Ninth
        Conference of Caribbean Historians, Cave Hill, Barbados,
        April 1977.

57   Reddock, Rhoda. "Indian Women and Indentureship in Trinidad
        and Tobago, 1845-1917: Freedom Denied."   Paper
        presented at the Third Conference on East Indians in the
        Caribbean, St. Augustine, Trinidad, August/September 1984.

58   Samaroo, Brinsley.   "Education as Socialization: Form and
        Content in the Syllabus in the Canadian Mission Pres-
        byterian School in Trinidad from the Late 19th Century."
        Paper presented at the Fifteenth Conference of Caribbean
        Historians, Mona, Jamaica, April 1983.

58A   _____. "The Mirror of War: Trinidad Newspaper Coverage
        of the First World War, 1914-1918." Paper presented at
        the Tenth Conference of Caribbean Historians, St. Thomas,
        U.S. Virgin Islands, 1978.

59   _____. "The Presbyterian Canadian Mission as an Agent of
        Integration in Trinidad during the 19th and 20th
        Centuries." *Caribbean Studies* 4:4 (1975), 41-55.

60   _____.   "The Trinidad Labour Party and the Moyne
        Commission, 1938." In *Politics, Society and Culture in the
        Caribbean: Selected Papers of the 14th Conference of
        Caribbean Historians*, Blanca G. Silvestrim, ed. San Juan,
        PR: University of Puerto Rico, 1983. Pp. 259-273.

61   _____. "The Vanguard of Indian Nationalism in Trinidad:
        The East Indian Weekly, 1928-1932." Paper presented at
        the Ninth Conference of Caribbean Historians, Cave Hill,
        Barbados, April 1977.

62   Sebastien, Raphael. "A Topology of the Caribbean Peasantry: The Development of the Peasantry in Trinidad, 1945-1917." *Social and Economic Studies* 29:2 (1980), 107-133.

63   Sheridan, Richard B. "Some Biographical and Historiographical Aspects of Eric Williams and his Capitalism and Slavery Book." Paper presented at the Conference on Capitalism and Slavery in the British West Indies: The Contribution of Eric Williams, Bellagio, Italy, May 1984.

64   Singh, Kelvin. "Adrian Cola Rienzi and the Labour Movement in Trinidad (1925-44)." Paper presented at the Eleventh Conference of Caribbean Historians, Curacao, April 1979. Also published in *Journal of Caribbean History* 16 (1982), 10-35.

65   _____. "The Diplomacy of the Patria-Patos Agreements of 1942." Paper presented at the Twelfth Conference of Caribbean Historians, St. Augustine, Trinidad, March/April 1980.

66   _____. "The Roots of Afro-Indian Conflict in Trinidad in the Indentureship Period." Paper presented at "East Indians in the Caribbean: A Symposium on Contemporary Economic and Political Issues," St. Augustine, Trinidad, September 1979.

67   Sutton, Paul. "Eric Williams as Scholar-Statesman: A Personal Appreciation." Paper presented at the Conference on Capitalism and Slavery in the British West Indies: The Contribution of Eric Williams, Bellagio, Italy, May 1984.

68   Temperley, Howard. "Eric Williams and the Abolitionists: A Study in Ambiguity." Paper presented at the Conference on Capitalism and Slavery in the British West Indies: The Contribution of Eric Williams, Bellagio, Italy, May 1984.

69   Tikasingh, Gerard. "Social Change in the Emerging Indian Community in Late 19th Century Trinidad." *Journal of Caribbean Studies* 1:2,3 (1980), 120-138.

70   _____. "The Representation of Indian Opinion in Trinidad, 1900-1921." Paper presented at "East Indians in the Caribbean: A Symposium on Contemporary Economic and Political Issues," St. Augustine, Trinidad, June 1975.

71   _____. "The Trinidad Press and the Issue of Immigration."
      Paper presented at the Ninth Conference of Caribbean
      Historians, Cave Hill, Barbados, April 1977.

72   Traboulay, David M. "The Indian Massacre of the Capuchins in
      Trinidad in 1699: A Fact in Trinidad's Economic
      Stagnation." *The Americas* 32:4 (April 1976), 544-548.

73   Trotman, D. "Protest in Post-Emancipation Trinidad: The
      Prisoner Riots of 1849." Paper presented at the Fifteenth
      Conference of Caribbean Historians, Mona, Jamaica, April
      1983.

74   _____. "The Yoruba and Orisha Workshop in Trinidad and
      British Guiana." *African Studies Review* 19:3 (September
      1976), 1-17.

75   _____. "Women and Crime in Late Nineteenth Century
      Trinidad." *Caribbean Quarterly* 30:3,4 (1984), 60-72.

76   Wilshire, Winston. "American Business Interests in Trinidad,
      1824-1906, from Consular Records." Paper presented at
      the Twelfth Conference of Caribbean Historians,
      St. Augustine, Trinidad, March/April 1980.

76A   _____. "The Commercial Development of Trinidad Lake
      Asphalt, 1888-1948." Paper presented at the Tenth
      Conference of Caribbean Historians, St. Thomas, U.S.
      Virgin Islands, 1978.

77   Winer, Lise. "Early Trinidad Creole: The Spectator Texts."
      English World-Wide 5:2 (1984), 181-210.

78   Winford, Donald. "'Creole' Culture and Language in Trinidad:
      A Socio-Historical Sketch." *Caribbean Studies* 15:3
      (October 1975), 31-56.

23. Al rescate del Caribe francés: Descripción de las colecciones de dos bibliotecas de la Ciudad de México

Marie-Claire F. de Figueroa

En tiempos difíciles surgen siempre ideas nuevas, métodos ingeniosos, brotes de imaginación, capaces de suplir las carencias de recursos, contrarrestar los efectos de estas carencias y descubrir caminos alternativos que conduzcan a la meta deseada. Para los países llamados del Tercer Mundo, la década de los ochenta no es precisamente alentadora en el campo intelectual. Los gobiernos luchan para que sus pueblos sobrevivan, para que el descontento no los sumerja. La clásica fórmula "panem et circenses" no ha envejecido; desgraciadamente, no incluye el maná espiritual, reservado para las épocas de vacas gordas. Sólo en tiempos de abundancia los encargados de los presupuestos se acuerdan de las necesidades intelectuales del pueblo en todos sus niveles y es cuando las bibliotecas pueden sacar algún provecho.

Para el Caribe en particular, el tiempo de abundancia ya pasó, y la recesión que los golpea, como a muchos, lo paraliza en sus actividades intelectuales: no hay presupuesto para las bibliotecas. Para evitar un desastroso estancamiento, varias soluciones están al alcance; una de ellas es el trueque ancestral: intercambiar los duplicados de una colección (o la publicación editada por una biblioteca) por algún material bibliográfico. Otra solución es el préstamo interbibliotecario o el envío de fotocopias. Para ésto, todos necesitamos saber de todos; de ahí la importancia de los catálogos colectivos. Pero la inversión en tiempo y recursos humanos es tal que muchas veces el resultado es desalentador: cuando existen catálogos, rara vez están actualizados, y los datos incluidos no siempre son veraces.

El propósito de este trabajo es describir los acervos de dos bibliotecas de México sobre la región del Caribe que más me interesa, por formar parte de la historia y del patrimonio de Francia, mi país de origen: el Caribe francés. Escogí el estudio de esta región por otra razón: su descuido total de parte de muchos bibliógrafos. Sentí la necesidad de rescatar esta "Cenicienta" del Caribe, el pariente pobre del área. Quisiera aprovechar para indicar unos ejemplos de una discriminación aparentemente deliberada de ciertos autores, quienes descartan de sus estudios, sin razón clara, el Caribe francés. No lo hago con un propósito rencoroso sino para ayudar a una toma de conciencia. Tal vez sea demasiado fuerte la palabra "deliberada," ya que según se vislumbra en la literatura, los bibliotecarios de las Antillas francesas se apartan o llegan en número muy reducido a las reuniones generales de las bibliotecas del Caribe. Según parece, existe poca comunicación entre las bibliotecas, tal vez porque los recursos son muy escasos y quizá también por la barrera del idioma. De todos modos, cuando se habla de unidad o de integración caribeña, es bien sabido que es muy artificial —¡siempre tenemos las "West Indies" por un lado y las "French West Indies" por otro!

Veamos en seguida unos ejemplos de este separatismo. El primero que lo denunció fue Eric Williams en 1954, en la introducción del artículo siguiente: "A Bibliography of Caribbean History: A Preliminary Essay" [I.12:208].*

International politics, in putting asunder what geography has joined together, has had the effect, in the field of historical research, of destroying the essential unity of Caribbean history and of segregating the scholars who have made this area their field of specialization. Historical research on the British West Indies has been generally distinguished by its ignorance and contempt of the contemporary French, Spanish, Dutch or Cuban material [. . .] the "parcellation" of the area is paralleled by the dispersation of the historical records. Linguistic difficulties aggravate a problem deeply noted in nationalism and insularity.

Los siguientes ejemplos vienen de los papeles del XXIV Seminario de la Adquisición de los Materiales Bibliotecarios de América Latina. En la introducción, el presidente Alma Jordan lamenta que "contributors solicited from the French and Dutch territories did not materialize to pull the strands together" [I.21:x]. Y durante la discusión en el Round Table on Caribbean Bibliographies, "The group wondered why the Netherlands and French West Indies were not included [in the *Caribbean Acronym List*], but felt that Mr. Freudenthal was probably writing only on the British Caribbean" [I.21:34]. Si el título no especificaba nada, bien podíamos esperar una lista de acrónimos de todo el Caribe.

En efecto, son muchas las obras que por su mismo título parecen incluir el Caribe en toda su extensión y, sin embargo, no es así. Veamos, por ejemplo, las "Bibliografías del Caribe" compiladas por el

---

*Este número refiere al apéndice, ítem y página de la citación.

Comité de Bibliografía de ACURIL, presentadas a la V Conferencia de ACURIL en Miami, en octubre de 1973:[1] entre los países citados no aparece ninguna región del Caribe francés en la bibliografía, aun cuando el título no especificaba esta limitación. Tampoco la presentación lo explica; no se puede sostener que el idioma fuera una barrera, ya que bibliografías en holandés sobre las Antillas holandesas están citadas.

Veamos por último la obra de Terry Dahlin y Reed Nelson: "Caribbean Religion: A Survey and Bibliography" [I.15]. Extrajimos lo siguiente de la presentación: "When considering the Caribbean area, the English-, Spanish- and Dutch-speaking Caribbean islands are emphasized, but some attention is also directed towards *adjacent*[2] countries . . ."

En cambio, cuando se habla de América Latina en general, y no aparece el Caribe francés, ya no se trata de discriminación. Si las ex-colonias no hispanas del Caribe están excluidas casi siempre de los estudios latinoamericanos, es porque tienen poco o ninguna relación en el diálogo y en los acontecimientos de América Latina. En efecto, no hay que olvidar que la población de esta región (incluyendo las Antillas británicas y holandesas) constituye menos del 2% de la de América Latina y ocupa menos del 1% del área geográfica.

Cerramos este paréntesis para proporcionar un esquema rápido de la ponencia. El desarrollo empezará con un esbozo geográfico-histórico, sin el cual no se entenderían cabalmente las otras secciones. En la parte principal del trabajo, descubriremos los nombres y las principales obras de los bibliógrafos pioneros que asentaron las bases sobre las cuales se edificaron las obras contemporáneas. En la segunda sección de esta parte principal, recordaremos los grandes temas de la colonia francesa, objeto de los estudios de los historiadores y de los bibliógrafos: esclavitud, negocios, plantaciones, religión, así como los temas de estudio de la época actual.

El trabajo no quedaría completo sin mencionar el estado de las bibliotecas y de la edición en algunos de los países del Caribe francés, así como las asociaciones científicas. Desgraciadamente, en varios casos no pudimos actualizar los datos por falta de información; por lo tanto, lo nuestro tampoco está muy actualizado: los resultados son parciales (en el sentido de incompletos), ya que las bibliotecas que sirvieron de fuente principal para este trabajo no lo tienen todo. Se trataba de aportar nuestro grano de arena, como parte de un conjunto que puede llegar a formarse con la ayuda de todos.

Finalmente, intentaremos concretizar unas recomendaciones, para evitar que se pierda lo más substancioso de este trabajo y de otros sobre el mismo tema. En los apéndices de este estudio, se agregó una bibliografía seleccionada, descriptiva del material encontrado en el acervo de la biblioteca "Daniel Cosío Villegas" de El Colegio de México, así como una bibliografía del material encontrado en el acervo de la biblioteca del Instituto Francés de América Latina (Institut Français d'Amérique Latine, IFAL) de la Ciudad de México.

Seleccionamos los acervos de estas dos bibliotecas porque son los más completos que existen en la capital y porque se complementan admirablemente. Una gran parte de la documentación de la biblioteca del IFAL no se encuentra en la biblioteca "Daniel Cosío Villegas" y viceversa. Pocas obras se duplican en versión original o en traducción. Por otra parte, es importante señalar que las obras y las revistas que componen el acervo del IFAL están solamente en francés mientras que en la biblioteca "Daniel Cosío Villegas" predominan las obras y revistas en inglés. Para no alargar el trabajo, las referencias del IFAL no se acompañaron de descripción.

Historia

Los Karibs fueron uno de los grupos étnicos descubiertos por los primeros colonizadores de las islas del Caribe y de los países cercanos. Desgraciadamente, no resistieron mucho tiempo a la crueldad de los invasores y no tardaron en extinguirse casi totalmente. Dejaron su nombre al mar que baña las costas orientales de los países de América Central, del Sureste de México y de la parte norte del continente sur, así como de todas las islas: Mar Caribe, región caribeña. En cuanto a las islas propiamente dichas, se les denomina la mayor parte del tiempo con el término de Antillas en español, Antilles en inglés y en francés, es decir, como lo indica su etimología latina "las islas de adelante." Los franceses las llaman también "Iles du Vent" o "Iles sous le Vent," de donde se deriva la palabra inglesa "Windward." Se acostumbra llamarlas también Indias occidentales (West Indies) en recuerdo de los viajes de Cristóbal Colón, quien estaba seguro de haber llegado a las Indias orientales. En cuanto a las posesiones francesas, se acostumbra en la literatura inglesa llamarlas French West Indies.

Cuando del Caribe se habla, pocas veces se encuentran nombrados estos DOM (Départements d'Outre-Mer) que forman parte de Francia, y como ya lo planteamos en la introducción, procuraremos sacarlos nuevamente a la luz, porque también tuvieron su época de esplendor. No nos limitaremos a los DOM: Santo Domingo merece un lugar en este trabajo por haber sido el objeto de múltiples estudios, tanto en francés como en inglés y español. No debemos olvidar que antes de convertirse en república de Haití formó parte del imperio francés durante un siglo. Veamos en seguida la lista de las regiones examinadas a lo largo de este trabajo: Martinica, Guadalupe, la Guyana francesa y la isla de Santo Domingo.

La Martinica es una isla volcánica situada a la mitad del arco de las Antillas más chicas, con una costa recortada y un terreno montañoso. Fue colonizada por europeos en 1635. Su nombre deriva de una vieja palabra karib que significa Isla de las flores. Dos acontecimientos importantes destacan en su historia: el primero fue el nacimiento de una niña llamada Josefina que se volvió emperatriz de los franceses por su matrimonio con Napoleón I; el otro fue la erupción del Monte Pelé, en 1902, que destruyó la ciudad de Saint-Pierre con su población entera de 20.000 habitantes.

Guadalupe fue colonizada por los franceses l'Olive y Duplessis en febrero de 1635; tomaron posesión de la isla en nombre de la Compagnie des Isles d'Amérique. El cultivo de la caña de azúcar se introdujo alrededor de 1650, y los franceses llevaron gran número de esclavos negros desde las costas de Africa occidental para trabajar en las plantaciones. Durante el período de la revolución francesa hubo una fuerte rebelión de esclavos; después, los ingleses ocuparon la isla por un corto período. Victor Hugues, enviado por la Convención francesa, volvió a ganarla para el gobierno revolucionario en 1794, fusiló y guillotinó buen número de colonos y pronunció la abolición de la esclavitud, que restableció Napoleón en 1802, pero fue definitivamente suprimida en 1848.

Para no extendernos demasiado, no describiremos en detalle las otras islas que dependen de la Guadalupe: Désirade, María Galante, Saint Barthélemy, Les Saintes, San Martín. San Kitts (nombre usual de Saint Christopher) fue colonizada por los franceses alrededor de 1627: se habían instalado en la isla en el extremo opuesto al que ocupaban los ingleses, sin que nadie se percatara del hecho al principio, pero los ingleses los expulsaron en 1713, con el tratado de Utrecht. Otras islas, tales como Santa Cruz, Tobago y Santa Lucía, estuvieron alternativamente en poder de ingleses y españoles. Como la influencia francesa fue de poca duración e importancia, no se estudiaron para este trabajo.

El conjunto de estas islas fue descubierto en 1493 por Cristóbal Colón, que puso el nombre de su caravela Marigalanda a la María Galante. En cuanto a Désirade fue una colonia de leprosos durante una temporada. Actualmente, al igual que Saint Barthélemy, tiene cultivos de algodón y vive del ganado y de la pesca. La caña de azúcar se cultiva en Désirade y en María Galante. Les Saintes se recuerda por la batalla que tuvo lugar el 12 de abril de 1782; fue la mayor victoria naval británica en las Antillas, que acabó definitivamente con la amenaza francesa para las posesiones inglesas del área. Compartieron San Martín holandeses y franceses, que se encontraron ahí por casualidad al mismo tiempo y se dividieron la isla en forma amistosa. En la actualidad exporta sal, algodón y ganado.

Martinica y Guadalupe fueron colonias de Francia hasta 1946, cuando escogieron ser parte integral de la república francesa bajo el nombre de Départements d'Outre-Mer (DOM). Su economía es bastante precaria, por dedicarse principalmente a la agricultura sin diversificación alguna: caña de azúcar y plátanos. Desprovistas de minerales y de industria (no la hay siquiera ligera), con una actividad pesquera muy rudimentaria, las islas se ven en la necesidad de importar la mayor parte de sus comestibles. Por otro lado, el clima, caracterizado por cataclismos naturales, nunca ha dejado de perturbar su economía. Sólo la industria hotelera está cobrando algo de importancia.

En la Guyana francesa se establecieron los franceses en 1676, después de dos intentos. La población progresó muy lentamente en el siglo XVIII, y las colonias desarrolladas con éxito por los Jesuitas desaparecieron después de la expulsión de la orden de la isla en 1767. En 1762, 12.000 personas fueron enviadas de Francia con promesas falsas, pero las condiciones eran tan duras que apenas 900 sobrevivieron al cabo de tres años. Pocas plantaciones de azúcar resistieron la abolición de la esclavitud en 1848. En 1852 se estableció la colonia penal, que recibió cerca de 70.000 convictos; el capitán Dreyfus [3] fue el más famoso de ellos. Se cerró en 1947. En 1946, el país eligió también el estatuto de DOM. En años recientes, el gobierno francés dotó a Guyana de varias escuelas, hospitales, vías de comunicación, etc. Pero dudamos de la bondad de los procedimientos franceses hacia la Guyana, ya que cerca de la ciudad de Kourou, instaló una base de lanzamiento de cohetes.

Haití no forma parte de las posesiones francesas en la actualidad, pero se incluye en nuestro estudio por su pasado histórico, ya que la antigua Saint Domingue fue francesa durante un siglo, desde 1697, cuando fue cedida por España, hasta 1804, año de su revolución por la cual se volvió República de Haití. Actualmente su lengua oficial sigue siendo el francés, aunque solamente 10% lo hablan; los demás hablan el criollo y la gran mayoría es analfabeta. Su economía, empobrecida por el régimen de los Duvalier, se reduce al cultivo de café, caña de azúcar y henequén. Sin embargo, tiene minas de bauxita y de cobre que forman una parte de sus exportaciones. Por lo menos 50% de sus importaciones provienen de Estados Unidos, que desde principios de siglo siguió de cerca los acontecimientos políticos de la isla, en parte para evitar una posible influencia de Cuba. Desde la huida de Duvalier, el país sigue padeciendo una fuerte inestabilidad política.

Bibliógrafos

En realidad, la mayor parte de nuestra bibliografía se refiere mucho más a la historia de estas islas; sin embargo, las guías bibliográficas modernas recogen también lo que se está escribiendo sobre las condiciones políticas, económicas y sociales actuales. En cuanto a la historia, vamos a hablar de algunos especialistas de las Antillas. Quizá el más importante especialista de las Antillas francesas sea Gabriel Debien. No sabemos mucho de su trayectoria académica; notamos que elaboró sus primeras bibliografías en el Institut Français d'Archéologie Orientale en El Cairo, Egipto, de donde tuvo que salir, como todos los franceses, al momento de la nacionalización del Canal de Suez. Después estuvo en Dakar como profesor de la Universidad. Posteriormente, encontramos su rastro en publicaciones de Haití (*Conjonction*), Guadalupe (*Bulletin de la Société d'Histoire de la Guadeloupe*). Siguen citados sus artículos en el *Handbook of Latin American Studies* [4] y otros índices hemerográficos.

Durante 20 años, Gabriel Debien publicó una interesantísima colección de bibliografías en la sección "Informaciones Bibliográficas Americanas" de la revista española *Anuario de Estudios Americanos* [I.25] y en una sección derivada de éste *Historiografía y Bibliografía Americanista* [I.26] en los volúmenes que aparecieron en 1954, 1958, 1960, 1963, 1967, 1968, 1971, 1972 y 1974. No son bibliografías comunes y corrientes; son realmente obras maestras que se leen como si fueran novelas históricas. Paralelamente a la lista de autores y de títulos, el autor pinta a grandes rasgos —es uno de sus méritos— la vida política, económica y social en las islas, vida de los colonos, vida de los esclavos. Nada de la aridez y del tedio de las bibliografías normales. El enorme interés radica en que Gabriel Debien *fait feu de tout bois*, es decir que utiliza cuantas fuentes tiene a la mano, y si no las tiene a la mano las busca y las lee. Escasas son las publicaciones que confiesa no haber leído. Señalamos a continuación la tipología de documentos incluidos a lo largo de sus numerosas bibliografías: trabajos universitarios como las tesis de maestría y las de doctorado; listas de las nuevas publicaciones periódicas, con sus principales características y estado de cada una a lo largo de su vida (a veces efímera, a veces duradera). Tal vez la característica más importante del contenido general es la abundancia de las obras de primera mano: documentos primarios tales como los de archivos y correspondencia (por ejemplo, la correspondencia general de los administradores), ensayos, notas, listas de pasaportes clasificados por puertos y conservados en los archivos nacionales; diarios náuticos y roles de la armada (con la descripción de los navíos, la lista del personal marinero, de los pasajeros del rey, de los de paga y de los contratados), minutas notariales de los siglos XVI, XVII y XVIII, donde se localizan los contratos de reclutamiento de los que se alquilaban para servir durante tres años; registros de los "certificados de identidad y de catolicidad"; registros parroquiales de las Antillas. Todas estas fuentes están descritas con gran minucia, datos curiosos, lenguaje muy pulido, a veces un tanto rebuscado. En varias ocasiones, el autor arremete contra las fuentes y los estudios norteamericanos, como podemos advertir en las dos citas siguientes:

> Avouons que nous n'avons pas cette fois poursuivi aussi méthodiquement les recherches dans les revues générales américaines. Elles ne présentent presque toujours que des articles de vulgarisation, et de quatrième main. Ils sont de mince apport. Leur récolte ne vaut pas la peine qu'elle donne. [I.25:20 (1963) 637]

> D'autres papiers, d'origine et d'interêt très divers sont aussi dans ce reposoir [Caribbean Acquisitions . . . by the University of Florida, 1964]. Je dis reposoir car on ne voit guère la curiosité des étudiants américains attirés vers ce miel. [I.25:22 (1965) 1018]

La mayor parte de sus bibliografías están muy bien estructuradas por capítulos y subcapítulos. Veamos, como ejemplo, una de las primeras, la de 1958 sobre Santo Domingo [I.25:15 (1958) 619-673]

I.   Bibliografía
    1.   Instrumentos bibliográficos
    2.   Reediciones
    3.   Repertorio de fuentes
    4.   Documentos en venta
    5.   Papeles pedidos, papeles encontrados
II.   El país
    1.   Viajes
    2.   Geografía y generalidades
    3.   Lengua y poesía
III. Historia religiosa
IV.   Esclavos
    1.   Para una demografía histórica de los esclavos
    2.   La trata
    3.   Legislación
    4.   Estudios locales
V.   Administradores, plantadores, plantaciones

VI.   La Revolución
        1. Estudios generales
        2. Constituyentes y colonos
        3. La insurrección de 1791
        4. Refugiados
        5. La expedición de 1802
        6. Toussaint L'Ouverture

La mayor parte de sus bibliografías sobre Saint Domingue/Haití siguen este modelo, prolongado posteriormente por dos secciones nuevas: Independencia—Hoy en día.

En ocasión de la celebración de los 150 años de su independencia, durante algún tiempo las obras sobre Haití proliferaron. Cabe señalar que Haití era la isla mejor provista en imprentas y la que más revistas publicaba. Guadalupe, Martinica y Guyana tuvieron también sus épocas de florecimiento cultural, pero siempre en un grado menor. Ciertos estudios de Gabriel Debien valen por la precisión de su análisis: estudio de los emigrados a las Antillas, por regiones de Francia de las cuales eran originarios; causas de las partidas: protestantes enviados en residencia vigilada (de Lorena, de los Cévennes, del Angoûmois . . .), malas cosechas en Normandía, etc.; estudio de los puertos franceses de donde salían los navíos de la trata de negros, los colonos y los contratados.

En sus introducciones a las bibliografías, el autor regresa constantemente a sus críticas de las fuentes y de sus autores: dispersión, desorden, heterogeneidad, multiplicación irracional de las revistas, muchas veces con corto destino, poca comunicación intelectual entre las islas (tienen más relaciones con Europa que entre sí); confusión frecuente de la literatura con la historia.

Me permitiré hacer una crítica al autor y a los editores de sus bibliografías. Muchas imprecisiones entorpecen a veces el texto: la naturaleza de ciertos documentos podría ser una causa; también el estilo llega a veces al borde de lo críptico, por el uso de metáforas obscuras que dejan duda sobre lo que quiso expresar. Por otra parte, las bibliografías que fueron traducidas al español contienen muchos galicismos. Reprocharía a los editores una edición muy descuidada, con gran cantidad de errores tipográficos. En cuanto al contenido, hubiera preferido menos citas sobre las otras Antillas (españolas, holandesas, británicas, americanas). A menudo era necesario para fomentar estudios comparativos, pero, como decimos en francés *trop, c'est trop.*

Hablaré más brevemente de los demás. El historiador Eric Williams elaboró una excelente bibliografía sobre la historia del Caribe

entre 1492 y 1898. Profesor en ciencias sociales y políticas en la
Howard University en Washington, D.C., fue "Deputy Chairman" de la
Comisión Caribeña del Consejo Caribeño de Investigación, presidente
de la Sociedad Histórica de Trinidad y Tobago, y Primer Ministro del
país. Compiló y editó series de documentos sobre la historia de las
Antillas británicas y fue editor de la revista *Caribbean Historical Review*.
En 1954 el número 3/4 de esta última publicó "A Bibliography of
Caribbean History: A Preliminary Essay," Parte 1, 1492-1898 [I.12]. La
introducción está citada al principio del presente trabajo, ya que fue el
primero o uno de los primeros en señalar la discriminación, entre los
investigadores, del material que no pertenece al ámbito anglo-
americano. Al principio de su artículo, Williams indica que no existe
todavía bibliografía caribeña sino intentos aislados limitados a regiones,
períodos o temas específicos. La lista que nos proporciona de estos
pioneros es corta pero indispensable. Su bibliografía se extiende
después en cinco períodos, de los cuales examinamos dos: la rivalidad
anglo-francesa (de 1656 a 1783) y la abolición de la esclavitud (de 1784
a 1898). Sus comentarios, las anotaciones a algunas referencias
específicas, son adiciones valiosas a su obra [I.12,14; II.20].

Uno de los escritores sobre el cual hace hincapié es el político del
siglo XVIII: Moreau de Saint Méry [I.44]. Cuatro años después,
Gabriel Debien retomará la misma opinión: "Todo estudio de Santo
Domingo comienza por Moreau de Saint Méry. [La edición de 1958
de su Descripción de la parte francesa de Santo Domingo] es al
documento fundamental de conocimiento cuando se quiere ver la
secuencia exacta del desarrollo de un distrito, de una cultura, de un
pueblo, o situar una plantación" [I.25:15(1958)623].

Max Bissainthe fue el gran bibliógrafo de Saint Domingue-Haití.
Director de la Biblioteca Nacional de Haití, fue también inspector
general de las bibliotecas de Haití. Trabajó sin descansar pero salió de
su país para ir a vivir a Estados Unidos, de donde siguió enviando
material bibliográfico. Su obra fue continuada por el bibliotecario del
Instituto Francés de Haití, Wilfrid Bertrand, y por Léon François
Hoffmann que publican regularmente listas actualizadas en la revista
franco-haitiana *Conjonction* [I.38,62].

Para la isla de la Martinica, unos investigadores del Centre
d'Etudes Régionales Antilles-Guyane (CERAG) recopilaron una
bibliografía muy completa que se publicó como suplemento de los
Cahiers du CERAG [I.30,34,55; II.73]. Para establecer listas sobre
Guadalupe y Guyana francesa, bastaría recorrer los capítulos escritos
por Gabriel Debien y las secciones bibliográficas de la revista
Caribbean Studies [I.61].

La gran especialista actual es sin duda Lambros Comitas, profesor de antropología y educación en el Teachers College de la Universidad de Columbia, Nueva York, y director en la misma universidad del Instituto de Estudios Latinoamericanos e Ibéricos. Autor de una gran obra *The Complete Caribbeana 1900-1975* [I.5], está encargado de las bibliografías de etnología en las secciones correspondientes del *Handbook of Latin American Studies* [I.8]. Las introducciones a las bibliografías son una excelente muestra del esmero y de la minucia con que compila la información. Finalmente, se debe mencionar la obra recientemente compilada por Lionel Loroña: *A Bibliography of Latin American and Caribbean Bibliographies: Annual Report 1985-1986.* [5] Ojalá tengamos una feliz sorpresa al hojearla cuando llegue a México.

Temas

Los grandes temas estudiados por los bibliógrafos fueron muchas veces comunes a todo el Caribe, especialmente durante la colonia francesa.   Posteriormente, cada región tomó un giro diferente, dependiendo un poco de los acontecimientos de su metrópoli. Después de los descubrimientos sucesivos de Cristóbal Colón, lo primero que se registra es la historia de los pioneros, nada menos que la de los bucaneros y la de los filibusteros, tantas veces confundidos. [6] Españoles, holandeses, ingleses, daneses, portugueses y franceses, cada uno trabajaba para su país. Algunos se establecieron en las islas; a éstos se sumaron posteriormente, en las Antillas francesas, los colonos y los "contratados" por tres años, venidos de la metrópoli. Fue el inicio de las grandes plantaciones, desde el siglo XVI. Escribió el historiador Eric Williams: "The history of the Caribbean is a history of sugar." [7] Pronto se hizo sentir una gran falta de mano de obra y se inició el comercio de los negreros, que durante tres siglos no interrumperían sus viajes triangulares: zarpaban de los puertos franceses (Dieppe en el Canal de la Mancha, Brest, Nantes, Rochefort, La Rochelle y Burdeos en el Atlántico), llegaban a las costas de África occidental para tomar esclavos (Guinea, Costa de Marfil, Senegal, etc.) y, de regreso, los desembarcaban en las Antillas, en donde los sobrevivientes se vendían en subasta a los plantadores (a veces moría más del 50% por las epidemias y la poca resistencia a unas condiciones de viaje infrahumanas). En las plantaciones, las condiciones de trabajo eran desiguales según los colonos que los hacían trabajar, pero, por lo general, los esclavos eran tratados muy mal; la mayor parte debían realizar faenas excesivamente duras, a cambio de las cuales recibían una mala alimentación y un alojamiento que carecía de la higiene más elemental. Sin embargo, hubo ciertos esfuerzos para proteger a los esclavos. Luis XIV emitió el famoso *Code Noir*, especie de Carta destinada a amparar a los esclavos y a controlar las relaciones sociales entre blancos y negros. En este código estaban cubiertos los aspectos siguientes: bienestar material y religioso, castigo por ofensas, derecho a apelar a las Cortes en caso de malos tratos de parte de los amos, emancipación y mezcla de razas. Desgraciadamente, pocas veces fue aplicada en toda su extensión; se respetó más en las islas pequeñas y en Guyana que en Santo Domingo en donde una larga tradición de violencia, de codicia y de crueldad, heredada tal vez de los bucaneros, era difícilmente compatible con el código.

Este tema de la esclavitud inspiró a muchos escritores, poetas y novelistas, y permitió denunciar a los historiadores, después de las odiseas de los navíos negreros y las condiciones precarias de la vida de los esclavos, los primeros resquebrajos del sistema; se empezaron o oír las primeras voces a favor de la abolición, Adam Smith en Inglaterra [8] y los fisiócratas en Francia. Los primeros esfuerzos de los colonos para liberar a sus esclavos, las fugas continuas de los que eran maltratados sin esperanza de liberación, las primeras rebeliones de las bandas de esclavos de Santo Domingo refugiadas en el norte de la isla en los albores de su independencia, fueron y siguen siendo objeto de numerosos estudios de historiadores, sociólogos, politólogos, etc. Los últimos años del siglo XVIII, "El siglo de las luces" [I.16], ven, al mismo tiempo, el fin de la epopeya de Toussaint L'Ouverture, primer héroe de la Independencia haitiana, y las contradicciones de una abolición de la esclavitud todavía inestable, entre el sí de la Convención durante la Revolución francesa, el no de Napoleón que restableció la esclavitud y finalmente el sí definitivo, en 1848.

El vaivén de los mercaderes entre Francia y las Antillas fue lo bastante notable como para favorecer el desarrollo de investigaciones históricas. En la mayor parte de los casos, los plantadores no lograban comprar y desarrollar sus plantaciones sin la edificación previa de una fortuna que les permitía entonces esta inversión nada trivial. La mayoría conseguía esta fortuna gracias al comercio. Existía toda una clase mercantilista, no siempre de lo más honesta, ya que evadía impuestos, burlaba reglamentos y aduanas, etc. Estos reglamentos eran muy estrictos; reservaban la exclusividad del comercio a la metrópoli, que aprovechaba para imponer sus condiciones financieras nada favorables a los colonos cada vez más descontentos, quienes trataron entonces de diversificar sus exportaciones, estableciendo tratos clandestinos con otros países.

Además de la vida de los comerciantes, se describió con gran lujo de detalles la vida de los colonos en las plantaciones. Algunos de los escritores modernos se esforzaron por destruir el mito de un lujo desenfrenado en las principales ciudades de las Antillas y en las grandes plantaciones. Según ellos, esto no corresponde a la realidad: el trabajo era muy duro, el rendimiento económico bastante parco, las condiciones climatológicas a veces fatales para la caña de azúcar, el café, las plantaciones de índigo y algodón. La vida era monótona y difícil, a pesar de la legendaria alegría criolla. Las calles de las ciudades estaban mal cuidadas y mal olientes, las casas carecían de higiene. Es cierto que algunos colonos poseían muebles de gran precio importados de Europa, y algunas esposas de colonos vestían magníficos atuendos, pero éstas eran excepciones; al final del siglo, la competencia de la remolacha azucarera con la caña de azúcar y la abolición de la esclavitud asestaron un duro golpe a muchos plantadores, que vieron llegar tiempos todavía más difíciles con problemas que, hasta la fecha, no han logrado superar.

Uno de los temas más atractivos para los historiadores de las Antillas es el de la religión, sobre todo la de los negros, que constituían la mayoría. ¡Cuántas obras se han escrito sobre el Vodú, religión afroantillana por excelencia! Mencionaremos aquí el nombre de Alfred Métraux [II.46,65], etnólogo francés, autor de numerosos libros sobre el tema. Es importante recordar también las obras sobre las misiones católicas francesas y, sobre todo, lo que se ha escrito sobre el protestantismo y los deportados en la época posterior a la revocación del Edicto de Nantes en 1685 (error político muy burdo de Luis XIV). Los que tenían parientes en las islas se reunían con ellos allá, donde se encontraban en residencia vigilada muy relativa. Acerca del protestantismo en Santo Domingo, Catts Pressoir escribe lo siguiente: "Les sources du protestantisme haïtien sont bien anglaises et américaines. Le protestantisme français n'a exercé sur nous qu'une action indirecte: par ses ouvrages religieux, son hymnologie, sa liturgie, ses journaux et ses revues." [9]

En cuanto a los temas actuales que hallamos con más frecuencia en los índices bibliográficos, giran alrededor de las condiciones políticas, económicas y sociales de la región. Brotes de independencia, problemas de índole agrícola, financiero o comercial, movimientos de población en el interior o hacia el exterior, son a grandes rasgos lo más significativo de los estudios sobre el Caribe francés de hoy.

Bibliotecas y colecciones

Inicio ahora la última sección, sobre el estado de las bibliotecas y de las colecciones en el Caribe francés, pero debo señalar de antemano que carezco de datos muy recientes sobre el particular. Me hubiera gustado encontrar, para el Caribe francés, unos artículos tan bien documentados y tan completos como los que escribió Alma Jordan en los años 70 sobre las bibliotecas del Caribe anglófono, sus finanzas, servicios, colecciones, edificios, usuarios, personal y sobre la profesión de bibliotecario. [10] Del mismo autor, citemos también *The Development of Library Service in the West Indies through Inter-Library Cooperation.* [11] No tenemos nada similar para el Caribe francés, pero podemos esbozar un panorama aceptable juntando artículos y datos recogidos aquí y allá.

Entre los países que abarca este estudio, Haití ha sido el de vanguardia en cuanto a bibliotecas, imprentas y edición. Cabe señalar aquí el excelente trabajo de Lygia Ballantyne: "Haitian Publications: An Acquisitions Guide and Bibliography," presentado en la reunión de SALALM en Pasadena en 1979 [I.21]. En su estudio, se extiende sobre el comercio de libros (editores, libreros, control bibliográfico), sobre las publicaciones oficiales, académicas y de los organismos oficiales, finalmente sobre las bibliotecas y los servicios de documentación.

Valerie Bloomfield en 1974 [I.1], Léon François Hoffmann en un número de *Conjonction* de 1977 [I.62] y Lygia Ballantyne en su trabajo de 1980 [I.36], concuerdan en que es muy difícil conseguir obras haitianas, porque se tiran a pocos ejemplares (unos centenares) que se agotan rápidamente. Afortunadamente, las ediciones Kraus Reprints, de Nedeln (Lichtenstein), las ediciones Fardin de Port-au-Prince, Lemeac de Montreal y el Club de los Amigos del Libro Haitiano han reeditado o reproducido buen número de textos. En el número de diciembre de 1975 de *Conjonction*, Wilfrid Bertrand, bibliotecario y compilador de las bibliografías editadas allí, hace el recuento de las bibliotecas públicas, universitarias, especializadas y escolares, y describe sus características físicas: locales, mobiliario, colecciones; un capítulo está dedicado a la estructura administrativa y funcional: personal, reglamentos, adquisiciones, clasificación y catalogación, servicios, estadísticas de asistencia. El cuadro descrito por W. Bertrand es pesimista porque, según él, existe un vicio de base, causa de una gran parte de los males padecidos por las bibliotecas haitianas: la falta de preparación de los bibliotecarios, que resulta en una mala organización general y un número de usuarios demasiado restringido. En 1976, se inauguró la nueva biblioteca del Instituto Francés de Haití y una descripción de sus servicios se encuentra en el número 132 de 1976 de *Conjonction*.

Para el resto de la región, tuve más dificultades al reunir documentación. Esta es una información sobre los archivos de Guadalupe:

Los Archivos fueron organizados en 1951. Siendo la Guadalupe un Departamento francés de ultramar, están supervisados de acuerdo con las leyes en vigor en la metrópoli. Todo el material anterior a 1920 está a la disposición de los investigadores. El edificio, a prueba de fuego, es de piedra y concreto con un techo especial para protegerse de los huracanes. Los estantes son de acero. En conección con los Archivos se encuentra una pequeña biblioteca histórica y administrativa, fundada en 1960. Además de estos archivos públicos, el archivista es responsable y supervisa el material de cada municipio. Se han microfilmado archivos que se refieren a la Guadalupe en Europa, especialmente en Francia y en Inglaterra . . . . [I.20:6] [12]

Por otra parte, el 14 de enero de 1966 se inauguró un sistema ambulante de libros establecido por el Consejo General de Guadalupe. Sus oficinas principales están situadas en Basse-Terre (Bibliothèque Centrale de Prêt de la Guadeloupe). Se encuentran también aquí los "Archives Départementales."

Para Martinica, tenemos una ponencia escrita en 1975 por Anne Marie Blanc sobre la formación del personal en las Antillas francesas [I.28]. Indica que la situación de las bibliotecas es similar en Guadalupe y Martinica, por lo que profundiza solamente sobre esta última. Enumera las diferentes bibliotecas con que cuenta, así como los servicios que presta a sus usuarios.

En cuanto a la Guyana francesa, es triste pensar que nunca ha sido un centro privilegiado de estudios; cuando uno se ocupa de su pasado, es la historia del presidio que viene a la mente. En cuanto a su presente, no hemos conseguido más datos sobre sus bibliotecas que los en *World of Learning*. El panorama de la enseñanza superior en los Departamentos franceses de ultramar (que incluyen las sociedades científicas e instituciones de investigación, además de las bibliotecas) publicado por *World of Learning*, completará los datos antes mencionados. [13]

Terminaremos por el Centre d'Etudes Régionales Antilles-Guyane (CERAG). Este centro, que depende de la Universidad de Burdeos, publica [14] *Les Cahiers du CERAG*, con una importante contribución a la historia, la política, la economía y la historia social y legislativa de las tres regiones. En el Apéndice I de esta ponencia, hemos resumido dos de ellos, uno sobre los problemas universitarios de las Antillas y de la Guyana francesa [I.30], y otro sobre la esclavitud en Guyana francesa en el siglo XVIII [I.34]. El cuaderno n° 22, sobre Burdeos, las Antillas (1830-1838) y la crisis económica y política de la esclavitud, tiene un interés especial. Para más detalles sobre el Centro, véase el artículo de R. Jouandet-Bernadat [I.29].

Como lo indicamos en nuestra última nota, no tenemos noticias de *Les Cahiers du CERAG*, desde 1982. Este silencio total de una revista de investigación seria y la imposibilidad de localizarla en el *Ulrich* [15] son una muestra de la poca publicidad que hacen los francoparlantes en la región. Son responsables en gran parte de su aislamiento, lo que disminuye seriamente el interés de los hispano y angloparlantes hacia ellos. El factor económico contribuye también al empobrecimiento general de los presupuestos, de las ideas, del personal y de las colecciones. De la misma manera que la Hispanic Division de la Biblioteca del Congreso envió a una investigadora para realizar una encuesta muy completa sobre el panorama bibliotecario y editorial de Haití, sería posible hacer algo similar para los DOM. Desde el punto de vista de la lógica, Francia sería el país indicado, pero "ojos que no ven, corazón que no siente"; también la distancia es un factor determinante.

Por otro lado, no se trataría solamente de hacer el recuento de las bibliotecas y de los acervos; se debe mejorar la preparación de los encargados de las colecciones y de los que atienden a los usuarios. Sería muy buena obra, tal vez en el marco de algún organismo internacional (OEA, UNESCO), enviar un especialista de habla francesa para organizar cursillos prácticos y capacitar más bibliotecarios con el fin de completar el personal reclutado por Francia o el personal de Haití. La unión hace la fuerza: sólo así se podrá superar las deficiencias que existen en el presente y evitar un mayor deterioro de las condiciones actuales.

Por último, como lo planteamos al principio, esperamos que los dos apéndices bibliográficos contribuyan a compensar la carencia de material de algunas bibliotecas sobre el Caribe francés, aportando una información útil y abundante a los estudiosos del tema.

NOTAS

1. Association of Caribbean University and Research Libraries, Committee on Bibliography, "Bibliografías del Caribe," [o Bibliografía de . . .] en *El Papel de la biblioteca en el desarrollo de un país: Documentos oficiales de la quinta conferencia anual de ACURIL* (San Juan, PR: Asociación de Bibliotecas Universitarias y de Investigación del Caribe, 1978).

2. Letra cursiva de la autora.

3. Alfred Dreyfus, acusado injustamente de hacer vendido secretos militares a Alemania y condenado a deportación perpetua a la isla del Diablo.

4. En el *Handbook of Latin American Studies* encontramos citada una última bibliografía: "Chronique bibliographique de l'histoire des Antilles françaises," *Bulletin de la Société d'Histoire de la Guadeloupe* 35 (janvier-avril 1978), 11-46.

5. Lionel Loroña, *Bibliography of Latin American and Caribbean Bibliographies: Annual Report, 1985-1986* (Madison, WI: Secretariat, Seminar on the Acquisition of Latin American Library Materials, Memorial Library, University of Wisconsin-Madison, 1986).

6. El término de bucaneros se refiere a los piratas que abordaban las islas para saquear a los campesinos, robándoles sobre todo el ganado; en cuanto a los filibusteros, eran los famosos corsarios que perseguían las embarcaciones enemigas y se apoderaban de ellas, así como de las mercancías que transportaban. A veces los bucaneros se volvían filibusteros. Se debe aclarar que estas definiciones varían de un autor a otro.

7. Eric Williams, "The Sugar Economy of the Caribbean," *Caribbean Historical Review* 2 (1951), 142.

8. Adam Smith, *Inquiry into the Nature and Causes of the Wealth of Nations* (London: Printed for W. Strahan and T. Cadell, 1776).

9. Catts Pressoir, *Le Protestantisme Haïtien*, vol. 1 (Port-au-Prince: Impr. de la Société Biblique et des Livres Religieux d'Haïti, 1945), 50.

10. Alma Jordan, "Libraries and Librarianship in the Commonwealth Caribbean," *Caribbean Quarterly* 18 (September 1972), 43-50, por un ejemplo.

11. Alma Jordan, *The Development of Library Service in the West Indies through Inter-Library Cooperation* (Metuchen, NJ: Scarecrow Press, 1970).

12. Texto original en inglés.

13. "French Overseas Departments," *The World of Learning 1988*, 38th ed. (London: Europa Publications, Ltd., 1987), 471-472.

14. Dejó de llegar a México en 1982 (no. 39). Ignoramos si se suspendió temporal o definitivamente .

15. No aparece en ninguna de las dos secciones del *Ulrich's International Periodicals Directory 1987-88*, 26th ed., 2 vols. (New York, NY: R. R. Bowker, 1987) y *Irregular Serials and Annuals 1987-88: An International Directory*, 13th ed. (New York, NY: R. R. Bowker, 1987).

APÉNDICE I

EL COLEGIO DE MÉXICO, A.C.
Biblioteca "Daniel Cosío Villegas"
Principales obras sobre el Caribe francés

Area del Caribe
Adquisición de libros

1. Bloomfield, Valerie. "Caribbean Acquisitions," en *Caribbean Studies*, 13,4 (Jan 1974), 86-110.

Desde la introducción, la autora, de nacionalidad inglesa, nos informa que la meta de su investigación es el Caribe no hispánico. Define las regiones estudiadas y de inmediato sabemos que Guyana y las Antillas francesas están incluidas. El artículo consiste en dos partes.

I. Caribbean in Prints. El comercio local de libros ha sido muy lento en desarrollarse aunque se vislumbra un poco mejor hoy en día. Sin embargo, la dispersión de las fuentes sigue siendo grande y los libros son de tiraje limitado. Unos cuadros resumen la producción de libros en el Caribe y la adquisición de libros caribeños. Las estadísticas son de 1969 y muestran perfectamente la diferencia de producción en cada país y la superioridad de las Antillas inglesas. En cuanto a editores, la autora especifica que la mayor parte de las publicaciones oficiales de las Antillas francesas se publican en París. Solamente unos cuantos documentos salen mimeografiados en las Antillas. En cuanto a Universidades e Institutos de investigación, el artículo menciona el Centre d'Etudes Régionales Antilles-Guyane en la Martinica y el Office de la Recherche Scientifique et Technique d'Outre Mer en Guyana. En cuanto a bibliotecas, la única mencionada es La Bibliothèque des Archives Départementales de la Guadeloupe. Dos asociaciones son citadas: Société d'Histoire de la Guadeloupe y Société d'Histoire de la Martinique; cada una publica un boletín.

II. Publications on the Caribbean. Estas dependen de las relaciones de los territorios con sus metrópolis y de ciertos factores culturales y geopolíticos. El aporte de los *emigrados* hacia Europa y Norteamérica no es despreciable y ha sido siempre bien recibido en las naciones a donde llegaron.

No hay que olvidar el turismo que desarrolló una abundante literatura de información en los países industrializados. La autora se extiende sobre las dos principales fuentes bibliográficas de la época y enfatiza sus similitudes y discrepancias: *Current Caribbean Bibliography* y la sección bibliográfica trimestral de *Caribbean Studies.*

Bibliografías

2. Arencibia, Yolanda, comp. *El Caribe, bibliografía selectiva.* Comp. por . . . y Ada Carracedo. La Habana: UNESCO, Oficina Regional de Cultura para América Latina y el Caribe, Centro de Documentación, 1983. (La Cultura en América Latina, Bibliografía, 7). 27 p.

Bibliografía seleccionada del material contenido en el Centro de Documentación arriba mencionado; 4 secciones: (A) Bibliografías temáticas, (B) Libros y folletos, (C) Artículos de revistas, (D) Otras fuentes (muy importantes).

La sección (B) Libros y folletos y la (C) Artículos de revistas recogen 40 referencias sobre el Caribe francófono sin contar las citas de interés general.

3. *Bibliografía actual del Caribe.* V. 1, 1951–. Comp. y edit. por el personal de la Biblioteca Regional del Caribe. Hato Rey, Puerto Rico: Biblioteca Regional del Caribe, Centro Norte-Sur. Títulos en inglés, francés y español.

La bibliografía es el producto de la colaboración de varias bibliotecas del Caribe, cuya lista aparece al principio. En los 1970 (no pudimos consultar nada de los 80) la participación del Caribe francófono se reducía a la de Haití. Así que el material sobre los demás países es parco, pero útil.

4. *Bulletin bibliographique Amérique Latine; analyse des publications françaises et recherche bibliographique automatisée sur le fichier FRANCIS.* Paris: Recherche sur les Civilisations, nº 1, 1981–. Anual.

Este boletín informa al público científico acerca de los trabajos sobre Ciencias Humanas en América Latina difundidos o editados en Francia. Contiene únicamente referencias a publicaciones en ciencias sociales y humanas en *lengua francesa.* Buenos análisis abajo de cada referencia.

5. Comitas, Lambros, comp. *The Complete Caribbeana, 1900-1975: A Bibliographic Guide to the Scholarly Literature* [comp. by] . . . , under the auspices of the Research Institute for the Study of Man. Millwood, NY: KTO, [c 1977]. 4 vols. Contenido: V. 1. People. V. 2. Institutions. V. 3. Resources. V. 4. Indexes.

Esta obra bibliográfica está organizada por temas con nueve secciones divididas a su vez en un total de 63 capítulos. Las secciones principales son las siguientes: Introducción al Caribe; El pasado; La población; Elementos de cultura; Salud, educación y bienestar; Política (Political Issues); Actividades e instituciones socioeconómicas; Ecología y geografía humana; Suelos, cosechas y ganado.

El material bibliográfico en francés y sobre áreas francesas es muy importante. A la inversa de muchas otras publicaciones, ésta excluye a Haití y a Santo Domingo precisamente para no duplicar las bibliografías que existen ya sobre la antigua Hispaniola. Todo lo demás tiene los elementos comunes a los de un estudio desde el punto de vista histórico, estructural y económico.

Es de señalar el esfuerzo del compilador para reunir lo que estuvo diseminado tanto tiempo y para atender lo que estuvo tan descuidado.

6. EE.UU. Department of the Army. Army Library. *Latin America and the Caribbean: Analytical Survey of Literature, 1969 ed.* Washington, DC: [GPO], 1969. 319 p. Ilus. 4 mapas (DA PAM 550-7).

La primera parte de la obra está formada por una bibliografía comentada en la cual Haití aparece bajo los aspectos siguientes: 1. Miscellaneous; 2. Borders and boundaries; 3. Haiti-Dominican Republic, 1963— conflict; 4. Government and politics. En la segunda parte, Haití y los países del Caribe francés tienen una ficha completa (Background Note) sobre población, historia, política y gobierno, economía, relaciones exteriores, etc. . . . y política de Estados Unidos con cada uno de ellos. Un mapa y una corta bibliografía completan cada una de estas fichas.

7. *HAPI. Hispanic American Periodicals Index*, 1974—. Los Angeles, CA: UCLA Latin American Center Publications. Anual. Editor, Barbara G. Valk.

Este índice hemerográfico proporciona poco material sobre el Caribe francés; se comprende en parte porque, de acuerdo con el título, éste no forma parte de América Latina. Sin embargo, no se puede aislar totalmente del conjunto caribeño: se encuentran algunas referencias interesantes. A primera vista las revistas que más material aportan son *Amérique Latine, Cahiers des Amériques Latines, Caribbean Studies, Journal de la Société des Américanistes* y para Haití: *Conjonction: Revue Franco-haïtienne.*

8. *Handbook of Latin American Studies.* N° 1, 1935—. Gainesville: University of Florida Press. Anual.

Esta excelente herramienta bibliográfica no decepciona porque sus estudios sobre el Caribe incluyen a la región de habla francesa sin discriminación alguna. Para conseguir material sobre las Antillas, se busca cada isla por su nombre así como por Greater Antilles, Lesser Antilles, French West Indies; finalmente se busca por French Guiana y Haití para estos dos países. Al principio de cada sección se encuentra un prefacio escrito por un especialista en la materia que expone a grandes rasgos los avances más recientes en las investigaciones y cita los trabajos sobresalientes. En la sección de Ciencias Sociales destaca Lambros Comitas que se encarga de las bibliografías de etnología en el Caribe.

9.   *ISLA. Information Services on Latin America.* V. 1—, n° 1—, 1970[?]. Oakland, CA. Mensual.

Se trata de un conjunto de recortes de la prensa norteamericana e inglesa organizados por regiones de América Latina. En la sección intitulada "Caribbean" se encuentran artículos sobre los Departamentos de Ultra Mar de Francia en el Caribe (Antillas y Guyana francesa) en gran mayoría sobre aspectos políticos y económicos.

10.   Lambert Gaborit, Michel. *Bibliographie latino-américaniste, 1959-1972.* México: IFAL, 1973. 159 p.

11.   Lambert Gaborit, Michel. *Bibliographie latino-américaniste; livres publiés en langue française, 1972-1982.* México: Universidad Autónoma Metropolitana-Azcapotzalco/IFAL, 1983. Sin pag.

Esta bibliografía y el número 10 se elaboraron a partir de bibliografías en existencia. El índice temático muy detallado y muy bien organizado es una excelente herramienta para el manejo de estas dos obras. A primera vista se da uno cuenta de que el Caribe francófono tiene un lugar bastante importante en esta bibliografía.

12.   Williams, Eric. "A Bibliography of Caribbean History: A Preliminary Essay; Part I, 1492-1898." *Caribbean Historical Review,* nos. 3-4 (Dec. 1954), 208-250.

El autor fue uno de los primeros en denunciar la diseminación de las fuentes debido a la heterogeneidad de las islas dispersadas por la política internacional.

Williams divida la historia del Caribe en 5 períodos y los que más nos interesan son el segundo: "La rivalidad anglo francesa, 1656-1783" y el tercero: "La abolición de la esclavitud, 1704-1898." (El autor termina su artículo después de este período sin abordar los últimos dos.) En lo que concierne a la rivalidad anglo francesa, la bibliografía, bastante abundante, está subdividida en los rubros siguientes: (a) Material documental, (b) Historia local, (c) Los mercantilistas, (d) Fuentes secundarias. Un capítulo muy importante de esta época es el de los primeros ataques en Europa de los abolicionistas en contra de los mercantilistas del imperialismo y de la esclavitud. Véase lo que escribieron los fisiócratas en Francia así como los ingleses, en particular Adam Smith (*Inquiry into the Nature and Causes of the Wealth of Nations*, London, 1776).

Las fuentes francesas para la abolición de la esclavitud son relativamente parcas si se comparan a las fuentes para las Antillas británicas. Pero lo que existe es excelente. Algunas nos aclaran el conflicto del siglo XIX entre el azúcar de caña y el azúcar de remolacha.

Por supuesto, el artículo de Williams no cita solamente las fuentes inglesas y francesas sino también fuentes españolas, holandesas y danesas ya que una parte de las Antillas pertenece o perteneció a estos países.

Catálogos

13. Texas University Library. *Recent Acquisitions for the Caribbean Islands (Excluding Cuba) and Guyana, French Guiana and Surinam of the Latin American Collection of the University of Texas Library.* Austin, TX. N° 1, 1962–.

Tabla de contenido por regiones. Fotocopia reducida de las fichas de las obras con la clasificación de la biblioteca de la Universidad de Texas en Austin.

Fuentes

14. Williams, Eric E. *Documents of West Indian History.* Port-of-Spain, PNM, 1963. V. 1, 1492-1655. From the Spanish discovery to the British conquest of Jamaica.

Son pocos los documentos reproducidos sobre las Antillas francesas pero son importantes. Aparecen en los últimos dos capítulos: cap. VII, "The International Struggle for the Caribbean" y cap. VIII, "The Early Organization of the Non-Spanish Colonies." Es una lástima que no se hayan publicado más documentos pero el conjunto de los demás es muy útil para un estudio comparativo entre las políticas de las diferentes potencias en juego: Inglaterra, España, Holanda, Francia.

Historia religiosa

15. Dahlin, Terry. "Caribbean Religion: A Survey and Bibliography" [by] . . . and Reed Nelson. Austin: University of Texas Library, SALALM Secretariat, 1979. Submitted for the 24th Seminar on the Acquisition of Latin American Library Materials, Los Angeles, June 17-22, 1979. 17 h. [También es parte del número 21.]

Se identificaron las bibliotecas de EE.UU. que contienen colecciones importantes sobre religión en el Caribe.

1. Obras sobre el Vodú en Princeton University. Princeton Theological Seminary. Speere Library.
2. En Library of Congress. Hispanic Division. Escritos de los padres católicos en el período colonial, descripción de las religiones caribeñas desde una óptica antropológica y sociológica.

"No single library is the Mecca for Caribbean religion researchers."

Este trabajo es incompleto ya que no menciona en su texto (solamente en la bibliografía) la emigración de los protestantes franceses que huyeron de Francia a causa de la Revocación del Edicto de Nantes en 1685. Los que tenían parientes en las islas francesas los alcanzaron allá.

De las 88 referencias, alrededor de 18 (quinta parte de las referencias, es una buena proporción), se refieren a las misiones católicas en Santo Domingo, Guadalupe, Martinica, la iglesia en el Caribe francés, el clero en la Guyana durante la Revolución francesa, el Vodú en Haití y en Martinica; el protestantismo en Martinica antes de la Revolución, el protestantismo en Haití.

Literatura

16. Carpentier, Alejo. *El siglo de las luces*; novela. México: Seix Barral, 1980. (Biblioteca Universal Formentor). 369 p.

Esta extraordinaria novela, tanto por su trama como por su estilo esplendoroso, relata la vida de Victor Hugues, personaje real de la Revolución francesa. De origen marsellés, había establecido un *comptoir* (gran almacén) en Port-au-Prince. Cuando los revolucionarios haitianos se lo quemaron, decidió entrar en la política de la Revolución francesa y, después de una temporada en Rochefort, regresó a las Antillas, más exactamente a la isla de Guadalupe, con el cargo de Comisario enviado por la Convención revolucionaria. Volvió a conquistar la Guadalupe caída en manos de los ingleses y, fiel imitador de Robespierre, instaló un régimen de terror en el cual la guillotina traída de Francia no jugaba el papel menor. Al principio firme y sincera, su actitud degeneró en contradicciones, especulaciones y cinismo. Denunciado en Francia, terminó su carrera política en Cayenne con el cargo de gobernador de la Guyana francesa.

Obras de referencia

17. *Encyclopaedia Universalis.* Paris, France, 1979. 20 vols.

Contiene una información muy detallada en cuanto a historia, geografía, condiciones políticas, económicas y sociales de cada uno de los países referidos; una lista de temas corolarios complementa el texto.

18. *The West Indies and the Caribbean Yearbook. Anuario comercial de las Antillas y Países del Caribe 1926-27—.* London: T. Skinner [etc.]. V. ilus. Título varía 1977—: Caribbean yearbook.

Compilación anual de datos y estadísticas del Caribe. Están incluidos los países del Caribe francés y francófono: Guadalupe, Martinica, Guyana francesa, Haití.

Población. Bibliografías.

19. Edmonston, Barry. *Population Research in Latin America and the Caribbean: A Reference Bibliography.* [Ann Arbor, Mich.] Published for the International Studies Program and the Latin American Studies Program, Cornell University by University Microfilms International, 1979. (Monograph Publishing Sponsor Series). 161 p.

Se trata de una obra en parte organizada a partir de referencias seleccionadas del *Population Index* y de otras bibliografías y a partir del material revisado en las universidades de Cornell, Stanford y Berkeley. La obra cubre las siguientes áreas: Estudios demográficos generales; Distribución de la población; Mortalidad; Fertilidad, matrimonio y la familia; Migración; Interrelaciones demográficas. Cada sección está dividida en subdivisiones geográficas. La que nos concierne se intitula "Caribbean." Pocas referencias sobre Antillas francesas y Guyana, pero las que hay son muy útiles.

Seminarios

21. *Caribbean Archives Conference, Mona, Jamaica, 1965.* Report of the . . . held at the University of the West Indies, Mona, Jamaica. Sept. 20-27, 1965. 32 h.

La isla de Guadalupe fue representada por J. P. Hervieu, Secretario de la Société d'Histoire de la Guadeloupe, que proporcionó una lista de materiales registrados en los Archivos de la Guadalupe, clasificada por grupos principales y fechas aproximativas. Los puntos principales tocados por la conferencia fueron los siguientes: (1) Uso y cuidado de los Archivos (Bajo la administración de Francia, los departamentos de los archivos como los de Guadalupe y de Martinica tienen poder de supervisión sobre los materiales departamentales y locales); (2) Disponibilidad de los Archivos (El representante de Guadalupe señaló que estaban reproduciendo materiales pero localizados en el extranjero. Reconoció que a menudo nadie se entera de estas actividades y se pierde la oportunidad de obtener una copia. También aprovechó para señalar la existencia en los Archives Départementales de Basse Terre de un material sumamente interesante que se refiere a la isla de Saint Barthélemy cuando estaba bajo la administración de Suecia, de 1784 a 1878); (3) Disponibilidad de los Archivos en el extranjero, es decir en la mayor parte de los casos, en las metrópolis (Aquí se indican los principales centros de Archivos en Francia); (4) Reproducción y canje de archivos (La Universidad de Florida empezó a ejecutar su proyecto de adquirir números de series caribeñas, los más antiguos posibles y ya se filmaron periódicos y materiales de otro tipo de la Guyana francesa, Guadalupe, Haití y Martinica); (5) Preservación y reparación de archivos (Se mencionó el *Bulletin d'Information sur la Pathologie des Documents* de los Archives Nationales Françaises); (6) Reclutamiento, formación y funciones del archivista.

21. *Seminar on the Acquisition of Latin American Library Materials*, 24. Los Angeles, EE.UU., 1979. Final report and working papers of the . . . Editor: Laurence Hallewell. Rapporteur général: Sonia Merubia, coord. by Suzanne Hodgman. Madison, WI: SALALM Secretariat, 1980. 354 p. A la cabeza de la portada: Windward, Leeward and Main: Caribbean Studies and Library Resources.

Esta obra debe citarse aunque no es capital para el Caribe francés. Sin embargo, es tan polifacética y con un material bibliográfico tan abundante que puede servir de guía y de base para cualquier trabajo sobre el Caribe en general.

En cuanto al Caribe francés en particular, encontramos mencionado el artículo de Lygia Ballantyne, "Haitian Publications" (véase en Ballantyne, Lygia), pero no aparece publicado allí. Por otra parte, podemos citar el artículo de Terry Dahlin y Reed Nelson sobre religión caribeña. A pesar de que el texto no menciona el Caribe francés, numerosas citas aparecen en la bibliografía final (véase Dahlin, Terry).

Tesis. Bibliografías.

22. Brown, Denise F., and Herman W. Konrad. *Directory of Canadian Theses on Latin American and Caribbean Topics, 1927-1980. Directorio de tesis canadienses sobre temas de la América Latina y del Caribe, 1927-1980.* [Calgary, Alberta, Canada]: Canadian Association for Latin American and Caribbean Studies, 1982. 77 p.

Es un trabajo excelente y muy completo. La mayor parte de las tesis se refieren al Caribe. En efecto, sobre un total de 724 citas, 350 giran alrededor de un aspecto específico de una de las islas o región del Caribe. 31 de ellas tienen que ver con relaciones especiales de Canadá con el Caribe y 35 se refieren a las condiciones sociales y económicas de las Antillas francesas (14 Martinica, 5 Guadalupe, 1 La Désirade, 1 María Galante, 12 Haití, 2 Las Antillas chicas en general).

23. Deal, Carl W., ed. *Latin America and the Caribbean: A Dissertation Bibliography.* [Ann Arbor, MI:] University Microfilms International [1977?]. 164 p.

Los grandes temas están divididos en subdivisiones geográficas. Las que nos interesan se intitulan French Overseas Departments and Haiti.

24. Pellegrin, Marie-Noelle. "Catalogue des thèses soutenues en France sur l'Amérique Latine de 1954 à 1969," en *Cahiers des Amériques Latines, Science de l'Homme* (jul-dic 1969), 145-195.

El artículo se refiere a las Antillas en general; es difícil definir exactamente la parte que le toca a la porción francesa. En cambio la compiladora trata individualmente Guadalupe, Martinica y Haití, este último siendo de lejos el más rico de todos.

Caribe francófono

Bibliografías

25. *Anuario de Estudios Americanos.* V. 1, 1944–. Sevilla: Consejo Superior de Investigaciones Científicas, 1944–. Anual. Publicaciones de la Escuela de Estudios Hispano-Americanos de la Universidad de Sevilla. Serie 1.

Esta revista presenta un conjunto de excelentes bibliografías publicadas por Gabriel Debien durante 20 años, cada dos o tres años desde 1954 hasta 1974. Se caracterizan por una abundancia de fuentes de primera mano, de descripciones de todo un contexto histórico en el cual se insertan, de comentarios múltiples y atinados, de detalles tan minuciosos como curiosos, a veces chuscos. Allí se encuentran incluidos todos los países del Caribe francés y también a menudo mucho material bibliográfico sobre las Antillas de otros idiosincrasias como referencias. (Véase una descripción más extensa en el texto de la ponencia.) Las primeras bibliografías están en el Anuario, las últimas en *Historiografía y Bibliografía Americanista* (véase en este título); algunas en ambas.

26. *Historiografía y Bibliografía Americanista, 1953–*. Sevilla. Anual. Publicaciones de la Escuela de Estudios Hispano-Americanos de Sevilla. Vols. para 1955– publicados como una sección del *Anuario de Estudios Americanos*. V. 12–. (1955–).
Véase *Anuario de Estudios Americanos*.

Catálogos

27. Paris. Bibliothèque Nationale. Département des Imprimés. *Catalogue de l'histoire de l'Amérique*, par George A. Barringer, bibliothécaire au Département des Imprimés. Paris, 1903-1911. 5 vols.
Se trata de la reproducción de una bibliografía manuscrita que reúne un importante material escrito sobre la historia de América. A continuación presentamos un extracto del contenido de los tomos que nos interesan:
Tome I: (1) Amérique en général: Bibliographie; Descriptions générales; Ethnographie; Histoires générales; Boucaniers; Périodiques et publications des sociétés historiques; Histoire religieuse; Esclavage; Moeurs et coutunes. (2) Canada; (3) Etats-Unis.
Tome IV: Antilles en général; Haïti; Guyane en général.

Bibliotecas

28. Blanc, Anne-Marie. "Exposé sur la formation des personnels de bibliothèques aux Antilles Françaises" [s.p.i.]. Trabajo presentado a la 7a Conferencia ACURIL, sep 21-26, 1975, Willemstad, Curazao. 25 h.
En esta ponencia la autora explica el esquema de la organización administrativa francesa en materia de bibliotecas; describe luego la formación profesional del personal de las bibliotecas francesas. Por otra parte nos indica que la situación de las bibliotecas es similar en Guadalupe y Martinica. Profundiza entonces únicamente sobre Martinica; enumera las diferentes bibliotecas con que cuenta y los servicios que prestan a sus usuarios.

Centros de investigación

29. Jouandet-Bernadat, R. "Le Centre d'Etudes Régionales Antilles-Guyane," en *Caribbean Studies*, 4, 3 (Oct 1964), 72-74.

Se encuentra en la sección IV intitulada: "Note on Institutions and Research." El artículo está en francés y proporciona un panorama de las investigaciones emprendidas por los miembros del Centro. Al mismo tiempo señala la especialización de cada uno y sus diplomas. El conjunto de los trabajos nos permite vislumbrar una gran diversificación de temas, todos centrados sobre "el conocimiento de las estructuras de la zona caribeña en la óptica de una lucha sistemática contra los fenómenos del subdesarrollo" (extractos de los estatutos).

Enseñanza superior

30. Problèmes universitaires des Antilles-Guyane françaises," en *Les Cahiers du CERAG*, 18, 4° trim (1969). 112 p.

Primera parte: "La Universidad de las Antillas: ¿Para qué?" por Jean Rosaz. El autor expone algunas ideas para organizar una Universidad de las Antillas francesas; ideas sobre su ideología, su propósito, las materias que se deberán enseñar, etc.

Segunda parte: (1) Plática con tres delegados del Centro de Estudios Superiores Literarios de Pointre à Pitre.

(2) Los estudiantes en Martinica (estudio sociodemográfico): características generales de la enseñanza superior. Descripción de dos institutos y estudio muy detallado en cuanto a los estudiantes y profesores, las condiciones materiales de trabajo, los locales (Biblioteca), horarios, exámenes y el porvenir de los estudiantes. La conclusión es bastante pesimista: el subdesarrollo de la enseñanza superior arriesga quedarse en esta etapa si no se define una política de conjunto racional y si no se coordinan los esfuerzos a nivel regional.

(3) Los alumnos de bachillerato del liceo (estudio socio-demográfico de las alumnas del liceo de Fort de France). Repartición por edad. Origen socioprofesional, etc. Múltiples cuadros estadísticos y análisis final de los resultados. Una de las conclusiones muestra la correlación entre el éxito escolar y la pertenencia a una categoría socioprofesional dada (más éxito en las categorías acomodadas).

Historia

31. Roberts, W. Adolphe. *The French in the West Indies.* Indianapolis: Bobbs-Merrill, 1942. 335 p.

Esta obra relata, paso a paso, las acciones tomadas por los franceses en el Caribe desde los primeros piratas durante el reino de

François 1er en el siglo XVI hasta la segunda guerra mundial. Este libro muy completo y lleno de vida se lee como una novela de aventuras. Las islas y las provincias del nuevo mundo pasan de mano en mano, los colonos y los esclavos están a la merced de gobernantes ambiciosos y caprichosos. La sucesión de guerras y tratados siembra desconcierto, incertidumbre y miedo en las poblaciones. El autor examina tanto las decisiones de los gobernantes en la metrópoli como las reacciones de los gobernantes en las islas y la de los gobernados. La obra se extiende más allá de las Antillas ya que considera también la conquista y pérdida de la Louisiana, la intervención en México, la construcción del Canal de Panamá, etc. Pero el núcleo de la obra gira alrededor del Caribe, y del Caribe francés en particular.

Literatura. Bibliografía.

32. Chanover, Pierre. "Martinique et Guadeloupe: A Check List of Modern Literature," en *Bulletin of the New York Public Library* (Oct 1970), 514-532.

La introducción se refiere a una de las fuentes principales para la elaboración de esta bibliografía: Jacques Gazin, *Eléments de bibliographie générale méthodique et historique de la Martinique* (Fort-de-France, Martinique: Imprimerie Antillaise, 1926; Paris: Librairie Ernest Leroux), pp. 110-118.

El autor señala que la mayor parte de los autores citados son negros, lo que demuestra hasta qué punto Africa está sólidamente arraigada en la literatura del Caribe francés.

33. Watson, Karl S., comp. *Literature of the English- and French-speaking West Indies in the University of Florida Libraries: A Bibliography.* Gainesville: University of Florida, Center for Latin American Studies, 1971. 26 p.

Tres páginas están dedicadas a la literatura de Martinica, Guadalupe y Guyana francesa. Haití no aparece en ningún lugar de la publicación. La sección que reseña algunas revistas cita solamente *Horizons Caraïbes* y *Parallèles*, las dos se publicaban mensualmente en Fort-de-France, Martinica.

Guyana

Esclavitud

34. Cardoso, Ciro Flamarion Santana. "Esclavage colonial et économie: contribution à l'étude des sociétés esclavagistes

d'Amérique à partir du cas de la Guyane française au 18è siècle,"
en *Cahiers du CERAG*, n° 39 (jul 1982), T. 1. 247 p.

Este documento reproduce una parte de la tesis de doctorado del
autor: "La Guyane française (1715-1817), aspects économiques et
sociaux: contribution à l'étude des sociétés esclavagistes d'Amérique."
La historia de la Guyana francesa es la historia de un fracaso que
permite entender mejor los mecanismos del caso típico descrito aquí.
El autor estudia, en el marco del mundo colonial francés, una sociedad
microscópica, una economía despreciable, muestra de un vasto
conjunto, ya que el mismo modelo rige todas las colonias de América
dotadas de plantaciones y de esclavos.

La primera parte proporciona una visión somera del medio geográfico, etnográfico e histórico en el cual se inscribe la colonización de
la Guyana; la segunda se refiere a su economía y la última a su
sociedad.

Política y gobierno

35. Schwarzbeck, Frank. "La Guyane: un département français comme
les autres?" en *Amérique Latine*, n° 11 (jul-sep 1982), 3-11.

El autor recuerda el estatuto político-jurídico de este país
continental del nuevo mundo, único en permanecer todavía ligado
totalmente a un país europeo. Expone los efectos económicos de la
"departamentalización" así como los intereses de Francia en Guyana.

Finalmente se muestran las diferentes alternativas que se ofrecen
a este país: dejarse anexar a Brasil, lo que no parecería imposible en
caso de pasividad excesiva de parte de Guyana o, lo que sería mucho
más deseable, buscar una mejor integración con sus vecinos del Caribe.
Mientras, necesita todavía el auxilio de Francia que debe hacer todo
para ayudarlo y prepararlo como país del Tercer Mundo a decidir de
su destino.

Haití/Santo Domingo

Bibliografías

36. Ballantyne, Lygia María F. C. *Haitian Publications: An
Acquisitions Guide and Bibliography.* [Madison:] University of
Wisconsin at Madison. Memorial Library. SALALM Secretariat,
1980. (Bibliography, 6). 52 p.

Esta bibliografía es el resultado de la investigación llevada a cabo
por la autora sobre la edición y distribución de libros en Haití y sobre
las posibilidades de adquisición de obras destinadas a completar las
colecciones del Hispanic Acquisitions Project de la Biblioteca del

Congreso de Washington. La primera parte trata del comercio de libros en Haití, de las publicaciones oficiales y académicas y de las publicaciones editadas por todas las organizaciones internacionales que prestan ayuda al país. Un estudio sobre los servicios de bibliotecas y documentación concluye esta primera parte. La segunda consta de 5 apéndices: Directorio de editores comerciales, de editores institucionales y de libreros susceptibles de hacer envíos al extranjero; hemerografía de periódicos, revistas y series en casi todos los temas; bibliografía de monografías haitianas de 1970 a 1979. El último apéndice lista obras publicadas por haitianos fuera del país o por extranjeros sobre temas haitianos.

37. Bayitch, S. A. *Latin America and the Caribbean: A Bibliographical Guide to Works in English.* Coral Gables: University of Miami Press, 1967. (University of Miami School of Law Interamerican Legal Studies, 10). 943 p. Título de la obra de 1961 LA: A Bibliographical Guide to Economy, History, Law, Politics and Society.

La única sección que se refiere al Caribe francés es la que trata de Haití, pp. 214-220 (ed. de 1961).

38. Bissainthe, Max. *Dictionnaire de bibliographie haïtienne.* Washington, DC: Scarecrow, 1951. 1052 p.

Obra de referencia por excelencia, base de cualquier investigación sobre este país desde sus orígenes (Hispaniola), en la época francesa (Saint Domingue) y en la época moderna hasta 1950 (Haití). Algunas citas están acompañadas de notas del autor. Una lista de publicaciones periódicas, una lista alfabética de periodistas y un índice por tema completan la bibliografía. Son 8.469 citas de obras y 885 citas de publicaciones periódicas. El autor fue director de la Biblioteca Nacional de Haití e Inspector General de las Bibliotecas.

39. Duvivier, Ulrick. *Bibliographie générale et méthodique d'Haïti.* Port-au-Prince: Imprimerie de l'Etat, 1941–. 2 vols.

La Biblioteca de El Colegio de México tiene solamente la 4a., 5a. y 6a. partes del 2do. volumen. La ausencia de índice global por una parte y del prefacio o de la introducción, por la otra, no permite informar al lector sobre el contenido de los volúmenes que faltan.

El índice parcial de este volumen indica su contenido del modo siguiente:

4a. parte: Ciencias jurídicas; Legislación; Código
5a. parte: Visitas y viajes; Esclavitud; Enfermedades

6a. parte: Literatura; Constituciones; Educación; Ciencias económicas y sociales; Prensa

La mayor parte de los capítulos se refieren sucesivamente a Haití y a Santo Domingo. Las obras citadas fueron en gran mayoría editadas en el siglo XIX. Algunas son del final del siglo XVII y otras del principio del XX. Es sorprendente el número de periódicos y revistas citados: el capítulo de prensa reseña alrededor de 630.

Esta obra está citada en el Catálogo de obras haitianas editado por la Librairie aux Livres pour Tous, en Port-au-Prince. Véase a Librairie . . . En cambio no aparece en la bibliografía de Lygia Ballantyne.

40. Librairie aux Livres pour Tous. Port-au-Prince. *Catalogue d'ouvrages haïtiens anciens [et] modernes*. Port-au-Prince, [s.f.]. Copia xerox. (Archivo CIDOC de documentos). 67 h.

Listas por orden alfabético do toda clase de documentos con su ficha bibliográfica y su precio (pero no se sabe de qué año). Ningún dato más, ya que este catálogo carece de prefacio o de alguna explicación complementaria.

41. Lugo, Américo. *Recopilación diplomática relativa a las colonias española y francesa de la isla de Santo Domingo 1649-1701*. Ciudad Trujillo: Edición del Gobierno Dominicano, 1944. (Col. Trujillo). Centenario de la República. (Documentos y Estudios Históricos. Serie III. Vol. I). 433 p.

Conjunto de documentos diplomáticos (memorias, cartas, proyectos, informes, etc.) cruzados entre las autoridades del Gobierno francés y sus agentes en la Isla de la Tortuga y Costa de Santo Domingo. Constituyen parte del resultado de las investigaciones efectuadas por el compilador en los archivos y bibliotecas de Francia. El gobierno dominicano encomendó al Dr. A. Lugo de 1911 a 1916 la misión de buscar fuentes de la Historia de Santo Domingo. Ciertas piezas están copiadas en toda su extensión; otras aparecen solamente como fragmentos. Algunas fueron resumidas y traducidas al español. Muchas están solamente mencionadas o registradas tal cual. Ahí se transparenta toda la historia de Santo Domingo en la segunda mitad del siglo XVII: invasión de los filibusteros y bucaneros y gobierno posterior de los enviados oficiales del gobierno de Francia.

42. Tardits, Claude. ["En hommage à Alfred Métraux"], en *L'Homme* (may-jun 1964), 49-62.

Se trata de un artículo que pone en evidencia todos los trabajos de Métraux sobre Haití. Gabriel Debien cita el artículo en la sección

"Informaciones Bibliográficas Americanas" de la revista *Anuario de Estudios Americanos*, vol. 21 (1964), 672-674. 36 referencias (Título del artículo de Gabriel Debien: "Antillas francesas").

43. Zimmerman, Irene. *Current National Bibliographies of Latin America: A State of the Art Study.* Gainesville: University of Florida, Center for Latin American Studies, 1971–. 139 p.

Haití es el único país tomado en consideración por la autora y se trata, una vez más, de una importante discriminación, por demás inexplicable ya que en el prefacio la autora nos señala que la costumbre al hablar de América Latina es "to refer to the twenty countries in the Western Hemisphere whose official language is Spanish, Portuguese or French." Ahora, para completar su estudio, anuncia que incluirá a Puerto Rico y al Caribe inglés. Más adelante informa al lector que dividirá los países en dos grupos: (1) "the ten Spanish- or Portuguese-speaking republics of South America, and (2) the 'Caribbean area' with the term used to include Mexico, Central America and the Antilles . . ."

Descripción y viajes

44. Moreau de Saint Méry, Médéric L. E. (1750-1819). *Descripción de la parte española de Santo Domingo*; trad. del francés por el Lic. C. Armando Rodríguez, por encargo del generalísimo Rafael L. Trujillo Molina, Presidente de la República Dominicana. Ciudad Trujillo: Montalvo, 1944. 491 p.

Como la "descripción de la parte francesa de Santo Domingo" no se pudo localizar, nos vemos en la obligación de citar por lo menos la descripción de la parte española para dar al lector una idea de la importancia de la obra. "El ilustre escritor y político martiniqueño visitó la ciudad de Santo Domingo en el año 1783. Fruto de sus sagaces observaciones y estudios fue la obra que traducimos, y que el autor publicó en dos volúmenes. En el primero, después de un Compendio histórico en que presenta la larga serie de depredaciones e invasiones de los occidentales en la parte española de la isla, entra en la descripción, pormenorizada, de la antigua colonia de España, abarcando en ella, minuciosamente, todo lo concerniente a la vida y costumbres de sus moradores. El segundo volumen trata, casi exclusivamente, de la Real Audiencia de Santo Domingo: de su creación y funcionamiento, de las leyes vigentes en la colonia, de los relativo al comercio, particularmente del negocio del ganado, principal medio de vida de los españoles-dominicanos, cuya vida campestre, en el hato, presenta vívidamente, haciendo observaciones que aún tendrán notoria utilidad. El autor señala, además, con lujo de detalles, las relaciones y divergencias entre las dos partes de la Isla, favoreciendo con sus votos en muchos aspectos, a la parte española." (Extracto del prefacio.) La referencia original de la descripción de la parte francesa de la isla es la siguiente: *Description topographique, physique, civile, politique et historique de la partie française de l'isle de Saint-Domingue.* Filadelfia, 1797-1798. 2 vols. en 4°. 788 y 856 pp.

Esclavitud

45. Fouchard, Jean. *Les marrons de la liberté.* Lettre-préface de Pierre-Henri Simon. Paris: l'Ecole, 1972. (Collection Histoire et Littérature Haïtiennes). 580 p.

Es la historia del origen de la comunidad haitiana a partir de la ruptura definitiva de las cadenas de la esclavitud. Es la historia del origen de la primera república negra del nuevo mundo, del crecimiento de sus masas, de la conquista del alfabetismo, de la evolución de las comunicaciones, de la agricultura, del bienestar social. La obra abunda en documentos sobre las condiciones en las cuales vivían los esclavos, verdaderas causas de las fugas cada vez más numerosas, y las analiza de tal modo que la historia se vuelve como lo dijo Cocteau: "uno de los medios más insolentes de decir la verdad."

Fuentes

46. Ménier, Marie Antoinette. "Les sources de l'histoire de la partie française de l'île de Saint Domingue aux Archives Nationales de France," en *Conjonction: Revue franco-haïtienne*, n° 140 (1978), 119-135.

La autora nos da la clave para entrar en el laberinto de los Archivos: enumera y describe brevemente cada serie y subserie con sus conjuntos de letras y números que sirven para la clasificación. Primera Serie "Colonias" B, correspondencia general a la salida, y C, correspondencia a la llegada: es decir, en B las cartas enviadas, en C las cartas recibidas. La serie F contiene la colección de Moreau de Saint Méry, el autor de . . . *La description de la partie française d'île de Saint Domingue, des lois et coutumes de l'Amérique sous le Vent.* La sección *Outre Mer*, iniciada en 1960, conserva el Depósito de los Expedientes Públicos de las Colonias y el Depósito de las Fortificaciones de las Colonias. Es difícil de entrar en el detalle de estos archivos por su inagotable riqueza.

47. St. Juste, Laurore. "Recherches haïtiennes dans les bibliothèques et archives américaines," en *Conjonction: Revue franco-haïtienne*, n° 141-142 (1979), 65-73.

En realidad las ricas colecciones que se mencionan allí se refieren solamente a los últimos años de Santo Domingo como posesión francesa, digamos a partir de 1775 hasta los principios de la 2a. década de nuestro siglo. En seguida enumeramos la lista de bibliotecas y archivos descritos: Biblioteca del Congreso en Washington, National Archives of the United States y New York Public Library. Uno de los departamentos más importantes de esta última es el "Schomburg Center for Research in Black Culture" que contiene fuentes impresas, fotografías y música, fuentes manuscritas, la colección Kurt Fischer y la colección Eugene Maxilien.

Historia

48. Logan, Rayford Whittingham. *Haiti and the Dominican Republic.* New York: Issued under the auspices of the Royal Institute of International Affairs [by] Oxford University, 1968. 220 p.

Este libro es la primera historia comparativa de Haití y de la República Dominicana desde sus orígenes coloniales hasta 1967. Está completado por dos apéndices que listan los nombres de los gobernantes y presidentes de los dos países. Una bibliografía seleccionada concluye la obra.

49. James, C. L. R. *The Black Jacobins: Toussaint L'Ouverture and the Santo Domingo Revolution.* 2 ed. rev. New York: Random House, [1963]. (Vintage Books). 426 p. Bibliografía, pp. 379-389.

Historia de la única rebelión de esclavos que tuvo éxito, y de la transformación de los esclavos en un pueblo capaz de organizarse y de desafiar a las naciones europeas más poderosas de su tiempo. El autor presenta al líder de tal revolución, el negro Toussaint L'Ouverture, no como el hombre que hizo la revolución sino como el hombre que fue hecho por ella. Se trata allí de una obra que aclara las bases históricas del presente drama de Haití.

Esta completada por una importante bibliografía.

Historia religiosa

50. Cabon, Adolphe. *Notes sur l'histoire religieuse d'Haïti de la Révolution au Concordat (1789-1860).* Port-au-Prince: Petit Séminaire Collège Saint Martial, 1933.

La revolución mencionada en el título es la Revolución francesa. La obra relata la historia religiosa de Haití desde *l'Ancien Régime* y sigue hasta 1860. Se trata aquí de un conjunto de notas muy detalladas que el autor publicó previamente en el *Bulletin de la Quinzaine,* revista bimensual del arzobispado de Port-au-Prince. La obra es también muy interesante desde el punto de vista de la política de los gobernantes en esa época y de las relaciones entre la iglesia incluyendo al Vaticano y el estado.

Historiografía

51. **Pressoir, Catts, Ernst Trouillot y Henock Trouillot.** *Historiographie d'Haïti.* México, 1953. (Instituto Panamericano de Geografía e Historia. Comisión de Historia, 66. Historiografías, 1). 298 p. Bibliografía, pp. 287-298.

Esta obra fue auspiciada por la IV Asamblea General del Instituto Panamericano de Geografía e Historia. Los autores agruparon en la primera parte los historiadores de la época española, en la segunda los de la época francesa, y en la tercera los de la época haitiana. Obra muy completa que incluye las biografías de los historiadores, la descripción de sus obras y el contexto histórico en el cual se insertan.

Lingüística

52. Pompilus, Pradel. *La langue française en Haïti.* Paris: Institut des Hautes Etudes de l'Amérique Latine, [1961]. Ouvrage publié avec le concours du Centre National de la Recherche Scientifique. 278 p.

Estudio de la lengua francesa de Haití tal como se fue transformando bajo la influencia de la geografía, de las costumbres y de diferentes circunstancias políticas y sociales. El autor nos da una descripción completa de este francés "dialectal" concentrándose sobre los rasgos característicos y esenciales. El estudio, limitado al período 1915-1959, abarca la fonología, la gramática y el vocabulario. Bibliografía importante al final de la obra.

Literatura. Bibliografía.

53. Hoffmann, Léon François. "Pour une bibliographie des études littéraires haïtiennes," en *Conjonction: Revue franco-haïtienne,* n° 152 (ene 1982), 43-57.

Este primer suplemento complementa y pone al corriente la bibliografía publicada en el n° 134, de jun-jul 1977. Incluye dos tipos de rubros: por una parte los que se refieren a los trabajos publicados desde esta fecha; por otra, los que se refieren a trabajos anteriores, pero que no se habían incluido en 1977.

Vida social y costumbres. Siglo XVIII.

54. Girod, François. *La vie quotidienne de la société créole: Saint Domingue au XVIIIè s.* Paris: Hachette, 1972. 238 p.

La parte francesa de la isla de Santo Domingo, situada en el centro de las grandes corrientes de comercio entre Europa y América, es cada vez menos el país de los bucaneros y de los filibusteros. Esta obra describe cómo viven los plantadores, los comerciantes y los especuladores que los reemplazaron. Describe también una sociedad en la cual coexisten los aristócratas del Estado Mayor y aventureros de toda calaña, frente a la masa de esclavos y libres. Describe por fin lo que existe tras el legendario encanto de la sociedad criolla, las duras realidades de este mundo en vía de extinción.

Martinica

Bibliografía

55. Jardel, Jean-Pierre, Maurice Nicolas y Claude Relouzat. *Bibliographie de la Martinique.* [Fort-de-France: Centre d'Etudes Régionales Antilles-Guyane (CERAG), 1969]. (Cuaderno especial del CERAG). 231 p.

Extensa bibliografía sobre la isla francesa de las Antillas. Cubre una multitud de aspectos además de los temas de siempre: sin enumerarlos basta decir que *todo* está ahí, lo que convierte a esta obra en una herramienta de mucha utilidad para los estudiantes y los investigadores y para todos los que quieren conocer el pasado de su región a fin de "definir y orientar mejor su futuro." Mencionaremos solamente algunos temas muy específicos de esta bibliografía: Fuentes bibliográficas; Inmigración; Historia (dividida por siglos); Derecho; Los cincuenta pasos geométricos; Justicia; Aduana; Turismo; etc.

Saint Barthélemy

Historia. Siglo XVIII.

56. Ekman, Ernst. St. Barthélemy and the French Revolution," en *Caribbean Studies*, 3, 4 (Jan 1964), 17-29.

Citamos este artículo por ser uno de los únicos que pudimos tener a la mano sobre esta isla tan poco conocida. El autor, de origen sueco, relata cómo los franceses la vendieron a Suecia a quien perteneció de 1784 a 1878. Su desarrollo fue mayor durante la ocupación sueca pero la isla resintió los cambios ocurridos durante el período de inestabilidad en la región, causada por la Revolución francesa y las acciones terroristas de Victor Hugues, comisionado por la Convención Nacional Francesa en la isla de Guadalupe. Pero el firme gobierno de éste y su sabia diplomacia con los sucesivos gobernadores de St. Barthélemy casi siempre lograron un buen entendimiento para el comercio de las islas interesadas.

Publicaciones periódicas

57. *Cahiers des Amériques Latines. Série Sciences de l'Homme.* Paris. N° 1—, 1968—. Irregular.

Los artículos publicados a lo largo de la revista desde 1968 no incluyen mucho. Durante nuestra revisión completa de la colección anotamos un artículo sobre "Le petit marronage à Saint Domingue" (N° 3, 1969); una crónica sobre unos expedientes de las Antillas "Papiers des Antilles" (N° 2, 1968 y N° 4, 1969) y un recuento de los estudios franceses sobre América Central y Antillas (N° 21-22, 1980).

Los méritos más grandes de esta revista, en cuanto a Antillas francesas se refiere, son el de incluir el material en su "Bibliographie américaniste française" y el de recopilar regularmente el catálogo de las tesis sustentadas en Francia sobre América Latina. Allí podemos encontrar listas importantes de tesis de Estado, de 3er Ciclo, de Universidad, y de Diplomas de Estudios Superiores y de Maestría, así como de *Mémoires* de Institutos universitarios, sobre las Antillas francesas en general y sobre Guadalupe, Martinica y Haití, en particular.

58. *El Caribe Contemporáneo.* México: UNAM, Facultad de Ciencias Políticas y Sociales, Centro de Estudios Latinoamericanos, Area del Caribe. V. 1—, n° 1—, marzo 1980—.

Ofrece estudios políticos, económicos y sociales sobre las diversas regiones que forman el Caribe. Las diferentes secciones, en particular la sección de artículos, están completadas por una muy importante sección bibliográfica que incluye una sección de reseñas de libros y artículos de revistas sobre el Caribe, y un comentario de tesis. Este último puede cubrir a veces varios años y darse de este modo un aire de catálogo completo sobre un país. Véase por ejemplo la lista de tesis de doctorado y otros *Mémoires* sobre Haití presentados en Canadá, EE.UU. y Francia de 1960 a 1980, publicada por Patrick D. Tardieu en el n° 6 de 1982.

59. *Caribbean Quarterly.* [Mona, Jamaica: University College of the West Indies. Extra Mural Department]. V. 1—, Apr-June 1949—. Trim.

Los problemas y temas expuestos en esta revista se refieren antes que todo a las Antillas de lengua inglesa. De los países que nos interesan, sólo Haití encuentra un lugar en la revista. Sin embargo, están citadas y reseñadas algunas obras sobre el Caribe francés en la sección de reseñas. Por otra parte, como singular excepción, el vol. 27, n° 4 (dic 1981) dedica un número completo a la literatura del Caribe francófono.

60. *Caribbean Review.* Miami: Florida International University, College of Arts and Sciences. V. 1, n° 1—v. 6, n° 4; [Jan-Mar] 1969—Oct-Dec 1974. 17 nos. Trim.

Revista multifacética en donde las Antillas francesas son abordadas tanto desde el punto de vista político, económico y social como desde la óptica literaria, artística o religiosa.

61. *Caribbean Studies.* [Río Piedras:] Institute of Caribbean Studies, University of Puerto Rico. V. 1—, Apr 1961—. Trim.

Esta revista es especialmente interesante por su bibliografía publicada regularmente en cada número.

En 1964 señalaba Gabriel Debien que casi todos los trabajos elaborados en Francia se hallaban fuera, los que era normal, ya que había y sigue habiendo poco intercambio de revistas de país a país. Se quejaba además de una falta de selectividad: *Il faut s'armer de la même patience résignée pour trouver son bien dans les trop copieuses listes de la Current Bibliography des 'Caribbean Studies.'* En otra ocasión se queja de que la bibliografía descuida la geografía y que, a final de cuentas, se seleccionan las referencias de acuerdo con la visión norteamericana.

Actualmente, la bibliografía sigue apareciendo con mucha regularidad y continuamente se tiene referencias sobre el Caribe de habla francesa.

62. *Conjonction: Revue Franco-haïtienne.* Port-au-Prince: Institut Français d'Haïti]. V. 1—, n° 1—, 1946. Irregular.

El gran mérito de esta revista publicada por el Instituto Francés de Haití, así como del bibliotecario-bibliógrafo Wilfrid Bertrand, es el de publicar regularmente la bibliografía nacional actualizada desde el principio de los 70s. En 1974 la bibliografía se divide on 4 rubros: obras publicadas en Port-au-Prince; obras reproducidas en 1974; obras haitianas publicadas en el extranjero; obras sobre Haití escritas por autores extranjeros (sobre todo por autores canadienses).

En los años posteriores las listas tendrán una organización diferente. Por lo general, la literatura y la historia continúan siendo las preocupaciones dominantes de los escritores haitianos. Es interesante notar que en el Vol. 130, por primera vez se publica una sección de obras en lengua criolla (sep 1976, pp. 83-92); en el Vol. 139 aparece un artículo bibliográfico de Charles Christophe: "Regards sur la jeune poésie haïtienne." Es un estudio sobre las corrientes poéticas y sus principales representantes en Haití en los años 60 (jul 1978, pp. 59-72); los artículos de Léon François Hoffmann: "Pour une bibliographie des études littéraires haïtiennes," proporcionan también mucha información bibliográfica sobre la literatura haitiana (nº 134, 1977, p. 3 y nº 152, ene 1982, pp. 43-57). Varias secciones bibliográficas están dedicadas a los trabajos de investigación en la Universidad Estatal de Haití. El nº 138 de mayo 1978 contiene el índice de los textos y artículos publicados en *Conjonction* y de todas las listas bibliográficas de Max Bissainthe y Wilfrid Bertrand. No hay que descuidar el aspecto polifacético de esta revista, que se interesa en todo lo relacionado con la vida haitiana: historia, sociología, etnología, antropología, literatura, turismo, etc.

63. *Jamaican Historical Review.* Kingston, Jamaica: Jamaica Historical Society. V. 1—, nº 1—, Jun 1945—. Irregular.

Esta revista estudia la historia de Jamaica en particular, pero también la historia de todas las Antillas y aun de los países que bordan el mar del Caribe. Pero es muy poco lo que se puede hallar sobre el Caribe francés.

64. *Journal de la Société des Américanistes.* Société des Américanistes de Paris. V. 1-5; nouv. sér. V. 1—, 1910—.

Esta revista, publicada por el Museo del Hombre en Paris, abarca los campos siguientes: Antropología, fisiología, patología, arqueología, etnografía, sociología, folclor, lingüística, historia, geografía, biografías. Los artículos aparecen en su lengua original: francés, inglés, español, portugués, alemán, italiano. En una rápida revisión de la colección de El Colegio, bastante completa, hemos detectado varios artículos sobre Guyana francesa, Martinica, Guadalupe y Haití.

Periódicamente salen abundantes bibliografías sobre los temas arriba mencionados, por sub-divisiones geográficas. En los últimos años, algunos números publican la portada de números recientes de revistas que cubren los mismos temas o temas colaterales.

65. *Notes et Etudes Documentaires*. Paris: La Documentation Française. Secrétariat Général du Gouvernement, 19 —, n° 1—. Catalogados monográficamente.

    N° 4060 (5-2-74) Lagrosillière (A). le département français de la Martinique.

    N° 4135-36-37 (22-11-74) Lasserre (G) *et al.* Le département français de la Guadeloupe.

66. *Problèmes d'Amérique Latine*. Paris: La Documentation Française, 19 —, n° 1—. 4 nos. al año. Subserie de: *Notes et Etudes Documentaires*.

Esta subserie de *Notes et Etudes Documentaires* catalogada monográficamente, presenta los artículos por países. En realidad cada número es una monografía sobre uno, dos o tres países.

No se escribió sobre las Antillas francesas en los 60. En los 70, un estudio sobre la economía de las Antillas habla muy poco de las Antillas francesas (nos. 3935-3936, oct 25, 1972). En cambio, un profesor de la McGill University de Montreal en Québec presenta un excelente análisis sobre la economía haitiana (nos. 4190-4191, may 22, 1975). En los 80, un extenso artículo sobre geopolítica de las Antillas contiene algunas referencias sobre las Antillas francesas (n° 71, 1er trimestre, 1984).

APÉNDICE II

INSTITUT FRANÇAIS D'AMÉRIQUE LATINE
Principales obras sobre el Caribe francés

Antillas

1. Revert, Eugène. *Entre les deux Amériques: le monde des Caraïbes.* Paris: Ed. Françaises, 1958.

Condiciones económicas

2. Crusol, Jean. *Economie insulaire de la Caraïbe. Aspects théoriques et pratiques du développement: Guadeloupe, Martinique, Barbade, Trinidad, Jamaïque, Puerto Rico.* Paris: Ed. Caribéennes, 1980.

Siglo XX

3. *Environnement caraïbe (Textes de L. S. Senghor, J. Benoist, C. G. Clarke, etc.).* Dakar: Enda, 1978. (Environnement africain—Cahiers d'études du milieu et d'aménagement du territoire).

Descripción y viajes

4. Hollier, Robert. *Antilles.* Paris: Seuil, 1976. (Col. Microcosme; Petite Planète).

5. Le Lomelin. *Kurun aux Antilles.* Paris: Flammarion, 1957.

6. Mitchell, Carleton. *Les îles caraïbes.* Traducido del inglés. Washington, DC/Paris: National Geographic society/Flammarion, 1976.

7. Ogrizek, Doré. *Mexique, Amérique Centrale, Antilles.* Paris: Odé, 1955.

8. Raspail, Jean. *Secouons le cocotier: mes libres voyages aux Antilles.* Paris: Laffont, 1973.

Siglo XVII

9. Labat, R. P. *Voyage aux îles de l'Amérique (Antilles), 1693-1705.* Paris: Seghers, 1979.

10. Labat, R. P. *Voyages aux îles de l'Amérique (Antilles), 1693-1705.* Paris: Duchartre, 1931. 2 vols.

Guías

11. *Antilles, Bahamas, Bermudes et Guyane française.* Paris: Vilo, 1973. (Guides modernes Fodor).

Descubrimiento y exploración

12. Doucet, Louis. *Quand les français cherchaient fortune aux Caraïbes.* Paris: Fayard, 1981.

Geografía

13. *Atlas des Départements d'Outre Mer*, realisé par le Centre d'Etudes de Géographie Tropicale du C.N.R.S. Bordeaux-Talence, 1975. 4 vols. T. 2. La Martinique.

14. Lasserre, Guy. *Les Amériques du Centre; Mexique, Amérique Centrale, Antilles, Guyane.* Paris: PUF, 1974.

Geografía física

15. Pagney, Pierre. *Le climat des Antilles.* Paris, 1966. (Travaux et Mémoires de l'Institut des Hautes Etudes de l'Amérique Latine).

Historia

16. Butel, Paul. *Les Caraïbes au temps des filibustiers, XVIè-XVIIè s.* Paris: Aubier-Montaigne, 1982.

17. Devèze, Michel. *Antilles-Guyane-La mer des Caraïbes de 1492 à 1789.* Paris: SEDES, 1977. (Regards sur l'histoire).

18. Julien, Ch. Audré. *Les français en Amérique, 1713-1784.* T. I. Le Traité d'Utrecht-Le Système de l'exclusif-Les îles. Paris: Centre de Documentation Universitaire, 1951. (Les cours de Sorbonne).

19. Pluchon, Pierre, dir. *Histoire des Antilles et de la Guyane.* Toulouse: Privat, 1982. (Univers de la France et des pays francophones, Série Histoire des Provinces).

20. Williams, Eric. *De Christophe Colomb à Fidel Castro: l'histoire des Caraïbes 1492-1969.* Paris: Présence Africaine, 1975.

Siglo XIX

21. Adelaïde-Merlande, Jacques. *Documents d'histoire antillaise et guyanaise, 1814-1914.* S.l., s.e., 1979.

Historia colonial

22. Cochin, Augustin. *L'abolition de l'esclavage*. Fort-de-France; Paris: Désormaux; L'Harmattan, 1979. (Col. Histoire de l'esclavage aux Antilles).

23. Schoelcher, Victor. *Polémique coloniale*. Fort-de-France; Paris: Désormaux; L'Harmattan, 1979. (Col. Les Antilles après l'abolition).

Historia económica

24. Chemin Dupontes, P. *Les petites Antilles: étude sur leur évolution économique (1820-1908)*. Fort-de-France; Paris: Désormaux; L'Harmattan, 1979. (Col. Les Antilles après l'abolition).

Historia religiosa

25. Rennard, J. *Histoire religieuse des Antilles françaises des origines à 1914 d'après des documents inédits*. Paris: Société de l'Histoire des Colonies Françaises, 1954. (Bibliothèque d'histoire coloniale).

Racismo

26. Souquet-Basiège, G. *Le préjugé de race aux Antilles françaises: étude historique*. Fort-de-France; Paris: Désormaux; L'Harmattan, 1979. (Col. Les Antilles après l'abolition).

Antillas en la literatura

27. Antoine, Régis. *Les écrivains français et les Antilles: des premiers pères blancs aux surréalistes noirs*. Paris: Maisonneuve et Larose, 1978.

Antillas francófonas

Civilización

28. Glissant, Edouard. *Le discours antillais*. Paris: Seuil, 1981.

Guadalupe

Condiciones económicas. Siglo XIX.

29. Schnakenbourg, Christian. *Histoire de l'industrie sucrière en Guadeloupe aux XIXè et XXè siècles*. Paris: L'Harmattan, 1980. T. I. La crise du système esclavagiste (1835-1847).

Descripción y viajes

30. Bourgois, Jean-Jacques. *Martinique et Guadeloupe: terre française des Antilles.* Paris: Horizons de France, 1958. (Visages du Monde).

31. Gérard, Bernard. *La Guadeloupe et ses îles, terre française.* (Texte en français, anglais et allemand). Boulogne, Seine: Delroisse, 1973.

32. Gillot-Pétré, Alain. *Voir les Antilles: Guadeloupe, Martinique.* Paris: Hachette-Réalités, 1980.

Martinica
Descripción y viajes

33. Gérard, Bernard, y Rose Rosette. *Martinique, terre française.* (Texte en français, anglais et allemand). Boulogne, Seine: Delroisse, 1973.

Historia económica. Siglo XVIII.

34. Banbuck, C. A. *Histoire politique, économique et sociale de la Martinique sous l'Ancien Régime (1635-1789).* Paris: Librairie des Sciences Politiques et Sociales, 1935.

Literatura

35. Tauriac, Michel. *Les années créoles.* Roman. Paris: La Table Ronde, 1984.

Vida política y social. Siglo XX.

36. Lépine, Edouard de. *La crise de février 1935 à la Martinique: la marche de la faim sur Fort-de-France.* Paris: L'Harmattan, 1980.

Guadalupe y Martinica
Vida política y social. Siglo XX.

37. Blaise, J., et al. *Culture et politique en Guadeloupe et Martinique.* Paris: Karthala, 1981.

Guyana Francesa
Geografía

38. Aubert de la Rue, E. *Reconnaissance géologique de la Guyane française méridionale, 1948-1949-1950, précédée d'un aperçu géographique.* Paris: Larose, 1953. (Ministère de la France d'Outre Mer).

Historia

39. Devèze, Michel. *Les Guyanes.* Paris: PUF, 1968. (Col. Que sais'je? no. 1315).

Vida política y social

40. Jolivet, Marie-José. *La question créole: essai de sociologie sur la Guyane française.* Paris: Ed. de l'Office de la Recherche Scientifique et Technique d'Outre Mer, 1982.

Haití

41. Cornevin, Robert. *Haïti.* Paris: PUF, 1982. (Col. Que sais'je? no. 1955).

42. Depestre, René. *Bonjour et adieu à la négritide.* Suivi de: *Travaux d'identité.* Essais. Paris: Laffont, 1980. (Chemins d'identité).

Civilización

43. Fouchard, Jean. *Langue et littérature des aborigènes d'Ayti.* Paris: L'Ecole, 1972. (Col. Histoire et littérature haïtienne).

Descripción y viajes

44. Bitter, Maurice. *Haïti.* Paris: Seuil, 1976. (Col. Microcosme-Petite Planète, 41).

45. Drot, Jean-Marie. *Journal de voyage chez les peintres de la fête et du vaudou en Haïti.* Genève: Skira, 1974. (Couleurs de la vie).

46. Métraux, Alfred. *Haïti: la terre, les hommes et les dieux.* Neuchâtel: La Baconnière, 1957.

47. Tarnowski, Raphaël, y J. J. Flori. *Haïti.* Boulogne, Seine: Delroisse, s.f.

Guías

48. Cornevin, Robert, y J. P. Bruneau. *Haïti-Saint Domingue.* Paris: Ed. Centre Delta, s.f. (Col. Les grands voyages).

Ejército

49. Delince, Kern. *Armée et politique en Haïti.* Paris: L'Harmattan, 1979.

Geografía

50. Pereira, Paul. *Géographie d'Haïti.* Cours supérieur et complémentaire. 1ᵉʳ volume comprenant un aperçu général sur l'île d'Haïti et géographie physique de la République d'Haïti. S.l., s.e., 1938.

Historia

51. Brutus, Timoléon C. *Rançon du génie ou la leçon de Toussaint L'Ouverture.* 2ᵉ vol. Port-au-Prince: Théodore, 1945. (Col. "Pro Patria").

52. Césaire, Aimé. *Toussaint L'Ouverture: la Révolution française et le problème colonial.* Paris: Club Français du Livre, 1960. (Précurseurs).

53. Dorsinville, Roger. *Toussaint L'Ouverture ou la vocation de la liberté.* Paris: Julliard, 1965. (Les Temps modernes).

54. James, P. I. R. *Les Jacobins noirs: Toussaint L'Ouverture et la révolution de Saint Domingue.* Trad. del inglés. Paris: Gallimard, 1949. (NRF-La suite des temps, 22).

55. Massoni, Pierre. *Haïti, reine des Antilles.* Paris: Nouvelles Ed. Latines, 1955.

56. Saint-Gérard, Yves. *Haïti: l'enfer au paradis: mal développement et troubles de l'identité culturelle.* Toulouse: Eché, 1984.

Siglos XVII y XVIII

57. Frostin, Ch. *Les révoltes blanches à Saint Domingue aux 17è, 18è siècles Haïti avant 1789.* Publié avec le concours du C.N.R.S. Paris: L'Ecole, 1975. (Col. Histoire et littérature haïtienne).

Siglo XIX

58. Price-Mars, Jean. *La République d'Haïti et la République Dominicaine. Les aspects divers d'un problème d'histoire, de géographie et d'ethnologie. Depuis les origines du peuplement de l'île antiléenne en 1492 jusqu'à l'évolution des deux Etats qui en partagent la souveraineté en 1953.* T. 2. Port-au-Prince, 1953. (Col. du Tricinquantenaire de l'Indépendence d'Haïti).

Literatura

59. Chavet, Marie. *Filles d'Haïti.* Paris: Fasquelle, 1954.

60. Colimon, Marie-Thérèse. *Fils de misère.* Roman. Port-au-Prince: Ed. Caraïbes, 1974.

61. Glissant, Edouard. *Malemort.* Paris: Seuil, 1975.

62. Hugo, Victor. *Bug-Jargal ou la révolution haïtienne.* Les deux versions du roman (1818 et 1826). Fort-de-France: Désormaux, 1979.

63. Metellus, Jean. *Jacmel au crépuscule.* Paris: Gallimard, 1981.

64. Peisson, Henry. *Port-au-Prince.* Roman. New York: Didier, 1944.

Religión

65. Métraux, Alfred. *Le vaudou haïtien.* Paris: Gallimard, 1958.

Vida política y social. Siglo XVIII.

66. Girod de Chantrans, Justin (1750-1841). *Voyage d'un suisse dans les colonies d'Amérique.* Paris: Jules Taillandier, 1980. (Bibliothèque Geographia).

Siglo XX

67. Hurbon, Laennec. *Culture et dictature en Haïti: l'imaginaire sous contrôle.* Paris: L'Harmattan, 1979. (Publié avec le concours du C.N.R.S.).

Vida social y costumbres. Siglo XVIII.

68. Girod, François. *La vie quotidienne de la société créole. Saint Domingue au 18è siècle.* Paris: Hachette, 1972. (Col. La vie quotidienne).

Anotamos a continuación la lista de las revistas indispensables para el estudio del Caribe francés y que forman parte del acervo del IFAL.

69. *Bibliographie Latino-Américaine d'Articles,* 1977—.

70. *Bulletin Bibliographique Amérique Latine (Analyse des publications françaises),* 1981—.

71. *Cahiers des Amériques Latines*, Série Sciences de l'Homme, 1967—.

72. *Cahiers D'Outre Mer: Revue de Géographie de Bordeaux*, 1948-1981.

73. *Cahiers du CERAG* (Centre d'Etudes Régionales Antilles-Guyane), 1978-1982.

74. *Conjonction: Revue franco-haïtienne*, 1962-1982.

75. *Journal de la Société des Américanistes*, 1912-1932, 1943-1982.

76. *Problèmes d'Amérique Latine*, 1977—.

Por último, queremos señalar que el personal del IFAL analiza buen número de publicaciones periódicas de tal suerte que su fichero analítico de artículos de revistas y de periódicos cuenta con un material muy interesante y actual sobre el Caribe francés.

24. Women in the Non-Hispanic Caribbean: A Selective Bibliography

Judith Selakoff

Abraham, Julian A. *The Female in the Police Force: A Consultation Done in Curacao*. Curacao, 1974[?]. 51 p.

Allman, James. "Conjugal Unions in Rural and Urban Haiti." *Social and Economic Studies* 34:1 (March 1985), 24-57.

Anderson, Patricia. "Women, Work and Development in the Caribbean." In Women, Work and Development. Cave Hill: Institute of Social and Economic Research (Eastern Caribbean), University of the West Indies, 1984. Pp. vii-xviii.

Andre, Jacques. "Le coq et la jarre: le sexuel et le feminin dan les sociétés Afro-Caribeenes." *L'Homme* 25:4 (October-December 1985), 49-76.

Antigua and Barbuda. Women's Desk. Women: Antigua and Barbuda. St. John's, 1984. 80 p.

Antrobus, Peggy. *Caribbean Women and Development: A Reassessment of Concepts, Perspectives and Issues*. Pinelands, St. Michael: Women and Development Unit, University of the West Indies, January 1985. 5 p.

_____. "Emerging Status of Jamaican Women." *Response* 9:6 (June 1977), 18-21.

_____. *Equality, Development and Peace: A Second Look at the Goals of the UN Decade for Women*. Pinelands, St. Michael: Women and Development Unit, University of the West Indies, 1983. 20 p.

_____. *Hanover Street: An Experiment to Train Women in Welding and Carpentry*. New York, NY: SEEDS, 1980. 15 p.

_____. *Institutions and Programmes for the Decade*. Pinelands, St. Michael: Women and Development Unit, University of the West Indies, March 1985. 4 p.

_____. "Women in Development: The Issues for the Caribbean." *Caribbean Educational Bulletin* 8:2 (May 1981), 1-7.

Bahamas. Department of Statistics. A Collection of Statistics on Women in the Bahamas, 1970-1982. Nassau, August 1982. 184 p.

_____. *Some Aspects of Fertility in New Providence.* Nassau, August 1981. 38 p.

Baptiste, Rhona. "Where We Are: Legal Rights of Women in the Caribbean." *Response* 9:6 (June 1977), 15-17.

Barbados Family Planning Association. *A Comparative Study of Contraceptive Prevalence in Antigua, Dominica, St. Lucia and St. Vincent.* Columbia, MD: Westinghouse Health Systems, 1983. 83 p.

Barbados. National Commission on the Status of Women. *Report.* St. Michael, Barbados: Government Printing Office, May 1978. 2 vols. in 3.

Bell, Robert R. "Marriage and Family Differences among Lower-Class Negro and East Indian Women in Trinidad." *Race* 12:1 (July 1970), 59-73.

Best, Ethel. *Economic Problems of the Women of the Virgin Islands of the United States.* U.S. Department of Labor, Women's Bureau, Publication 42. Washington, DC: United States Government Printing Office, 1936. 24 p.

"Beyond a Decade." *Women Speak!* 18 (July/December 1985), 3-35. Special Issue.

Bilby, Kenneth. "Black Women and Survival: A Maroon Case." In *The Black Woman Cross-Culturally*, Filomina C. Steady, ed. Cambridge, MA: Schenkman, 1981. Pp. 451-467.

Bird, Edris. "The Role of Women in Social and Economic Development in the Caribbean." *Report on Consultation on Social and Economic Development in the Eastern Caribbean Held in St. Vincent, Nov. 26-30, 1968.* Port-of-Spain: Superservice Printing Co., 1968. Pp. 21-24.

_____. "Adult Education and the Advancement of Women in the West Indies." *Convergence* 8:1 (1975), 57-67.

Bissett-Johnson, A. "West Indian Views of Palm Tree Justice and Section 17 of the Married Women's Property Act." *International and Comparative Law Quarterly* 14:1 (January 1965), 308-312.

Bland, Anthony. "How Constructive Is the Trust? The Use of the Concept in Relation to Property Rights of the De Facto Spouses: A Comparative Study." West Indian Law Journal (October 1977), 34-48.

Blume, Sheila. "Alcoholism in Women." *Proceedings of the Caribbean Institute on Alcoholism, St. Thomas, June 17-26, 1975, and June 1-12, 1976.* St. Thomas: College of the Virgin Islands, 1977. Pp. 63-69.

Bolles, A. Lynn. "'Goin' Abroad': Working Class Jamaican Women and Migration." In *Female Immigrants to the United States: Caribbean, Latin American, and African Experiences*, Delores M. Mortimer and Roy S. Bryce-Laporte, eds. Washington, DC: Research Institute on Immigration and Ethnic Studies, Smithsonian Institution, 1981. Pp. 56-84.

_____. "IMF Destabilization: The Impact on Working Class Jamaican Women." *Transafrica Forum* 2:1 (Summer 1983), 63-75.

_____. "The Impact of Working Class Women's Employment on Household Organization in Kingston, Jamaica." Ph.D. diss., Rutgers University, 1981. Ann Arbor, MI: University Microfilms, 1981. 264 p.

Bouchereau, Madeleine. "Haïti et ses femmes: une étude d'évolution culturelle." Ph.D. diss., Bryn Mawr College, 1941. Ann Arbor, MI: University Microfilms, 1941. 349 p.

Brana-Shute, Gary. "Mothers in Uniform: The Children's Police of Suriname." *Urban Anthropology* 10:1 (Spring 1981), 71-88.

Brodber, Erna. *Perceptions of Caribbean Women.* Introduction by Merle Hodge. Women in the Caribbean Project, Vol. 4. Cave Hill: Institute of Social and Economic Research (Eastern Caribbean), University of the West Indies, 1982. 62 p.

Brody, Eugene B. *Sex, Contraception and Motherhood in Jamaica.* Cambridge, MA: Harvard University Press, 1981. 278 p.

_____. *The Meaning of First Coitus in Relation to Later Reproductive Performance in Jamaica Women.* Montreal, n.d. 41 p.

Buchanan, Susan H. "Profile of a Haitian Migrant Woman." In *Female Immigrants to the United States: Caribbean, Latin American, and African Experiences*, Delores M. Mortimer and Roy S. Bryce-Laporte, eds. Washington, DC: Research Institute on Immigration and Ethnic Studies, Smithsonian Institution, 1981. Pp. 112-142.

Bullard, M. Kenyon. "Hide and Secrete: Women's Sexual Magic in Belize." *Journal of Sexual Research* 10:4 (November 1974), 259-265.

Burgess, Judith A. "Migration and Sex Roles: A Comparison of Black and Indian Trinidadians in New York City." In *Female*

Immigrants to the United States: Caribbean, Latin American, and African Experiences, Delores M. Mortimer and Roy S. Bryce-Laporte, eds. Washington, DC: Research Institute on Immigration and Ethnic Studies, Smithsonian Institution, 1981. Pp. 85-111.

Bush, Barbara. "Towards Emancipation: Slave Women and Resistance to Coercive Labor Regimes in the British West Indian Colonies, 1790-1838." *Slavery and Abolition* 5:3 (December 1985), 222-243.

_____. "White 'Ladies,' Coloured 'Favourites' and 'Black 'Wenches': Some Considerations on Sex, Race and Class Factors in Social Relations in White Creole Society in the British Caribbean." *Slavery and Abolition* 2:3 (December 1981), 245-262.

Byrne, Joycelin. *Levels of Fertility in the Commonwealth Caribbean, 1921-1965*. Kingston: Institute of Social and Economic Research, University of the West Indies, 1972. 84 p.

Cannon, Jo Ann. "Mating Patterns as Environmental Adaptations in Dominica, British West Indies." Ph.D. diss., University of California, Los Angeles, 1970. Ann Arbor, MI: University Microfilms, 1971. 189 p.

"Caribbean Woman." *Savacou* 13 (Gemini 1977), v-90. Special issue.

Celma, Cecile. "Les femmes au travail à la Martinique (XVII-XX siècles): première approche. *Dossiers de l'Outre Mer (Bulletin d'Information du CENADDOM)* 82 (1st trimestre 1986), 24-31.

Centre d'Entraide et d'Etudes des Antillais, Guyannais, Reunionnais. "Femmes et mères Antillaises: faits, témoignages et représentations." *Dossiers de l'Outre Mer (Bulletin d'Information du CENADDOM)* 82 (1st trimestre 1986), 95-103.

Clarendon, Hannah. *Women and Food Production*. Pinelands, St. Michael: Women and Development Unit, University of the West Indies, April 1985. 3 p.

Clark, Bori S., comp. *Trinidad Women Speak*. Introduction by Patricia Mohammed. Redlands, CA: Libros Latinos, 1981. 71 p.

Clarke, Roberta. "Dim Light at the End of the Tunnel: A Critique of the Integration of Women in Development Approach." *Bulletin of Eastern Caribbean Affairs* 11:2 (May/June 1985), 51-60.

Cohen Stuart, Bertie A., comp. Women in the Caribbean: A Bibliography. Leiden: Department of Caribbean Studies, Royal Institute of Linguistics and Anthropology, 1979. 163 p.

Cole, Joyce. "Official Ideology and the Education of Women in the English-speaking Caribbean, 1835-1945, with Special Reference to

Barbados." In *Women and Education*. Cave Hill: Institute of Social and Economic Research (Eastern Caribbean), University of the West Indies, 1982. Pp. 1-34.

Coleridge, P. E. "Vrouwenleven in Paramaribo." In *Suriname in Stroomlijnen*, J. van de Walle and H. de Wit, eds. Amsterdam: Wereld Bibliotheek, 1978. Pp. 86-93.

Comhaire, Suzanne-Sylvain. "La paysanne de la région de Kenscoff (Haïti)." In *La Femme de Couleur en Amérique Latine*, Roger Bastide, ed. Paris: Editions Anthropos, 1974. Pp. 149-170.

"Conflict and Protest." *Women Speak!* 19,20 (April/August 1986), 2-40. Special Issue.

Cropper, Angela. The Integration of Women in Development of Windward and Leeward Islands of the Caribbean: A Situation Study. Discussion, Analysis and Statistical Tables. Pinelands, St. Michael: Women and Development Unit, University of the West Indies, March 1980. 62 p.

Cuthbert, Marlene, ed. *The Role of Women in Caribbean Development*. Bridgetown, Barbados: CADEC (Caribbean Ecumenical Consultation for Development), 1971. 56 p.

Dagenais, Huguette. "L'apport méconnu des femmes à la vie économique et social aux Antilles: le cas de la Guadeloupe." *Anthropologie et Sociétés* 8:2 (1984), 179-187.

Daly, Stephanie. *The Developing Legal Status of Women in Trinidad and Tobago*. Port-of-Spain: National Commission on the Status of Women, 1982. 136 p.

Drayton, Kathleen. "Women and Education." In *Women and Education*. Cave Hill: Institute of Social and Economic Research (Eastern Caribbean), University of the West Indies, 1982. Pp. vii-xiv.

_____. *Women in Social Development: Health and Education in the Commonwealth Caribbean over the Decade for Women*. Pinelands, St. Michael: Women and Development Unit, University of the West Indies, August 1985. 10 p.

_____. "Women, Power and the Social Construct of Reality." *Bulletin of Eastern Caribbean Affairs* 9:2 (May/June 1983), 15-24.

Duncan, Neville. *Women and Politics in Barbados, 1948-1981*. Women in the Caribbean Project, vol. 3. Cave Hill: Institute of Social and Economic Research (Eastern Caribbean), University of the West Indies, 1983. 68 p.

Durant-Gonzalez, Victoria. "Higglering: Rural Women and the Internal Market." In *Rural Development in the Caribbean.* P. I. Gomes, ed. New York, NY: St. Martin's Press, 1985. Pp. 103-122.

_____. "Role and Status of Rural Jamaican Women: Higglering and Mothering." Ph.D. diss., University of California, Berkeley, 1976. Ann Arbor, MI: University Microfilms, 1977. 212 p.

_____. "The Occupation of Higglering." *Jamaica Journal* 16:3 (August 1983), 2-12.

_____. "The Realm of Female Familial Responsibility." In *Women and the Family.* Cave Hill: Institute of Social and Economic Research (Eastern Caribbean), University of the West Indies, 1982. Pp. 1-27.

_____. *Women and Industry.* Pinelands, St. Michael: Women and Development Unit, University of the West Indies, March 1985. 3 p.

Edwards, Melvin R. *Jamaican Higglers: Their Significance and Potential.* Swansea, Wales: Centre for Developing Studies, University College of Swansea, University of Wales, May 1980. 58 p.

Ellis, Patricia. *From Silent Beneficiaries to Active Participants and Contributors to the Development Process.* Pinelands, St. Michael: Women and Development Unit, University of the West Indies, August 1983. 13 p.

_____. "How Extension Services Can Enhance the Role of Women in Agricultural Development." *Cajanus* 17:1 (1984), 8-15.

_____. *Mini Courses in Social Studies: An Introduction to Women's Studies Prepared for Social Studies Education.* Pinelands, St. Michael: Women and Development Unit, University of the West Indies, February 1981. 10 p.

_____. "Non-formal Education, Women, and Development in the English-speaking Caribbean." *Bulletin of Eastern Caribbean Affairs* 11:2 (May/June 1985), 23-33.

_____. *The Role of Women in Rural Development. The Rose Hall Experience: Bottom Up Development in Action.* Pinelands, St. Michael: Women and Development Unit, University of the West Indies, August 1983. 32 p.

_____. *Women, Adult Education and Literacy: A Caribbean Perspective.* Pinelands, St. Michael: Women and Development Unit, University of the West Indies, January 1985. 5 p.

_____. *Women and Adult Non-formal Education: The Use of Participatory Methods in a Community Based Adult Education Programme in Rose Hall, St. Vincent.* Pinelands, St. Michael: Women and Development Unit, University of the West Indies, May 1982. 17 p.

"End of the UN Decade for Women, 1975-1985." *Bulletin of Eastern Caribbean Affairs* 11:2 (May/June 1985), 1-60.

Fanon, Frederique. "L'emploi des femmes à la Martinique." *Dossiers de l'Outre Mer (Bulletin d'Information du CENADDOM)* 82 (1st trimestre 1986), 57-64.

Foner, Nancy. "Male and Female: Jamaican Migrants in London." *Anthropological Quarterly* 49:1 (January 1976), 28-35.

_____. "Women, Work, and Migration: Jamaicans in London." Urban Anthropology 4:3 (1975), 229-249.

Ford-Smith, Honor. "Sistren: Explaining Women's Problems through Drama." *Jamaica Journal* 19:1 (February/April 1986), 2-12.

Forde, Norma M. *The Status of Women in Barbados: What Has Been Done since 1978.* Cave Hill: Institute of Social and Economic Research (Eastern Caribbean), University of the West Indies, 1980. 53 p.

_____. "What Has Been Done? A Re-assessment of the Barbados National Commission Report and Recommendations." *West Indian Law Journal* (March 1981), 45-62.

_____. *Women and the Law.* Cave Hill: Institute of Social and Economic Research (Eastern Caribbean), University of the West Indies, 1981. 125 p.

Fortunat, F. *Les déterminants proches de la fécondité en Haïti.* Voorburg, Netherlands: International Statistical Institute, December 1984. 77 p.

Gautier, Arlette. *Les soeurs de solitude: la condition féminine dans l'esclavage aux Antilles du XVII au XIX siècle.* Paris: Editions Caribéennes, 1985. 285 p.

_____. "La vie des esclaves Antillaises." *Dossiers de l'Outre Mer (Bulletin d'Information du CENADDOM)* 82 (1st trimestre 1986), 71-72.

Gervais, Françoise. "Le sport, l'activité physique et la femme Martiniquaise." *Dossiers de l'Outre Mer (Bulletin d'Information du CENADDOM)* 82 (1st trimestre 1986), 83-88.

Gibson, Evette. "Underemployment and Unemployment of Caribbean Women." *Bulletin of Eastern Caribbean Affairs* 11:2 (May/June 1985), 39-45.

Gill, Margaret. "Women, Work and Development in Barbados, 1946-1970." In Women, Work and Development. Cave Hill: Institute of Social and Economic Research (Eastern Caribbean), University of the West Indies, 1984. Pp. 1-40.

Goossen, Jean. "The Migration of French West Indian Women to Metropolitan France." *Anthropological Quarterly* 49:1 (January 1976), 45-52.

Gordon, Monica H. "Caribbean Migration: A Perspective on Women." In Female Immigrants to the United States: Caribbean, Latin American, and African Experiences, Delores M. Mortimer and Roy S. Bryce-Laporte, eds. Washington, DC: Research Institute on Immigration and Ethnic Studies, Smithsonian Institution, 1981. Pp. 14-55.

Griffith, David C. "Women, Remittances, and Reproduction." *American Ethnologist* 12:4 (1985), 676-690.

Groot, Silvia W. de. "Maroon Women as Ancestors, Priests and Mediums in Suriname." *Slavery and Abolition* 7:2 (September 1986), 160-174.

Gussler, Judith D. "Adaptive Strategies and Social Networks of Women in St. Kitts." In *A World of Women: Anthropological Studies of Women in Societies of the World*, Erika Bourguignon, ed. New York, NY: Praeger, 1980). Pp. 185-209.

Guy, Henry A. *Women in the Caribbean: A Record of Career Women in the Caribbean: Their Background, Service and Achievements.* Kingston: The Author, 1966. 173 p.

Hamilton, Jill. *Women of the Barbados: Amerindian Era to mid-20th Century.* Bridgetown: The Author, 1981. 91 p.

Hamilton, Marlene A. "Sex-Incongruous Occupational Roles." *Social and Economic Studies* 34:1 (March 1985), 97-111.

Haniff, Nesha Z. "Successful Caribbean Women: We Had the Courage and the Vision." Ph.D. diss., University of Michigan, 1983. Ann Arbor, MI: University Microfilms, 1984. 160 p.

Harewood, Jack. *Family Planning in Trinidad and Tobago in 1970: Preliminary Report on the Family Planning Survey–Females.* St. Augustine: Institute of Social and Economic Research (Eastern Caribbean), University of the West Indies, 1971. 61 p.

_____. *Unions and Partners in Guyana: Paper Prepared for Discussion at the WPS Caribbean Seminar in Trinidad, September 6-8, 1982.* N.p., 1982. 96 p.

_____. *What Our Women Know, Think and Do About Birth Control: A Graphic Summary of the Results of the Family Planning Survey-Females.* St. Augustine: Institute of Social and Economic Research (Eastern Caribbean), University of the West Indies, 1972. 42 p.

Harris-Coleman, Valerie. "Women in an Independent Antigua and Barbuda." *Everybody's Magazine* 5:8 (December 1981), 22-25.

Henney, Jeannette H. "Sex and Status: Women in St. Vincent." In *A World of Women: Anthropological Studies of Women in Societies of the World*, Erika Bourguignon, ed. New York, NY: Praeger, 1980). Pp. 161-183.

Henry, Frances. "The Status of Women in Caribbean Societies: An Overview of Their Social, Economic and Sexual Roles." *Social and Economic Studies* 24:2 (June 1975), 165-198.

Holder, Joyce. "Caribbean Women in Community Development." *Response* 9:6 (June 1977), 22-24.

Holzberg, Carol S. In Celebration of Jamaican Jewish Women: An Extended History of the Jewish Ladies Organization. N.p., 1980. 31 p.

Homiak, John. "The Hucksters of Dominica." *Grassroots Development* 10:1 (1986), 30-37.

Hope, Margaret. *Journey in the Shaping.* Cave Hill: Women and Development Unit, University of the West Indies, n.d. 59 p.

Inter-American Institute of Agricultural Sciences (IICA). Committee for Rural Women and Development. *Rural Women: A Caribbean Bibliography with Special Reference to Jamaica.* San José, Costa Rica, 1980. 29 p.

Jackson-Christmas, June. "'I'm Sick and Tired of Being Sick and Tired': Black Women and Health Care in the 80's." Pinelands, St. Michael: Women and Development Unit, University of the West Indies, March 1986. 5 p.

Jackson, Jean. "Stresses Affecting Women and Their Families." *Women and the Family.* Cave Hill: Institute of Social and Economic Research (Eastern Caribbean), University of the West Indies, 1972. Pp. 28-61.

Jacquet, Alain. "Les freins psycho-sociologiques à l'évolution de la condition féminine en Guadeloupe." *Dossiers de l'Outre Mer (Bulletin d'Information du CENADDOM)* 82 (1st trimestre 1986), 111-120.

Jagan, Janet. "Women United: Stand Up and Fight." *Thunder* 16:1 (1st quarter 1984), 3-9.

Jamaica. Information Service. *Jamaica Women*. Kingston, n.d. Unpaged.

Joseph, Rita S. "The Significance of the Grenada Revolution to Women in Grenada." *Bulletin of Eastern Caribbean Affairs* 7:1 (March/April 1981), 16-19.

Justus, Joyce. *Increasing Educational and Economic Options of Jamaican Adolescent Females: A Study of Policy Implications for Reducing Fertility and Raising Female Status*. New York, NY: Research Institute for the Study of Man, 1980. 129 p.

————. "Women's Role in West Indian Society." In *The Black Woman Cross-Culturally*, Filomina C. Steady, ed. Cambridge, MA: Schenkman, 1981. Pp. 431-450.

Katzin, Margaret Fisher. "Higglers of Jamaica." Ph.D. diss., Northwestern University, 1958. Ann Arbor, MI: University Microfilms, 1958. 238 p.

————. "The Business of Higglering in Jamaica." In *People and Cultures of the Caribbean: An Anthropological Reader*, Michael M. Horowitz, ed. New York, NY: Natural History Press for the American Museum of Natural History, 1971. Pp. 340-381.

————. "The Jamaican Country Higgler." In *Work and Family Life: West Indian Perspectives*, Lambros Comitas, ed. New York, NY: Anchor Books, 1973. Pp. 3-25.

————. "The Jamaican Higgler." *Social and Economic Studies* 8:4 (December 1959), 421-440.

Kerns, Virginia R. "Daughter Bring In: Ceremonial and Social Organization of the Black Carib of Belize." Ph.D. diss., University of Illinois at Urbana-Champaign, 1977. Ann Arbor, MI: University Microfilms, 1977. 363 p.

————. *Women and the Ancestors: Black Carib Kinship and Ritual*. Urbana, IL: University of Illinois Press, 1983. 229 p.

Knudson, Barbara. *The Economic Role of Women in Small Scale Agriculture in the Eastern Caribbean–St. Lucia*. Pinelands, St. Michael: Women and Development Unit, University of the West Indies, 1985. 92 p.

Kruijer, Gerardus Johannes. "Family Size and Family Planning: A Pilot Survey among Jamaican Mothers." *West-Indische Gids* 38:3-4 (December 1958), 144-150.

Latin American and Caribbean Women's Collective. *Slaves of Slaves: The Challenge of Latin American Women.* Chap. 4, "Guadeloupe and Martinique: Ethnocide and Traditional Employment." Translated by Michael Pallis. London: Zed Press, 1980. Pp. 59-64.

Latortue, Regine. "The Black Woman in Haitian Society and Literature." In *The Black Woman Cross-Culturally*, Filomina C. Steady, ed. Cambridge, MA: Schenkman, 1981. Pp. 535-560.

Leo-Rhynie, Elsa A. "Professional Jamaican Women—Equal or Not?" *Caribbean Quarterly* 29:2,3 (September-December 1983), 70-85.

Leridon, Henri. *Fécondité et famille en Martinique; faits, attitudes et opinions.* Institut National d'Etudes Démographiques. Travaux et documents. Cahier no. 56. Paris: Presses Universitaires de France, 1976. 186 p.

————. "Fertility in Martinique." *Natural History* 79:1 (January 1970), 57-59.

Manley, Beverley. *Caribbean Women and the Political Process.* Pinelands, St. Michael: Women and Development Unit, University of the West Indies, February 1985. 5 p.

————. *Women and the Process of Social Change.* Pinelands, St. Michael: Women and Development Unit, University of the West Indies, September 1985. 4 p.

Mason, Beverley J. "Jamaican Working-Class Women: Producers and Reproducers." *Review of Black Political Economy* 14:2-3 (Fall-Winter 1985-86), 250-277.

Massiah, Joycelin. "Abortion and Public Opinion in Barbados." *Bulletin of Eastern Caribbean Affairs* 3:11-12 (January/February 1978), 11-18.

————. *Employed Women in Barbados: A Demographic Profile, 1946-1970.* Cave Hill: Institute of Social and Economic Research, University of the West Indies, 1984. 131 p.

————. "Establishing a Programme of Women and Development Studies in the University of the West Indies." *Social and Economic Studies* 35:1 (March 1986), 151-197.

————. "Indicators of Women in Development: A Preliminary Framework for the Caribbean." In *Women, Work and Development.* Cave Hill: Institute of Social and Economic Research

(Eastern Caribbean), University of the West Indies, 1984. Pp. 41-129.

_____. "The Status of Women in Barbados: Some Considerations." *Bulletin of Eastern Caribbean Affairs* 2:9 (November 1976), 1-5.

_____. "The UN Decade for Women: Perspectives from the Commonwealth Caribbean." *Bulletin of Eastern Caribbean Affairs* 11:2 (May/June 1985), 1-9.

_____. *Women in the Caribbean: An Annotated Bibliography: A Guide to Material Available in Barbados.* Cave Hill: Institute of Social and Economic Research (Eastern Caribbean), University of the West Indies, April 1979. 133 p.

_____. *Women as Heads of Households in the Caribbean: Family Structure and Feminine Status.* Paris: UNESCO, 1983. 69 p.

_____. "Women in the Caribbean: Research Problems and Needs." *Bulletin of Eastern Caribbean Affairs* 7:3 (July/August 1981), 16-22.

_____. "Women Who Held Households." In *Women and the Family.* Cave Hill: Institute of Social and Economic Research (Eastern Caribbean), University of the West Indies, 1982. Pp. 62-130.

Mathurin, Lucille. "A Historical Study of Women in Jamaica from 1655-1844." Ph.D. diss., University of the West Indies, 1974. Kingston, 1974. 489 p.

_____. "The Arrivals of Black Women." *Jamaica Journal* 9:2-3 (1975), 2-7.

_____. *The Rebel Woman in the British West Indies during Slavery.* Kingston: African-Caribbean Publications, 1975. 41 p.

_____. "Reluctant Matriarchs." *Savacou* 13 (Gemini 1977), 1-7.

Maugé, Michelene E. "Against the Odds: An Examination of Background, Motivation and Achievement of Successful Black Women of West Indian Descent." M.A. thesis, Boston University, 1982. Boston, MA, 1982. 98 p.

Maze, Brian L. "The Selective Utilization of Legal Avenues of Assistance by Women on the Caribbean Island of St. Kitts in the British Leewards." Ph.D. diss., Ohio State University, 1985. Ann Arbor, MI: University Microfilms, 1985. 357 p.

McClean, A. Wendell A. "The Economic Role of Women in the Development of the Caribbean." *Bulletin of Eastern Caribbean Affairs* 4:6 (January/February 1979), 11-16.

McKenzie, Hermione. "Caribbean Women: Yesterday, Today, Tomorrow." *Savacou* 13 (Gemini 1977), vii-xiv.

————. "Women and the Family in Caribbean Society." In *Women and the Family*. Cave Hill: Institute of Social and Economic Research (Eastern Caribbean), University of the West Indies, 1982. Pp. vii-xv.

Miller, Errol L. "Self-Evaluation among Jamaican High School Girls." *Social and Economic Studies* 22:4 (December 1973), 407-426.

Mintz, Sidney W. "Economic Role and Cultural Tradition." In *The Black Woman Cross-Culturally*, Filomina C. Steady, ed. Cambridge, MA: Schenkman, 1981. Pp. 515-534.

————. "The Employment of Capital by Market Women in Haiti." In *Capital, Saving, and Credit in Peasant Societies*, Raymond Firth, ed. London: George Allen and Unwin, 1964. Pp. 256-286.

————. "Les rôles économiques et la tradition culturelle." In *La Femme de Couleur en Amérique Latine*, Roger Bastide, ed. Paris: Editions Anthropos, 1974. Pp. 115-148.

————. "La utilización del capital por las vendedoras de mercado en Haití." *América Indígena* 42:3 (1982), 409-447.

Mohammed, Patricia. "Educational Attainment of Women in Trinidad-Tobago, 1946-1980." In *Women and Education*. Cave Hill: Institute of Social and Economic Research (Eastern Caribbean), University of the West Indies, 1982. Pp. 35-77.

————. *The Woman's Movement in Trinidad and Tobago since the 1960's*. Pinelands, St. Michael: Women and Development Unit, University of the West Indies, 1985. 2 pts. 9 p.

Morin, Françoise. "La femme haïtienne en diaspora." In *La Femme de Couleur en Amérique Latine*, Roger Bastide, ed. Paris: Editions Anthropos, 1974. Pp. 211-220.

Morrissey, Mike. *Women in Jamaica: A Contribution to International Women's Year*. Kingston: Jamaica Department of Statistics, n.d. 3 p.

Moses, Yolanda T. "Female Status and Male Dominance in Montserrat, West Indies." Ph.D. diss., University of California, Riverside, 1976. Ann Arbor, MI: University Microfilms, 1976. 267 p.

————. "Female Status, the Family, and Male Dominance in the West Indian Community." In *The Black Woman Cross-Culturally*, Filomina C. Steady, ed. Cambridge, MA: Schenkman, 1981. Pp. 499-513.

_____. "What Price Education: The Working Women of Montserrat." *Council on Anthropology in Education Quarterly* 7 (1975), 13-16.

Nag, Moni. "Patterns of Mating Behaviour, Emigration and Contraceptives as Factors Affecting Human Fertility in Barbados." *Social and Economic Studies* 20:2 (June 1971), 111-133.

Nielsen Allen, Corinne A. "Factors Influencing Life Decision and Attitudes toward Life Decisions: An Intergenerational Study of Crucian Women (Virgin Islands)." Ph.D. diss., Indiana United Nations, 1983. Ann Arbor, MI: University Microfilms, 1984. 200 p.

Nicholson, Marteen. "Migration of Caribbean Women in the Health Care Field: A Case Study of Jamaican Nurses.' Ph.D. diss., City University of New York, 1985. Ann Arbor, MI: University Microfilms, 1986. 163 p.

Osei, G. K. *Caribbean Women: Their History and Habits.* London: Africa Publication Society, 1979. 191 p.

Ostrowsky, Bernice J. "Peasant Marketing in Antigua." M.A. thesis, Brandeis University, 1969. Waltham, MA, 1969. 63 p.

Pau-Langevin, George. "La femme Antillaise dans l'émigration." *Dossiers de l'Outre Mer (Bulletin d'Information du CENADDOM)* 82 (1st trimestre 1986), 121-126.

Perinbaum, B. Marie. "The Parrot and the Phoenix: Frantz Fanon's View of the West Indian and Algerian Woman." *Savacou* 13 (Gemini 1977), 7-13.

Pollock, Nancy J. "Women and the Division of Labor: A Jamaican Example." *American Anthropologist* 74:3 (June 1972), 689-692.

Powell, Dorian. *Contraceptive Use in Jamaica: The Social, Economic and Cultural Context.* Mona: Institute of Social and Economic Research, University of the West Indies, 1978. 88 p.

_____. "Female Labour Force Participation and Fertility: An Exploratory Study of Jamaican Women." *Social and Economic Studies* 25:3 (September 1976), 234-258.

_____. "Network Analysis: A Suggested Model for the Study of Women and the Family in the Caribbean." In *Women and the Family.* Cave Hill: Institute of Social and Economic Research (Eastern Caribbean), University of the West Indies, 1982. Pp. 131-162.

_____. "The Role of Women in the Caribbean." *Social and Economic Studies* 33:2 (June 1984), 97-122.

Prescod-Roberts, Margaret. *Black Women: Bringing It All Back Home.* Bristol, England: Falling-Wall Press, 1980. 48 p.

Price, Sally. *Co-wives and Calabashes.* Ann Arbor, MI: University of Michigan Press, 1984. 224 p.

————. "Sexism and the Construction of Reality: An Afro-American Example." *American Ethnologist* 10:3 (August 1983), 460-476.

————. "The Role of Women in the Caribbean." *Social and Economic Studies* 33:2 (June 1984), 97-122.

————. "Wives, Husbands, and More Wives: Sexual Opportunities among the Saramaka." *Caribbean Review* 12:3 (August 1983), 26-29, 54-58.

Reddock, Rhoda. "Productivity in the Workplace and Domestic Responsibility." *Bulletin of Eastern Caribbean Affairs* 11:2 (May/June 1985), 16-23.

Regional Seminar on "The Participation of Women in Economic, Social and Political Development: Obstacles that Hinder Their Integration; Country Paper on Jamaica." Buenos Aires, March 22-30, 1976. n.p., n.d. 21 p.

Roberts, George W. *Fertility Differentials in Trinidad.* Vienna: Working Committee of the International Population Conference, 1959. 7 p.

————. *Fertility and Mating in Four West Indian Populations: Trinidad and Tobago, Barbados, St. Vincent, Jamaica.* Kingston: Institute of Social and Economic Research, University of the West Indies, 1975. 341 p.

————. "Mating among East Indian and Non-Indian Women in Trinidad." *Social and Economic Studies* 11:3 (September 1982), 203-240.

————. *Reproduction and Family in Jamaica.* Kingston, n.d. 370 p.

————. *Women in Jamaica: Patterns of Reproduction and Family.* Millwood, NY: KTO Press, 1978. 346 p.

Rowe, Maureen. "The Woman in Rastafari." *Caribbean Quarterly* 26:4 (December 1980), 13-21.

Safa, Helen I. "The CBI and Women Workers." *Cultural Survival Quarterly* 8:2 (Summer 1984), 57-59.

Seebraran, Lynette. "Rape in Trinidad and Tobago." *The Lawyer* 1:3 (January-March 1979), 17-25.

Shorey-Bryan, Norma. "The Making of Male/Female Relationships in the Caribbean." *Bulletin of Eastern Caribbean Affairs* 11:2 (May/June 1985), 34-38.

_____. *The Status of Male/Female Relationships.* Pinelands, St. Michael: Women and Development Unit, University of the West Indies, May 1985. 4 p.

Silvera, Makeda. *Silenced: Makeda Silvera Talks with West Indian Women about Their Lives and Struggles as Domestic Workers in Canada.* Toronto: Williams-Wallace, 1983. 132 p.

Sinclair, Sonja A. "Socio-biological Perspectives of Female Reproduction in Jamaica." Ph.D. diss., University of Surrey, April 1981. Surrey, 1981. 396 p.

Singh, Jotis. *Selected Aspects of Guyanese Fertility: Education, Mating and Race.* Canberra: Development Studies Centre, Australian National University, 1980. 49 p.

Smith, Janet D. "The Caribbean Woman as Dominant: Fact or Fiction?" *Microstate Studies* 4 (1981), 22-36.

Spence, Eleanor Jean. "Marketing Activities and Household Activities of Country Hawkers in Barbados." M.A. thesis, Department of Sociology and Anthropology, McGill University, 1964. Montreal, 1964. 129 p.

Standing, Guy. *Migration, Labour Force Absorption and Mobility: Women in Kingston, Jamaica.* Geneva: International Labour Organization, October 1978. 28 p.

_____. *Unemployment and Female Labour: A Study of Labour Supply in Kingston, Jamaica.* New York, NY: St. Martin's Press, 1981. 364 p.

Stavrakis, Olga. "Women, Agriculture and Development in the Maya Lowlands: Profit or Progress?" *Belizean Studies* 8:5 (September 1980), 20-28.

Stycos, J. Mayone. *The Control of Human Fertility in Jamaica.* Ithaca, NY: Cornell University Press, 1964. 129 p.

Sutton, Constance R. "Social Inequality and Sexual Status in Barbados." *Sexual Stratification: A Cross-Cultural View.* New York, NY: Columbia University Press, 1977. Pp. 292-325.

_____. "Women, Knowledge and Power." In *Women Cross-Culturally: Change and Challenge*, Ruby Roehrlich-Levitt, ed. The Hague: Mouton, 1975. Pp. 581-600.

Talbot, Sylvia R. "Contemporary Issues in the Ordination of Women in the Caribbean." *Caribbean Journal of Religious Studies* 2:2 (September 1979), 8-24.

Tarer, George. "Les femmes battues: un phénomène de société en Guadeloupe." *Dossiers de l'Outre Mer (Bulletin d'Information du CENADDOM)* 82 (1st trimestre 1986), 107-110.

Teilhet-Fisk, Jehane. "Djuka Women and Men's Art." *African Arts* 17:2 (February 1984), 64-66.

Texeira, Gail. "Amerindian Women: Lowest Rung of Society." *Thunder* 18:3 (3d quarter 1986), 28-34.

Thoden van Velzen, H. U. E. "Female Religious Responses to Male Prosperity in Turn-of-the-Century Bush Negro Societies." *Nieuwe West-Indische Gids/New West Indian Guide* 56:1,2 (1982), 43-68.

Thorpe, Marjorie. "The Problem of Culture Identification in Crick Crack Monkey." *Savacou* 13 (Gemini 1977), 31-38.

Trinidad and Tobago. Central Statistical Office. *Trinidad and Tobago Fertility Survey, 1977*, Vol. 1, *Country Report*. Port-of-Spain, 1980. 153 p.

Turittin, Jane. "'We Don't Look for Prejudice': Migrant Mobility among Lower Status West Indian Women from Montserrat." In *Two Nations, Many Cultures! Ethnic Groups in Canada*, Jean L. Elliott, ed. Scarborough, Ontario: Prentice-Hall of Canada, 1979. Pp. 311-324.

United States. Agency for International Development. Office of Development Information and Utilization. *Selected Statistical Data by Sex: Latin America, Guyana.* Washington, DC, 1981. 48 p.

_____. *Selected Statistical Data by Sex: Latin America, Haiti.* Washington, DC, 1981. 47 p.

_____. *Selected Statistical Data by Sex: Latin America, Jamaica.* Washington, DC, 1981. 49 p.

University of the West Indies. Extra-Mural Department. *Caribbean Resource Kit for Women.* Pinelands, St. Michael: Women and Development Unit; New York, NY: International Women's Tribune Center, March 1982. Various paging.

_____. *Planning for Women in Rural Development: A Source Book for the Caribbean.* Pinelands, St. Michael: Women and Development Unit, University of the West Indies; New York, NY: Population Council of New York, 1985. 112 p.

_____. Institute of Social and Economic Research (Eastern Caribbean). *Report on Planning Workshop for Project Women in the Caribbean, September 24-27, 1979.* Cave Hill, 1979. 35 p.

Uri, Alex. "Market Women in Guadeloupe." *Response* 9:6 (June 1977), 12-14.

Vance, Carole S. "Female Employment and Fertility in Barbados." Ph.D. diss., Columbia University, 1979. New York, NY, 1979. Various paging.

Vassoigne, Yolene de. "La femme dans la société antillaise 'Française.'" In *La Femme de Couleur en Amérique Latine*, Roger Bastide, ed. Paris: Editions Anthropos, 1974. Pp. 193-209.

Veeder, Nancy W. "Prenatal Care Utilization and Persistence Patterns in a Developing Nation: A Study of One Hundred and Eighty-five Pregnant Women Attending Two Prenatal Clinics in Kingston, Jamaica, West Indies." Ph.D. diss., Florence Heller Graduate School for Advanced Studies in Social Welfare, Brandeis University, 1974. Ann Arbor, MI: University Microfilms, 1974. 247 p.

"Violence against Women." *Women Speak!* 19 (March 1983), 2-22. Special issue.

Waterman, Kathy Ann. "The Gentle Arm of the Law." *People* 8:3 (October-November 1983), 30-35.

Williams, Cheryl. *The Role of Women in Caribbean Culture*. Pinelands, St. Michael: Women and Development Unit, University of the West Indies, June 1985. 4 p.

_____. "The Role of Women in Caribbean Culture." *Bulletin of Eastern Caribbean Affairs* 11:2 (May/June 1985), 46-50.

"Women and Aging." *Women Speak!* 8 (September 1982), 3-17. Special issue.

"Women and Agriculture." *Women Speak!* 7 (May 1982), 1-17. Special issue.

"Women and Credit." *Women Speak!* 14 (May 1984), 3-17. Special issue.

"Women and Disability." *Women Speak!* 15 (July 1984), 3-23. Special issue.

Women and Education. Cave Hill: Institute of Social and Economic Research (Eastern Caribbean), University of the West Indies, 1982. 77 p.

Women and the Family. Cave Hill: Institute of Social and Economic Research (Eastern Caribbean), University of the West Indies, 1982. 77 p.

"Women and the Law." *Women Speak!* 15 (July 1984), 3-24. Special issue.

"Women and the Media." *Women Speak!* 13 (January 1984), 3-14. Special issue.

Women, Work and Development. Cave Hill: Institute of Social and Economic Research (Eastern Caribbean), University of the West Indies, 1984.

Women's Progressive Organization (Guyana). *Forward with the Women's Struggle.* Georgetown, October 1983. 39 p.

World Fertility Survey. *Evaluation of the Guyana Fertility Survey, 1975,* by Sundat Balkaran. Voorburg, Netherlands: International Statistical Institute; London: World Fertility Survey, February 1982. 37 p.

_____. *The Guyana Fertility Survey, 1975.* Voorburg, Netherlands: International Statistical Institute; London: World Fertility Survey, March 1980. 37 p.

_____. *The Haiti Fertility Survey, 1977: A Summary of Findings.* Voorburg, Netherlands: International Statistical Institute; London: World Fertility Survey, September 1981. 17 p.

_____. *The Jamaica Fertility Survey, 1975-76: A Summary of Findings.* Voorburg, Netherlands: International Statistical Institute; London: World Fertility Survey, June 1980. 10 p.

"Young Women!" *Women Speak!* 12 (October 1983), 3-20. Special issue.

25. A Search for New Interpretations: The Puerto Rican Experience

Thomas Mathews

To place in proper perspective my remarks and, in a sense, offer some authority to my observations, it may be argued that *Puerto Rican Politics and the New Deal*,[1] published by the University of Florida Press in 1960, initiated the process we have under review today. After this work came a long list of publications by writers like Truman Clark, Robert Anderson, Henry Wells, Surendra Bhana, and others.[2] Almost all of these works were based on research in the National Archives, Presidential Libraries, and other depositories of government reports and documents.

Most of these works carved out limited periods of the current century. There were also other works published in the sixties and seventies which followed the pattern established by Lidio Cruz Monclova and dealt with the Spanish period of colonial control of Puerto Rico. The works of Loida Figueroa and Germán Delgado Pasapera[3] are examples of this type of history.

As could have been expected these studies of the fifties and sixties produced a reaction. This reaction in the students of the sixties and seventies has fermented into the output of the late seventies and early eighties. Some of these new writers of the history of Puerto Rico, like Carmen Rafucci, Juan Rodriguez Cruz, Isabel Picó, and Humberto García, were students of mine at one time or another. Others like Angel Quintero Rivera, Andrés Ramos Mattei, Guillermo Baralt, Francisco Scarano came from different influences, but all in one way or another reacted to the earlier histories by forging new viewpoints and offering valid material for expanded insights.

As James L. Dietz, himself a recent contributor[4] to the new history, has shown in a review article,[5] these new historians have made a conscious effort to incorporate into Puerto Rican history the "unknowns," the nameless ones. Thus Quintero[6] writes about the laborer, Baralt[7] about the rebellious slave, Marcia Rivera[8] about the woman, Fernando Picó[9] about the sharecropper or *agregado*, or Samuel Silva[10] about the social critics in the churches.

Furthermore, although Dietz does not mention it, many of these studies place Puerto Rican history on the wider stage of the Caribbean region. Thus the labor struggles of the thirties are seen against the backdrop of labor unrest in the English-speaking West Indies. Slave revolts in Puerto Rico are examined in the light of similar explosions of violence in Haiti or Guadeloupe. Humberto Garcia Muñiz[11] looks at the militarization of the colony of Puerto Rico within the proper perspective of global conflict and the big-power struggle for strategic geopolitical advantages.

One must give proper recognition to the work of Professor Gordon Lewis[12] which in almost every way pointed toward the new focus which most of these studies have chosen to emphasize.

Care must be taken to stress that for the most part there is little evidence of the rewriting of history by the new historians. It is rather that the new historians are amplifying, rounding out, and achieving a more proper perspective of history than had been possible by those of us who were initiating the process a generation ago. For example, my own case might be used to illustrate the point. Blanca Silvestrini[13] and Angel Quintero have brought out new important material which my original work did not include. However, the original framework has not been altered. As Dietz puts it: "The micro-micro studies characteristic of much of the new history depend upon the broad sweep of the old history to frame them, in the same way that the old histories are incomplete without the results of the research of the 1970s."[14]

Before closing allow me to do what a historian should never do: look into the future. In the immediate future the Organization of American States will publish the multivolume history of the Americas which includes a volume on the Caribbean. The editors are Guillermo Morón of Venezuela and John Oglesby of Canada. If you live long enough you may see the multivolume history of the Caribbean to be published by UNESCO. This cooperative effort of five volumes is a work produced by the historians of the Association of Caribbean Historians formed by Jamaicans, Venezuelans, Haitians, Puerto Ricans, Cubans, and Dominicans among many others.

The Center for the Study of Puerto Rican Reality (CEREP) that has published most of the works of the new historians is currently preparing publications that will aim at the wider nonuniversity community with books generously illustrated about the workers, women, the freed slaves, and sharecroppers. CEREP is also in the process of organizing an economic databank which will supply economic and social statistics for the new generation of historians.

NOTES

1. Thomas B. Mathews, *Puerto Rican Politics and the New Deal* (Gainesville, FL: University of Florida Press, 1960).

2. Truman R. Clark, *Puerto Rico and the United States, 1917-1933* (Pittsburgh, PA: University of Pittsburgh Press, 1975); Robert William Anderson, *Party Politics in Puerto Rico* (Stanford, CA: Stanford University Press, 1965); Henry Wells, *The Modernization of Puerto Rico* (Cambridge, MA: Harvard University Press, 1969); Surendra Bhana, *The United States and the Development of the Puerto Rican Status Question, 1936-1968* (Lawrence, KS: University Press of Kansas, 1975). This is not a complete listing of this type of study.

3. For an example of this type of study see Loida Figueroa, *Breve historia de Puerto Rico, segunda parte: desde el crepúsculo del dominio español hasta la antesala de la Ley Foraker, c1892-1900* (Río Piedras, PR: Editorial Edil, 1977).

4. James L. Dietz, *Economic History of Puerto Rico* (Princeton, NJ: Princeton University Press, 1986).

5. Idem, "Puerto Rico's New History," *Latin American Research Review* 19 (1984), 210-222.

6. Angel Quintero Rivera, *Workers' Struggle in Puerto Rico: A Documentary History* (New York, NY: Monthly Review Press, 1976).

7. Guillermo A. Baralt, *Esclavos rebeldes: conspiraciones y sublevaciones de esclavos en Puerto Rico, 1795-1873* (Río Piedras, PR: Ediciones Huracán, 1981).

8. Edna Acosta-Belén, *La mujer en la sociedad puertorriqueña* (Río Piedras, PR: Ediciones Huracán, 1981).

9. Fernando Picó, *Amargo café* (Río Piedras, PR: Ediciones Huracán, 1981).

10. Samuel Silva Gotay, *El pensamiento cristiano revolucionario en América Latina y el Caribe* (Salamanca: Sígueme, 1981).

11. Humberto García Muñiz, "Jamaica: las fuerzas de seguridad, ¿Fiel de la balanza en el futuro? " *Secuencia* (Mexico), (Septiembre/Diciembre 1986), 118-150.

12. Gordon Lewis, *Puerto Rico: Freedom and Power in the Caribbean* (New York, NY: Monthly Review Press, 1963).

13. Blanca Silvestrini de Pacheco, *Los trabajadores puertorriqueños y el Partido Socialista, 1932-1940* (Río Piedras, PR: Editorial Universitaria, 1979).

14. Dietz, "Puerto Rico's New History," p. 211.

26. Agrarian Reform in Central America: A Bibliography of Bibliographies

Nelly S. González and Scott Jacob

Introduction

The implementation of agrarian reform in Central America has been attempted to improve the social, economic, and political conditions of the rural poor and of the host country. From the point of view of economics, allocating land to the landless peasantry was seen as a way to lower rural unemployment and slow the rate of farm-to-city migration. Also, agricultural productivity has been thought to be improved through the farming of small plots of land gained through the expropriation and redistribution of large privately owned lands. From a political viewpoint, agrarian reform has been used to garner political support from the rural poor and placate domestic movements at conflict with the government in power. This attempt to include the landless poor, indigenous peoples and tenant farmers, into the political process through land ownership has been seen as a way to strike at the social inequality that predominates Latin America. Each of these measures has at some time been implemented to improve the rural conditions within Central America. [1]

Agrarian reform in Central America began after World War II with most of the activity occurring in the 1960s. A brief overview here notes some of the actions taken by the individual countries. Costa Rica implemented a modest program in the 1960s by legalizing the ownership of lands held by squatters with the hope of preventing further squatting and protecting virgin land. Political expediency caused the El Salvadoran administration of 1980 to implement a limited reform project designed to transfer lands to the rural poor. The 1979 Nicaraguan revolution has spent considerable time and energy implementing a reform policy that has combined both capitalist and socialist land reform ideologies. Guatemalan land reform legislation passed in 1949 had little impact owing to ineffective administrative implementation. Peasant agitation in Honduras attributable to large layoffs by foreign agribusiness firms in the early 1960s brought about agrarian reform legislation. The 1962 Panamanian agrarian reform legislation attempted to provide the rural poor with land for cultivation. [2]

In some cases land reform has proved successful, but other attempts have failed miserably. One constant throughout these attempts has been the numerous works written on the topic. Although the major interest in land tenure and agrarian reform has been on Mexico, Brazil, and the Andean Region, Central America's land reforms have also been observed, recorded, and commented upon. This interest has spawned a large body of literature on agrarian reform and land tenure.

With these and the following points in mind, a compilation of the bibliographies focusing on agrarian reform will be of help to the research community attempting further study on agrarian reform in Central America. One, the multidisciplinary aspect of agrarian reform literature hinders the finding of these works. A collection of these works provides a source that each discipline can turn to for its own specialized study. Two, while agrarian reform may not be seen as the powerful change agent it was, there is still strong interest in the topic as shown by monograph and journal articles produced in the 1980s. [3] Three, Russell King noted that just three bibliographies on the topic issues by the Food and Agricultural Association of the United Nations contained over 10,000 references. [4] These are only a few of the bibliographies published on the topic of land tenure and agrarian reform in Latin America. This paper compiles a listing of bibliographies on agrarian reform and related topics.

Definition

That land reform has been applied in so many ways has led to various interpretations of the term. Doreen Warriner pointed out the traditional definition of the term as meaning the redistribution of property or rights in land for the benefit of small farmers and agricultural laborers. But she also notes that any improvement in the institutions of land tenure or agricultural organization also can be considered as land reform. [5] The issue of land reform is one that is touched upon by a variety of disciplines, in particular law, agriculture, sociology, and economics. Each area is an integral part of the land reform process.

Scope

Only bibliographies and related sources that include lists of materials on agrarian reform in Central America fall within the scope of this annotated bibliography. Bibliographies have been selected from

monographic works, journal articles, indexes, and catalogs, with
emphasis on the years 1946 to the present. Here Central America
includes the Spanish-speaking countries of Costa Rica, El Salvador,
Guatemala, Honduras, Nicaragua, and Panama.

Methodology

The entries included have been selected through keyword-in-title
and subject field searches of the University of Illinois Library online
catalog, Arthur E. Gropp and Haydée Piedracueva's editions of *A
Bibliography of Latin American Bibliographies*, and the *Catalog of the
Nettie Lee Benson Latin American Collection*. Subject terms successfully
searched on the online system were "Land reform—Bibliography";
"Land reform—Latin America—Bibliography"; "Land use—Bibliography";
"Land tenure—Latin America—Bibliography." [6] Search terms in the
Gropp and Piedracueva, and the Benson Collection were "Land
reform"; "Land reform—Latin America—Bibliography"; "Land
tenure—Bibliography"; and "Land use."   These searches identified
works that in some cases mentioned other works that are also included
here.

Lionel Loroña's *Bibliography of Latin American and Caribbean
Bibliographies* (1984-85, 1985-86) was also searched for pertinent
bibliographies, but none were found. This may imply that the interest
in compiling bibliographies on land reform is waning. With this
noticeable drop-off, the time is appropriate to collate the existing
bibliographies on this topic.

The bibliographies selected for this work are filed according to the
American Library Association 1980 Filing Rules.

Annotations

Annotations are descriptive in nature. Information includes most
of the following points: basic bibliographic information, coverage of the
literature on Central America land reform, special emphasis of the
bibliography, number of pages, number of citations, and inclusion of
indexes.

Bibliographies of Special Note

Although the annotations adequately describe each of the works
listed, certain publications deserve special mention as they provided
exceptional coverage of a specific aspect of the topic.

General coverage of land reform can be found in the Wisconsin
Land Tenure Center bibliographies *Agrarian Reform and Land Tenure*
and *Agrarian Reform in Latin America: An Annotated Bibliography*;

Thomas F. Carrol, *Land Tenure and Land Reform in Latin America*; Maruja Uribe Contreras, *Bibliografía selectiva sobre reforma agraria en América Latina*; *Catalog of the Nettie Lee Benson Latin American Collection*; and the *Bibliographic Guide to Latin American Studies*.

Legal publications and legislation of the individual countries coverage are in Teresa J. Anderson, *Sources for Legal and Social Science Research on Latin America*; S. A. Baytich, *Latin America: A Bibliographical Guide to Economy, History, Law, Politics, and Society*; Confederación Universitaria Centroamericana, *Documentación Socioeconómica centroamericana*; Margarita Castillo and María José Galrão, *Bibliografía agrícola de Costa Rica*; and Uribe and Carrol's works, mentioned above.

Government publications can be found in the Food and Agriculture Organization of the United Nations, *Bibliography on Land Tenure*; IICA-CIDIA's *Indice agrícola de América Latina y el Caribe*; and *Bibliographic Guide to Government Publications: Foreign*. Social and economic aspects are covered by Ramón Oqueli, *Bibliografía sociopolítica de Honduras*; D. Neil Snarr and Leonard Brown, "Social and Economic Change in Central America and Panama," in *International Review of Modern Sociology*; and *HAPI: Hispanic American Periodicals Index*.

The area of agriculture is covered in M. Bazlul Karim, *The Green Revolution: An International Bibliography*; *Bibliography of Agriculture*; Margarita Castillo and María José Galrão, *Bibliografía agrícola de Costa Rica*; M. E. Lassany, *Agriculture in Central America, 1970-1983*; and the CAB International publication, *Rural Development Abstracts* and *World Agricultural Economics and Rural Sociology Abstracts*.

NOTES

1. Peter Dorner and Dan Kanel, "The Economic Case for Land Reform: Employment, Income Distribution, and Productivity," in *Land Reform in Latin America: Issues and Cases*, ed. Peter Dorner (Madison, WI: Land Economics for the Land Tenure Center at the University of Wisconsin-Madison, 1971), pp. 41-56. The authors outline several reasons and measures for implementation of agrarian reform in this region.

2. Pablo Casanova, ed., *Historia política de los campesinos latinoamericanos*, vol. 3 (Mexico: Siglo Veintiuno, 1985). The initiation of agrarian reform in each of the Central American countries is chronicled here.

3. An initial survey of the FBR (Full Bibliographic Record) online system at the University of Illinois under the subject headings "Agriculture and state–Country," "Land reform–Country," "Land tenure–Country," and "Land use–Country" collated 37 monographs on the topic of land reform since 1980. All six Central American countries are individually covered here. A similar search in *Hispanic American Periodicals Index*, 1980-1984, located 71 items using the headings listed above and also "Land settlement–Country." Thus interest on the topic is still strong.

4. King Russell, *Land Reform: A World Survey* (Boulder, CO: Westview Press, 1977), p. 3.

5. Doreen Warriner, *Land Reform in Principle and Practice* (Oxford: Oxford University Press, 1969), pp. xiii-xiv.

6. The following related subject headings found on the online system were not utilized in the search because "Agrarian reform" is a See reference to "Land reform" and the other headings are too broad for this search: "Agrarian reform," "Land reform," "Beneficiaries," "Economic policy," and "Social policy."

BIBLIOGRAPHY

1. Anderson, Teresa J. *Sources for Legal and Social Science Research on Latin America: Land Tenure and Agrarian Reform*. Madison, WI: Land Tenure Center, 1970. 34 p.

Informative work that describes and evaluates materials on agrarian reform through 1970. Covers institutional sources for research in the field, e.g., bibliographies, periodicals, books, and journal articles. Appendixes list addresses for international, Latin American, and United States sources for agrarian reform.

2. Asociación Costarricense de Bibliotecarios. *Anuario bibliográfico costarricense*. San José, Costa Rica: (s.n.), 1958–.

Subject headings covering materials on land reform are: Derecho agrario, Cooperativas, and Derechos. Arrangement is by subject. No annotations. Author (corporate and personal) index.

3. Bayitch, S. A. *Latin America: A Bibliographical Guide to Economy, History, Law, Politics, and Society*. University of Miami School of Law. Interamerican Studies 6. Coral Gables, FL: University of Miami Press, 1961. 335 p.

Selective research guide includes only works in English. Of interest here are the large number of legal citations that cover cooperatives, agriculture, constitutions, land, and property from 1900 to 1960, all items that relate to agrarian reform in Central America. Divided in five chapters: Bibliographical and Reference Works, General Information on Latin America, Background Information, Guide by Subject, and Guide by Country. No annotations. Subject index.

4. Bercaw, Louise O., and Annie M. Hannay. *Bibliography on Land Utilization, 1918-1936*. U.S. Department of Agriculture Miscellaneous Publication 284. Washington, DC: United States Government Printing Office, 1938. 1,508 p.

Early land use. Lists government declarations and legislation for countries in Central America during the 1930s. Arrangement by country.

5.   *Bibliographic Guide to Latin American Studies, 1984.*   3 vols. Boston, MA: G. K. Hall & Co., 1978–.

Annual publication of new acquisitions cataloged at the University of Texas Nettie Lee Benson Latin American Collection and the Library of Congress. No annotations. Access by author, title, and subject.

6.   *Bibliographic Guide to Government Publications: Foreign, 1986.* 3 vols. Boston, MA: G. K. Hall & Co., 1981–.

Compilation of foreign government publications cataloged by The Research Libraries of the New York Public Library and the Library of Congress. Includes nonbook materials. Pertinent subject headings are "Land reform"; "Land reform—Law and legislation"; "Land use"; "Land use, Rural"; "Agriculture and state." No annotations. Access by author, title, and subject.

7.   *Bibliography of Agriculture.*   Phoenix, AZ: Oryx Press, 1986. Monthly.

Lists foreign and domestic journal articles, pamphlets, reports, proceedings, and monographs in the field of agriculture.   Author (corporate and personal) and subject indexes.

8.   Bushong, Allen D.   *Doctoral Dissertations on Pan American Topics Accepted by United States and Canadian Colleges and Universities, 1961-1965: Bibliography and Analysis.* Austin, TX: *Latin American Research Review,* 1967.   Supplement to Volume II, No. 2.   70 p.

Lists doctoral dissertations on Pan American topics. Arranged by geographical region, then by subject.   Central America and Mexico occupy one region.   Updated by Nelly S. González's *Doctoral Dissertations on Latin America and the Caribbean, 1966-1970.*   No annotations.

9.   Carrol, Thomas F.   *Land Tenure and Land Tenure in Latin America: A Selective Annotated Bibliography.* 2d ed. Washington, DC: Inter-American Development Bank, 1965.   474 p.

Of importance here are the selective listing of agrarian reform legislation for the individual Central American countries in Appendix IV and the four general aspects of land reform that make up the first chapter of this work (Historical Accounts of Land Tenure,

Theoretical and Conceptual Papers, Agrarian Structure: Description and Analysis, and Land Reform: Policy and Analysis). Extensive reviewing of materials by subject area experts helped in the selection of the materials. Annotations included for works considered to be of special importance. Works located in the following libraries are noted: Library of Congress, the University of Wisconsin Libraries, the Pan American Union Library, and the ESCOLATINA in Chile. Arrangement by country with the majority of works published from 1940 to 1960. Author (corporate and personal) index.

10. Castillo, Margarita, and María José Galrão. *Bibliografía agrícola de Costa Rica.* Documentación e Información Agrícola 83 (Rev.). San José, Costa Rica: IICA, SEPSA, 1980. 431 p.

Revision of the like-titled 1972 publication includes 8,100 citations of books, pamphlets, theses, and other works covering agriculture in Costa Rica, spanning the time period 1945 to 1980. Of the sixteen chapters divided by subject, three are on agrarian reform in Costa Rica: Geografía e Historia, Administración y Legislación, and Economía, Desarrollo y Sociología Rural. Documents noted by an asterisk can be obtained for $.20 a page from the specified institute. No annotations. Author (corporate and personal) index.

11. *Catalog of the Nettie Lee Benson Latin American Collection.* 3 vols. 4th supplement. Boston: G. K. Hall and Co., 1977.

Represents the holdings of one of the largest Latin American collections in existence. Annually updated by the *Bibliographic Guide to Latin American Studies.* No annotations. Access by author, title, and subject.

12. Centro Latinoamericano de Investigaciones en Ciéncias Sociales. *Estrucura y reforma en América Latina: Bibliografía.* Rio de Janeiro: Serviço de Documentação de CENTRO, 1962. Lvs. 50.

Arrangement by country beginning with a list of general bibliographical sources followed by a list on Latin America as a whole. Includes journal articles and reports. Central America coverage includes references to economics and sociology, agrarian law, colonization, agro-economics, and agrarian reform with Guatemala receiving the most citations with twenty.

13. Confederación Universitaria Centroamericana/Centro de Documentación Económica y Social de Centroamérica. *Documentación socioeconómica centroamericana.* 1983. C, No. 7. 146 p.

Index of articles in periodicals which is made up of 150 entries listing works related to the social and economic situation in Central America. Materials on agrarian reform can be found under the following terms: "Campesino," "Cooperativas," "Desarrollo rural," "Legislación agraria," "Reforma agraria," and "Tenencia de la tierra." Consists largely of institutional and governmental studies and reports from the late 1970s. Index provides keyword terms for each item, enabling quick subject access. Abstracts included for each work. Author index.

14. Deal, Carl W., ed. *Latin America and the Caribbean: A Dissertation Bibliography*. Ann Arbor, MI: University Microfilms International, 1978. 164 p.

Compilation of dissertations from the United States which supplements Nelly S. González's *Doctoral Dissertations on Latin America and the Caribbean, 1966-1970*. Follows *Dissertation Abstracts* format. Pertinent subject headings are "Agriculture—Country"; "Economics—Country"; "Sociology—Country". Author index.

15. _____. *Latin America and the Caribbean II: A Dissertation Bibliography*. Ann Arbor, MI: University Microfilms International, 1980. 78 p.

Update of Deal's *Latin America and the Caribbean: A Dissertation Bibliography* listed above. Updated quarterly by *Research Update* published by University Microfilms International under the subject heading "Latin America" and online on Dissertation Abstracts.

16. Delgado, Oscar. *Bibliografía latinoamericana sobre reforma agraria y tenencia de la tierra, 1950-1961*. México, DF: N.p., 1962. 37 p.

Selective bibliography lists over 500 annotated works predominantly from Latin American of which only publications from Costa Rica, Guatemala, and Nicaragua represent Central America. Special subject coverage enhances this work, e.g., agrarian social history and rural sociology. Author (corporate and personal) index.

17. DeSelms Langstaff, Eleanor. *Panama*. World Bibliographical Series, Volume 14. Santa Barbara, CA: ABC/Clio Press, 1982. 184 p.

Journal articles or issues and monographs make up 641 items providing a general overview of Panama. Work divided into numerous chapters. Those that relate to agrarian reform in Panama are History, Economy and Economic Planning, and Agriculture. Annotations are descriptive. Works included published between 1950 and 1980 with some older works included when appropriate. Bibliography and Bibliographies chapter lists fifteen bibliographical works related to Panama. Author (corporate and personal) and subject indexes.

18. Food and Agriculture Organization. *Bibliography on Land Settlement*. Rome: FAO, 1976, c1977. 146 p.

Update of the next entry. Cites mostly journal articles about individuals and governmental bodies implementing land settlement programs, an important aspect of agrarian reform. Central America receives nominal but adequate coverage, i.e., 50 items. Arrangement by country. Author (corporate and personal) and periodical indexes.

19. Food and Agriculture Organization of the United Nations (FAO)—Rural Institutions Division. *Bibliography on Land Tenure*. Rome: FAO, 1955. 386 p. Supplement published in 1959. 282 p.

The strength of this work is the listing of U.N. organization materials on agrarian reform. Owing to the worldwide scope of this bibliography, Central America receives limited coverage. The general section on Latin America does note many of the major writers on this topic in the 1950s. A supplement issued in 1959 follows the same format as this edition.

20. Franklin, Woodman B. *Guatemala*. World Bibliographical Series, Volume 9. Santa Barbara, CA: Clio Press, 1981. 109 p.

Follows series format described in DeSelms Langstaff's *Panama*. Excellent source for students with little background to improve their breadth of knowledge on Guatemala. Chapters containing pertinent materials on agrarian reform in Guatemala are Geography, History, Economics, and Agriculture and Fishing. Author (corporate and personal), title, and subject indexes.

21. González, Nelly S. *Doctoral Dissertations on Latin America and the Caribbean: An Analysis and Bibliography of Dissertations Accepted at American and Canadian Universities, 1966-1970*. Publication No. 10. Urbana, IL: Consortium of Latin American Studies Programs, 1980. 201 p.

Source for dissertations on topics dealing with Latin America. Updates Allen D. Bushong's *Doctoral Dissertations on Pan American Topics Accepted by United States and Canadian Colleges and Universities, 1961-1965*. Follows the *Dissertation Abstracts* format.

22. _____. "A Meta-Bibliography: Colonos, Campesinos, and Colonizadores." In *Latin American Economic Issues*. SALALM XXVI, Tulane University, New Orleans, LA. Los Angeles, CA: UCLA Latin American Center Publications, 1981. Pp. 78-119.

Annotated sources on agrarian reform and related topics in Latin America. Majority of works are from the 1960s to the present, with older works included when they offer the most complete source of information. Arrangement by general bibliography followed by country and subject groupings.

23. Gropp, Arthur E., comp. *A Bibliography of Latin American Bibliographies*. Metuchen, NJ: Scarecrow Press, 1968. 515 p. Supplement, 1971. 227 p.

Over 4,000 bibliographies listed in this and the next compilation of bibliographies on Latin America. Brief annotations included for many entries. They update the Library of Congress's *Bibliography of Latin American Bibliographies* (1942). Included are monographs, indexes, catalogs, articles, and general books containing bibliographies. Pertinent subject headings are "Agrarian reform" and "Land tenure." Author (corporate and personal) and subject indexes.

24. Gropp, Arthur E. *A Bibliography of Latin American Bibliographies Published in Periodicals*. 2 vols. Metuchen, NJ: Scarecrow Press, 1976. 1,031 p.

See preceding entry. Cites selected bibliographies from journal articles. Subject headings include "Land tenure," "Land tenure and reform," "Agrarian reform," and "Land settlement."

25. Guerra, D'Almeida. *Indicações bibliográficas sobre reforma agrária*. Serie Documentária 14. Rio de Janeiro, Brazil: Ministério da Agricultura, 1961. 36 p.

Compilation separated into groupings of monographs, pamphlets, articles, and studies from the 1940s and 1950s. Arrangement hinders access by subject or country. Brazil receives the most complete coverage, Central America is briefly covered.

26. *HAPI: Hispanic American Periodicals Index, 1970-1974*. 3 vols. Los Angeles, CA: University of California: UCLA Latin American Center Publications, 1984.

A major source for locating journal articles and book reviews on events in Latin America. Coverage is from 1970 through 1974. Over 240 journals are indexed. Arrangement by subject area. Pertinent headings: "Peasants," "Land use," "Land reform," and "Land tenure." No annotations.

27. *HAPI: Hispanic American Periodicals Index.* Los Angeles, CA: University of California: UCLA Latin American Center Publications, 1978–. (Covering journals published 1975 to date. Annual.)

The annual compilation of the preceding work.

28. *Handbook of Latin American Studies.* No. 45: *Social Sciences.* Cambridge, MA: Harvard University Press, 1983–.

Cites works selected for their usefulness and importance in their field by a board of experts in each field. Brief annotations included. Works all available from the Nettie Lee Benson Collection. Published annually since 1936, alternating every year between the humanities and the social sciences. Access by field of study, e.g., anthropology.

29. *Indice agrícola de América Latina y el Caribe.* San José, Costa Rica: IICA, CIDIA. Quarterly. Continues *Bibliografía agrícola latinoamericana y del Caribe* (1966-1974).

Index of technical materials produced in Latin America. Subject areas including land reform literature are "History," "Administration," "Legislation," "Development," and "Rural sociology." No annotations.

30. Inter-American Committee for Agricultural Development. *Inventory of Information Basic to the Planning of Agricultural Development in Latin America.* Washington, DC: Pan American Union: General Secretariat, Organization of American States, 1964. 78 p.

OAS publication consisting of over 5,000 books, articles, and comments from 1950 through 1964 on the topic of agricultural development. Chapters Agricultural Institutions, and Land Use and Agricultural Production contain materials on agrarian reform. Central American countries individually covered in each chapter. No annotations. Author (corporate and personal) index.

31. *Interpaks Resource Center Materials.* Urbana, IL: University of Illinois at Champaign-Urbana, 1985. Bimonthly.

Foreign and domestic works on international agriculture make up this serial, includes working papers. Cumulative author and subject index and annotations are invaluable here.

32. Jiménez Muñoz, Dina. *Bibliografía retrospectiva sobre política agraria en Costa Rica, 1948-1978.* San José, 1980. 528 p.

Collection of 2,641 entries ranging from newspaper and journal articles to legislation and theses. Work divided into seven chapters of which Desarrollo e Historia Económica, Estructura Agraria, Condiciones de Vida, and Seguridad Social provide the best coverage of agrarian reform in Costa Rica. Each citation notes general bibliographic information along with subject headings and location of the work in one of the five identified Costa Rican libraries. Three appendixes included, with the third listing annotated works of special significance. Subject and author (corporate and personal) indexes are included following each chapter.

33. Kasim, M. Bazlul, comp. *The Green Revolution: An International Bibliography.* Bibliographies and Indexes in Economics and Economic History 2. New York, NY: Greenwood Press, 1986. 288 p.

Cites over 2,000 monographs, journal articles, and reports available in English which cover the development and implementation of technology in agriculture during the 1960s and 1970s. Overview of Latin American agrarian reform works can be found under the regional heading of Latin America in General Works. Selective annotations included. Author (corporate and personal) and subject indexes.

34. Kruse, David Samuel, and Richard Swedberg. *El Salvador: Bibliography and Research Guide.* Cambridge, MA: Camino, 1982. 233 p.

Cites topical journal articles and U.S. Congressional hearings on economic and military assistance to El Salvador during the 1970s. In Chapter Three 90 works cover agrarian reform with brief annotations for selected works considered to be important. Chapter Seven covers the Salvadorean economy and social structure, an excellent background resource. Included is a section on resources for locating new materials on El Salvador covering periodicals, organizations, and audiovisual materials. Author index.

35. Lassany, M. E. *Agriculture in Central America, 1970-1983.* Quick Bibliography Series, National Agricultural Library 1983). No. Nal-Bibl. 84-04. 22 p.

Derived from online searches of the AGRICOLA database, this bibliography focuses on the current state of agriculture in Central America. No annotations or indexes.

36. Latin American Center for Research in the Social Sciences.
See Centro Latinoamericano de Investigaciones en Ciéncias Sociales.

37. Lichtenberg, Garland G. *Bibliography of Agricultural Colonization in Latin America.* S.l.: S.n., c1961? Lvs. 22.

Brief compilation of journal articles concentrates on agricultural colonization. Each Central American country receives limited coverage. No annotations.

38. Loroña, Lionel V., comp. *Bibliography of Latin American and Caribbean Bibliographies. Annual Report, 1982-1983-.* Madison, WI: SALALM Secretariat, 1984-.

Update of Arthur E. Gropp's *A Bibliography of Latin American Bibliographies Published in Periodicals.* Arranged by subject areas and published annually. Items cited are bibliographies and bibliographic journal articles. A five-year compilation was published in 1987. No annotations. Author (personal) and subject indexes.

39. Nikhjavani, Mehran. *Agrarian Reform in Latin America: The Role of Marketing and Credit.* Bibliography Series No. 6. Montreal, Quebec: Centre for Developing-Area Studies, 1977. 46 p.

Offers limited coverage of Central America (Panama is excluded), but the economic viewpoint expressed here is unique. The majority of the works are from the 1970s and arrangement is by subject area, e.g., Co-operatives and Credit. Annotated. Author (corporate and personal) and country indexes.

40. Oqueli, Ramon. *Bibliografía sociopolítica de Honduras.* Colección Cuadernos Universitarios 15. Tegucigalpa: Editorial Universitaria, 1981. 106 p.

Collection of works predominantly published in Honduras during the 1970s. Included are government declarations and legislation.

41. *Rural Development Abstracts.* Farnham, England: CAB International, 1978-. Quarterly.

A United Kingdom publication from the Commonwealth Agricultural Bureau that lists a variety of materials including dissertations. Abstracts of each citation available in print or from CAB online database. Author (corporate and personal) and subject indexes.

42. *Rural Extension Education and Training Abstracts.* Farnham, England: CAB International, 1978-. Quarterly.

Provides descriptive abstracts on rural education and training. Arrangement by region with Central America located in the America region. Abstracts available through the CAB online database. Author (corporate and personal) and subject indexes.

43. Snarr, D. Neil, and Leonard Brown. "Social and Economic Change in Central America and Panama: An Annotated Bibliography." *International Review of Modern Sociology.* Vol. 2. New Delhi: Vikas, 1972. Pp. 102-115.

Journal articles, studies, and conference papers that reflect social and political changes of the 1960s in Central America. Guatemala, Costa Rica, and Panama receive most of the coverage. Descriptive annotations aid in identifying works dealing with agrarian reform and related topics.

44. Specher, Ana María de León de, Aracelly Kisanda Mérida González, and Silvia Patricia Muralles Castro. *Bibliografía agrícola de Guatemala.* Guatemala: Universidad de San Carlos de Guatemala. Facultad de Agronomía: Centro de Documentación e Información Agrícola, 1985. 192 p.

Compiled for the use of students, faculty, and researchers in Guatemala and abroad studying the agricultural sciences. Arrangement of 3,578 references for the years 1980-1984 is by broad subject categories, with the chapter Economía, Desarrollo y Sociología Rural containing materials on agrarian reform. No annotations. Author (corporate and personal) and product indexes.

45. Uribe Contreras, Maruja, and Guillermo Isaza Vélez. *Bibliografía selectiva sobre reforma agraria en América Latina.* Bogotá: IICA, 1972. 381 p.

Extensive collection of Latin American materials that reflect the strong interest in agrarian reform in Latin America. The 1,995 entries cover the years 1964-1971. Two sections of special interest are Agrarian Reform Legislation and Philosophy of Agrarian Reform. Chapters K and L cover agrarian reform and agrarian rights, respectively, providing coverage of each Central American country. Author (corporate and personal) and subject indexes.

46. Villegas, Carmen, comp. *Bibliografía sobre colonización de América Latina.* Documentación e Información Agrícola 80. Turrialba, Costa Rica: CIDIA, 1980. 124 p.

The 1,539 items deal with colonization of the agricultural regions of Latin America between the years 1947 and 1979. Included are conference papers and theses. Arrangement by country with each of the Central American countries represented. Citations noted with an asterisk can be obtained through the reproduction service of the CIDIA (Centro Interamericano de Documentación, Información y Comunicación Agrícola) in Turrialba, Costa Rica. No annotations provided. Author (corporate and personal) and subject indexes.

47. West, H. W., and O. H. M. Sawyer. *Land Administration: A Bibliography for Developing Countries.* Cambridge, Great Britain: University of Cambridge, 1975. 292 p.

Uneven coverage of the Central America region. Included are works on Costa Rica and Guatemala not found in the Land Tenure Center's *Agrarian Reform in Latin America*, while El Salvador receives no coverage. Consists mainly of U.S. and British journal articles published between 1960 and 1973 and a limited number of government publications. Entries arranged by region and within each region by country. Author (corporate and personal) and country indexes.

48. White, Sylvia, and Gregory DeYoung. *A Bibliography of Sources Relating to Urban and Regional Planning in Costa Rica.* Public Administration Series: Bibliography, P-1014. Monticello, IL: Vance Bibliography, 1982. 26 p.

Purpose of this work is to aid urban and rural planners in Costa Rica. Divided into three sections: primary sources, supporting studies, and background information, all of which include materials that relate to agrarian reform. No index.

49. Wisconsin, University of. Land Tenure Center. *Agrarian Reform and Land Tenure.* Training and Method Series Number 4. Madison, WI: Land Tenure Center, 1965. 112 p.

Research-oriented work that provides laws and regulations, journal articles, and monographs. Includes subject coverage of agricultural finance, taxation and agriculture, and agricultural statistics. Bibliographic sources and master journal subscription list cited. Author (corporate and personal) and subject indexes.

50. _____. *Agrarian Reform in Latin America: An Annotated Bibliography.* Madison, WI: Land Tenure Center, 1974. 667 p.

The most extensive bibliography on agrarian reform at this time. Critical annotations helpful in evaluating each work. Central American coverage adequate. As an update to the 1965 bibliography by the Land Tenure Center, the majority of the materials have been produced since that time, although items published before 1964 included when not covered earlier. Included are dissertations, studies, legislation, and a listing of journals cited. Author (corporate and personal) and subject indexes.

51. _____. *Catalog.* Madison, WI: Land Tenure Center, 1987[?].

Soon to be published, this catalog will be an excellent source on the topic of agrarian reform.

52. Woodward, Jr., Ralph Lee. *Nicaragua.* World Bibliographical Series, Volume 44. Santa Barbara, CA: Clio Press, 1983. 245 p.

Follows the series format described in DeSelms Langstaff's *Panama.* Emphasizes works in English, although works from Nicaragua included. Chapters providing coverage of land tenure and agrarian reform are Geography, History, Politics, and Agriculture. Monographic works predominate, with journal articles and some dissertations/theses included. Author (corporate and personal), title, and subject indexes.

53. *World Agricultural Economics and Rural Sociology Abstracts.* Farnham, England: CAB International, 1958–. Monthly.

Monographs, journal articles, dissertations, and reports on land use can be located under the subject heading "Development and agrarian reform." Online searching available through the CAB database. Descriptive abstracts. Author (corporate and personal) and subject indexes.

Part Six
Cuba

27. Analyzing Social Change and Movements: Historical Writings on Nineteenth-Century Cuba

Rebecca J. Scott

The history of Cuba in the nineteenth century is contested terrain. [1] Protagonists and antagonists of the Cuban Revolution and the subsequent transformation of the Cuban state interpret and reinterpret Cuba's colonial past in support of competing visions of Cuban nationality. For some, the examination of the nineteenth century yields confirmation of the willful creation of economic dependency, the depth of Cuban nationalism, and the persistence of class struggle, and such history helps to give meaning to postrevolutionary transformations. [2] For others, by contrast, a rereading of the history of Cuba's relations with the rest of the world, or a reinterpretation of the thought of José Martí, can challenge the role of each of these in the legitimation of postrevolutionary politics. [3] Somewhat independent from these polarities, still other scholars have taken Cuba as a testing ground for competing hypotheses about the character of slavery in a colonial society, and as a setting in which to examine social transformations. [4] But virtually all scholars of Cuba study and write about the colonial period with a continued awareness of the upheaval to follow in the twentieth century, and the search for the "roots of revolution" lies, implicitly or explicitly, behind much scholarship on the nineteenth century.

Author's Note: I would like to thank Louis A. Pérez, Jr. for initial discussions of Cuban historiography that stimulated the undertaking of this essay. I am very grateful to numerous Cuban scholars who generously shared copies of their work and thoughts on current Cuban scholarship during my visit to the island in April and May of 1987. Particular thanks are due to María del Carmen Barcia, Ramón de Armas, Walterio Carbonell, Pedro Deschamps Chapeaux, Tomás Fernández Robaina, Bernardo Iglesias, Fe Iglesias, Zoila Lapique, Julio LeRiverend, Juan Francisco González, Enrique López Mesa, Manuel Moreno Fraginals, Franciso Pérez Guzmán, Rodolfo Sarracino, Eduardo Torres Cuevas, Carlos Venegas, Cintio Vitier, and Oscar Zanetti. I am also very grateful to Jean Stubbs, a British scholar long resident in Cuba, and to Jordi Maluquer de Motes Bernet, of Barcelona, for their reflections and insights.

Taken as a whole, this scholarship has explored social, political, and economic aspects of Cuba's nineteenth-century history. Analyses of sugar and slavery, for example, are juxtaposed with accounts of the rise of nationalism and the outbreak of anticolonial struggle; analyses of patterns of credit and landowning provide a background to the understanding of the impact of U.S. intervention at the turn of the century. In practice, however, the social and the political have remained somewhat detached from each other. There are points of significant intersection—such as the examination of the behavior of the planter class, or exploration of Spain's linked economic and political commitment to the maintenance of colonial rule.[5] But studies that systematically unite the political with the economic and social remain very rare.[6]

One might begin, for example, with the observation that the anticolonial conflicts in Cuba were vast social movements, drawing on thousands of participants. But what were the lived experiences—of work, of poverty, of frustration, of dislocation—that moved those thousands to rebel? What did they imagine that they were doing? How did they interpret the successes and failures of their efforts?

The difficulty in addressing this kind of question does not rest solely on a lack of knowledge about broad economic and social trends in the nineteenth century. The social and economic history of Cuba has attracted the attention of excellent historians within Cuba, and has yielded the magisterial study of slavery and plantation society by Manuel Moreno Fraginals, *El ingenio*, and the penetrating works of the late Juan Pérez de la Riva, as well as subtle studies by others of such subjects as landholding, railways, and technology.[7] Scholars both within and outside Cuba have used government documents, plantation inventories, manuscript censuses, notarial archives, and land records to analyze the growth of a prosperous sugar economic, its transformation under stress from slavery to wage labor, and its combination of resilience and vulnerability.[8]

The documents and studies that have enabled us to understand Cuba's slave economic as a whole may not, however, be sufficient to illuminate fundamental questions about the character of nineteenth-century society and the behavior of its members. For this we clearly need regional analyses that can encompass the full range of activities—slave and nonslave, oriented toward export, the internal market, or subsistence—of Cuba's varied provinces. If we are to understand the patterns of political mobilization we will have to move beyond the categories of slave and *hacendado*, peasant and artisan, to explore the varied circumstances under which members of these groups lived, worked, and interacted in different ecological, political, and social settings.

The prospects for such study are encouraging.   Teams of researchers in Matanzas and Santa Clara have already begun to explore in detail not only the economic history of each region but the links between them, reflected in flows of cattle in one direction and capital in the other.   At the same time, detailed research on the eastern region of the island (called Santiago de Cuba in the latter part of the nineteenth century, and Oriente thereafter) continues. [9]

In addition to regional studies that draw on notarial records and oral sources as well as governmental and estate documents, it may be helpful to attempt new readings of old texts.   An innovative move in this direction has been taken by Arcadio Díaz Quiñones, who examines Cuban historical and nationalist texts as elements of a "discurso de la nación," a discourse that draws, for example, on shared presumptions about civilization and barbarism that bear close examination. [10]   This approach now rests primarily on an examination of classic texts, but it could profitably be extended by exploring such sources as minor autobiographies, war memoirs, song lyrics, and legal depositions, asking what they reflect about the developing consciousness of different groups of Cubans in this period. [11]   Indeed, such an extension of the method may be essential if one aims at an exploration of national perception and consciousness, rather than an explication of elite conceptions.

The problem, then, is not simply the lack of sufficient social historical research, but rather the failure of most existing works to engage directly a question that underlies Cuba's political history: How were these vast social transformations experienced by those who participated in them?   This question, in turn, has multiple dimensions: did the increasing commercialization of agriculture drive peasants off the land in the last decades of the nineteenth century, and, if so, what were the mechanisms and dimensions of this phenomenon?   Were the rebels and bandits of this period characteristically drawn from displaced groups?   Or did railways, for example, which assisted in the growth of the sugar industry, at the same time stimulate small-scale production by improving access to markets?   How did sugar workers, many of them recent Spanish immigrants, respond to the turmoil that engulfed the island in the 1890s?   How did the abolition of slavery affect levels of wages, salaries, and taxes, and how were such changes perceived by those who had been slaves as well as by those who had been free?

Rather than extending such a list of questions indefinitely, what I do in this essay is identify a series of specific historical issues for which the linkage between the socioeconomic and the political has not yet been fully developed, and suggest ways of framing or reframing our interpretive questions about these issues in order to encourage such linkages. I will in each case make some preliminary suggestions of sources that might usefully be drawn upon by scholars, in hopes that such suggestions can be of use both to researchers and to those who work on the acquisition of supporting library materials.

I

The first is the examination of banditry and related informal kinds of social protest, phenomena that by their nature force one to seek connections between the social and the political. In recent years several authors, both inside and outside Cuba, have explored the nature of Cuban banditry. Rosalie Schwartz implicitly challenges the applicability of Eric Hobsbawm's notion of social banditry to the Cuban case, and doubts whether the commercialization of Agriculture drove peasants into outlawry. She is inclined to emphasize the opportunism of bandits, and their willingness to participate in, rather than reject, the market economy. [12] Louis Pérez, by contrast, argued in a 1985 essay that the upsurge of banditry in the late 1880s and 1890s, a period of expansion in the sugar industry, is evidence of a strong link between proletarianization and social upheaval. On this view, banditry is one of the precursors of insurgency, and draws on many of the same felt grievances. [13] In a more recent work Pérez has expanded the focus to explore important distinctions within the rural population, and has examined the patterns of alliances that shaped popular perceptions of bandits. [14] In a brilliant and highly interdisciplinary thesis, María Poumier draws on popular imagery as well as documentary evidence to analyze the figure of Manuel García. While she makes use of Hobsbawn's concept of the social bandit, she downplays direct economic forces, and places great emphasis on García's symbolic appeal as a figure who could challenge authority with impunity. [15] Julio Angel Carreras, in a somewhat ambivalent article, gives evidence of the social content of certain bandit actions, but generally portrays banditry in the early years of the twentieth century as part of a larger picture of criminality and corruption. [16]

It is by now clear that no simple, dichotomous view of Cuban banditry will suffice: one cannot simply ask whether the bandits were rebels or opportunists, friend or foe of the rural population. One must ask instead how they emerged, how they behaved, how they were perceived, and in what ways they were incorporated into larger social struggles. But there remains the difficulty of locating and defining what we are really looking for in seeking the social context and

meaning of banditry. Can we find the *links* between the social transformations that seem to spawn banditry, and the bandits themselves?
Is it possible to trace biographies individuals, and profiles of
communities, in such a way that we determine the processes that
underlay the shift to outlawry?

As important as the antecedents of any given bandit group are the
forces that sustain such groups and permit them to survive in the face
of government repression. If, indeed, commercialization of agriculture
displaced peasants, we might ask: what were the forms of support that
such displaced peasants provided to bandits, and what kinds of support
were provided by other sectors? The fact that banditry arose in a
colonial context, and was later transformed in a neocolonial one, was
undoubtedly of significance in the choice of targets and enemies. It
should, moreover, be possible to conjoin social and political inquiry to
locate the moments and the mechanisms by which some bandits were
mobilized into the independence struggle. [17]

Inquiry into these questions will clearly involve prolonged archival
research, and each scholar must do that work following his or her own
instincts. But there may be some kinds of sources that could be
acquired or duplicated that would broaden the field of inquiry into
these questions. Spanish authorities in Cuba, for example, had a
striking tendency to write self-justificatory memoirs, published in small
numbers and often difficult to obtain. The Spanish government in
Cuba also periodically published transcriptions of correspondence
relating to conspiracies and uprisings, volumes of extraordinary
usefulness. A systematic effort to locate these, and reproduce them on
microfilm or microfiche, would open up new sources to systematic
study. [18] Governor Camilo Polavieja, moreover, not only wrote
memoirs but also retained his personal papers, which his descendants
subsequently deposited in the Archivo General de Indias. These
include extraordinarily useful documents on banditry and rebellion, and
on his bitter efforts to extinguish both. [19] Explorations of manuscript
and printed materials generated by the repression of banditry can open
the way for a linkage of Spanish and Cuban perspectives on the
phenomenon of banditry itself.

The point, then, is to seek additional ways of linking theoretical
formulations about social transformation with empirical data about
bandits and their activities. This may then open up the way to the
next phase, which is to understand the nationalist movements
themselves.

II

In addition to debating the social character of Cuban banditry, historians have debated the character of the Cuban wars for independence. Analysts have disagreed on the relative weight of, on the one hand, nationalism, and, on the other, ideals of social revolution and transformation. They have explored varied and competing attitudes among separatists toward the United States. Much of this discussion has centered on specific leaders of the movements for independence, and on exegesis of their thought. Other work has explored the evolution of policy, and the forces impinging on those who formulated policy. [20] But if we try to go beyond explicit policy to an analysis of the wars as social movements we encounter the same difficulty: how do the "tensions" and "contradictions" of Cuban colonial society translate themselves not just into a political critique but into a motivation for action by thousands of Cubans?

Several recent works suggest possible avenues for pursuing such analysis. Tadeusz Lepkowski has studied the social composition of the insurrectionist movement in Cuba in 1869, using lists of suspects from the Cuban archives. [21] This kind of close examination of participants helps to illuminate the cross-class alliances that are known to have existed, while it underlines the relative absence of slaves in the movement at this early date. It also enables one to make important regional distinctions. Similarly, María Dolores Domingo Acebrón examines the responses of different Cuban landholders to the Ten Years' War, using documentation from the Real Academic de Historia in Madria. [22] Francisco Pérez Guzman and Rodolfo Sarrancino, in their study of the "Guerra Chiquita," note the participation of slaves in the conflicts. [23] But we are still a long way from developing a full portrait of the component parts of nineteenth-century revolutionary consciousness.

The task of constructing a full history of the insurgent movements in Cuba will obviously have to be a collaborative one, and it would be very useful if more of the printed and manuscript raw material were available outside the few libraries where it is now located. There are, for example, several rare publications that could lend themselves to systematic analysis, such as the partial listing compiled of participants in the War for Independence, which contains biographical sketches of some of those who were killed. [24] At the same time, such a project may require a redefining of sources, as one turns to songs, to oral history, and to fiction to complement the portrait of insurgency that emerges from military records.

The voluminous Cuban material in the Archivo Histórico Nacional in Madrid, which includes detailed information on individual insurgents, is at present being cataloged by the staff of the Sección de Ultramar; when available, that published catalog will be enormously valuable. Any effort to microfilm Cuban newspapers, periodicals, and pamphlets of the nineteenth century—a worthy enterprise on several counts—would also provide raw material for understanding the Cuban countryside in the last decades of the nineteenth century. [25]

One of the major open questions about the insurgency is the role played by Afro-Cubans. We know that role to have been a significant one, but we still lack detailed understanding of the internal dynamics of the movement, and of the relations between black, white, and mulatto soldiers, or the relevance of prior slave experience to the decision to participate in the armed struggle. Tomás Fernández Robaina's extraordinary new *Bibliografía de temas afrocubanos* provides hundreds of citations to the Afro-Cuban press; a systematic effort to locate, preserve, and duplicate the materials that this bibliography identifies would help to open the way to an exploration of this question. [26]

Perhaps the most important source for a study of the social history of the 1895-1898 conflict will be the holdings of the Fondo Ejército Libertador in the Archivo Nacional de Cuba. The extraordinary set of documents—containing service records of those who fought in the liberation army, and in some cases correspondence concerning their participation—remains almost untouched. Systematic efforts to examine the composition of specific regiments, linking them to the regions in which they arose, would be a logical first step. [27]

The aim in this case is to do what scholars have always found most difficult: to understand the social history of major political movements. There are a few examples from history and sociology of such successful attempts at analysis. One may hope that the Cuban wars for independence, with their complexity and rich documentation, might afford the possibility of adding to that select set of works.

III

A third, and equally complex, area of research that might lend itself to exploration from a combined social and political perspective is the period of occupation of Cuba by the United States. We have already a fine recent history of this period, Louis Pérez's *Cuba Between Empires*, as well as useful older works. [28] By beginning to explore the social context of the first occupation, Pérez's work suggests a whole new range of questions: what was the character of popular perceptions of the occupation army, and what kinds of response did occupation forces meet in the countryside? [29] When the United States encouraged the formation of a Rural Guard, and explicitly excluded blacks from participation, how did this shape race relations in the countryside? What kinds of initiatives did Cubans attempt within the framework of U.S. domination, in an effort to shape the character of occupation rule? A suggestive new article by Hebert Pérez Concepción, for example, uses documents from the Archivo Histórico Provincial of Santiago de Cuba to emphasize the initiatives of Cubans during the occupation period, and further research in Cuban archives should yield additional insights into the interplay of occupiers and occupied. [30]

The sources that might help move scholarship forward on this question are perhaps less elusive than one might think. The United States, after all, is the repository of the great bulk of the official documentation on the occupation of Cuba, though this is by no means the only kind of appropriate material. A systematic effort to reproduce out-of-print finding aids and catalogs of the holdings of the U.S. National Archives on this period would be a good start, enabling scholars to use those sources more efficiently. Similarly, the printed briefs and claims presented to the U.S. Spanish Treaty Claims Commission are a gold mine of information about social conditions during the war and the early occupation period, yet they are quite difficult to locate outside of Washington, DC. [31]

For the most intriguing questions about Cuban behavior during the occupation, there is obviously no substitute for research in Cuba, but a wider distribution of Cuban publications, particularly some of the materials now being produced in Santiago de Cuba, would help to open the channels of communication. While the contents of the Cuban National Archives are relatively well known to scholars as a result of years of publications by the archives, those of the Santiago Archives are more of a mystery. An effort to locate and reproduce any available finding aids would be very useful. [32] These archival materials might be usefully complemented by an examination of the local press during this period—a task that would, again, be facilitated by the microfilming of key newspapers.

It should by now be possible for scholarship on the occupation to move away from the exploration of the motives of the occupiers, which have been carefully examined by Pérez and others, and move toward the experiences of the occupied. The aim here would be to see the two groups interactively, thus linking not only political and social history but the history of rulers and ruled. Again, a regional focus that moves us beyond Havana—and Washington—is essential, as is the exploitation of the widest possible range of texts, including oral tradition, songs, and local ephemera of various kinds.

IV

The agenda set forth in this essay is obviously just one historian's imagining of the potential for new scholarship. To the extent that I am exhorting myself and my colleagues to attempt to analyze political movements in their social and economic context, I am to a degree uttering a recommendation so obvious that it would seem to go without saying. But to the extent that I am challenging us to ask the most difficult questions about human choices and actions in the past, and to move beyond our tendency to study one more price series, one more sugar plantation, or one more conspiracy, the exhortation may nonetheless be worthwhile. And if this essay suggests some of the kinds of sources that would make it possible to meet the challenge, and enables researchers and bibliographers to join forces in locating those sources, then I trust that the enterprise will have been worthwhile.

NOTES

1. For a systematic examination of Cuban historiography since the Revolution, see Louis A. Pérez, Jr., *Historiography in the Revolution: A Bibliography of Cuban Scholarship, 1959-1979* (New York, NY: Garland Publishing, 1982) and his "Twenty-five Years of Cuban Historiography: A Retrospect," presented at the meetings of the Latin American Studies Association, Boston, October 1986, and forthcoming in *Cuban Studies*. See also two special numbers of the *Revista de la Biblioteca Nacional "José Martí"* devoted largely to historiography: Año 76/ 3ra. época-vol. XXVII, Enero-abril 1985, Número 1 and Mayo-augusto 1985, Número 2.

2. A famous, and vivid, call by a Cuban scholar for a sophisticated history consonant with a new revolutionary reality is the essay by Manuel Moreno Fraginals, "La historia como arma," first published in *Casa de las Américas* 7 (January-February 1967), and reprinted in his collection of essays, *La historia como arma y otros estudios sobre esclavos, ingenios y plantaciones* (Barcelona: Editorial Crítica, 1983). A substantial portion of Cuban scholarship since the revolution has been framed explicitly as an exploration of the roots of the social, economic, and political ills that characterized prerevolutionary society, though of course the research itself goes in many directions and can lead to varying conclusions.

3. For a polemical and revisionist view of Cuban nationalism, see Carlos Alberto Montaner, "The Roots of Anti-Americanism in Cuba: Sovereignty in an Age of World Cultural Homogeneity," *Caribbean Review* 13 (Spring 1984), 13-16, 42-46. The amount of writing on José Martí is, of course, vast, and some of it challenges the portrait of Martí that emerges from postrevolutionary scholarship. See most recently Enrico Mario Santí's provocative essay, "José Martí and the Cuban Revolution," *Cuban Studies* 16 (1986), 139-150. Santí is highly critical of what he perceives as the "ultimately distorting teleological reading of Cuban history."

4. See, for example, Manuel Moreno Fraginals, Stanley L. Engerman, and Herbert S. Klein, "The Level and Structure of Slave Prices on Cuban Plantations in the Mid-Nineteenth Century: Some Comparative Perspectives," *American Historical Review* 88

(December 1983), 1201-1218; and Herbert Klein and Stanley L. Engerman, "Del trabajo esclavo al trabajo libre: notas en torno a un modelo económico comparativo," *HISLA (Revista Latinamericana de Historia Económica y Social* 1 (1983), 41-55, also appearing in Manuel Moreno Fraginals, Frank Moya Pons, and Stanley L. Engerman, eds., *Between Slavery and Free Labor: The Spanish-speaking Caribbean in the Nineteenth Century* (Baltimore, MD: The Johns Hopkins University Press, 1985).

5. On planters, see, for example, María del Carmen Barcia, "La Ley de Vientres Libres y los intereses esclavistas," *Santiago* 59 (September 1985), 127-136; and Robert Paquette, "The Conspiracy of La Escalera: Colonial Society and Politics in Cuba in the Age of Revolution," Ph.D. thesis, The University of Rochester, 1982. On Spanish interests in Cuba see the work of Jordi Maluquer de Motes, including, most recently, "Abolicionisme i esclavisme a Espanya," *Avenç* (Barcelona) 101 (February 1987), 38-45.

6. An innovative essay that does accomplish this, for a slightly later period, is Louis A. Pérez, Jr., "Politics, Peasants, and People of Color: The 1912 'Race War' in Cuba Reconsidered," *Hispanic American Historical Review* 66 (August 1986), 509-539. See also his *Lords of the Mountain: Banditry and Peasant Protest in Cuba, 1878-1918* (University of Pittsburgh Press, forthcoming).

7. See Manuel Moreno Fraginals, *El ingenio: complejo económico social cubano del azúcar* (Havana: Editorial de Ciencias Sociales, 1978); Juan Pérez de la Riva, *El barracón y otros ensayos* (Havana: Editorial de Ciencias Sociales, 1975); the works of Fe Iglesias García, including "Algunos aspectos de la distribución de la tierra en 1899" *Santiago* 40 (December 1980), 119-178; "Características de la población cubana en 1862," *Revista de la Biblioteca Nacional José Martí*, 3d ser., 22 (September-December 1980), 89-110; "El censo cubano de 1877 y sus diferentes versiones," *Santiago* 34 (June 1979), 167-214; and "Azúcar, esclavitud y tecnología (Segunda mitad del siglo XIX)," *Santiago* 61 (March 1986), 113-131; the works of Oscar Zanetti Lecuona, including, most recently, "Esclavitud i treball lliure: La questió laboral als ferrocarrils cubans, 1837-1867," *Avenç* 101 (February 1987), 17-23, which is taken from his larger study of Cuban railways, scheduled to appear in 1987; and Gert J. Oostinde, "La burguesía cubana y sus caminos de hierro, 1830-1868," *Boletín de Estudios Latino-Americanos y del Caribe* (Amsterdam) 37 (December 1984), 99-115.

8. Manuel Moreno Fraginals pioneered the use of account books in the first edition of *El ingenio* in 1964. Franklin Knight's *Slave Society in Cuba during the Nineteenth Century* (Madison, WI: University of Wisconsin Press, 1970) was an early and influential English-language study, drawing heavily on sources in Spanish archives. My own *Slave Emancipation in Cuba: The Transition to Free Labor, 1860-1899* (Princeton, NJ: Princeton University Press, 1985) explores the dynamics of the breakdown of slavery, and uses judicial records as well as plantation accounts. John Dumoulin contributed an important essay on the sugar industry: John Dumoulin, "El primer desarrollo del movimiento obrero y la formación del proletariado en el sector azucarero; Cruces 1886-1902," *Islas* 48 (May-August 1974), 3-66. Pedro Deschamps Chapeux has explored Afro-Cuban history in detail in a series of books and articles, most notably *El negro en la economía habanera del siglo XIX* (Havana: Unión de Escritores y Artistas de Cuba, 1971). Verena Martínez-Alier's *Marriage, Class and Colour in Nineteenth-Century Cuba* (Cambridge, MA: Cambridge University Press, 1974) is a perceptive study of "race relations" in a social context. More recently, Laird Bergad has used notarial archives to explore the development of sugar regions. See Laird Bergad, "Land Tenure, Slave Ownership, and Income Distribution in Nineteenth-Century Cuba: Colón and Cárdenas, 1859-1876," presented to the Symposium on Caribbean Economic History, 7-8 November 1986, University of the West Indies, Mona, Jamaica.

9. I am indebted to Professor Juan Francisco González, of the Instituto Superior Pedagógico Juan Marinello in Matanzas, for discussing these projects with me. Professor González is coordinating the studies on Matanzas; those on Santa Clara are coordinated by Professor Hernán Venegas Delgado of the Universidad Central de las Vilas. See, e.g., Iván Santos Víctores and Hernán Venegas Delgado, "Un siglo de historia local: el barrio

de Arango (1825-1933)," *Islas* 63 (May-August 1979), 3-64. Other essays based on these projects can be found in the journal *Islas*, published in Santa Clara, and in *Cuadernos de Historia Matancero*, published in Matanzas. The North American historian Laird Bergad is also conducting detailed research on Matanzas. Work on the eastern regions of the island often appears in the journal *Santiago* and, increasingly, in the journal *Del Caribe*. For overviews of regional historical studies in Cuba see Hernán Venegas Delgado, "Veinticinco años de historia regional en Cuba revolucionaria (1959-1983)," *Revista de la Biblioteca Nacional José Martí* 76,3ª época (May-August 1985), 5-32, and Julio LeRiverend, "Variaciones sobre el mismo tema: historia nacional e historia regional," *Del Caribe* 2:6 (1986), 90-98.

10. See his essay on the Cuban "discurso de la nación," forthcoming in the *Anuario de Estudios Americanos*. My thinking on this subject has been stimulated by conversations both with Arcadio Díaz, of the Romance Languages Department at Princeton University, and with Cintio Vitier, of the Centro de Estudios Martianos in Havana. The "textualization" of Cuban history clearly goes against the grain of prevailing approaches to history within Cuba. While it is a helpful counterforce to the hagiographic tendencies within certain areas of Cuban scholarship, the treating of historical themes as texts created by members of the *ciudad letrada* has its limitations for those interested in history as a lived experience of an entire population.

11. Agnes I. Lugo-Ortiz, of the Department of Romance Languages at Princeton University, is currently preparing a dissertation that examines nineteenth-century Cuban biographical texts for insights into the development of nationalism.

12. Rosalie Schwartz, "Bandits and Rebels in Cuban Independence: Predators, Patriots, and Pariahs," *Biblioteca Americana* 1 (November 1982), 91-130.

13. Louise A. Pérez, Jr., "Vagrants, Beggars, and Bandits: Social Origins of Cuban Separatism, 1878-1895," *American Historical Review* 90 (December 1985), 1092-1121.

14. Louis A. Pérez, Jr., "The Pursuit of Pacification: Banditry and the United States' Occupation of Cuba, 1889-1902," *Journal of Latin American Studies* 18 (November 1986), 313-332.

15. See María Poumier-Taquechel, *Contribution à l'étude du banditisme social à Cuba: L'histoire et le mythe de Manuel Garcia 'Rey de los Campos de Cuba' (1851-1895)* (Paris: Harmattan, 1986).

16. Julio Angel Carreras, "El bandolerismo en la República burguesa." *Santiago* 50 (Junio 1983), 145-161.

17. This inquiry will in some cases lead us to the nineteenth-century emigré community, and to processes of politicization in Tampa and Key West. On Manuel García's conversion, see Pérez, "Vagrants, Beggars, and Bandits," p. 1120. On emigré separatism, see Gerald E. Poyo, "Evolution of Cuban Separatist Thought in the Emigré Communities of the United States, 1848-1895," *Hispanic American Historical Review* 66 (August 1986), 485-507.

18. See, e.g., Camilo Polavieja, *Relación documentada de mi política en Cuba* (Madrid: Imprenta de Emilio Minuesa, 1898); *Conspiración e la raza de color descubierta en Santiago de Cuba el 10 de diciembre de 1880 siendo comandante general de la provincia el Exmo. Sr. Teniente General Don Camilo Polavieja y Castillo* (Santiago de Cuba: Sección Tipográfica del Estado Mayor, 1880); Valeriano Weyler y Nicolau, *Mi mando en Cuba (10 febrero 1896 a 31 octubre 1897)* (Madrid: F. González Rojas, 1910-1911).

19. These are located in the Archivo General de Indias, Sevilla, Sección de Diversos, Archivo Polavieja. Portions translated in the appendix to Poumier's thesis.

20. The best recent analysis of these themes is Louis A. Pérez, Jr., *Cuba Between Empires, 1878-1902* (Pittsburgh, PA: University of Pittsburgh Press, 1983).

21. Tadeusz Lepkowski, "Cuba, 1869: desafectos al gobierno e insurrectos," *Estudioso Latinoamericanos* (Poland) 9 (1982/1984), 125-148.

22. María Dolores Domingo Acebrón, "Los hacendados cubanos antes la Guerra de los Diez Años: 1868-1878," *Revista de Indias* 43 (July-December 1983), 707-727.

23. Francisco Pérez Guzmán and Rodolfo Sarracino, *La Guerra Chiquita: una experiencia necesaria* (Havana: Editorial Letras Cubanas, 1982), chap. 9.

24. Cuba, Ejército, Inspección General, *Indice alfabético y defunciones del ejército libertador de Cuba, guerra de independencia* (Havana, 1901). The inadequacies of this listing become immediately apparent when one examines the Fondo Ejército Libertador in the Cuban archives. It can, however, serve as a point of entry for the collective biography of insurgents.

25. A compendious guide to the literature on the wars for independence, one that can serve to identify material worth seeking out and duplicating, is Araceli García Caranza, comp., *Bibliografía de la Guerra de Independencia (1895-1898)* (Havana: Editorial Orbe, for the Departamento Colección Cubana, Biblioteca Nacional José Martí, 1976). One important source of periodical literature from this period, material badly inn need of preservation and duplication, is the Biblioteca del Instituto de Literatura y Lingüística de la Academia de Ciencias, Havana.

26. Tomás Fernández Robaina, ed., *Bibliografía de temas afrocubanos* (Havana: Biblioteca Nacional José Martí, Dpto. de Investigaciones Bibliográficas, 1985).

27. For an idea of some of the contents of this *fondo*, see Barnardo Iglesias Delgado and René González Barrios, "Presencia extranjera en la Guerra del 95: Estudio del Primer Cuerpo del Ejército Libertador," forthcoming in the *Boletín del Archivo Nacional* (Havana). For the Ten Years' War another useful source, which has been examined by Manuel Moreno Fraginals, is the *fondo* Bienes Embargados. The Spanish colonial government, in confiscating the goods of suspected rebels, give their property a permanence in the records which it might not have had otherwise, and which enables us to explore the structure of the insurgent movements.

28. See, e.g., David F. Healy, *The United States in Cuba, 1898-1902* (Madison, WI: University of Wisconsin Press, 1963).

29. On this point, see also Pérez, "Pursuit of Pacification."

30. Hebert Pérez Concepción, "Esencia y forma del gobierno interventor norteamericano en el Departamento Oriental de Cuba: 1899-1902," *Del Caribe* 1 (1983), 21-34.

31. The case files of the Spanish Treaty Claims Commission are located in Record Group 76, entry 352 of the U.S. National Archives. A complete set of the printed briefs is located in entry 353 of the same reference group; scattered volumes also appear in other libraries.

32. The same could be said of other regional archives, particularly those of Matanzas. Some news of the regional archives appears in the *Boletín del Archivo Nacional*, which has recently resumed publication. A brief overview of the Santiago holdings is Julio Corbea, "Fuentes documentales para la historia de Santiago de Cuba (siglo XIX)," *Del Caribe* 2:6 (1986), 103-107.

28. Publicaciones periódicas del exilio cubano

Esperanza B. de Varona

Los cubanos por razones políticas han tenido que abandonar su patria y emigrar como exiliados a otros países durante diversas luchas por su libertad. Principalmente en este nuevo exilio, arribaron a los E.U.A., país que acogió y abrió sus puertas al pueblo cubano, perseguido por el régimen imperante en Cuba desde 1959.

Pocas fuentes de información bibliográfica quedaron como testimonio de otros exilios. Es por esta razón que en este éxodo, bibliotecarias cubanas exiliadas, que pertenecían y aún continúan en la facultad de la Biblioteca de la Universidad de Miami se dieran a la tarea de recoger para el futuro todo el material a su alcance producido por este exilio.

El material es diverso en su forma, pero similar en su contenido, todos orientados a propagar la verdad de lo ocurrido en Cuba. Entre estos materiales encontramos materiales impresos y no impresos. Entre los impresos, además de los libros publicados, tenemos las publicaciones periódicas que incluyen revistas, boletines y periódicas, mayormente conocidos como los "Periodiquitos de Exilio."

La mayor concentración de cubanos se encuentran en el estado de la Florida y es en Miami, la llamada "Capital del Exilio," donde la mayor cantidad de estas publicaciones se originaron y aún continúan publicándose, a través de los 28 años de exilio. La Universidad de Miami que está situada en esta área posee la mayor colección de estas publicaciones periódicas del exilio. En la bibliografía publicada recientemente por SALALM, titulada *Cuban Exile Periodicals at the University of Miami Library: An Annotated Bibliography,* [1] están descritos los 665 títulos de las publicaciones periódicas que la Biblioteca de la Universidad tenía en su colección hasta abril 1, 1986. Desde esa fecha hasta el presente la biblioteca ha recibido cerca de 80 nuevos títulos, haciendo un total de cerca de 250.000 ejemplares incluidos en esta colección.

El criterio establecido para incluir una publicación en esta colección es que tiene que estar editada, dirigida o publicada por cubanos refugiados, por cubano-americanos o por miembros de una nueva generación que ahora surge, los nacidos de padres cubanos y que continúan fieles a las tradiciones cubanas inculcadas por sus padres. Las 665 citas bibliográficas están en orden alfabético por título, seguidas por una lista de directores y cuatro índices: cronológico, geográfico (por ciudad), geográfico (por país) y un índice de materias. Cada cita bibliográfica está precedida por un código convencional (una letra y un número); la letra representa la primera letra del título y el número corresponde al orden consecutivo dentro de cada letra. La numeración y la fecha del inicio de cada publicación es ofrecido seguido por un guión si la publicación todavía continúa; si ya ha cesado de publicarse se escribe la fecha. La verificación del cese de las publicaciones en la mayoría de los casos se obtuvo directamente de los editores, directores o colaboradores de las distintas publicaciones. Esta fechas ofrecidas no indican que la biblioteca posee los ejemplares de esas fechas en su colección.

La fuente de información bibliográfica se ha tomado de la cabecera editorial de cada publicación y en su ausencia la información procede de la primera página.

Las anotaciones ofrecidas por cada título son las siguientes: frecuencia, editor (cuando es ofrecida), idioma, variaciones en el título, subtítulo, medida y anotación por materia cuando la publicación no tiene subtítulo. Todas las fechas de las anotaciones son escritas en español, excepto cuando la publicación es en inglés.

Como característica de estas publicaciones podemos señalar que la frecuencia es generalmente irregular, debido en la gran mayoría de los casos, que no contaban con el apoyo económico necesario para poder publicarse regularmente. Así vemos publicaciones como *Cuba Libre* editada por Isodoro Rodríguez Martín, publicado en Miami, que consta de un solo número (vol. 1, no. 1, nov. 1986).

Como característica interesante de estas publicaciones es que en su gran mayoría se han repartido gratuitamente en mercados y comercios latinos, habiéndose publicado gracias a la ayuda recibida por anunciantes y colaboradores y sólo unas pocas se obtienen por subscripción.

Esta colección es de gran importancia porque a través de estas fuentes primarias de información, los eruditos e investigadores pueden analizar los cambios ocurridos dentro de la comunidad cubana desde el comienzo de éxodo en 1959 hasta el presente. Estas publicaciones reflejan diferentes aspectos del exilio cubano: intereses políticos, el deseo de mantener vivo el retorno a la patria lejana, el interés por conservar el patrimonio cubano en tierras extranjeras divulgando sus raíces históricas, literarias folklóricas, científicas, musicales, artísticas, religiosas, etc. Así como también demuestran el impacto socio-económico e histórico que los cubanos exiliados han tenido en muchas áreas de los Estados Unidos de América, principalmente en el estado de la Florida y particularmente en el área del Gran Miami. Los cubanos se han establecido en distintas áreas metropolitanas de los E.U.A., por lo que la información ofrecida en estas publicaciones abarca áreas bastante amplias. El tópico general de estas publicaciones es polémico y político en esencia, así como también reflejan intereses nacionales e internacionales. Un factor importante es que esta colección sirve como medio de comunicación para aquellos hispano-hablantes que no pueden leer o escribir mucho inglés, por lo que la mayoría son escritas en español.

Para terminar, voy a citar a Gastón Baquero, distinguido erudito periodista cubano, actualmente exiliado en España, que en un artículo titulado "El Periodismo heroico de exilio," publicado en *El Miami Herald*, edición en español, nov. 4, 1985, p. 9, describe estas publicaciones como "el periodismo heroico del exilio, el hecho con el alma, más que con recursos materiales . . .".

NOTA

1. Esperanza B. de Varona, *Cuban Exile Periodicals at the University of Miami Library: An Annotated Bibliography*, Seminar on the Acquisition of Latin American Library Materials Bibliography and Reference Series, no. 19 (Madison, WI: SALALM Secretariat, 1987).

29. The Cuban Information System, University of Miami

Sara M. Sánchez

The Cuban Information System, a project of the Research Institute for Cuban Studies, Graduate School of International Studies, University of Miami, is a highly specialized, extensive, interdisciplinary collection of databases, focusing on Cuba and Cubans abroad. It is particularly, although not exclusively, aimed at assisting the researcher of life in Cuba after 1959.

Other Similar Print Sources

None as comprehensive, specialized, or specific in subject access. The *Indice General de Publicaciones Periódicas Cubanas*, published by Cuba's National Library since 1970, is a wide bibliographic source for about one hundred Cuban publications, with very general subject headings lacking depth. The *Granma* index is based on the weekly supplement. It appears with considerable time lag.

Cuban Information System Databases
*Cuban Periodicals**

History, Economics, Political Science, Ideology, Sociology, Social Welfare, Socioeconomic Indicators and Demography, Education, Military Science, Culture and Arts, Public Health, Industries, Technology, Communication and Transportation, Labor, Agriculture, Foreign and Domestic Policy, International Relations.

*Oral History Collection***

Index of the recorded testimonies of the Cuban-American emigre community reminiscing life in Cuba and the exile experience, as perceived by the elite and the common man. Categories are geared to contributing insights from the early republican period to the present

---

*Developed under grant from USIA's Radio Martí Program.

**See Chapter 30, below: Graciella Cruz-Taura, Index to the Cuban Oral History Collection.

and to issues of cultural continuity and class relations (blacks, women, immigrants and the rural population).

Experts on Cuba

Data file on leading experts on Cuba, pointing to their research specialties.

Cuban Biographical Dictionary

Based on Professor Jaime Suchlicki's historical and biographical research on Cuban personalities, including proper names and corporate sources, associations and other pertinent items. It is an alphabetical listing.

Ancillary Subject Areas for Cuban Periodicals Database

Science (including pure, natural, medical and behavioral sciences), Ecology, Folklore, Criminology, Laws and Legislation, Literature, Music (classical and popular), Dance, Sports and Recreation, Trade.

Type of Source Documents

Chronologies, Cuban biographical data, periodicals, tapes, speeches, lectures, emphasis on substantive articles in Cuban periodicals, stressing historical, socioeconomic, political and cultural issues. Addresses of leading specialists; includes reports and results of meetings and conferences, relevant authored and anonymous papers.

Selection Policy

Aims to produce a vast, comprehensive information database on Cuban studies. The Cuban Periodicals Database, in particular, emphasizes current or contemporary events since 1959; but will eventually cover selected general interest publications, like *Bohemia*, from pre-revolutionary times. As a general policy, it stresses substantive, relevant articles dealing with Cuba or Cubans, excluding articles about other nations not having connection with that country.

Language of Source Documents

Spanish and English.

Dates Covered

Cuban Periodicals Database

Started with 1985 issues of publications in descending chronological order from the most current to the earliest. Database indexing aims to reach the date of inception of each publication. Periodicals selected for initiation of indexing project: *Granma, Bohemia, Verde Olivo.* By December 1987, daily edition of *Granma* was indexed through 1978.

Oral History Collection Database

Covers material on Cuban exile community taped since 1970.

File of Experts on Cuba

As current as possible.

Biographical Dictionary

Covering from early Cuban history to current Central Party Committee members. Data online updated periodically.

Size of Cuban Periodicals Database (as of December 1987)

Records Online:	20,584
Articles Indexed:	39,000

Update Frequency of Cuban Periodicals Database

Weekly inputs.

Number and Type of Subject Entries

Standardized, thesaurus-based controlled vocabulary consisting mainly of simple terms, sometimes pre-coordinated. Based on fundamental principles of facet analysis, with general, relevant clusters of categories and descriptor terms grouped together. Free search provided with key subject words in the title and frequently in sub-title (if entry is not too long). Controlled vocabulary descriptors and identifiers (for proper names of persons, places, corporate sources, organizations, and "buzz" words). Capacity to combine these descriptor terms and identifiers, using Boolean logic (and/or operators) to retrieve coordinated terms.

Search Guides Available to Researchers

Printed Subject Guide to Index Terms (alphabetical listing and taxonomic listing by categories). *List of Geographical Terms. Authority List* for acronyms used (corporate or organizational identifier terms). *Authority List for Proper Names* (in progress). List of related terms, not used terms, broader and narrower terms, plus scope notes for descriptors (in progress). Thesaurus available online and in printed form.

Type of Record

Full bibliographical citation containing up to two authors, title and subtitle; periodical title; year of publication, issue number, date and pagination. There is a special field for relevant remarks or notes on a document cited.

Level of Indexing Specificity

Medium. An average of 6 descriptors/identifiers per document.

Strengths

Strong and comprehensive in its in-depth coverage of Cuban materials both from Cuba and from the exile community.

Capacity to combine any term, whether descriptor or identifier, utilizing Boolean logic to increase the specificity of the postings retrieved.

Specific key words compose the controlled vocabulary rather than multi-term headings.

Includes a variety of formats: periodicals, speeches, reports, biographical, historical, chronological material (and others as listed above).

Very specific in the use of identifiers: proper names of Cuban personalities, government leaders, Cuban Communist Party members, organizations, conferences, assemblies and other meetings, as well as in the use of current "buzz" words, such as *Guerra de Todo el Pueblo*.

Currency.

Weaknesses

Citations printed out do not conform to L.C. bibliographic standards, i.e., author's name is not in inverted form; surname appears last. Hence, it is not possible to obtain an alphabetical bibliography-type listing of citations.

Organizations and other corporate names are retrieved by the corresponding acronym, hence acronyms listing must be consulted.

Although the program is user-friendly, the specific highly controlled vocabulary makes it somewhat difficult for any user not familiar with Cuban terminology to research.

Lacks abstracts on content. If interested, user must have access to the article.

30. Index to the Cuban Oral History Collection

Graciella Cruz-Taura

As part of the Cuban Archives, the University of Miami houses the Cuban Oral History Collection. This paper describes an initiative of the Research Institute for Cuban Studies to integrate the content descriptions of the existing collection into the Cuban Information System, thus establishing bibliographic availability to an important research collection heretofore largely unknown to the academic community.

The Cuban Information System* is a standardized, extensive, interdisciplinary system of databases; Cuban periodicals are being indexed on one of these databases. Following the thesaurus construction methodology suggested by the American National Standards Institute, a thesaurus has been developed by the Cuban Information System staff to index Cuban periodicals. Similarly, a thesaurus has been designed for the Cuban Oral History Collection database. Based on fundamental principles of facet analysis, this thesaurus, derived from the main thesaurus used for periodicals, is being developed to meet the specific needs of orally transmitted information.

Conceptual Framework

As a result of improved recording techniques, oral history has become a particularly valuable tool for historians in recent decades. It is the best suited method to capture, for contemporary and future scholars, valuable information that would otherwise be irretrievably lost. The theoretical frame of reference for the Cuban Oral History Collection is based on the premise that oral historiography is an ancient art, rediscovered by the academic community in recent decades with the appearance of the tape recorder. Furthermore, the interviewer plays a historian's role, as oral history is a selection and a first interpretation of information recorded with two particular historical

---

*See Chapter 29, above: Sara M. Sánchez, Description of Cuban Information System, University of Miami.

perspectives interacting. A relationship is developed between the historian-interviewer and the informant based on each other's Weltanschauung and idea of history.

Beyond the possibilities researchers find in the actual tapes and transcriptions, each interview is an entity in itself, structured by the language and interactions of the participants, but especially structured ideologically by the message it conveys. Oral history is predominantly based on reminiscences, which are not thoughts said at random but "part of an organized whole of memories that tend to project a consistent image of the narrator and in many cases, a justification of his or her life." [1] A selection process takes place in the human mind based on other life experiences and on the historical consciousness felt by both, the interviewer and the interviewee.

The Cuban Oral History Collection covers a wide range of topics that fall basically into two categories. First, there are interviews of people who have played a role in Cuban affairs publicly or as seekers of change. Like most oral history projects now undertaken by American presidential libraries, this category complements written histories by adding or revising information. In many ways, it can be described as an oral history of the elite. Nevertheless, oral history as a method may provide its greatest potentialities in the second category: records capturing the perceptions of the ordinary citizen, whose views, "by virtue of being historically inarticulate, have been overlooked in most studies of the past." [2] Folkloric and popular culture elements are captured within the scope of this subject area, also important as the interviewee is becoming assimilated into a new social order.

Alice Kessler-Harris's experiences interviewing immigrant women revealed contradictions between the immigrant's actions and attitudes toward family patterns in America, as observed during the course of the interview. [3] Such experience exemplifies how oral history leads the analyst toward the conflict between historical and mythic visions of the past and to an understanding of the tensions felt by the immigrant in the process of adapting to life in the United States.

Appraisal Guidelines

Given the volume of tapes to be processed, it is essential to utilize a cost-effective method to make them accessible to researchers. Selection criteria have been established, as it would be unreasonable to devise plans to index all the existing tapes at this time, and since they will increase in number as a result of future acquisitions. Index guidelines are as follows for subject matter.

The Early Republican Period

This section includes the following:

Interviews with families of past presidents of Cuba, providing fuller insights into their lives. Cuban republican politics included a presidential system that, until 1935, operated within the constraints of the Platt Amendment. Insights into how Cuban presidents perceived their powers during and after Platt are crucial to an understanding of Cuban politics during this period.

Interviews with families of patriots of Cuba's independence wars. As a topic, the struggle for independence has traditionally dominated written Cuban historiography. The perceptions of those who fought the wars should contribute to reinterpretations of a subject that continues to fascinate historians specializing in Cuba.

Interviews with former senators, representatives, cabinet members, party and labor leaders, delegates to the Constitutional Assembly of 1940, and senior civil service staff, namely, people who served under the aforementioned officials. The "lost republic" is an obvious focus here, but a very thorny and complex subject. Corruption and gangsterism undermined the system perhaps to a much greater extent than socioeconomic deprivation. This is an important clue in the preamble to revolution.

Cultural Continuity

Turmoil has characterized Cuban history throughout the twentieth century. In the 1920s, political protest arose in reaction to the cultural discontinuity brought about by the devastation left by Cuba's independence wars, by U.S. economic penetration, and by the question of denationalization. Beginning with the Generation of 1923, the experiences of prison, human rights violations, counterrevolutionary activities, and political exile cover the entire span of Cuban history. As such, the recorded memories of those who suffered should be made accessible along with their views of Cuban social realities. The question of cultural continuity is directly related to the immigrant experience in the United States and to the assimilation process. The Cuban Oral History Collection should facilitate in-depth examination of the value structure of Cuban society and identify those conceptual landmarks that may be useful to researchers concerned with longitudinal (generational) and/or cross-sectional (Cubans vs. Cuban-Americans) contrasts in attitudes, normative orientations, and values. Revealing the evolution of colloquial Cuban Spanish and the influence of English, the oral history collection is creating a record of the speech patterns of the five or six generations of this century.

Within this section, the Index classifies interviews within categories:

Minority issues and ethnic politics as they affect Cuban-Americans in the United States, for example, immigration laws, bilingualism in the schools.

Events elsewhere in the world that involve Cuba or in which Cuban exiles and Cuban-Americans have attempted to influence U.S. public opinion and foreign policy makers, for example, the situation in Nicaragua, aid to the Contras, Angola.

Cuban and Cuban-American perceptions or image of U.S. affairs and life.

Class Relations

This section consists of interviews on the average person's perception of events and forces that shaped Cuban's social development. The scope of this subject requires the following, at times overlapping, dimensions:

Black History—To collect the daily experiences of blacks is of great importance to scholars specializing in race relations. Ethnologist Carlos Moore is now conducting research in Miami on the experiences of black Cuban-Americans. He has already expressed interest in contributing to the enhancement of the Cuban Oral History Collection.

Rural Cuba—This section encompasses recordings capturing the folklore and traditions of the countryside, now being eroded by exile and life in urban America.

Immigration—Cuba received large numbers of immigrants throughout this century, many of whom subsequently were compelled to settle in the United States. Spaniards headed the list, but important communities were also formed by Jews and Chinese. The impact of these immigrations on Cuba's social structure remains to be studied with more specificity, particularly in reference to the aforementioned observations on cultural continuity.

Women in Cuba—Claiming to represent all women, middle- and upper-class Cuban feminists place Cuba as a hemispheric leader in legislation for women's rights. The social and political consciousness of Cuban-American women must be studied against this background.

Indexing Methodology

Headed by bibliographic data, the tape is indexed by timed content blocks, for which specific descriptor terms and identifiers are chosen. Descriptors are controlled by a thesaurus, developed following

American National Standards Institute guidelines; authority lists are kept for the identifiers.

When an interview has been indexed, the indexer prepares an abstract of the tape as a whole. The abstract includes background to the interview; it points to the main ideas discussed, as an aid to prospective users in deciding if they wish to listen to the desired excerpts.

The system allows searches by date, by interviewer(s), by interviewee(s) or by any combination of Boolean logic applied to the search and retrieval process—AND, OR, AND NOT, OR NOT, in a continuous string applied against both descriptor terms and identifier terms in combination. The researcher then needs to listen only to the pertinent time block.

The output of a search request will be printed as well as viewable on the monitor screen and will contain a full description of the oral history information found, including abstract. Most importantly, it will contain the time segment on the recorded media where a match of the Boolean logic combination of descriptor/identifier terms was found. This enables the requestor to find directly where an occurrence of the request could be found on the recorded media.

This Index synthesizes the Cuban Information System's experience indexing periodicals and its experience in retrieval with the TAPE (Timed Access to Pertinent Excerpts) System, now used by the State Historical Society of Wisconsin. [4] Unlike TAPE, however, no abstract is prepared for each block. The descriptors/identifiers suffice to facilitate retrieval, providing a system that is significantly more cost-effective.

Samples

The following two samples represent the search as it appears on the monitor screen and subsequently on the hard copy. The first was broadcast by various Miami radio stations and by USIA's Radio Martí Program to Cuba. The second collects the testimony of a Cuban refugee as she adapts to life in the United States. It is part of an assimilation study, now undergoing its third phase, directed by sociologist Juan Clark, which interviews every three years immigrants who arrived during the Mariel Boatlift.

Sample I

INTERVIEWEE(S):___Manuel Sánchez Pérez___ REPOS:___FUM___
INTERVIEWER(S):___Carlos Alberto Montaner___ ACC. NO._____
TITLE:_____Cuba Uncensored_____
LENGTH:___2 Hr. 5 Min. 43 Sec._____
DATE:_____23 January 1986_____ PLACE:___Madrid, Spain_____
REMARKS:_____

ABSTRACT

Interview with Manuel Sánchez Pérez, Vice-Minister of CEATM, upon his defection and failed kidnap attempt by Cuba's security forces in Spain. Analysis of the basic problems faced by the Cuban economy. Comparison of trade with socialist and capitalist blocs. Inefficiency of economic system inhibits any reform measures. Castro's personal coercive attitude controls decision-making process. Soviet attitude toward Cuba's poor economic management and the skepticism of Cuba's technocrats to solve the problems. Concern over changes in Soviet leadership. Comparison of the Castro brothers in respect to politics, the economy, Soviet subordination. Socialist models implemented. Discrepancies, changes in ruling class. *Fidelismo* over historical communism. Cuba's possible return to the Western bloc and its domestic repercussions. The meaning of Mariel. Cuban youth today—ideology, perspectives and frustrations. Institutional characteristics of the Communist party, state security and armed forces. Control of information re Angola, Ethiopia, Grenada. Castro's personality. Post-Castro Cuba. USSR options. Foreign investments. U.S. image as presented to the Cuban people by the regime.

SECTION	DESCRIPTORS	IDENTIFIERS

Side A: Part I

(A) 3:0:30   Political asylum   Spain
                 Dissidents

(B) 0:12:45   Kidnappings   DSE
                 Corruption   Fidel Castro

SECTION		DESCRIPTORS	IDENTIFIERS
(C)	0:12:00	Raw materials Foreign trade Socialist countries	
(D)	0:15:32	Nutrition Imports Agricultural production	Fidel Castro Osmani Cienfuegos
(E)	0:18:24	Economic assistance Negotiations Socialist countries Technicians Bureaucracy Deficit Budget	USSR Fidel Castro FAR
(F)	0:26:31		"Viajes de la Comunidad" Mariel Fidel Castro

Side A: Part II

(A)	0:28:22	Domestic policy	Raúl Castro FAR
(B)	0:29:50	Economic policy Socialist countries	
(C)	0:31:02	Destitutions Deficiencies Repression	Ramiro Valdés Osmani Cienfuegos Guillermo García MITRANS MININT Juan Almeida
(D)	0:34:25	Moral incentives	Fidel Castro USSR 1960 + Raúl Castro

SECTION	DESCRIPTORS	IDENTIFIERS
(E) 0:36:08	Communist parties History	Aníbal Escalante Microfaction PSP Carlos Rafael Rodríguez Isidoro Malmierca
(F) 0:37:13		Raúl Castro Mikhail Gorbachev USSR
(G) 0:40:45	Emigration Repression Exiles	Mariel Embassy of Peru Fidel Castro "Viajes de la Comunidad"
(H) 0:45:23	Suicides Planning Destitutions Corruption	Osvaldo Dorticós JUCEPLAN Fidel Castro MINJUS DSE
(I) 0:50:00	Suicides Youth	
(J) 0:51:36	Destitutions Intellectuals Economy Economic incentives	Humberto Pérez Raúl Castro
(K) 0:53:54	Destitutions Youth Revolution Ideology Conduct	Antonio Pérez Herrero

SECTION	DESCRIPTORS	IDENTIFIERS

Side B: Part III

(A)	0:00:00	Appointments	Carlos Rafael Rodríguez Juan Almeida Armando Hart José Abrahantes Sergio del Valle
(B)	0:2:14	Leaders Communist parties	CCPCC Raúl Castro Osmani Cienfuegos
(C)	0:2:43	Armed forces Internal security	DSE ANPP
(D)	0:3:07	Dissidents	Politburo CCPCC
(E)	0:4:58	People's power	
(F)	0:5:42	Political structure Domestic policy Organizations	Roberto Veiga FMC Vilma Espín FMC Armando Costa CDR Jesús Montané Humberto Pérez Pepín Naranjo
(G)	0:8:23	Troops Internationalism Foreign policy	Angola SMO
(H)	0:17:22	Conflicts Control of information Officials Leaders	Ethiopia Eritrea Somalia

SECTION	DESCRIPTORS	IDENTIFIERS
(I) 0:20:41	Troops Troop withdrawals Deficiencies Armed forces Appointments Trials Military intelligence	Grenada Maurice Bishop Tortoló Méndez Cominche Fidel Castro
(J) 0:28:00		Embassy of Peru Nicaragua Fidel Castro
(K) 0:31:37	Foreign policy International relations Emigration Capitalism Enterprises National economy Developmental strategies Free market Foreign debt	U.S.A. Politburo CCPCC Fidel Castro USSR
(L) 0:38:15	Propaganda Public opinion Leaders Revolutions Ideology	U.S.A. Fidel Castro
(M) 0:43:34	Books Testimonies Dissidents	

Sample II

INTERVIEWEE(S):__Estella Martínez_____ REPOS:__FUM_____
INTERVIEWER(S):__Juan Clark_____ ACC. NO._____
TITLE:_____--------
LENGTH:__29 Min. 20 Sec._____
DATE:____7 January 1986_____ PLACE:__Miami, Florida____
REMARKS:_Phase Two (1983) of Mariel Assimilation Project____

ABSTRACT

Three years after arriving on the Mariel Boatlift, this woman tells of the difficulties of adjusting to life in America and compares living conditions to those of Cuba. With a son in jail, she shows lack of knowledge of the U.S. judicial system and of her constitutional rights.

SECTION	DESCRIPTORS	IDENTIFIERS
(A) 0:0:42	Exiles	Embassy of Peru
(B) 0:2:18	Youth Conditions of life Crimes	U.S.A.
(C) 0:6:26	Prisons Sentences Courts Letters Deportation Family	Krome Atlanta Nancy Reagan
(D) 0:13:19	Immigration Democracy Judicial branch Laws Prisons Deportation	Ronald Reagan Robert Graham U.S. Congress INS

SECTION	DESCRIPTORS	IDENTIFIERS
(E) 0:18:46	Hunger Strikes Prisons Immigration Solidarity Exiles Deportation	Atlanta Prison INS Mariel Cuban Americans
(F) 0:26:19	Labor Communism Exiles Working conditions Unemployment	U.S.A. Mariel

NOTES

1. Jan Vansina, *Oral Tradition as History* (Madison, WI: University of Wisconsin Press, 1985), p. 8

2. David Henige, *Oral Historiography* (London: Longman, 1982), p. 107.

3. Ronald J. Grele, ed., *Envelopes of Sound: Six Practitioners Discuss the Method, Theory and Practice of Oral History and Oral Testimony* (Chicago, IL: Precedent Publishing, 1975), pp. 56-67.

4. Dale E. Treleven, "Oral History, Audio Technology, and the TAPE System," *International Journal of Oral History* 2 (February 1981), 26-45.

Acronyms

AABDFC	Association des Archivistes Bibliotecaires Documentalistes Francophones de la Caraïbe (Association of French-speaking Caribbean Archivists, Librarians and Documentalists)
AACR2	Anglo-American Cataloging Rules, 2d edition
ABIESI	Asociación de Bibliotecarios de Instituciones de Enseñanza Superior e Investigación (Mexico)
ABUD	Asociación de Bibliotecas Universitarias Dominicanas
ACT	Association for Caribbean Transformation
ACRL	Association of College and Research Libraries
ACURIL	Association of Caribbean University Research and Institutional Libraries
AGRIS	International Information System for the Agricultural Sciences and Technology (FAO)
ANPP	Asemblea Nacional del Poder Popular (Cuba)
ANUEIS	Asociación Nacional de Universidades e Instituciones de Enseñanza Superior (Mexico)
APEC	Acción Pro-Educación y Cultura, Inc. (Dominican Republic)
ARL	Association of Research Libraries
ASIS	American Society for Information Science
ASLIB	Association of Special Libraries and Information Bureaus (U.K.)

ASSODOC	Association des Documentalistes-Bibliothécaires de Centres de Documentation et d'Information des Etablissements Secondaires (Association of Documentalist-Librarians of Documentation and Information Centers in Secondary Education)
AVM	Audio visual material
CAB	Commonwealth Agricultural Bureau
CADEC	Caribbean Ecumenical Consultation for Development
CAGRIS	Caribbean Information System for the Agricultural Sciences
CARDI	Caribbean Agricultural Development Institute Information Network
CARICOM	Caribbean Community
CARIRI	Caribbean Industrial Research Institute (Trinidad)
CARISPLAN	Caribbean Information System for Economic and Social Planning
CARNEID	Caribbean Network for Education and Innovation
CARPIN	Caribbean Information System for Patents
CARSTIN	Caribbean Network for the Exchange of Information and Experience in Science and Technology
CARTIS	Caribbean Trade Information System
CBIN	Caribbean Basin Information Network
CCOH	Catalogue collectif des ouvrages haïtiens
CCPCC	Comité Central del Partido Comunista de Cuba
CD-ROM	Compact disk read-only memory
CDCC	Caribbean Development and Cooperation Committee
CDR	Comité de Defensa de la Revolución (Cuba)

CDS	Computerized Documentation System (UNESCO)
CEATM	Comité Estatal de Abastecimiento Técnico-Material (Cuba)
CEIS	Caribbean Energy Information System
CENTROMIDCA	Centro Taller Regional de Restauración y Microfilmación de Documentos para el Caribe y Centroamérica (Inter-American Center for Restoration and Microfilming of Books, Documents, and Photographs)
CERAG	Centre d'Etudes Régionales Antilles-Guyane
CEREP	Center for the Study of Puerto Rican Reality
CERLAL	Centro Regional para el Fomento del Libro en América Latina
CICH	Centro de Información Científica y Humanística (UNAM)
CIDA	Comité Interamericano de Desarrollo Agrícola (Inter-American Committee for Agricultural Development)
CIDIA	Centro Interamericano de Documentación, Información y Comunicación Agrícola (IICA)
CIDOC	Centro Intercultural de Documentación (Mexico)
CIESPAL	Centro Internacional de Estudios Superiores de Periodismo para América Latina (Ecuador)
CONACYT	Consejo Nacional de Ciencia y Tecnología (Mexico)
CONSER	Conversion of Serials (U.S.A.)
CTCS	Caribbean Technology Consultancy Service
DAG	Disaster Action Group
DEVSIS	Development Sciences Information System (Canada)

DISC	Project to Develop Integrated Information Systems in the English-Speaking Caribbean
DLS/UWI	Department of Library Studies, University of the West Indies
DOM	Départements d'Outre Mer (France)
DRA	Data Research Associates (St. Louis, MO)
DSE	Departamento de Seguridad del Estado (Cuba)
DUP	Disponibilidad Universal de Publicaciones (Universal Availability of Publications)
ECLAC	Economic Commission for Latin America and the Caribbean (United Nations)
EEC	European Economic Community
EE.UU.	Estados Unidos (United States of America)
E.U.A.	Estados Unidos Americanos (United States of America)
FAR	Fuerzas Armadas Revolucionaria (Cuba)
FAO	Food and Agricultural Organization (of the United Nations)
FBR	Full bibliographic record (University of Illinois)
FIAB	Federación Internacional de Asociaciones de Bibliotecarios
FMC	Federación de Mujeres Cubanas
FUM	University of Miami, Florida
IABNSB	Instituto Autónomo Biblioteca Nacional y de Servicios de Bibliotecas (Venezuela)
ICA	International Council on Archives (UNESCO)
ICAITI	Instituto Centroamericano de Investigación y Tecnología Industrial (Center for Information for Industry) (Guatemala)

ICFES	Instituto Colombiano para el Fomento de la Educación Superior
IDRC	International Development Research Centre (Canada)
IFAL	Institut Français d'Amérique Latine (Mexico City)
IFLA	International Federation of Library Associations
IICA	Instituto Interamericano de Ciencias Agrícolas (Inter-American Institute on Agriculture) (OAS)
ILIS	Integrated Library and Information Services
INAGHEI	Institut National d'Administration de Gestion et des Hautes Etudes Internationales (Haiti)
INFOLAC	Information Networks and System for Development in Latin America and the Caribbean
INID	International agreed Numbers for Identification of Data
INS	Immigration and Naturalization Service (U.S.)
INSEE	Institut National de la Statistique et des Etudes Economiques (France)
ISBN	International Standard Book Number
ISIS	Integrated Scientific Information System
ISO	International Organization for Standardization (UN)
JUCEPLAN	Junta Central de Planificación (Cuba)
LAMP	Latin American Microfilming Project
LDC	Least (or Less) Developed Country
LIFENET	Library Involvement for Education Network
MARC	Machine-readable cataloging
MININT	Ministerio del Interior (Cuba)

MINJUS	Ministerio de Justicia (Cuba)
MITRANS	Ministerio de Transporte (Cuba)
NBLC	Dutch Centre for Public Libraries and Literature
NCSU	North Carolina State University, Raleigh
NEH	National Endowment for the Humanities (U.S.A.)
NOTIS	Northwestern Online Total Integrated System (U.S.A.)
NPO	National Preservation Office (U.K.)
OAS	Organization of American States
OCLC	Online Computer Library Center (U.S.A.)
OEA	Organización de los Estados Americanos (Organization of American States)
OECD	Organization for Economic Cooperation and Development
OECS	Organization of Eastern Caribbean States
PAU	Pan American Union
PGI	Programme général d'information (Programa General de Información) (General Information Programme) (UNESCO)
P.I.	Principal Investigator
PILI	Proyecto Interamericano de Literatura Infantil (Inter-American Project on Children's Literature) (OAS)
PNM	People's National Movement (Trinidad and Tobago)
PNUD	Programa de las Naciones Unidas para el Desarrollo (United Nations Development Program)
POC	Products of combustion

PRILINET	Puerto Rico Information Library Network
PROMIS	Agricultural Production and Marketing Information System
PSP	Partido Socialista Popular (Cuba)
PVA	Polyvinyl acetate
RECON	Retrospective conversion
SALALM	Seminar on the Acquisition of Latin American Library Materials
SCONUL	Standing Conference of National and University Libraries (U.K.)
SDI	Selective dissemination of information
SECOBI	Servicio de Consulta a Bancos de Información (Mexico)
SENARC	Servicio Nacional de Revistas Científicas (Mexico)
SEP	Secretaría de Educación Pública (Mexico)
SEPSA	Secretaría Ejecutiva de Planificación Sectorial Agropecuaria de Recursos Naturales Renovables (Costa Rica)
SIRAG	Service Interrégionale Antilles Guyane (INSEE)
SMO	Servicio militar obligatorio (Cuba)
STP	UNESCO Division of Science and Technology Policies
TAPE	Timed Access to Pertinent Excerpts
TOM	Territoires d'outre mer (France)
UAP	Universal Availability of Publications (IFLA)
UBIC	Unidad de Bibliotecas de Investigación Científica (Mexico)
UCLA	University of California, Los Angeles

U.K.	United Kingdom
UKAEA	United Kingdom Atomic Energy Authority
U.N.	United Nations
UNAM	Universidad Nacional Autónoma de México
UNC	University of North Carolina, Chapel Hill
UNDP	United Nations Development Program
UNECLAC	United Nations Economic Commission for Latin America and the Caribbean
UNESCO	United Nations Educational, Scientific and Cultural Organization
UNISIST	Universal System for Information in Science and Technology (UNESCO)
UPR	University of Puerto Rico
U.S.A.	United States of America
USIA	United States Information Agency
USSR	Union of Soviet Socialist Republics
UTCat	University of Texas online Catalog
UTLAS	UTLAS International (Canada), formerly University of Toronto Library Automation System
U.W.I.	University of the West Indies

About the Authors

ELSA BARBERENA BLASQUEZ is Jefe de la Unidad de Bibliotecas de Investigación Científica at the Universidad Autónoma de México, Mexico City.

SUSAN SHATTUCK BENSON is Senior Specialist, Development of Libraries, Archives and Mass Media, Division of Cultural Heritage, Department of Cultural Affairs, Organization of American States.

VIRGINIA BETANCOURT VALVERDE is Directora, Instituto Autónomo Biblioteca Nacional y de Servicios de Bibliotecas, Caracas, Venezuela.

NEL BRETNEY is Head of cataloging at the Main Library, University of the West Indies, Cave Hill, Barbados.

ELLEN H. BROW is Book Selector for Ibero-America, Harvard College Library.

ANTONITO GORDIANO CROES is currently Minister of Welfare for Aruba. He also serves as Secretary-General of the Aruba's People Party.

GRACIELLA CRUZ-TAURA is Associate Director, Research Institute for Cuban Studies, University of Miami, Florida.

DAPHNE DOUGLAS is Head of the Department of Library Studies, University of the West Indies, Kingston, Jamaica.

MARIE-CLAIRE F. DE FIGUEROA is Coordinator of the Unidad de Documentación del Programa México—Estados Unidos, El Colegio de México, Mexico City.

NELLY S. GONZALEZ is Head, Latin American Library Services Unit at the University of Illinois, Champaign-Urbana.

MINA JANE GROTHEY, President of SALALM in 1986-1987, is Ibero-American Reference Librarian at the General Library of the University of New Mexico, Albuquerque.

LAURA GUTIERREZ-WITT is Head of the Nettie Lee Benson Latin American Collection, University of Texas at Austin.

DAN C. HAZEN is Librarian for Hispanic Collections, University of California, Berkeley. He served as President of SALALM in 1984-1985.

SCOTT JACOB is a librarian at Dickinson College, Carlisle, Pennsylvania.

DEBORAH JAKUBS is Ibero-American/General Bibliographer at Duke University, Durham, North Carolina.

THOMAS MATHEWS is Secretary General, Association of Caribbean Universities, Río Piedras Puerto Rico.

MARIANO A. MAURA is currently working on a Ph.D. at the University of Pittsburgh. At the time of the conference he was teaching at the Graduate School of Librarianship of the University of Puerto Rico, Río Piedras.

FRANÇOISE MONTBRUN is Director, Bibliothèque Universitaire de Guadeloupe, part of the Bibliothèque Universitaire Antilles-Guyane.

ALAN MOSS is Acquisitions Librarian, Main Library, University of the West Indies, Barbados.

MAUREEN C. NEWTON is a documentalist with the Caribbean Community Secretariat.

MARY NOONAN is Project Leader for Customer Support, Dynix Inc., Provo, Utah.

ROBIN MURRAY PRICE is Deputy Librarian and Curator of the American Collections, Wellcome Institute for the History of Medicine, London.

WILMA PRIMUS is Project Coordinator for the Caribbean Documentation Centre, Economic Commission for Latin America and the Caribbean, Port of Spain, Trinidad.

VERONICA REGUS is Directora General de la Biblioteca de la Universidad Central del Este, San Pedro de Macorís, Dominican Republic.

DICK REUMER is Director, Dutch Centre for Public Libraries and Literature, The Hague.

MARGARET D. ROUSE-JONES is a historian and librarian at the West Indies Collection, University of the West Indies, St. Augustine, Trinidad.

SARA M. SANCHEZ is Bibliographer/Subject Specialist for the Graduate School of International Studies, University of Miami Library.

REBECCA J. SCOTT is Associate Professor, Department of History, University of Michigan, Ann Arbor.

JUDITH SELAKOFF is the Librarian for the Research Institute for the Study of Man located in New York City.

YVONNE V. STEPHENSON is University Librarian at the University of Guyana, Greater Georgetown.

BARBARA G. VALK is Coordinator of Bibliographic Development, Latin American Center, University of California, Los Angeles. She also edits the *Hispanic American Periodicals Index* and served as President of SALALM in 1981-1982.

ALICE VAN ROMONDT, President of ACURIL in 1986-1987, was Director of the National Library of Aruba at the time of the meeting.

ESPERANZA B. DE VARONA works in the Archives and Special Collections Department of Richter Library, University of Miami, Florida.

SABINE ZEHRER is a librarian at the Ibero-Amerikanisches Institut in Berlin.

Program of Substantive Panels and Workshops

Sunday, May 10

8:00-7:30   Committee Meetings

8:00-9:00   Conference Opening Session
Rapporteur: Peter J. de la Garza, Library of Congress

Monday, May 11

9:00-10:00   Conference Session I
Keynote Panel on Recession Management Strategies
Chair: Michael Gill, University of the West Indies, Cave Hill, Barbados

Dr. Mito Croes, Minister of Education Libraries and Cultural Affairs, Aruba

Elsa Barbarena, Universidad Nacional Autónoma, Mexico

Laura Gutiérrez-Witt, University of Texas at Austin

Yvonne Stephenson, University of Guyana

Virginia Betancourt, Instituto Autónomo Biblioteca Nacional, Caracas, Venezuela

Rapporteur: Karen J. Lindvall-Larson, University of California, San Diego

10:00-2:00   *Organization of American States: Roundtable on Caribbean Cooperative Microfilming Project*
(Closed meeting of librarians and archivists of the English-speaking Caribbean; observers welcome)

Conducted by Barclay Ogden, Director of Library Conservation Department, University of California Library System

Moderator: Susan Shattuck Benson, Senior Specialist, Development of Libraries, Archives and Mass Media, Organization of American States

11:45-12:30 ACURIL Business Meeting

12:30-2:00 ACURIL Past Presidents Luncheon
Chair: Marie Françoise Bernabé

2:00-3:00 Workshops, Set I

I.1 *Development of an Index Language and a Database for Spanish-Language Materials*
Chair: Sara M. Sánchez, University of Miami
Speaker: David Batty, Catholic University of America
Discussant: Graciella Cruz-Taura, University of Miami
Rapporteur: Barbara Parker, University of Massachusetts-Amherst

I.2 *Preservation and Conservation*
Moderator: Mark Grover, Brigham Young University
Mary Noonan, Dynix, Inc., Provo, Utah
Robin Price, Wellcome Institute for the History of Medicine, London, England
Richard D. Smith, Wei T'o Associates, Matteson, Illinois
Rapporteur: Shelley J. Miller, University of Kansas

I.3 *Latin American Bibliography: Printed Products and Prospects for Database Development*
Moderator: Nelly S. González, University of Illinois at Urbana-Champaign
Ludwig Lauerhass, Jr., University of California, Los Angeles: "Disciplinary Bibliographies: *Latin America, a Guide to the Historical Literature*."
Dolores M. Martin, Editor, *Handbook of Latin American Studies*: "Caribbean Bibliography and the *Handbook of Latin American Studies*: Past Trends and Future Prospects."
George F. Elmendorf, Latin American Bibliographic Foundation: "Country and Regional Bibliographies: The *Nicaraguan National Bibliography*, A Case Study."

Marie-Claire F. de Figueroa, El Colegio de México: "Al rescate del Caribe Francés: descripción de las colecciones de dos bibliotecas de la ciudad de México."

Rapporteur: Angela M. Carreño, New York University

3:45-5:00   Workshops, Set II

II.1 *Recession Management Strategies: University and Special Libraries*

Michael Gill, University of the West Indies, Cave Hill, Barbados

Thomas Niehaus, Tulane University

C. Jared Loewenstein, University of Virginia

Vere Achong, General Hospital, Trinidad and Tobago

Yvonne Stephenson, University of Guyana

II.2 *Recession Management Strategies: Public and National Libraries*

Jeanette Allis, U.S. Virgin Islands

Virginia Betancourt, Instituto Autónomo Biblioteca Nacional, Caracas, Venezuela

Tuesday, May 12

9:00-12:00   Conference Session II

Panel on Strategies for Resource Sharing

Moderator: Mina Jane Grothey, University of New Mexico

Dick Reumer, Nederlands Bibliotheek en Lektuur Centrum, Netherlands

Verónica Regus, Universidad Central del Este, República Dominicana

Françoise Montbrun, Bibliothèque Universitaire Antilles-Guyane, Guadeloupe

Daphne Douglas, University of the West Indies, Mona, Jamaica

Mariano Maura, Universidad de Puerto Rico, Río Piedras

Deborah Jakubs, Duke University

Rapporteurs: Blanca Hodge, Philipsburg Jubilee Library, St. Maarten

Olivia Figueroa, Aruba

1:30-2:00   Inter-American Development Bank Video Presentation (in Spanish)

2:00-3:00   Workshops, Set I

I.1 *Bookdealers*

Alan Moss, Barbados

Valerie Mwalilino, Schomburg Center for Research in Black Culture, New York

Robert Davies, Services Complètes d'Editions, Canada

Rapporteur: Sheila A. Milam, Arizona State University

I.2 *Indexing*

Barbara Valk, University of California, Los Angeles: "See *HAPI* Run: Procedures for Preparing the *Hispanic American Periodicals Index*."

I.3 *Fugitive Materials, Monies and Research Packages on Cuban Political Prisoners and Cuban Exile Periodicals*

Danilo H. Figueredo, New York Public Library

Esperanza D. de Varona, University of Miami Library

Luisa Pérez, Miami-Dade Public Library

Lesbia O. Varona, University of Miami Library

Rapporteur: Rosa Q. Mesa, University of Florida

3:45-5:00   Workshops, Set II

II.1 *Acquisition of Government Publications*

Eudora Loh, University of California, Los Angeles

Sabine Zehrer, Ibero-Amerikanisches Institut, Berlin, Germany

Alan Moss, Barbados

Roberto Brauning, Inter-American Development Bank

Rapporteur: Marcia Nurse, Barbados National Library

II.2 *Interlibrary Loan, Gifts and Exchanges*

Noris Vásquez, Universidad de Puerto Rico, Río Piedras

Marie Françoise Bernabé, Bibliothèque Universitaire Antilles-Guyane, Martinique

Rapporteur: Rachel B. Miller, University of Kansas

II.3 *Right or ROM? Assessing New Technology for Reference Services in Academic and Research Libraries*

Moderator: Norma Corral, University of California, Los Angeles

Teresa Portilla, University of California, Los Angeles

Pamela Howard, Arizona State University

Patricia Wade, University of California, Los Angeles

Shirley Evelyn, University of the West Indies, St. Augustine, Trinidad and Tobago

Rapporteur: Robert Vaughn, College of the Virgin Islands

7:00-10:00   Latin American Microfilming Project (LAMP)

Laura Gutierrez-Witt, University of Texas at Austin

Wednesday, May 13

9:00-12:00   Conference Session III

Grantsmanship Panel

Chair: Guust van Wesemael, IFLA

Susan Shattuck Benson, OAS

Dennis Irvine, UNESCO

Maureen Newton, CARICOM

John R. Hébert, Library of Congress

TBA, L'Agence de Cooperation Culturelle et Technique (LACCT)

Rapporteurs:

Winnie Stegeman, Curaçao Public Library

Laura D. Loring, University of Southern California

1:30-2:00   Inter-American Development Bank Video Presentation (in English)

2:00-3:15   Workshops, Set I

I.1 *Cataloguing Issues and Developments*

Moderator: Gayle Williams, University of New Mexico

Nel Bretney, University of the West Indies, Cave Hill, Barbados: "Building a Caribbean Bibliographic Database: The View from a Cataloguer's Desk."

I.2 *Recession Management Strategies: University and Special Libraries* (continued from Monday afternoon workshop)

Michael Gill, University of the West Indies, Cave Hill, Barbados

Thomas Niehaus, Tulane University

C. Jared Loewenstein, University of Virginia

Vere Achong, General Hospital, Trinidad and Tobago

Yvonne Stephenson, University of Guyana

II.3 *Recession Management Strategies: Public and National Libraries* (continued from Monday afternoon workshop)

Jeanette Allis, U.S. Virgin Islands

Virginia Betancourt, Instituto Autónomo Biblioteca Nacional, Caracas, Venezuela

3:45-5:00   Workshops, Set II
"How To" Discussions

II.1 *Grants: Caribbean*

Wilma Primus, Economic Commission for Latin America and the Caribbean, Port of Spain, Trinidad

II.2 *Grants to Support Information Resources in Latin American Studies: A North American Perspective*

Moderator: Dan Hazen, University of California, Berkeley

Ellen Brow, Harvard College Library: "Getting Started."

Barbara Valk, University of California, Los Angeles: "Preparing an Application."

Dan Hazen, University of California, Berkeley: "Funding in a Broader Context."

II.3 *Latin American/Caribbean Cataloging Backlogs: Management and Priority Perspectives: Open Discussion*

Gayle Williams, University of New Mexico

All interested parties encouraged to participate

Thursday, May 14

9:00-12:00   Conference Session IV

The Search for New Interpretations: Historiography of the Caribbean

Arthur E. Burt, Howard University: "The Caribbean Search for Independence: The Clash of Conflicting Ideologies."

Benjamín Nistal-Moret, National Park Service, Southeast Preservation Center: "The Fortifications of San Juan Bautista de Puerto Rico as Engineering and Architectural Historiography, 1530-1940."

Margaret D. Rouse-Jones, University of the West Indies, St. Augustine, Trinidad: "Recent Research in the History of Trinidad and Tobago: A Review Of Journal and Conference Literature, 1975-1985."

Rebecca J. Scott, University of Michigan: "Analyzing Social Change and Social Movements: Recent Historiography on Nineteenth Century Cuba."

Thomas Mathews, Association of Caribbean Universities

Discussants:

Graciella Cruz-Taura, University of Miami

Peter J. Johnson, Princeton University

Kenneth Ingram, Jamaica

Rapporteurs:

Pamela F. Howard, Arizona State University

Sylvania Golphin, Florence Williams Public Library, Christiansted, St. Croix, U.S. Virgin Islands

12:00-12:30 ACURIL Business Meeting
(Election)

2:00   Afternoon and Evening Free
Optional Tours of Local Libraries

7:00-10:00   SALALM Executive Board

Friday, May 15

9:00-10:00   ACURIL Standing Committees

10:30-12:30   Conference Session V

10:30-11:30   Reports on Recession Management Workshops
              Chair: Alice van Romondt, Aruba National Library
              Rapporteur: Peter S. Bushnell, University of Florida

11:30-12:30   Joint Resolutions
              Chair: Mina Jane Grothey, University of New Mexico
              Almaluces Figueroa: ACURIL (Spanish)
              Lynette Hutchinson: ACURIL (English)
              Françoise Montbrun: ACURIL (French)
              Blanca Hodge: ACURIL (Dutch)
              Mark Grover: SALALM

2:00-3:00   SALALM Business and Membership Meeting

2:00-4:00   ACURIL Executive Council

3:30-6:00   SALALM Executive Board

7:00-8:00   Conference Closing Session
              Rapporteur: Charles S. Fineman, Northwestern University

Saturday, May 16

9:00   ACURIL Executive Council